Poverty and landlessness in rural Asia

PHILLIPS MEMORIAL
LIBRARY
PROVIDENCE COLLEGE

D1313612

International Labour Office
Geneva

HC
415
P6
P68

Copyright © International Labour Organisation 1977

Publications of the International Labour Office enjoy copyright under Protocol 2 of the Universal Copyright Convention. Nevertheless, short excerpts from them may be reproduced without authorisation, on condition that the source is indicated. For rights of reproduction or translation, application should be made to the Editorial and Translation Branch, International Labour Office, CH-1211 Geneva 22, Switzerland. The International Labour Office welcomes such applications.

ISBN 92-2-101766-4 (limp cover)
ISBN 92-2-101767-2 (hard cover)

First published 1977
Second impression 1980

The designations employed in ILO publications and the presentation of material therein do not imply the expression of any opinion whatsoever on the part of the International Labour Office concerning the legal status of any country or territory or of its authorities, or concerning the delimitation of its frontiers.
The responsibility for opinions expressed in signed articles, studies and other contributions rests solely with their authors, and publication does not constitute an endorsement by the International Labour Office of the opinions expressed in them.

ILO publications can be obtained through major booksellers or ILO local offices in many countries, or direct from ILO Publications, International Labour Office, CH-1211 Geneva 22, Switzerland. A catalogue or list of new publications will be sent free of charge from the above address.

Printed in Switzerland

FOREWORD

This is the first major research study to be published under the rural component of the ILO's World Employment Programme.

During the 1960s national income per head in developing countries grew rapidly by historical standards and many of the growth targets which had been set for the United Nations Strategy for the First Development Decade were achieved or exceeded. But in many countries the lives of the mass of the people did not greatly improve and there was growing concern for the widening gap between rich and poor nations and groups of people. Two main reasons for this failure were adduced: the excessive concentration of development in modern sector enclaves which typically were capital intensive and had few linkages with the traditional rural and informal sectors in which most people worked and (partly but not exclusively as a result of this) the failure of employment opportunities to keep up with the rapid expansion of the population of working age. It became evident that rapid over-all growth, as measured by indicators such as gross national product, could not be relied upon automatically to increase employment and earning opportunities for the mass of the people.

It was this growing realisation that led the ILO to launch in 1969 its World Employment Programme (WEP). The Programme's original rationale was that one of the most effective means of ensuring that higher incomes and living standards were achieved for the masses was to provide them with more work opportunities and more productive work to do. It was argued that this approach would be compatible with high rates of economic growth, as higher domestic incomes would increase domestic demand and thus stimulate production. The original objective of the WEP was thus to provide assistance to member States in the elaboration of policies which would enable national planners and decision makers to reduce unemployment and underemployment by accelerating the creation of productive income-earning opportunities.

The technical assistance and advisory services provided to ILO member States in the employment field are complemented by a research programme which is designed to achieve a better understanding of the nature and causes

V

of the unemployment problem, to elaborate and promote comprehensive employment-oriented development strategies, and to integrate such results into the national decision-making process. The research activities of the World Employment Programme were initially focused on issues such as the relationship between population growth and employment, the scope for adopting more labour-intensive and therefore capital-saving technologies, the effects of trade expansion on employment, the links between education systems and the labour market, urban employment problems, and the relationship between income distribution and employment.

The focus of WEP research activities has, however, progressively shifted from methods of creating higher levels of productive employment to the need to attack mass poverty more directly where it exists, that is to say primarily in the traditional rural and in the so-called urban informal sectors of developing countries. Thus the rural employment component of the WEP was initiated in 1975, in response to a recommendation of the Eighth Session of the ILO Advisory Committee on Rural Development (Geneva, 1974) and a Resolution concerning rural development adopted by the International Labour Conference in June 1975. Additional impetus to ILO research in rural development was given by the conclusions of the Eighth ILO Asian Regional Conference (Colombo, October 1975), which considered my report on *The poor in Asian development: an ILO programme*, and by those of the World Employment Conference (Geneva, June 1976) which considered my report *Employment, growth and basic needs: a one-world problem*.

The World Employment Conference in fact adopted a Declaration of Principles and Programme of Action which stressed the need for national development strategies to focus on increasing the incomes of the lowest income groups, especially in the rural sector. It recommended that the basic needs of these groups should be met primarily by the generation of productive employment with a view to reaching full employment by the year 2000. The Conference further declared that this employment must be freely chosen, and emphasised that the rural poor themselves should effectively participate in policy making and programme implementation, and that rural workers must be encouraged and helped to organise in order to make such participation possible.

The present volume is intended as a contribution to the debate on the strategies and policies recommended by the World Employment Conference. As indicated in the Preface, an attempt has been made to document the assertion that during the past quarter of a century the standard of living of the poorest groups in rural areas has declined in many parts of Asia. The national monographs were commissioned from various authors, with the objective of describing as systematically and objectively as possible the situation of the rural masses in the country or region concerned. A chapter is also included on the Chinese experience, despite the problem, well known to sinologists, of incomplete sources of data and other information.

No attempt has been made to examine systematically issues of human rights enshrined in ILO standards and in the Declaration of Principles and

Programme of Action adopted by the World Employment Conference, such as the right to freely chosen employment or the right of rural workers to organise and to participate in policy making, as this study focuses on drawing an economic profile of the rural masses. The ILO assumes no responsibility, moreover, for the views expressed by the authors of the case studies.

As far as the ILO is concerned, it will draw on the data assembled for this study in its further efforts to assist governments, employers' and workers' organisations to give effect to the conclusions of the World Employment Conference through the design and implementation of national development strategies having as a primary objective the promotion of employment and the satisfaction of the basic needs of the poor, particularly in rural areas.

Geneva, January 1977

Francis Blanchard,
Director-General,
International Labour Office.

CONTENTS

Part III: The Chinese experience

PREFACE

It is increasingly recognised that the rural areas of Asia are in crisis. Food scarcity is chronic, episodically becoming so severe as to lead to famine. Population growth is rapid and landlessness is rising.

Various hypotheses have been put forward to explain this crisis: unfavourable weather cycles, slow growth, a bias in favour of urban areas, the demographic explosion. None of these explanations seems to be complete or fully convincing. In the past quarter of a century, or roughly during the period when most of Asia has achieved its independence, the number of the rural poor has increased and in many instances their standard of living has tended to fall. Perhaps surprisingly, this has occurred irrespective of whether growth has been rapid or slow, or agriculture has expanded swiftly or sluggishly.

An attempt has been made in this volume to describe the situation of the rural poor in Asian countries and to trace the causes for the decline in the well-being of the peasantry in many parts of Asia. Part I comments on the facts available, analyses briefly the situation and deals with some of the basic issues. In Chapters 2 to 11, which form Part II, statistical evidence has been assembled from six countries of South and Southeast Asia as well as from four of the major states of India. In all these studies there is at least a strong presumption that the standard of living of the poorest groups in rural areas has deteriorated over time. Evidently, growth as such is not at fault, but the pattern of growth and the policies pursued are shown to have been of signal importance.

In Part III an attempt has been made to describe the Chinese experience in dealing with problems of rural poverty and inequality.

Except for Chapter 3 (which is a revision based on earlier work) all the studies were specially undertaken for inclusion in this volume, which is a product of collective effort. Much of the conceptual framework and the editorial work were done by Keith Griffin and Azizur Rahman Khan who were, together with two of the other authors (Lee and Palmer), at the ILO in Geneva throughout the period of research; two others were able to spend a brief period there for discussions (Naseem and Nayyar). With the remaining two,

1

the dialogue was only through correspondence (Kurien and Rajaraman). The chapter on the Indian state of Punjab is a revised, extended version of a paper first published in the *Journal of Development Studies*, in July 1975, and gratitude is expressed to the editors and the publisher of the journal for permission to include it. The fact that close contact was established among so many of the contributors was a great advantage.

In addition to the authors many others contributed to the completion of the present volume. Thanks are due to L. R. Khan, Anisur Rahman and Abdus Salek who provided valuable comments on the Bangladesh study. Albert Berry was very helpful in commenting on the Philippines study, and Stephan Guisinger was a valuable critic of the Pakistan study. Deepak Nayyar made many suggestions which helped to improve the chapter on Uttar Pradesh, while Franklyn Joseph and R. Srinivasan served as research assistants for the Tamil Nadu study. Gilbert Etienne and Akbar Noman provided helpful comments on the China study.

The work was conducted under the auspices of the World Employment Programme and is part of a continuing research effort at the International Labour Office. It is hoped in the near future to undertake studies of a similar type in other regions of the world.

The studies in this volume were financed from a grant provided by the Swedish Government to whom the ILO is much indebted for the support it has given not only to this project but to the entire rural development programme of the ILO.

MAIN AREAS REFERRED TO IN THIS STUDY

1 Pakistan
2 India
   2a Punjab State
   2b Uttar Pradesh
   2c Bihar
   2d Tamil Nadu
3 Bangladesh
4 Sri Lanka
5 Malaysia
   5a West
   5b East
6 Indonesia
   6a Java
7 Philippines
8 China

PART I

FACTS, METHODS AND ANALYSIS

RURAL POVERTY: TRENDS AND EXPLANATIONS

1

In this part an attempt has been made to analyse the facts and the trends concerning rural poverty as they emerge from the case studies presented in the following chapters. The results are not uniform and generalisations are therefore avoided. However, some trends are clearly visible which suggest that sustained growth in a country can be accompanied by continuing poverty of certain groups of people, in that their income in real terms remains stagnant or is even falling. This observation demonstrates that even under conditions of over-all growth its benefits do not always "trickle down" to those most in need.

In fact, some of the case studies seem to support the view that in certain Asian countries the incomes of the rural poor have been falling absolutely or that the proportion of the rural population living below a designated "poverty line" has been increasing, or both. In any case there are indications that the process of growth may have tended to increase relative inequality. On the basis of such findings many observers accordingly advocate a redistribution of the increments of output toward the poor as the main means of improving material well-being. In the light of contemporary experience, however, it seems clear that such a policy of income redistribution will result in a noticeable improvement of the conditions of the rural poor only after a long period, particularly under conditions of high rates of population growth. Others, therefore, go further and argue that only a redistribution of wealth, particularly of landed wealth, through agrarian reforms and similar measures, will be able to stop the process of impoverishment of sections of the rural population within any reasonable period. Much will depend on local conditions, the availability of land, rates of growth and demographic trends, but the studies confirm that energetic policy measures are required to change existing trends in large parts of rural Asia.

SCOPE AND METHODS

South and Southeast Asia are the natural points of departure for an inquiry into the problem of rural poverty. These regions contain an extremely high proportion of the world's rural population, and many of the people living there suffer from appallingly low standards of living.[1]

In Part II ten empirical studies of trends in rural poverty in seven major "market" (i.e. non-socialist) economies of the region are presented. Apart from the special case of Taiwan the only major market economies of South and Southeast Asia that have not been covered are those of Thailand, Burma and Nepal. In these three cases the distribution of rural income and the incidence of rural poverty are unlikely to be very different from the rest of South and Southeast Asia. Although studies could not be carried out because of inadequate documentation, it is unlikely that these countries achieved significant success in reducing rural poverty in recent decades. In one sense, circumstances in these countries were less favourable than in most of the countries that have been studied in that over the decade ending in the mid-1970s, food production per head in Nepal and Burma actually declined while that in Thailand remained unchanged. In most of the seven countries that have been studied, in contrast, there was some increase in food output per head over the same period.

The story is different for Taiwan. It appears that income inequality in rural Taiwan is much less than in the rest of Asia and that inequality and poverty have declined in recent decades.[2] It might appear to be unfortunate, therefore, that its experience has not been treated in the present set of studies, since it could serve as an illustration of an alternative pattern to the cases presented in Part II. Indeed, the replicability of the Taiwanese experience elsewhere in Asia remains a possibility to be considered seriously. Taiwan, however, is in many ways a unique case which differs from the major contemporary economies of Asia. For half a century, until the end of the Second World War, it was part of the economy of the leading industrial power in Asia and was the beneficiary of a considerable amount of Japanese investment in infrastructure and irrigation facilities. Moreover, after it became the seat of the Nationalist Government in 1949 it received substantial external assistance. These factors enabled Taiwan to achieve a quick recovery after the war and a rapid rate of growth of non-agricultural activities. As a result, improvements in agriculture, and in the rural economy more generally, were easier to bring about. Finally, it proved to be possible in Taiwan to overcome the many obstacles that hinder land reform elsewhere in Asia. In fact that which distinguishes Taiwan from the Asian countries discussed in Part II is the fact that the authorities in Taiwan were able to carry out a highly egalitarian land reform.

In Part III an attempt is made to describe the Chinese experience in creating an egalitarian rural income distribution through land reform and collectivisation and thereby provide the reader with a basis for comparison

---

[1] See also ILO: Report of the Director-General to the Eighth Asian Regional Conference (Colombo, September/October 1975): *The poor in Asian development: an ILO programme* (Geneva, 1975).

[2] Keith Griffin: *Land concentration and rural poverty* (London, Macmillan, 1976), Ch. 7.

with the experiences discussed in Part II. In this connection a word of warning must be added. Unlike the other case studies which have been prepared on the basis of the authors' own research and for which considerable statistical material was readily available, there is a serious lack of income distribution statistics and other relevant data for China. In so far as material is available at all, it relates mostly to specific regions or communes. This makes it difficult to come to conclusions valid for the country as a whole. The other socialist countries in the region have all been afflicted by war in recent years or have become socialist only in the current decade. Thus it is both more difficult and less useful to analyse their experience.

Some preliminary remarks

In the eight studies in Part II an attempt is made to determine the trends in the absolute and relative incomes of the rural poor in seven Asian countries. Together, these seven countries account for about 70 per cent of the rural population of the non-socialist developing world. Since their average income is below that of the rest of the underdeveloped market economy countries, it is not unlikely that their share of the poor of the non-socialist developing world is even greater.

In each of the seven countries the scope and method of analysis had to be adapted to the available statistical information. Considerable differences in the quantity and quality of evidence are therefore inevitable. And yet some broad generalisations about trends are possible.

In general the authors of the studies tried to cover as many years as possible and to bring the story forward as close to the present as possible. Attempts were made to overcome distortions due to weather cycles and to incorporate the most up-to-date information. But here too it was impossible to ensure uniformity. The periods covered vary from ten to twenty-five years. In each case, however, the analysis includes the period during which the new technology of the so-called Green Revolution was adopted.

The most outstanding facts to be noted are the worsening distribution of income and the declining real income of the rural poor at least in a number of cases. Those studies which contain the relevant data show that the shares of the lower decile groups in aggregate income and consumption have been declining even during periods of relatively rapid agricultural growth. There are significant differences from country to country as regards the proportion of population that has been adversely affected, but in each country for which data exist, a substantial proportion of the lowest income groups appears to have experienced a decline in their share of real income over time.

Indeed, the evidence from the case studies points to an even stronger conclusion. In each case a significant proportion of low income households experienced an absolute decline in real income.

This fact emerged from two separate types of measurements that were attempted in the case studies. First, a level of real income was defined below which all households were classified as poor. In most studies this "poverty line" was derived from an estimate of the level of income necessary to ensure a minimum diet, although the case studies differ widely as to what should be the contents of a minimum diet—which brings an element of incomparability into the picture. In each case, however, it was found that the proportion of the population below the "poverty line" has been increasing over time. Second, the real incomes of decile or quintile groups at different points of time was calculated, and here it was found that the real incomes of the lowest decile or quintile groups have been declining. Once again, the range over which this has occurred differs from one country to another.

The other major empirical finding concerns the trend in real wages of agricultural labourers. In most of the countries for which measurements could be obtained real wages either remained constant or there appeared to have been a downward trend. On the other hand, there are some cases, as in the Indian state of Punjab, for example, where some measurements suggest that there was an increase in real wages of agricultural labourers. In general, this sort of comparison is difficult since the results are very sensitive to the wage series selected, the nature of the cost-of-living index used to convert nominal wages into real wages and the choice of the base year. In Chapter 3 one finds, for example, an indication that the proportion of agricultural labourers below the poverty line in the Punjab increased during the period when real wages showed an upward trend. An explanation of these contradictory trends may be that there was a change in the occupational distribution of the wage earners included in the average wage index. In fact, the occupations of agricultural labourers do seem to have changed significantly as a result of the widespread adoption of capital-intensive farming techniques, especially by the labour-hiring, larger farmers. The importance of skilled labour and of operators of mechanical equipment has increased considerably. The rise in demand for workers of this type, given the initial shortage of skills, undoubtedly led to a relatively rapid increase in their wages. On the other hand, the balance between the supply and demand for more traditional types of labour became increasingly unfavourable over time, and consequently their wages failed to rise.

In Chapter 12 it is postulated that the major improvement in the distribution of income in rural China occurred mainly as a result of the early land reforms. These reforms did not in themselves constitute a process of socialist transformation; their main initial purpose was to promote individual cultivation based on private land ownership. Indeed, the reduction of inequality in China since the early land reforms has been a slow and difficult process, although it is probable that without collectivisation it would have been difficult to prevent a tendency toward polarisation of income and wealth.

The countries studied in Part II are all characterised by a highly unequal distribution of land ownership. Statistical information usually relates to the distribution of farm size, i.e. to the area farmed and not the area owned. It is generally known that the ownership distribution is less equal than the distribution of farm size.[1] Of the seven countries studied, the degree of inequality is perhaps the least in Bangladesh, but even there the bottom 20 per cent of the holdings account for only 3 per cent of the land while the top 10 per cent of the holdings account for over 35 per cent of the land. The Gini concentration ratio is 0.5.[2] In the other six countries the distribution is less equal. For example, the Gini concentration ratios of the distribution of land holding for Pakistan, India and the Philippines have been estimated to be around 0.6.[3]

Although there is some form of land reform legislation in nearly all of the countries studied progress towards redistribution of land during the periods considered in Part II has not been such as could have contributed to a sizeable reduction of inequality in land ownership. The effects of land reform measures initiated in the early 1970s in Pakistan, the Philippines and Sri Lanka could not unfortunately be taken into account, since the relevant data are not yet available. However, it must be feared that the redistributions resulting from these reforms have not been sufficient to bring about significantly greater equality in land ownership.[4]

The continuation of the highly unequal ownership of land during a period of rapid demographic growth has resulted in increased landlessness and near-landlessness. Due to the lack of statistical data in these countries it is very difficult to obtain a time series on the number of landless workers. In those cases where information is available a marked trend towards increased landlessness can be discerned (see Chapters 4 and 7 for examples).

Methodological aspects

In the process of preparing the country reports several important methodological problems were noted in relation to studies concerned with the measurement of changes in the distribution of income. It is important to recognise these methodological problems in order to resolve the conflicting claims that are sometimes put forward on the basis of the same information.

A common practice is to construct indices of inequality (e.g. Gini coefficients) from the distribution of money income and then to derive conclusions about changes in the distribution of income by comparing such indices over time. Occasionally the money incomes of various groups are deflated by an over-all index of the cost of living (based on average consumption weights of all groups) in order to obtain distributions of "real income" at different times. Both procedures yield the same results, of course, since the second method

---

[1] See, for example, Chapter 7 for some evidence of this.

[2] These estimates for Bangladesh are based on the 1967-68 Master Survey of Agriculture.

[3] These estimates, for 1960, are reported in IBRD: *Land reform* (World Bank Paper, Rural Development Series), July 1974.

[4] See Chapter 8 and also Zubeda M. Ahmad (ed.): *Land reform in Asia, with particular reference to Pakistan, the Philippines and Thailand* (Geneva, ILO, 1976; mimeographed World Employment Programme research working paper; restricted).

merely involves deflating the incomes of all individuals or households by the same factor. If, however, the composition of consumption differs between income groups and if relative prices change over time, then both practices can produce seriously biased estimates.

A simple example will illustrate this. Assume a simple economy in which there are two income groups, poor and rich. In the base year 0, the poor consume 10 kg of rice (a necessity) and 1 m of silk (a luxury), while the rich consume 10 kg of rice and 20 m of silk. In the base year the price of rice is 2 rupees per kg and the price of silk is 2 rupees per m. In a later year the consumption of the two groups and the price of silk remain exactly the same as before, while the price of rice rises to 4 rupees per kg. On the assumption that neither group saves, money incomes and income shares of the two groups in the two years would look as follows:

Group	Year 0		Year t	
	Income (Rupees)	Income share (Percentage)	Income (Rupees)	Income share (Percentage)
Poor	22	27	42	34
Rich	60	73	80	66

Although the real incomes have remained exactly the same as before, the share of money income of the poor has increased in year t as compared to the base year. If all incomes in year t are deflated by the over-all cost-of-living index based on the average consumption weight for all groups, (which, in the present case, is 148.78 for year t with year 0 as the base) the "real incomes" would be as follows:

Group	Real income (Rupees)	Income share (Percentage)
Poor	28.23	34
Rich	53.77	66

Once again, the figures imply a redistribution of "real income" in favour of the poor although, in reality, the real incomes of the two groups have remained exactly the same as before. This false conclusion arises from the application of the same cost-of-living index to the two groups despite the fact that their real costs of living have changed at vastly different rates. The reasons for this, in turn, are that their consumption patterns are different and that relative prices have altered over time. In the present example, the cost-of-living index of the poor rises to 190.9 while that of the rich rises only to 133.3. If these group-specific indices are applied to the money incomes of the relevant groups in year t, then the constancy of real incomes and income shares over time becomes readily apparent.

It is well known that the proportion of income spent on food rises as income falls. Indeed, as some of the country studies indicate, the percentages of income spent on food by the bottom and top quintiles of the population can be dramatically different. The poorest groups frequently spend as much as 70 per cent of their income on food while the richest often spend less than 40 per cent. It is also well known that during the last two decades food has tended to become relatively more expensive compared to consumption goods in general. In such a situation a comparison over time of Gini coefficients calculated from the distribution of money income or of "real income" obtained by deflating money income by the over-all cost-of-living index is misleading. Such a comparison understates any deterioration in the distribution of income that may have occurred and exaggerates any improvement.[1] Unfortunately, the procedures referred to above have been widely applied to derive conclusions about changes in the distribution of income. A number of studies in Part II, notably that on Sri Lanka in Chapter 8, have shown how the use of questionable methods may lead to false conclusions about improvements in the distribution of income in some countries.

The same problem frequently arises when measuring trends in real wages. One of the most difficult questions to decide is which cost-of-living index should be used to deflate nominal wage rates. Too frequently, the general cost-of-living index has been used for this purpose. Reference is again made to the case of Sri Lanka in Chapter 8 for a critical discussion of this issue. As is indicated in a number of the case studies, in the past two decades in almost every country for which data are available, the cost of living for the lower income groups has increased faster than the general cost of living. The reason for this is that the prices of food and other wage goods have increased faster than the average.

Another important problem that is neglected in many other studies of income distribution is the different needs of different social groups. In Chapter 7 it is argued that the occupational status of the low income groups in an underdeveloped rural economy is such that poor workers must work much harder than persons belonging to higher income groups. Yet few studies make an allowance for the amount of calories and other items of consumption required by persons in different job and income categories. If incomes were calculated, say, on the basis of the calories required by workers during the process of production, then the indices of inequality would be considerably greater than those usually given.

One final methodological point must be mentioned, if only to demonstrate the somewhat rigid position that some economists take. It has been argued that measurements of the distribution of current income, such as those given in Part II, are not acceptable because it is expected life-time income, rather

---

[1] Note that the same bias will affect international comparisons of Gini coefficients if relative international prices differ between countries.

than observed current income, which is the true indicator of welfare. In some cases the argument ends on this note of agnosticism; in other cases, however, the argument is taken further and it is claimed that the distribution of current consumption, rather than current income, is the better measure of expected lifetime income.

It is difficult to make such generalisations when referring to contemporary developing countries. A great deal more must be known, for example, about the ways in which households accommodate differences between current consumption and income. In general, low income groups tend to consume more than they earn, and it is likely that this occurs, not because expected lifetime income is so high as to make it desirable to have an intertemporal allocation of consumption different from that of income, but because the requirements for physical survival are in excess of current income. It also seems highly likely that the most important mechanism for financing an excess of current consumption over current income is borrowing and the sale of the meagre assets owned by these income groups.

Notwithstanding this problem nearly all of the authors of the studies in Part II have not rejected the evidence on the distribution of consumption but have used it, along with, and in some cases in preference to, other evidence.

ANALYSIS

A salient characteristic of the countries studied is that many of the resources needed for development are at hand, unutilised or poorly utilised. Foremost among these are the intelligence, ingenuity and effort of the labour force itself. It has long been known that part, usually a small part, of the rural workforce is often openly unemployed, particularly during the slack season in regions where multiple cropping is not practised. In addition, a larger part of the workforce may be underemployed in the sense that it is engaged in tasks with a very low level of productivity. More important, perhaps, is the low productivity and occasionally low intensity of work arising from the poor motivation, poor health and injustice that are often found in rural areas. The exploitation and inequality from which the majority of the rural population suffers is demoralising, engenders resentment and stifles initiative and creativity. The effect is not only to lower current output below its potential but to reduce the capacity and willingness of the population to innovate. Where conditions are so severe that children of the poor continue to suffer from protein deficiency and general malnutrition, intelligence is permanently impaired and creative talent is destroyed. In societies where material deprivation is less acute, effects on initiative and innovation may be similar because of the psychological consequences of an ill-conceived incentive system and the sociological consequences of a social structure which permits most of the economic surplus to be captured by a small minority.

Labour is not the only resource that is poorly utilised; in many countries land and other natural resources are not efficiently exploited. Especially on the larger farms, the length of the fallow period is excessively long, the degree of cropping intensity is too low and the amount of land in natural pastures is high. At the same time, many of the smallest farmers are forced to over-exploit their land, with the result that useful land is destroyed through exhaustion of soil fertility. Economic systems of the type described above result not only in poor use of part of its human resources, but also in poor use (and even destruction) of part of its natural resources.

Underutilisation of labour and land often is accompanied by underutilisation of capital. Large irrigation facilities are not used to capacity; irrigation canals and drainage ditches are allowed to fall into disrepair; fish ponds are permitted to become overgrown with weeds; mechanical equipment becomes inoperative because of poor maintenance and lack of spare parts. Furthermore, much of the savings potential of the peasantry remains untapped and hence the rate of accumulation of capital remains lower than necessary.

Latent within these inefficiencies and inequities are possibilities for higher output, faster growth and greater equality. This potential for rural development, however, has lain dormant. Instead of growing prosperity for those most in need there has been increasing poverty for many. The crucial question is: why?

Poverty and food production

It is certainly not the case that the increasing poverty of many of the poor is mainly due to general stagnation in Asia, or, worse, economic decline. On the contrary, all but one of the seven countries surveyed have enjoyed a rise in average incomes in recent years, and in some instances the rise has been quite rapid. Only in Bangladesh have average incomes fallen, and the interesting question there is how, despite the decline in the average, the upper income groups were able to improve their living standards. In a sense, Bangladesh is the most dramatic illustration of what is happening in the rest of Asia: in countries where average incomes have increased, the poor have tended to become poorer and the rich richer; in Bangladesh, where average incomes have fallen, the rich have nevertheless become richer while the incomes of the poor have fallen faster than the average.

Excluding Bangladesh, between 1960 and 1973, gross national products per head increased between 1.3 per cent a year (in India) and 3.9 per cent (in Malaysia). In other words, during this period the level of income, on average, increased about 18 per cent in India and 65 per cent in Malaysia. Yet the incomes of the poor fell in both countries, as well as in those which experienced intermediate rates of growth.

The claim that the growing poverty of Asia is due to a world food shortage, or to a failure of food production in Asia to keep up with the expanding population, must be questioned. While it would be wrong to deny the seriousness of the periodic food scarcities which beset the world, particularly in South

Poverty and landlessness in rural Asia

Table 1. Growth of GNP per head, 1960-73

Country	Percentage growth per annum
Bangladesh	−0.2
India	1.3
Indonesia	2.4
Malaysia	3.9
Pakistan	3.4
Philippines	2.3
Sri Lanka	2.0

Source: *World Bank Atlas*, 1975. Because of differences in the period covered, the growth rates in this table sometimes differ from those reported in the individual chapters.

Figure 1. Food output per head, 1955-74
(index: 1961-65=100)

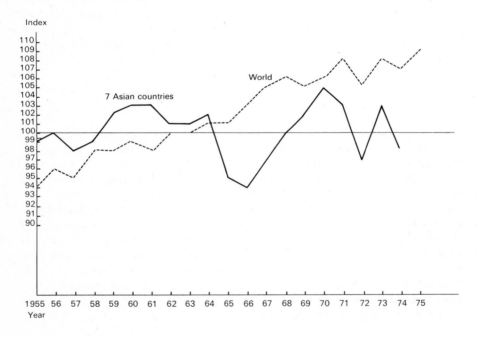

Asia, it would be an improper simplification to use food shortages as the explanation for increasing poverty in rural areas of Asia. In fact many serious scholars recognise, as one has said, "that there is little reason to anticipate severe food supply limitations in the medium-term future".[1]

---

[1] Lance Taylor: "The Misconstrued Crisis: Lester Brown and World Food", in *World Development*, Nov./Dec. 1975, p. 832.

Figure 2. Cereal output per head, 1955-74
(kilograms per annum)

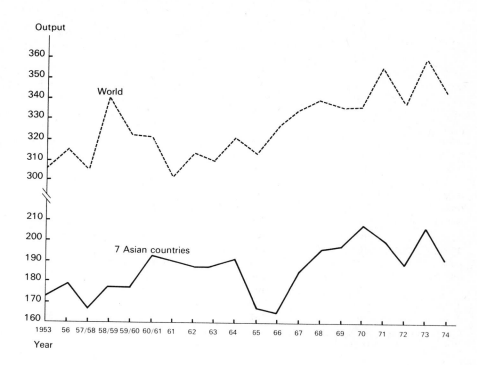

As can be seen from figure 1, world food production per head has modestly but noticeably increased during the last two decades, as, incidentally, has total agricultural production per head. There have, of course, been periods of harvest failure, notably in 1972, but even then there was significantly more food available per person than, say, a decade earlier. There certainly is no evidence that the world is moving toward a Malthusian trap.[1] When the poor starve, it is not mainly because there is no food but because they do not have the wherewithal to acquire food. In other words, the problem of world hunger cannot be solved merely by attempting to increase production. The solution requires better distribution and more productive employment both to increase incentives to expand output and create effective demand for greater food output.

Similarly, there is no clear tendency for food production per head in Asia to fall. The evolution of a weighted average of the seven countries included in

---

[1] For a popular statement of the neo-Malthusian position see Lester Brown: *By bread alone* (New York, Praeger, 1974).

Table 2. Food and cereal output per head in seven Asian countries and in the world, 1955-74

| Year | Food (index: 1961-65 = 100) | | Cereals (kg per annum) | |
	Seven Asian countries	The world	Seven Asian countries	The world
1955	99	94	173	306
1956	100	96	179	315
1957	98	95	166	304
1958	99	98	177	339
1959	102	98	177	322
1960	103	99	192	321
1961	103	98	190	301
1962	101	100	187	313
1963	101	100	188	310
1964	102	101	191	320
1965	95	101	167	312
1966	94	103	165	326
1967	97	105	184	334
1968	100	106	195	339
1969	102	105	197	336
1970	105	106	208	336
1971	103	108	200	355
1972	97	105	188	338
1973	103	108	207	360
1974	98	107	190	343

Sources: FAO: *Production Yearbook*, various years; idem: *Monthly Bulletin of Agricultural Economics and Statistics*, Nov. 1975; United Nations: *Demographic Yearbook*, various years.

Table 3. Growth of population (1960-73) and food production (1952-74) (per cent per annum)

Country	Food production	Population
Bangladesh	2.0	2.6
India	2.3	2.3
Indonesia	2.5	2.0
Malaysia (West)	5.6	2.6
Pakistan	3.0	2.9
Philippines	3.4	3.0
Sri Lanka	3.7	2.3

Sources: Food production data obtained from FAO; population growth rates reproduced from *World Bank Atlas*, 1975.

this study is traced in figure 1. It can be seen that, if anything, there is a slow tendency for production per head to rise, although this is not statistically significant. Equally clear are the dramatic fluctuations around this trend.

Estimates of total food production in the underdeveloped countries of Asia often are not very accurate. More reliable are data on the main food items, notably cereals, and accordingly the evolution of cereal output per head during the last 20 years is shown in figure 2. It can be seen that in the world as a whole and, more important, even in the seven Asian countries concerned, output per head has increased. The trend rate of growth of cereal output per head in these seven countries has been 0.7 per cent a year, and this estimate is highly significant statistically. Thus the increase in poverty that has been described has been associated, not with a fall, but with a rise in cereal production per head, the main component of the diet of the poor.

The data from which figures 1 and 2 were constructed are reported in table 2.

If one examines the countries individually, it transpires that in only one of them did population expand faster than domestic food production. This was in Bangladesh where, as has been seen, even GNP per head has been falling. In India population and food production have grown at about the same rate, while cereal production has expanded faster than the population; in Pakistan food production may have grown fractionally faster than the population and cereal production significantly faster. In all the other countries studied food production clearly has increased faster than the population, and in some countries, notably Sri Lanka and Malaysia, the difference in growth rates has been rather large.

Thus only in the countries refered to above on the South Asian sub-continent has the production of food per head failed to rise in the last two decades or so; elsewhere food has become increasingly plentiful. Of course, if China is excluded most of the population of Asia is concentrated in the sub-continent and this accounts for the sluggish movement of the weighted average of the seven countries. Only in Bangladesh, however, could one conceivably argue that the trends in food production explain the trends in poverty that have been indicated. But since poverty has increased even in countries which enjoyed a rapid expansion of food production, one must conclude that the connection between the two is tenuous.[1]

The structure of the economy

The answer to why the poverty of the poorest groups of the rural population has increased has more to do with the structure of the economy than its rate of growth. One structural feature common to all the countries studied is a high degree of inequality, as can be seen in table 4. Data from the six countries on which information is available suggest that in the economy as a whole the richest 20 per cent of households receive about half the income, whereas

---

[1] It is for this reason that the argument that "the nutrition problem is ... primarily a *poverty* problem: a problem of ineffective supply" (Leonard Joy: "Food and Nutrition Planning", in *Journal of Agricultural Economics*, Jan. 1973, pp. 1-22) seems to be more relevant than the statement that "the raising of agricultural output remains of paramount importance and that the solving of distributional problems is secondary ..." (Deepak Lal: "The Agrarian Question", in *South Asian Review*, July/Oct. 1975, p. 399).

Table 4. Income shares of decile groups

Country and year	Entire economy		Rural areas	
	Poorest 40%	Richest 20%	Poorest 40%	Richest 20%
Bangladesh (1963/64)	18.0	44.5	18.5	43.0
India (1963-65)	16.0	52.0	20.0	42.0
Malaysia (1970)	11.6	56.0	12.4	45.7
Pakistan (1963/64)	17.5	45.5	18.0	43.0
Philippines (1971)	11.6	53.8	13.3	51.0
Sri Lanka (1973)	15.1	45.9	17.0	42.7

Sources: Bangladesh and Pakistan: Asbjorn Bergan: "Personal Income Distribution and Personal Saving in Pakistan", in *Pakistan Development Review*, Summer 1967. India: P. D. Ojha and V. V. Bhatt: "Patterns of Income Distribution in India: 1953-55 to 1963-65", in T. N. Srinivasan and P. K. Bardhan (eds.): *Poverty and income distribution in India* (Statistical Publishing Society, Calcutta, 1974). Philippines: Hollis Chenery et al.: *Redistribution with growth* (Oxford University Press, 1974), table I.1, p. 8 and Ch. 11. Malaysia and Sri Lanka: ibid., Chapters 9 and 8 respectively.

the poorest 40 per cent receive between 12 and 18 per cent of total income. The bottom 20 per cent fare even worse, receiving between 3.8 and about 7 per cent of the income.

The degree of income inequality in rural areas, also reported in table 4, is somewhat less than in the urban areas and, hence, less unequal than the average for the economy. None the less, the degree of inequality is considerable. These differences should not be unduly stressed, however, as the data are not very precise.[1]

The counterpart to the compression of the income of the poor is the concentration of the economic surplus in the hands of a minority. The methods of disposal of this surplus, in turn, largely determine the pace and composition of economic growth. The preferences of the upper income groups as between present consumption and savings will affect the rate of accumulation. The pattern of demand, itself strongly influenced by the distribution of income, will determine in large part the sectors into which investment flows. And the set of relative factor prices which confront those who invest the surplus will have an effect on the methods of production that are used, the amount of employment that is generated, the productivity of that employment and the distribution of income.

The structure of factor markets is such that the unequal distribution of income arising from an unequal distribution of productive assets is reinforced by the operations of the price mechanism. Those who have access to the organised capital market are able to obtain finance capital for investment on relatively favourable terms.[2] Indeed, when nominal rates of interest are adjusted for inflation, the real rate of interest paid by large investors often is negative. This introduces a strong bias in favour of investment in the more capital-intensive sectors and in the more capital-intensive methods of pro-

---

[1] In fact, from the available alternative estimates of the distribution of income in India the data which present the lowest degree of inequality have been quoted.

[2] See, for example, Ronald I. McKinnon: *Money and capital in economic development* (Washington, The Brookings Institution, 1973).

duction. As a result, the demand for labour is lower than it otherwise would have been. Paradoxically, the relatively high productivity of labour associated with the more mechanised processes may lead to higher wages for those who find employment in the sector, thereby further reducing the demand for labour.

This pattern of investment is accentuated in countries where a system of protection is combined with a foreign exchange rate that is overvalued and import permits for foreign equipment consequently must be allocated through a rationing device of some sort.[1] The contrived cheapening of imported goods relative to domestic labour introduces an additional bias in favour of capital intensity, and tends to raise the share of profits in national income while reducing the demand for labour.

The capital markets operate in such a way that a small minority of the labour force is equipped with excessively capital-intensive techniques, given the relative availabilities of investible resources and labour. At the same time, the majority of the labour force (in urban as well as in rural areas) is forced to work with techniques which are insufficiently capital intensive. As a result, the productivity and incomes of the majority are exceptionally low compared to those employed in the so-called modern, capital-intensive sector. Crude "guesstimates" from Indonesia, for example, suggest that in the modern sector it costs about $5,000 to equip each additional worker. Expansion of employment in this sector provides for about 12 per cent of the new entrants into the labour force and absorbs over 70 per cent of the surplus allocated to investment. As a result, the investible surplus available for those who enter the informal urban sector and rural occupations is less than $300 per worker.

Price-cum-rationing mechanisms also are present in other parts of the economy. In fact most markets for intermediate goods and services operate in a fashion parallel to that of the capital market. For instance, electric power typically is distributed highly unevenly, many rural areas being excluded from the national network. Efficient transportation services are available to only a relatively few producers, and many rural areas are thus isolated from the main currents of commerce. Within the rural areas, technical assistance is concentrated on the large farmers and research programmes often are oriented toward their needs. Finally, even the labour market operates to the disadvantage of the poor, monopsonistic elements being present in many localities, often associated with a high degree of concentration of land ownership.[2]

The initially high degree of inequality of income and wealth, the concentration of the economic surplus in relatively few hands, and the fragmented allocative mechanisms constitute a socio-economic context in which powerful dynamic forces tend to perpetuate and even accentuate low standards of

---

[1] See I. M. D. Little, T. Scitovsky and M. F. Scott: *Industry and trade in some developing countries: a comparative study* (London, Oxford University Press, 1970).

[2] See Keith Griffin: *Land concentration and rural poverty*, op. cit.

living of a significant proportion of the rural population. Three such forces, or processes occurring through time, should be mentioned.

First, there is private investment. The volume of such investment is low in proportion to the economic surplus appropriated by those who control the national wealth. Although some of this investment is located in rural areas, much of it is channelled into the urban areas, notwithstanding the fact that as regards the countries studied the urban population accounts for as little as 10 per cent of the total in Bangladesh and about 30 per cent in the most urbanised country, Malaysia. This "urban bias"[1] in the pattern of investment often takes the form, as has been noted, of highly mechanised projects in which the share of wages in value added is relatively low. As a result, the rate of employment creation in the capital-intensive sector is slow, sometimes not even as fast as the rate of growth of the labour force. In the Philippines, for example, the proportion of the labour force engaged in manufacturing fell from 13 per cent in 1957 to less than 10 per cent a decade and a half later.[2] In Sri Lanka the situation was even worse: between 1959 and 1968 total employment increased less than 2 per cent a year whereas the labour force grew about 2.9 per cent a year.[3]

Those unable to obtain employment in the capital-intensive activities must seek a livelihood either in the urban informal sector or in rural areas, or become openly unemployed. If the labour force entering these categories expands faster than the rate of accumulation in the informal sector and rural areas combined, there are likely to be downward pressures on the real incomes of the most vulnerable workers in the most vulnerable sectors.

Moreover, these pressures are sometimes reinforced by trends in state investment which often is supportive of the large and capital-intensive private sector enterprises.

Second, the process of technical innovation has frequently a labour-saving bias in the activities in which most of the investment occurs. Part of the explanation for this is that the pattern of innovation is certain to be affected by the set of relative factor prices which large investors confront. It has already been noted that these factor prices encourage the adoption of relatively mechanised techniques which economise on labour. Another part of the explanation is that the economies under study are dependent for much of their innovation on imported foreign technology. This technology was developed in economies where labour is relatively scarce in relation to capital, and hence their exportation to countries where the opposite conditions prevail is likely to diminish still further the amount of employment created per unit of investment.

---

[1] See Michael Lipton: "Urban Bias and Food Supply in Poor Countries", in *Food Policy*, Nov. 1975.

[2] ILO: *Sharing in development: a programme of employment, equity and growth for the Philippines* (Geneva, 1974), tables 77 and 78, pp. 433 and 434.

[3] idem: *Matching employment opportunities and expectations: a programme of action for Ceylon* (Geneva, 1971), p. 48.

Thus in activities where most of the surplus is invested—in manufacturing, on the large mechanised farms, in ports, airports and highways development—there is a danger that the process of innovation will be increasingly labour-displacing. In the rest of the economy, however, where most of the labour force is occupied, the investible surplus is small and producers are forced by circumstances to seek land and capital saving innovations. At times this process may be pushed so far that the ratio of labour to land and capital begins to rise and a process of increasing poverty, declining labour productivity and "agricultural involution" is initiated.[1]

Whether and to what extent this happens depends, of course, upon the third dynamic process: demographic forces. Given the structure of the economy as it has been described and the resulting nature of the processes of accumulation and innovation, the faster the rates of growth of the population and labour force, the stronger will be the tendency for the standard of living of some groups to fall. Unfortunately, without exception rough estimates indicate that present rates of demographic expansion in the seven Asian countries are high. The slowest estimated rate of population growth is 2 per cent a year (in Indonesia), while the fastest is about 3 per cent (in Pakistan and the Philippines).

However, rapid population growth is certainly not the only cause of the increasing poverty of some sections of the rural population in Asia. Equally important causes seem to be the unequal ownership of land and other productive assets, allocative mechanisms which discriminate in favour of the owners of wealth, and a pattern of investment and technical change which is biased against labour.

Because of the rate and pattern of accumulation and innovation the amount of labour that can be readily absorbed in urban areas and in non-farm rural activities is relatively small—far smaller than the increase in the labour force. Agricultural production is characterised by diminishing returns to labour, which of course in principle could be offset by high rates of investment and technical change. Unfortunately, however, investment in agriculture has been modest, especially on the small farms, yet the sector has been forced to carry a large fraction of the annual increase in the labour force.

As a result, the tendency toward diminishing returns and falling labour productivity has not always been compensated by rising investment. As the land-man ratio has fallen, the level and share of rents has increased while the wage share, real wages and the number of days employed per person have tended to fall. In other words at the going terms of agricultural remuneration, the demand for labour has increased less rapidly than the supply and hence the standard of living of those who depend on work as a source of income has fallen. This has affected some plantation workers, unskilled landless agricul-

---

[1] Clifford Geertz: *Agricultural involution: the process of ecological change in Indonesia* (Berkeley, University of California Press, 1963).

tural labourers, pure tenants and some small landowners who have to supplement their income by engaging in paid labour.

Unemployment

A view once commonly held was that a major symptom of poverty is unemployment. The most recent evidence has shown, however, that there is relatively little open unemployment in rural areas although in some localities seasonal unemployment can be severe. In urban areas measured rates of open unemployment are much higher, but there is no evidence that the rate of unemployment has increased in the course of time.[1] Growing poverty is not necessarily associated with growing unemployment. Indeed it is noteworthy that in none of the empirical studies of Asia was unemployment cited as a prominent cause of poverty.

In broad terms unemployment is, first, an urban phenomenon and, second, a phenomenon of the middle class. The very poor cannot afford to be unemployed; they must obtain a source of livelihood even if this implies pitifully low earnings. It is found over and over again that education is positively correlated with unemployment. As an ILO report on Sri Lanka put it: "generally speaking, the more a young person has been educated, the greater the likelihood that he or she will be unemployed ...".[2] It is also found that unemployment rates often are higher among women than among men, although this appears not to be the case in India.[3] Again, it is noted that unemployment is much higher than average among the younger members of the workforce. Lastly, unemployment rates tend to be higher for dependants and those who are not heads of households than for the primary breadwinner. For example, in the Philippines in 1972 the unemployment rate among heads of households was 2.1 per cent whereas the unemployment rate among other workers was 9.3 per cent.[4]

Those who must find employment are likely to do so by entering the flexible income sector, i.e. the informal sector. For many years it was thought that wages or incomes in rural areas were institutionally fixed. The studies carried out for this work have shown, however, that inflation can easily erode the purchasing power of nominal wages, so that real wage rates can be highly flexible downwards. Moreover, in more than one instance, even nominal wages in rural areas have been known to fall.

---

[1] See, for example, David Turnham: *The employment problem in less developed countries: a review of evidence* (Paris, OECD, 1971).

[2] ILO: *Matching employment opportunities and expectations: a programme of action for Ceylon,* op. cit., Vol. 1. See also Mark Blaug: "The Unemployment of the Educated in India", in Richard Jolly, Emanuel de Kadt, Hans Singer and Fiona Wilson (eds.): *Third world employment* (Harmondsworth, Middlesex, Penguin Books, 1973).

[3] Turnham, op. cit.

[4] ILO: *Sharing in development: a programme of employment, equity and growth for the Philippines*, op. cit., table 1, p. 6.

A similar assumption of wage rigidity has been made as regards the urban areas, implying that entrants into the urban labour force had either to find one of the few jobs with a high, fixed wage or become openly unemployed. It is now known, however, that even in the modern sector real wages are flexible downwards. A study in Pakistan, for example, indicated that during the period 1954 to 1966-67 real wages in industry declined about 11 per cent.[1] Flexibility in the informal urban sector is even greater, of course.

Thus most of the poor are not unemployed and many of the unemployed are not poor. The people at the bottom of the consumption scale typically have jobs, although they are always on the alert for more rewarding opportunities. In fact there is a great deal of geographical and job mobility among the poor. Small landowners become temporary wage labourers during the slack season; landless workers from, say, Bihar, migrate to the more prosperous rural areas of western Uttar Pradesh; some rural residents (individuals as well as entire households) abandon the countryside and move to the city. Labour is continuously reallocated in response to income differentials between different regions and betweeen job categories to which the poor have access.

The process of migration results in the gradual elimination of the income differentials which initially provoked it. In particular, the exodus from the countryside tends to undermine income levels in the informal urban sector and reduce them to the levels prevailing in the rural areas. There is a strong presumption, of course, that the migrants benefit from migration, but the benefits are likely to be marginal. In effect, the movement of labour represents little more than a shuffling around of poverty. As long as the economic structure remains as has been described, with its income distribution and resource allocation mechanism intact, the major function of rural to urban migration is to spread the growing poverty of the countryside to the towns.

SOME BASIC ISSUES

On the basis of the findings of the country studies the problem of rural poverty and its main causes have been described in the preceding sections. In the following sections some main issues which are of immediate importance in finding solutions for overcoming the poverty crisis will be discussed. First, some observations on the nature of poverty will be made.

The well-being of an individual, household or collectivity depends on many things — the level of money income and of prices, the volume of production for self-consumption, the distribution of purchasing power, the allocation of government expenditure, the extent of participation in making the important decisions which affect one's life, the extent to which society is divided into classes and the degree of social mobility. Well-being, in other

---

[1] Keith Griffin and Azizur Rahman Khan (eds.): *Growth and inequality in Pakistan* (London, Macmillan, 1972), Ch. 9 and the Commentary to Part Four.

words, is a multi-dimensional concept; it depends in part on the absolute level of real income and consumption, in part on the relative distribution of income, wealth, power and social status, and in part on the ease with which it is possible to move from one occupation or social category to another. To express it in yet another way, the notion of well-being contains both stock and flow elements, both absolute and relative dimensions, and both static and dynamic characteristics.

It has long been recognised that the notion of well-being is too complex to be reduced to a single index number. Thomas Carlyle,[1] for example, writing in 1839, asked "What constitutes the well-being of a man?" In part, he said, it is wages and the amount of bread his wages will buy, but he then added that man does not live by bread alone.

Can the labourer, by thrift and industry, hope to rise to mastership; or is such hope cut off from him? How is he related to his employer — by bonds of friendliness and mutual help, or by hostility, opposition and chains of mutual necessity alone? ... With hunger preying on him, his contentment is likely to be small! But even with abundance, his discontent, his real misery may be great. The labourer's feelings, his notion of being justly dealt with or unjustly; his wholesome composure, frugality, prosperity in the one case, his acrid unrest, recklessness, gin-drinking, and gradual ruin in the other — how shall figures of arithmetic represent all this?

The answer, of course, is that they cannot and it would be idle to pretend that the "figures of arithmetic" in this volume do more than illuminate a small part of the problem of the lack of well-being of much of mankind. None the less, by assuming everything else is equal, it has often been argued that a rise in national income per head (for the nation) or in disposable income (for the family) is indicative of an increase in welfare and a decline in poverty. Tables of GNP per head and rates of growth of GNP have been widely used to assess the extent of international poverty and the rate at which welfare is rising. Within nations, "poverty lines" have been drawn, as is done in some of the chapters which follow, with the implication, presumably, that poverty will have been eliminated once those below the line are able to rise above it.

Increasingly, however, it has become accepted that income per head is an inadequate measure of well-being and that poverty is not an absolute concept that can be delineated by a poverty line. A family below the poverty line in the United States obviously would not be considered poor in Nigeria, for example. Similarly, a household in England earning 50 pounds a week in 1970 would be well above the poverty line, whereas an identical household with the same real income in 1978 might be considered rather poor. The point of these simple illustrations is that one's well-being or prosperity is relative; it is intimately related to the standard of living of one's neighbours.

Once this point is fully accepted, the idea that some items are absolute necessities, or that poverty is inversely related to income, must be abandoned. This was clear to Adam Smith two centuries ago when he stated that "By

---

[1] Thomas Carlyle: *Past and present* (London, Dent, Edition of 1882, reissued in 1967).

necessities I understand not only the commodities which are indispensably necesary for the support of life, but whatever the custom of the country renders it indecent for creditable people, even of the lowest order, to be without."[1] If "custom" determines "necessities", and if poverty is defined in relative terms, then the reduction of poverty by merely raising the average level of income will not be enough to achieve the well-being of the individual. The wider notion of poverty implies that over and above material needs there are other "necessities" which determine, together with food, shelter, clothing and health, the well-being of a person. In this sense poverty can only be eradicated when the needs for education, social mobility, participation, human working conditions, etc., are satisfied. Individual and collective freedom and respect for human rights and dignity constitute an inseparable part of a person's well-being.

The distribution of wages

It is often claimed that inequality is necessary in order to provide incentives, to encourage the labour force to increase its skills (and hence income) through training and education and to induce an efficient allocation of resources. When, however, one examines the evidence, incomplete though it is, it appears that inequality of earnings is one of the mechanisms perpetuating low income among the poor rather than a device for its alleviation.

It is often claimed that the large wage differentials observed in many underdeveloped economies — sometimes known as "wage cliffs" — are necessary in order to provide incentives and ensure the most productive use of resources. No doubt there is some truth in this argument. On the other hand, the effect of any given differential depends in part on the social context. In fact, in some circumstances earnings inequalities, apart from being undesirable in themselves, may reduce efficiency and growth. For example, in countries where the distribution of income is a mere reflection of social, caste or ethnic divisions in society, the incentive effect of earnings differentials on the mobility of labour and individual enterprise will be weak. If the social structure is rigid, rewards will be dissociated from effort and ability, and consequently wage inequality will perform no useful economic function whatever.

The greater the degree of social mobility in a country, the more effective will be wage differentials in ensuring an efficient allocation of resources. Thus the acceptability, or not, of a given degree of earnings inequality cannot be determined in isolation from the social and political system. If equality of opportunity and social mobility are considerable, earnings inequality may be more tolerable. On the other hand, if social mobility and equality of opportunity are not present, inequality simply adds insult to injury. A system which

---

[1] Adam Smith: *The wealth of nations* (Oxford, Clarendon Press, 1880), Book 5, Ch. 2, Part II, p. 466.

combines restricted education opportunities with wage inequality is far more objectionable than a more fluid system in which all have access to knowledge and education but in which inequality still prevails. One of the sad things about so many of the developing countries is that the wage structure provides potentially strong signals to acquire skills and training, yet the social and educational systems inhibit workers from responding to them. As a result, normal economic forces are frustrated and inequality is needlessly perpetuated. Indeed, as has been seen, in many countries poverty has increased. Thus, it cannot be claimed that wage inequality will necessarily provide incentives and ensure an efficient functioning of the economy. Logic and experience refute this.

Inequality and accumulation

Sometimes it is argued that inequality is essential in order to ensure a rapid rate of accumulation of capital and hence the eventual eradication of poverty through growth. The fact that growth does not automatically reduce poverty has already been noted.

A few further remarks regarding the relationship between inequality and investment may, however, be called for. First, the evidence on the connection between aggregate savings and income per head will be reviewed; next, unconventional ways of increasing investment will be considered, to be followed by some comments on the relationship between inequality and household savings.

It is important that the issue of inequality and accumulation be placed in a wide social context and that it not be confined to a discussion of individual or household savings decisions. The role of the State in mobilising resources is obviously relevant, since the effects of the distribution of income on savings are likely to be confined largely to savings originating in the household sector. Thus the larger public sector (and private corporate sector) savings as a proportion of the total, the smaller, *a priori*, will be the effects of changes in the distribution of income on aggregate saving and accumulation.

A major feature of developing countries is the comparatively low rate of domestic savings. The average gross savings rate is about 16 per cent,[1] and the net rate would be, say, approximately 12 per cent, with considerable variation around this average.

Although a high savings rate is not a sufficient condition for rapid growth, most economists are agreed that growth cannot be sustained without investment. It is useful to begin, therefore, by considering briefly why savings rates are relatively low in developing countries. A common view is that countries are poor because they do not save, and they do not save because they are

---

[1] See United Nations: *World economic survey, 1969-1970* (New York, 1971).

poor.[1] If this vicious circle of poverty does in practice operate, one would expect consumption as a percentage of GNP to be much higher in poor countries than in rich. In fact the relationship is rather weak.

Professor Kuznets examined the data for a large number of countries for the period following the Second World War. He organised these countries into seven groups in accordance with their income per head and then estimated private consumption as a percentage of GNP for each group. He found that in Group I — which includes the United Kingdom and the United States — private consumption accounted for about 65 per cent of GNP. On the other hand, in Group VII — which includes extremely poor countries such as Burma and Nigeria — the percentage was only slightly higher, viz. 73.1 per cent. Kuznets said: "it is surprising that the range of the share of private consumption expenditures for countries by per capita income is so narrow".[2] Even more surprising to those who believe in the vicious circle hypothesis is that within the groups of developing countries there is no association between the private consumption ratio and income per head. Group III (which includes Argentina and Chile) and Group IV (which includes Turkey and Columbia) both had a higher share of private consumption in GNP than the poorest countries in Group VII.

In a recent study Chenery and Syrquin examined the relationship between private consumption and income per head.[3] They too found a moderate inverse relationship and considerable variance.

Earlier Kuznets examined long-run trends in investment and savings in the few countries which had reliable data extending back to the nineteenth century. He concluded from this research that:

the rather simple relations assumed in much economic analysis—close association between levels of income and the savings proportions, and between capital formation proportions and the rate of growth—are not confirmed by the long-term records. The relation between capital formation and per capita income (as a determinant) and the rate of growth (as an effect) is too irregular and variable to warrant being given much weight in any realistic analysis. The association between national capital formation proportions or savings rates and levels of income is not close.[4]

There are no simple formulae for increasing savings and improving the performance of the public sector, but there are a few cases in which rapid progress would be possible. Too often, however, these opportunities are

---

[1] See Ragnar Nurkse: *Problems of capital formation in underdeveloped countries* (London, Oxford University Press, 1957).

[2] Simon Kuznets: "Quantitative Aspects of the Economic Growth of Nations, VII: The Share and Structure of Consumption", in *Economic Development and Cultural Change*, Jan. 1962, Part II, p. 5. Also see H. Houthakker: "On Some Determinants of Saving in Developed and Underdeveloped Countries", in E. A. G. Robinson (ed.): *Problems in economic development* (London, Macmillan, 1965).

[3] Hollis B. Chenery and Moises Syrquin: *Patterns of development, 1950-1970* (London, Oxford University Press, 1975), table 5, p. 38.

[4] Simon Kuznets: "Quantitative Aspects of the Economic Growth of Nations, V: Capital Formation Proportions: International Comparisons for Recent Years", in *Economic Development and Cultural Change*, July 1960, Part II, pp. 55-56.

overlooked. One reason for this, at least in part, is that conventional economic theory and the policy prescriptions derived from it are not always readily applicable in the developing countries. Take four examples where this appears to be true.

First, in some instances a judicious and discriminating rise in consumption will lead to increased productivity and output. This possibility, until recently, was seldom considered. In conventional economic thought expenditure is divided into two broad categories—expenditure on consumption and on capital goods. Spending on the latter accelerates growth, whereas spending on the former does not. It is now known, however, that expenditure on some items usually classified as consumption can, in some circumstances, raise output per man-hour.[1] Increased food consumption among the very poor and those suffering from malnutrition, more extensive preventive health measures, and expenditure on certain types of training and education and on improvement of industrial relations can result in greater energy and morale, less time lost as a result of illness and increased knowledge and skill—and thus contribute to accelerating growth.

One must not, of course, merely switch food, health and education expenditure from the consumption category to the investment category. They are quite different, even though they may be productive. Additional food consumption, for example, will raise productivity only over a certain range. It is obvious that most Argentinians would not produce more if they ate more food, but the same is not true for the landless labourers of Bangladesh. Similarly, more expenditure on personal curative medicine (e.g. surgery) would have a much smaller impact on aggregate output in, say, Java, than an equivalent sum spent on public health measures (e.g. village water supplies). Again, expansion of the classical-literary style educational system in a given country might have a negative impact on growth (since it diverts people into less productive activities), whereas the provision of technical training could be very productive.

The problem in many developing countries is still that public consumption either is channelled into unproductive activities, e.g. subsidised air transport, or is not sufficiently selective, e.g. food subsidies. The establishment of catering institutions in public and private enterprises might be a more effective way of ensuring that low-income workers receive an adequate diet than the price controls and general subsidies used in many developing countries.

Second, it sometimes is possible to increase investment not only by reducing consumption but also by reducing the amount of idle or unproductive labour time. Often labour is badly utilised and in some areas seasonal unemployment is severe. Thus unskilled manpower is not scarce and is waiting to be mobilised and reorganised for development. Experience shows that this

---

[1] Indeed, elaborate theories have been constructed on this premise. See for example James A. Mirrlees: "A Pure Theory of Underdeveloped Economies", in Lloyd G. Reynolds (ed.): *Agriculture in development theory* (New Haven, Conn., Yale University Press, 1975).

"surplus" labour can be organised and that it can be used to accelerate capital formation in rural areas. There are many tasks in the countryside which consist largely of earthmoving and simple construction—for example, irrigation ditches and earth dams, field terracing, drainage, school construction—and if these tasks can be accomplished by using underemployed labour in the slack periods of the year, a high rate of investment can be obtained at low real cost in terms of consumption. In most cases additional investment and faster growth can be achieved by working longer and harder, and this need not imply a reduction in current consumption. On the contrary, such a strategy is likely to lead to a quick and significant increase in the material well-being of the labourers who work on such projects.

The argument for a selective increase in consumption and a reduction in involuntary leisure as ways of accelerating growth does not imply that there is no need to raise domestic savings. What must be guarded against, however, is the tendency to assume that savings and investment are two separate decisions taken by separate groups in the community. Most simple models are based on the assumption that it is households which save and firms which invest, and these two independent decisions are reconciled through variations in the rate of interest and level of income.

In many developing countries, however, savings and investment are interdependent and there is no capital market, or only a rather rudimentary one, to bring the two groups together. In these conditions savings and investment are indistinguishable; they are the same thing. A peasant accumulates capital in the form of livestock by not slaughtering as many of his animals as are born. A small businessman increases the size of his firm by diverting part of his cash flow into the purchase of equipment rather than spending it on consumption goods. In other words, many of those who save do so in order to invest, and were there no desire to invest no savings would be forthcoming. This suggests that, until capital markets are fully developed, one way of increasing saving, and a third way of accelerating development, is to increase incentives and opportunities to invest. That is, instead of concentrating on reducing consumption, more attention should be devoted to policies which increase investment opportunities and incentives. The latter are likely to entail greater equality rather than the former.

Finally, consideration must be given to the relationship between income inequality and savings, as it is usually posed. Unlike the discussion above, the argument in favour of an unequal distribution of income is couched in very narrow terms and is based on the supposition that a household's marginal propensity to save increases with its average income. It follows, then, that the more unequal is disposable household income, the higher is the rate of household saving.

This supposition is not undisputed and the empirical evidence is at least inconclusive.[1] Indeed there are a number of studies which have shown that in

---

[1] See, for example, Keith Griffin and Azizur Rahman Khan (eds.): *Growth and inequality in Pakistan*, op. cit., pp. 199-207.

rural areas the distinction between rich and poor households is less significant in explaining savings behaviour than the distinction between landless labourers and cultivating households. A study in Haryana, India, indicates that there is no systematic relationship between the degree of inequality in rural areas and the savings ratio.[1] Another study in the Indian Punjab and in Haryana showed that there was no tendency for large farmers to save proportionately more than medium and small farmers.[2] On the other hand, numerous studies have shown that non-cultivating rural households save a negligible proportion of their income whereas cultivating households, including secure tenants, save a significant amount. There is a suggestion that in Indonesia the marginal and average savings ratio varies positively with the proportion of total income originating from owned land,[3] but most studies indicate that the savings rates of tenants and small farmers are comparable with those of large farmers. Research in Taiwan, for instance, revealed that the marginal savings rates of large and small farmers were not significantly different.[4]

The conclusion, then, is that under prevailing conditions the connection between inequality and household savings is very weak and perhaps non-existent. The link between inequality and corporate or public savings is, if possible, even more tenuous. In short, an unequal distribution of income cannot be justified on grounds of increasing the rate of accumulation. Nor, it is suggested, should it be justified on grounds of incentives. It is contended that there is no valid economic argument in favour of inequality. There are, however, powerful arguments against it—and it is to these that attention is now directed.

Equality and prosperity

In most rural areas of the Third World poverty is intimately related to the degree of land concentration.[5] A reduction in the inequality of land-ownership through a redistribution of landed property in favour of landless workers, tenants and small farmers would contribute directly to the alleviation of the most acute forms of poverty. Moreover, a redistribution of land through the creation of small holdings is likely to reduce poverty indirectly by increasing production and total income.

---

[1] K. N. Raj, D. K. Grover and D. S. Nandlal: "Investment and Saving Pattern in Irrigated and Unirrigated Zones of Haryana State", in *Indian Journal of Agricultural Economics*, Oct.-Dec. 1969.

[2] A. S. Kahlon and Harbhajan Singh Bal: *Factors associated with farm and farm family investment pattern in Ludhiana (Punjab) and Hissar (Haryana) Districts: (1966-67 through 1969-70)* (Department of Economics and Sociology, Punjab Agricultural University, Ludhiana), n.d.

[3] Allan C. Kelly and Jeffrey G. Williamson: "Household Saving Behaviour in the Developing Economies: The Indonesian Case", in *Economic Development and Cultural Change*, Apr. 1968.

[4] Marcia L. Ong, Dale W. Adams and I. J. Singh: "Voluntary Rural Savings Capacities in Taiwan 1960 to 1970" (Economics and Sociology Occasional Paper No. 175, Ohio State University).

[5] See Keith Griffin: *Land concentration and rural poverty*, op. cit.

The reason for this is that small farmers typically use production technologies, cropping patterns and rotation systems which are more productive than those used by large farmers. Specifically, small farmers tend to cultivate any given crop with more labour-intensive techniques. They also tend to choose a composition of crop and livestock activities which is more labour intensive. Finally, small farmers tend to use their land more intensively, even at risk of exhausting soil fertility. It is often found that as the size of farm increases, the proportion of the land which is uncultivated, in fallow or in natural pastures also increases.

As a result, employment per hectare rises, and output per worker falls, as the average size of farm declines. Similarly, yields and value added per hectare rise as the average size of farm declines. These tendencies have been observed in developing countries throughout the world, including several countries in Asia, notably Bangladesh,[1] Malaysia,[2] Sri Lanka, Indonesia and Thailand,[3] Pakistan, India and the Philippines.[4]

The inverse relationship between farm size and output per hectare is thus well established. Moreover, the evidence indicates that the relationship cannot be attributed to differences in land quality, soil fertility or the presence of irrigation, although these factors will also have to be taken into account. The differences in employment and output per hectare are largely due to differences in the behaviour of farmers, not to environmental differences. Even on a crop-by-crop basis, it appears that yields decline as farm size increases. The relationship is reinforced, however, by changes in the output mix.

It is increasingly becoming accepted that the explanation for the inverse relationship is systematic differences in relative factor prices which small and large farmers confront.[5] Interest rates on borrowed capital and the rental price of land are usually higher for the smaller farmers, while the wage rates for labour are sometimes higher for the larger farmer. As a result, the incentive system induces farmers to shift towards relatively higher land/labour and capital/labour ratios as the size of farm increases. These tendencies are often accentuated by public sector agencies which channel their services (technical assistance, credit, etc.) disproportionately toward the larger farmers.

The larger farmers, in consequence, often appear to be more innovative or "progressive". Indeed, studies of the Green Revolution have shown that the larger farmers were usually the first to introduce the new seed-fertiliser technology. Despite the adoption of high-yielding varieties, however, value

---

[1] Azizur Rahman Khan: *The economy of Bangladesh* (London, Macmillan, 1972), pp. 131-136.

[2] For evidence on the inverse relationship between size of farm and yields of rubber in Malaysia, see Colin Barlow and Chan Chee-Kheong: "Towards an Optimum Size of Rubber Holding" (paper presented at the Natural Rubber Conference, Kuala Lumpur, 1968).

[3] Keith Griffin: *The political economy of agrarian change* (London, Macmillan, 1974, pp. 39-45).

[4] R. Albert Berry and William R. Cline: *Farm size, factor productivity and technical change in developing countries* (Washington, DC, World Bank, 1976; mimeographed).

[5] See, for example, ibid. and Keith Griffin: *The political economy of agrarian change*, op. cit.

added per hectare continues to be less on the large farms than on the small; the high degree of labour intensity on the small farms more than compensates for the higher degree of capital intensity on the large.

It is important not to romanticise about the peasantry or exaggerate their comparatively higher total factor productivity. The intensity with which small farmers cultivate their land is mainly a reflection of the severe scarcity of resources complementary to their labour. In a sense, much of the peasantry is forced to engage in self-exploitation on small holdings because this is the only means of survival. Be that as it may, it follows from this analysis that a redistribution of land to small cultivators would increase both employment and output. In this connection it must, however, be noted that the land resources available for redistribution are in a number of cases relatively limited.

A reduction in inequality, therefore, if brought about through a redistribution of landed property and supported by subsidiary measures such as the provision of credit and marketing facilities, is likely to raise total production and is certain to raise the incomes of the poor. Indeed, it has been rightly stated that "rural development cannot be said to have begun without land reform."[1]

Under certain circumstances land redistribution may also lead to an increase in the rate of growth of production. Dynamic processes affecting the rate of growth, however, are rather unpredictable and their discussion necessarily remains somewhat speculative.

The chances that land reforms will initiate a process of cumulative development and a sustained reduction in poverty are particularly great where redistributive measures have been introduced as a direct result of organised pressure from the peasantry. Thus, the participation of the peasantry is essential, first, in order to ensure that a substantial initial redistribution occurs and, second, to ensure that land redistribution becomes not just an end in itself but a stimulus to further progress.[2] It is becoming more and more widely recognised that rural development, to be successful, must be not only for the people concerned but also by them.

Because of differences in historical circumstances and in the extent of participation by the poor, it is impossible to generalise about the effects of redistribution on growth. Most observers now believe, however, that "it is difficult to identify clear evidence of a trade-off between growth, however defined or measured, and distribution."[3] Yet the view may be becoming more widely accepted that the most effective way to redistribute income in

---

[1] Wahidul Haque, Niranjan Mehta, Anisur Rahman and Ponna Wignaraja: *Towards a theory of rural development* (United Nations, Asian Development Institute, 1975), p. 96.

[2] The importance of participation by the beneficiaries of reform is stressed by Joost B. W. Kuitenbrouwer: *Premises and implications of a unified approach to development analysis and planning* (United Nations, ESCAP, SD/SP/Ex In-3, 1975).

[3] Hollis Chenery et al.: *Redistribution with growth* (London, Oxford University Press, 1974), p. 255.

this connection is to redistribute wealth. An analysis of the historical experience of selected countries in Asia and elsewhere has led some observers to conclude that "in all cases, successful redistribution seems to have been preceded or accompanied by changes in the structure of asset ownership, particularly by land reform."[1]

The main conclusions to be drawn from the above discussion might be as follows. First, it is desirable and necessary that the mass of the population actively participate in the formulation and implementation of policies to reduce poverty. Second, a redistribution of productive assets, notably land, is likely to be an essential component of any development strategy designed to improve the living standards of the very poor and to reduce inequality. Third, land reform is likely to result not only in greater equality but also in higher output. Fourth, there is no reason to believe that it will reduce the rate of growth of agricultural output. It may, indeed, increase it in the longer run.

Undoubtedly the key to greater prosperity for the poor is a combination of greater equality and faster growth. This was well illustrated in a recent report prepared by the International Labour Office.[2]

In that report minimum consumption objectives—basic needs—were established for food, housing, education and, implicitly, for health. These specific items were used as a proxy for the larger basket of basic needs and this basket, in turn, was converted into an income equivalent by estimating from household expenditure data the level of income necessary to satisfy the household's basic needs. It was assumed that the objective is to meet the basic needs of the poorest 20 per cent or so of the population, most of whom are in rural areas, within one generation. This target implies that by the year 2000 all households except those with an income below the average of the lowest quintile would have met their basic needs. It was further assumed, optimistically perhaps, that the population would follow the United Nations low growth rate projection, implying a rapid fall in the rate of demographic expansion.

Calculations were first made of the rate of growth that would be necessary until the year 2000 to achieve the basic needs target, assuming no redistribution occurred. In the case of China the required rate of growth turned out to be 6.0 per cent per annum. Given that the China growth rate was 6.3 per cent a year between 1965 and 1973 such a strategy for achieving basic needs would seem to be feasible. In the case of the other medium- and low-income countries of Asia, however, the required rate of growth was much higher, namely 9.7 per cent a year. Since the recent rate of growth of these countries is much lower than this—the weighted average for the seven countries included in this volume is 4.4 per cent during the period 1965-73—it cannot be expected that on the basis of current growth rates alone

---

[1] Chenery et al., op. cit.

[2] ILO: *Employment, growth and basic needs: a one-world problem* (Geneva, 1976), Ch. 2.

the poor will be enabled to attain their basic needs, particularly if present high population growth rates do not fall as assumed in the model. Indeed, as the findings of the study suggest, the modest growth that has been achieved so far has resulted, in some countries, in a tendency for the very poor to become absolutely poorer. This would mean that some additional redistributive measures would be necessary.

Next, assuming countries were able to grow at the rate of 6 per cent per annum for a generation, the growth rate being that of the International Strategy adopted by the United Nations for the Second Development Decade, calculations were made of the amount of redistribution that would be necessary to achieve the basic needs targets. Specifically, estimates were made of what the share of the poorest 20 per cent of households would have to become by the year 2000 in order to meet the objectives. In the case of most medium- and low-income countries of Asia, the basic needs of the population could be met only if 6 per cent growth were combined with a redistribution of income such as to raise the share of the poorest quintile from 5.3 per cent at present to 14.3 per cent. That is, the share of the poor would have to increase nearly three times. Evidently such a strategy is not feasible.

Finally, the rate of growth that would be required to satisfy basic needs within the stipulated time was recalculated on the assumption that income be redistributed until the share of the poorest 20 per cent reached 11.3 per cent.[1] Under this assumption an annual rate of growth of 7.2 per cent would be needed in the medium- and low-income countries of Asia to enable them to meet the basic needs objective within a generation.

The model on which the growth calculations were based did not require a distinction between an initial, once-for-all redistribution and a series of annual incremental redistributions; all that was specified in the model was the distribution of income at the end of the period, i.e. the year 2000. In the practical application of the model, however, a large initial redistribution would be preferable, since the sooner redistribution occurs the higher will be the standard of living of the poor in the intervening years between the initiation of a basic needs strategy and its completion.

The model was concerned only with the distribution of income. In practice, however, measures which attempt to redistribute income without affecting the distribution of wealth seem to be difficult to implement. This is partly because it is difficult to confine the effects of standard price, subsidy, tax and expenditure policies to a particular group and partly because the effects of many standard economic policies ultimately are neutralised by offsetting forces set in motion by the policies themselves.[2] For example, the benefits of a rural road building programme cannot be limited to small farmers; they

---

[1] This figure corresponds to the share of the poorest quintile in China. See *Employment, growth and basic needs ...*, op. cit., p. 42.

[2] See Keith Griffin: *Land concentration and rural poverty*, op. cit., Introduction.

inevitably "spill over" or "leak" to large farmers as well. Similarly, the imposition of a minimum wage for landless agricultural labourers will have multifarious implications for, say, the costs of agricultural production, the demand for labour, the level of food prices and of prices in general—all of which may to a certain extent counteract the effects of the legislation on the distribution of income. Thus because of leakages and countervailing forces the only way to alter substantially the distribution of income is by altering the distribution of wealth. In agricultural countries this implies above all the need for land reform.

PART II

POVERTY AND LANDLESSNESS
IN RURAL ASIA

RURAL POVERTY AND
LANDLESSNESS IN PAKISTAN

2

S. M. Naseem

The people of Pakistan[1] have, on average, a higher level of income than those living in the two other major countries of the subcontinent. The population of the country, which was 63.2 million in 1974-75, is estimated to be growing at a rate of 3 per cent per annum. The amount of land available per person, however, is among the highest in Asia.[2] Industrial growth during the past 25 years has been consistently high and has transformed Pakistan into a semi-industrialised country—although most of the industries are based on processing agricultural raw materials. Since the mid-1960s the agricultural sector also has experienced rapid growth through the spread of the Green Revolution. The mechanics of the growth process, however, have created inter-regional, inter-sectoral and inter-personal disparities of income.

Although the secession of Bangladesh in 1971 was the consequence of a complex set of economic, political, social, cultural and geographical circumstances, the rapid industrial growth of the then West Pakistan, when set alongside the stagnation of the then East Pakistan, helped to precipitate the separation. But such inter-regional tensions were only one aspect of the unbalanced and inegalitarian growth in the former undivided Pakistan. Inter-sectoral and inter-personal income inequalities created within West Pakistan became prominent once the thorny question of the relationship between the two major regions was solved.

Agriculture has been the mainstay of Pakistan's economy. In addition to employing 55 per cent of the labour force[3] it has constituted the foundation on which the industrial sector rests (textiles and food processing accounting for the major share in value added) and, through its exports, agriculture has earned most of the country's foreign exchange. As in most Asian countries,

---

[1] Before December 1971 Pakistan consisted of the present States of Pakistan and Bangladesh (then known as East Pakistan). However, the term Pakistan in this chapter, even for the pre-1971 period, refers to the present State of Pakistan only (known as West Pakistan before December 1971).

[2] The amount of cultivated land per agricultural family of 5.5 persons is about 7½ acres.

[3] This estimate is based on the 1967-68 Labour Force Sample Survey.

the development strategy in Pakistan has tended to be urban-biased and the improvement of conditions in the rural areas has received rather low priority. The advent of the Green Revolution, however, has brought prosperity to those who own land and are capable of investing in the new agricultural inputs. Government subsidies and extension services have helped the new techniques to become more widely adopted. Agricultural stagnation has definitely ended and the country's goal of food self-sufficiency is becoming a reality.

These developments in Pakistan's rural areas may induce one to take the view that everyone's well-being has improved. Whether this has been the case will be examined in this study. It will be shown who the people are who suffer most from poverty, where are they concentrated and whether poverty in rural areas has increased over time. The findings will not tell much about who has gained from growth and to what extent. It is obvious, however, that, since average incomes and output per head have been rising, the final outcome was not a zero-sum game.

In the first part of the study the movements in rural poverty over time are described. In the second part rural poverty is related to the distribution of the ownership of land and an attempt is made to identify the occupational structure of the rural poor. In the third part the trends in landlessness and related factors and their effects on poverty are examined. Lastly, the regional dimension of the poverty problem is described.

TRENDS IN RURAL POVERTY IN PAKISTAN

The most important source of data for detemining trends in rural poverty in Pakistan is the Household Surveys of Income and Expenditure (formerly the Quarterly Surveys of Current Economic Conditions) carried out by the Central Statistical Office. These are available for 1963-64, 1966-67 and from 1968-69 to 1971-72, after which they were discontinued. Before 1963-64 two surveys were undertaken in the years 1960 and 1961, but their scope was much more limited and they have since become inaccessible. The main empirical basis for the study, therefore, will be the Household Income and Expenditure Surveys from 1963-64 to 1971-72. From the point of view of making policy deductions, the experience of the 1960s would seem to be most interesting, since it was then that a well-articulated policy was enforced of promoting growth regardless of its social and distributional consequences. After the reduction of Pakistan to its present size in 1971, and after the inevitable transition period of readjustment, many changes were made in the general orientation of policy. Although little time has elapsed since these changes were introduced, an attempt is made, on the basis of incomplete data, to evaluate the possible impact they might have had on the extent of rural poverty in Pakistan.

A basic step in determining the extent of poverty, as well as trends in the extent of poverty, is the selection of an income or consumption norm for the individual or the household. This norm should reflect a minimum below which existence is intolerable. The selection of such a poverty line, of course, is rather arbitrary. In most exercises concerned with developing countries the poverty lines are related to the absorption of a minimum diet based on nutritional requirements. The logic of such exercises is that since food is the most basic of the basic needs, the attainment of an adequate diet commands priority over other needs. Moreover, it is possible that other needs can largely be satisfied by maintaining a proper relationship between food consumption and total consumption. Another reason for working with dietary minima is that it is conceptually (as well as practically) difficult to work with similar norms for other basic needs, e.g. clothing, housing, medical and other services.

Following the above reasoning, the poverty line is defined as the total consumption expenditure of households (or individuals) at which the stipulated amount of food is purchased. This level of total expenditure, at the constant prices of a particular year, is then used to estimate the number or proportion of people living in poverty. That is, those with an income less than the amount associated with the purchase of an adequate diet are classified as the poor.

The regularity implied by Engel's law between food and non-food consumption expenditures should not lead one to neglect cross-cultural differences in the consumption of non-food items. In other words, the assumption that those who are adequately fed also receive an adequate amount of other goods and services (by their own or somebody else's standard) may not necessarily be true. In addition, one should not exclude the possibility that there are significant consumption externalities in regard to both food and non-food items. The consumption pattern of the relatively affluent, for example, may influence the preferences of the poor in such a way that their physiological well-being is reduced below what it otherwise could have been.

A number of attempts have been made by nutritional experts to define a balanced diet which ensures an adequate supply of basic nutrients to the human body. Such diets have also taken into account relevant climatic, ecological and sociological factors, as well as the tastes of the specific population groups for which they are recommended. The two diets frequently mentioned on the Indian subcontinent are those recommended by the FAO and Sukhatme. The Nutrition Cell of the Planning Division of the Government of Pakistan also has developed a normative diet based on local conditions. These three diets are described in table 5.

These standard diets are very expensive and are beyond the reach of all except the very high-income groups in a country such as Pakistan. They provide for a relatively low percentage of calories to be derived from cereals, which are the cheapest source of calories. Thus, in Pakistan, wheat flour is the cheapest source; pulses and rice, although much more expensive than wheat as a source of calories, are much cheaper than meat, milk, vegetables and fruits. Whereas the standard diets supply only 60-70 per cent of the

Table 5.   Some recommended diets

Item	Kilograms per person per day recommended by:		
	Sukhatme	FAO	Planning Division
Cereals	0.403	0.395	0.411 (0.343 wheat; 0.068 rice)
Pulses	0.104	0.075	0.025
Starch roots	0.046	0.160	–
Sugar	0.050	0.035	0.078 (0.024 refined; 0.054 raw)
Milk	0.201	0.098	0.171
Fish and eggs	0.019	0.027	–
Meat	0.007	0.036	0.018
Fruits and vegetables	0.137	0.225	0.093
Oils and fats	0.018	0.016	0.016

Source: P. V. Sukhatme: *Feeding India's growing millions* (London, Asia Publishing House, 1965); FAO: *Monthly Bulletin of Agricultural Economics and Statistics*, Jan. 1973; and an unpublished source from the Planning Division, Government of Pakistan.

calorie intake through the consumption of cereals, actual consumption patterns in rural Pakistan reveal that about 80-90 per cent of the calorific intake is derived from cereals. Given that calorie consumption is itself inadequate, this implies that for a given level of calories the actual diets are seriously deficient in other nutrients for which cereals are a poor source compared to the standard recommended diets.

It is well known that the distribution of consumption tends to be less unequal than that of income, savings rates being proportional to income. The distribution of expenditure on food also is less unequal than that of total consumption and the distribution of expenditure on cereals is even less unequal than that of food consumption because of the relative concentration on cereals by the poorer groups. A low proportion of food expenditure to total expenditure implies greater availability of other goods and services and a low proportion of calories obtained from cereals indicates that other nutrient requirements are being better met. This, together with the fact (pointed out in Chapter 7) that the calorie requirements of poorer households are likely to be higher than average because the poor engage in more arduous work, suggests that inequalities in the distribution of calories grossly understate disparities in economic welfare.

The data on calorie consumption were estimated for the various income groups from the Household Surveys of Income and Expenditure of the various years. Data on household expenditure for these groups were also tabulated. Since these latter data are at current prices it was necessary to convert them into constant prices of a certain year. For this purpose a Laspeyre price index for each of the 11 income groups in the 1963-64 Survey was prepared by using that year's expenditure weights for each group.[1] The

[1] These indices are shown in S. M. Naseem: *Rural poverty and landlessness in Pakistan: dimensions and trends* (Geneva, ILO, 1976; mimeographed World Employment Programme research working paper; restricted).

base year of the price relatives of this index is 1959-60. By deflating the household expenditures by these group-specific cost of living indices all expenditure was converted into 1959-60 constant values.

The next step was to identify a poverty line—a level of consumption per head at the constant prices of 1959-60 which would enable an average rural household to obtain the minimum calorie intake per head. The regression of daily calorie intake per head (K) on monthly consumption expenditure at 1959-60 prices per head (C) produced the following fit on the basis of pooled data from the five Household Surveys (altogether 56 pairs of observations were obtained on calorie intake per head and consumption expenditure per head based on grouped data from the six Surveys):

$$\log K = 2.7403 + 0.3887 \log C; R^2 = 0.77$$

For an average Pakistani a daily intake of 2,100 calories is believed to be the minimum requirement. From the above equation it is found that a monthly consumption per head of Rs. 31.41 at 1959-60 prices would be necessary to enable a rural household in Pakistan to obtain a daily intake per person of 2,100 calories. It would be a little absurd, however, to use such a "high" poverty line. In 1963-64, the first of the years for which information is available on the distribution of consumption and calories, over 85 per cent of the rural households in Pakistan (or 80 per cent of the population) were below this norm. Thus it must be concluded that for Pakistan a level of income that ensures adequate calorie consumption, but almost certainly implies serious deficiency in non-calorie nutritional requirements, is too high to be used as a realistic poverty line.

Instead, three different poverty levels respectively representing the amounts of income that permit the intake of 95 per cent, 92 per cent and 90 per cent of the minimum required calories have been used. Thus poverty line I, the highest of the three levels, represents Rs. 27.53 at 1959-60 prices. This level of income would permit the intake of 1,995 calories (95 per cent of the requirement) per head per day according to the above regression equation. Poverty line II, the intermediate level, represents Rs. 25.35 at 1959-60 prices. This is consistent with a daily calorie intake per head of 1,932 (92 per cent of the requirement). Poverty line III, representing Rs. 23.95 at 1959-60 prices, is consistent with a daily calorie intake per head of 1,890 (90 per cent of the requirement), and the lowest of the three levels.[1]

The percentage of population and households below the poverty lines in different years is given in table 6. The percentage of the population (households) lying below a poverty line was derived by plotting a curve with the cumulative percentage distribution of the population (households) below given levels of expenditure per head on one axis and corresponding expenditure per head at constant prices on the other and by drawing a perpendicular

---

[1] The cost of the Sukhatme diet shown in table 5 is Rs. 20.1 at 1959-60 prices. Since food accounts for about 70 per cent of total consumption expenditure for the low-income groups in 1963-64, the use of this diet as the minimum norm implies a poverty line of Rs. 28.7, which is considerably higher than any of the poverty lines noted here.

Table 6.   Incidence of poverty in rural Pakistan
(Percentages)

Year	Below poverty line I (95 per cent of minimum of 2100 calories)		Below poverty line II (92 per cent of minimum of 2100 calories)		Below poverty line III (90 per cent of minimum of 2100 calories)	
	Households	Population	Households	Population	Households	Population
1963-64	79	72	62	54	54	45
1966-67	73	64	63	52	55	44
1968-69	74	64	63	53	56	46
1969-70	76	68	56	46	45	36
1970-71	79	71	58	47	48	38
1971-72	82	74	65	55	54	43

on the latter at the level of consumption expenditure per head corresponding to the poverty line. The intersection of the perpendicular with the plotted curve shows the percentage of the population (households) lying below the stipulated poverty line.[1]

The results presented in table 6 consist of six sets of data based on three poverty lines—three lines each for households and population. The proportion of the population below a poverty line is lower than the proportion of households below a poverty line and this is especially noticeable for the lower poverty lines. This phenomenon reflects the fact that the poorer households are generally smaller in size than the average.

The proportion of households below poverty line I drops after the base year and rises steadily thereafter. The trend appears to be upwards. The proportion of households below poverty lines II and III shows no definite trend; except for a temporary drop in the late 1960s it remains essentially unchanged. These conclusions also generally apply to the proportion of the population below the poverty lines.

Thus, the proportion of households and people in poverty, if poverty is defined in terms of a level of expenditure consistent with the intake of 95 per cent of the minimum calorie requirement, appears to have increased over the years. When poverty is defined in more extreme and intolerable terms (e.g. as the level of expenditure permitting the intake of no more than 90 per cent of the minimum required calories) it appears to have remained roughly unchanged in percentage terms over the years. Of course, the absolute numbers of households and population below each poverty line have increased over the years.

The above trends in poverty need to be contrasted with the over-all growth of the rural economy. During the period under consideration Paki-

---

[1] In practice, the percentages of population and households were located by linear interpolations. Such interpolations were necessary because information was available about only some points of the distribution and not about the entire distribution. In general such interpolation biases the estimates of poverty downwards. It is to be hoped that the bias is roughly of the same degree in all years. Since the primary concern was with change over time the downward bias of the level of poverty did not cause undue worry.

stan experienced a rapid expansion in agricultural production and income. From the second half of the 1960s the country experienced a remarkable spread of the Green Revolution. Although periodic fluctuations occurred as a result of variable weather conditions and other factors, the over-all trends of production and income were strongly upwards. None the less, poverty failed to decline. Consequently, the distribution of expenditure and income must have worsened.

DISTRIBUTION OF LAND, TENURIAL STATUS AND POVERTY

The estimates of poverty in the preceding section were based on data on total expenditure derived from household income and expenditure surveys. Although they illuminate the extent and trend of rural poverty, they help very little in identifying who are the rural poor. The main source of livelihood for the majority of households is, of course, land. Although a majority of households is engaged in the cultivation of land, only a minority actually owns the land. Thus, according to the Population Census of 1961, out of the 6.5 million rural households, 4.87 million were cultivating land either as owners or tenants, or both. Of these, only 1.97 million cultivators were tenants renting all land. An estimated 0.61 million rural households consisted of landless agricultural labourers and 1.04 million were engaged in non-farm occupations. The economic condition of these various groups can be determined with varying degrees of accuracy.

So far as the cultivating households are concerned, the 1960 Census of Agriculture gives the size distribution of holdings cultivated by three tenurial groups, viz. owners, owners-cum-tenants and tenants. Table 7 gives the distribution of farms by three major size groups and for the three main tenurial categories.

The picture presented in table 7 is very aggregative but none the less shows the high degree of concentration of holdings, especially among the owner and owner-cum-tenant farms. The Gini concentration ratios for land distribution, derived from the detailed distribution shown in the Census of Agriculture, are as follows:

All farms	0.61
Owner farms	0.71
Owner-cum-tenant farms	0.55
Tenant farms	0.54

How many of the 4.87 million land-operating rural households were below the poverty line? This is not an easy question to answer. The Census of Agriculture does not contain a distribution of income or expenditure according to the size of holdings. Nor is it possible to determine on an *a priori* basis the minimum size of farm holding that would keep a household above the poverty line. However, some rough approximations can be attempted.

Table 7. Number and area of farms, by size and tenure
(Percentages)

Farm size	Owner farms		Owner-cum-tenant farms		Tenant farms		All farms	
	No.	Area	No.	Area	No.	Area	No.	Area
Small farms (under 5 acres)	25	4	6	2	19	4	50	10
Medium farms (5 to 25 acres)	13	15	9	11	20	22	42	48
Large farms (over 25 acres)	3	19	2	10	3	13	8	42
Total	41	38	17	23	42	39	100	100

Source: *Pakistan Census of Agriculture 1960*, Vol. II: West Pakistan.

There are very wide variations in the productivity and cropping pattern of land in the various parts of Pakistan. It is, therefore, impossible to work with a single figure for all regions. However, in order to obtain a conservative estimate of the extent of rural poverty one may use as a yardstick the size holding in a relatively more productive area which provides a subsistence level of living for an average household. An IBRD Survey[1] in 1966 estimated that an average family in one of the Canal Districts (which are the most productive agricultural regions of the Punjab) would require 5 acres for subsistence. This can be taken as the minimum size for owner-cultivators. For tenants the figure would be 10 acres, since 50 per cent of the produce is given as the landlord's share. For owner-cum-tenants the figure used is 6.4 acres, since owner-cum-tenants typically own 56.6 per cent of the land they farm.

This produces the following estimate of the number and proportion of farm households below subsistence level by tenurial status:

	Number in thousands	Percentage
Owners	1,201	60.3
Owner-cum-tenants	294	38.0
Tenants	1,359	67.1
Total	2,854	58.7

This, it must be repeated, is a very conservative estimate as the subsistence farm size in a Canal Colony district in the Punjab has been used as the basis of the calculation. In non-irrigated, *barani* (rain-fed) and arid areas of Pakistan the minimum size of farm is likely to be considerably higher.

To complete the picture of rural poverty in 1961 there must be added to this category the 0.6 million landless agricultural labourers who are generally regarded as being on the lowest rung of the economic ladder in the rural

[1] IBRD (International Bank for Reconstruction and Development): *Programme for the development of irrigation and agriculture in West Pakistan: a comprehensive report* (May 1966).

Table 8.   Income per head and per year of different occupational groups in the
Punjab, 1970-71
(Rupees)

Occupational group	Eckert survey	Punjab Board of Economic Inquiry survey
Large farmers	1 102	933
Small farmers	318	633
Tenants	200	343
Agricultural labourers		180
Permanent	192	
Casual	173	
Artisans		253
Mueens (menial workers)		225
Shopkeepers		327

Source: J. B. Eckert: *Rural labour in Punjab, a survey report* (Lahore, 1972); Punjab Board of Economic Inquiry: *Farm accounts and family budgets of cultivators in the Punjab, 1970-71* (Lahore, 1973).

areas.[1] This leaves 1.04 million households in the rural areas which were engaged in non-farm occupations. On the basis of a conservative estimate that half of these households were poor, the following is the aggregate picture of the composition of poor households: farming households, 2.85 million; landless labour households, 0.61 million; non-farm households, 0.52 million; making a total of 3.98 million.

Thus out of a total of 6.5 million households in 1961 about 3.98 million or 61 per cent of the households were poor. This estimate is close to the estimated proportion of households below the middle poverty line in table 6.

A further idea of the relative position of the different groups in the rural economy in a more recent year can be obtained by comparing average incomes of these groups as estimated from two surveys conducted in 1970-71 in the Punjab. These estimates are reported in table 8. The categories of the two surveys are not always comparable, but both of them make it clear that the "landed" classes are relatively much better off than the others and that landless agricultural labourers are at the extreme end of the income scale. Their average income is well below any realistic poverty line.

CHANGES DURING THE 1960s AND EARLY 1970s

Knowledge of changes in land distribution and its effect on occupational structure and rural income distribution since 1960-61 is rather limited. In 1972 both an agricultural and a population census were carried out but, unfortunately, the results of neither have been officially released so far. Ana-

---

[1] According to the 1961 population census the number of landless labourers was 0.61 million. The corresponding figure according to the 1951 census was 0.14 million. Thus between 1951 and 1961 the increase in the number of landless workers was nearly 350 per cent.

lysis of these trends will therefore be limited by the non-availability of this important set of data. When these censuses become available it will be necessary to compare the present analysis with the new evidence.

Two significant structural changes have taken place since the beginning of the 1960s. These are likely to have affected the distribution of land by different tenurial and size groups. The first consists of two land reforms carried out under Martial Law Regulations in 1959 and 1972. The second is the introduction, with government encouragement and subsidies, of a set of technological innovations associated with the Green Revolution which resulted in an increase in agricultural productivity.

Land reforms

The effects of land reforms on tenurial status and land distribution and, hence, on incomes and levels of living in the rural areas can be both direct and indirect. The direct effects consist of providing security of tenure and of land redistribution in favour of tenants, small peasants and landless labourers. The indirect effects consist of pre-emptive and sometimes fictitious transfers of land by larger landowners. Land reforms may also induce a trend towards self-cultivation of land, the substitution of tenant farming by farming with hired labour and the substitution of hired labour by family labour.

Before 1959, land reform laws were intended mainly to provide security of tenure and occupancy rights to tenants. The Martial Law Regulation of 1959 (MLR 64) was the first piece of legislation which provided for a ceiling on land holdings—500 acres of irrigated or 1,000 acres of non-irrigated land. The impact of this ceiling was considerably softened by the granting of a number of exemptions, such as permission to transfer to heirs 18,000 Produce Index Units[1] of land equivalent (thereby effectively increasing the ceiling by roughly 50 per cent). In addition, there was an exemption of 150 acres for orchards and an exemption for stud and livestock farms. Compensation to the landowners was provided at a rate varying from 1 to 5 rupees per PIU, depending on the area of land resumed, in 50 half-yearly equal instalments.

The effects of the 1959 land reform measures on the pattern of ownership can be judged by the fact that 5,064 landowners declared land in excess of 500 acres, amounting to 2.35 million acres. According to the estimates prepared by the Planning Commission at that time there were 6,061 landowners with land in excess of 500 acres on 7.5 million acres. Of the total resumed land of 2.35 million acres, 755,000 acres were sold to 196,000 sitting tenants (an average of 3.85 acres per tenant) and 100,000 acres to 4,000 small landowners (25 acres per farmer).

---

[1] A Produce Index Unit (PIU) is the value attached to the quality of land and it varied from 5 for an acre of waste land in Baluchistan to 120 for an acre of double-cropped land in the fertile districts of Punjab.

Thus a total of 200,000 families benefited from the land reforms out of an estimated 2.5 million subsistence farmer households, or about 8 per cent of such households. The sale price of land was about one-fifth of the ruling market price. It may be conjectured that a substantial amount of such land was resold by the allottees to larger farmers.

The philosophy of the 1959 land reforms was clearly stated by the Land Reforms Commission:[1]

... in determining the extent of the ceiling, social justice has not been the only criterion before us... the ends of social justice, in the sense of securing land for the entire landless population, thus being almost unattainable, what we thought prudent was to fix the ceiling at a level which will on the one hand eradicate the feudalistic elements from the existing tenure structure, and on the other, by causing the minimum necessary disturbance of the social edifice, lead to a harmonious changeover and at the same time, by providing incentives at all levels, conduce to greater production.

The land reforms announced in early 1972 were considerably more far-reaching than those of 1959. The ceilings for irrigated and unirrigated land were reduced to 150 and 300 acres, respectively, or to an area equivalent to 15,000 PIUs, whichever is greater. The owner was allowed to retain an additional area equivalent to 3,000 PIUs if he owned a tubewell or tractor as of 20 December 1971. The ceiling was later reduced to 12,000 PIUs and the tubewell and tractor supplement to 2,000 PIUs. The 1972 reforms also ended the exemptions given to orchards, stud and livestock farms and, what was perhaps the most radical measure, they provided no compensation to those whose land was taken away.

The total area resumed under the 1972 land reforms by 31 October 1974 was only 879,000 acres, or a little over a third of the area resumed under the 1959 reforms. It is widely suspected that the declarations were very low and that large owners concealed and illegally transferred vast amounts of land. It has been estimated that at least 2.8 million acres of land should have been forthcoming as resumable land if the land reforms laws had been implemented effectively, and moreover, that the 1972 land reforms, even if their full potential is realised, will benefit no more than 16 per cent of the tenants under the most optimistic assumptions.[2]

The Martial Law Regulation of 1972 gives priority in land redistribution to those tenants already farming the resumed acreage. Completely landless tenants were to receive 12.5 acres of land. Tenants who had some land were to receive additional land to bring their total to this "subsistence" farm size. In the event, only 50,306 small farmers and tenants received a total area of 446,950 acres, or an average of 8.9 acres.

The preceding discussion of land reform measures indicates that a total of only 250,000 farm families, or only 5 per cent of the farming families in 1960,

---

[1] Land Reforms Commission: *Report of the Land Reforms Commission for West Pakistan* (Lahore, January 1959), p. 30.

[2] R. Herring and M. Ghaffar Chaudhry: "The 1972 Land Reforms in Pakistan and their Economic Implications", in *Pakistan Development Review*, XIII-3, 1974, pp. 245-279.

were favourably affected by the two land reforms through direct redistribution of land. Whether those families continued to retain the land and whether the land was always sufficient to pull them above the subsistence level cannot be determined from the existing data. In any event, neither of the two land reform measures helped to improve the lot of the landless labourers directly. Moreover, to the extent that the land reforms, or fear of future reforms, induced absentee landlords to cultivate their land themselves, they may have led to a displacement of tenants.

The effect of technological changes

Pakistan's agricultural sector tended to stagnate in the 1950s when growth rates of output were below that of the population. Growth accelerated during the Second Five-Year Plan (1960-65), however, to 3.4 per cent a year, thereby outpacing the population growth rate by between 0.5 and 1 per cent. During the Third Five-Year Plan (1965-70) agricultural growth accelerated further, despite a serious drought and the war with India, and achieved an average rate of growth of 4.1 per cent. Since 1970 agricultural growth has been disrupted by disturbed political and economic conditions during 1970-72, by heavy flooding in 1973, by the lowest ever canal discharges in 1974-75 and by the mishap in the gigantic Tarbela dam. Nevertheless, the growth trend has continued and the agricultural economy has regained its vitality.

Among the sources of agricultural growth in Pakistan, water resource development (especially tubewells) and, since 1965, fertilisers and new seeds have played prominent roles. In addition, the Government has been active in providing incentives for higher production through increases in support prices for major crops, subsidies to yield-augmenting inputs of fertilisers, seeds and insecticides and through the provision of subsidised credit for capital inputs such as tubewells and tractors. It has been the Government's policy to reverse the unfavourable terms of trade against agriculture and this policy has been largely successful.

The employment and income distribution effects of the new technological innovations in Pakistan agriculture depend on the extent of the diffusion of new inputs among different classes of farmers. The inputs of tubewells, fertilisers and new seeds require a considerable amount of investment on the part of farmers. The ability to reap the benefits of the new technological breakthrough thus depends on the ability to mobilise enough funds, either through savings or borrowing, to undertake such investment. Although the technology itself is not biased in favour of large farmers, since there are no significant scale economies and the rates of return on investment are fairly high, institutional arrangements such as access to credit and scarce inputs do give large farmers an advantage. The high incidence of tenancy may also reduce incentives to invest in these inputs.

In Pakistan, where land ownership is highly concentrated and bureaucratic controls are widespread, access to the key inputs is directly proportional to the size of one's landholding. Whether it is the transmittal of knowledge through the extension services, access to credit, or securing additional canal water supplies, the distribution of services is primarily in favour of the large landowners. Even the co-operatives and other Government Departments tend to discriminate against the small farmers.

Many studies of the Green Revolution in Pakistan have shown, however, that despite the bias of the administrative setting there has been broad-based participation of small farmers in at least the initial stages of the seed-fertiliser revolution.[1] There is some evidence which shows that small farmers have lagged a year or so behind the larger farmers in adopting the new techniques and that their application of fertiliser per acre has been lower than that of larger farmers.

As regards tubewells, however, the diffusion of technology has been less uniform. Subsidised credit available for the purchase of tubewells has gone mainly to large farmers, because of strict standards of creditworthiness imposed by the lending agencies, the greater familiarity of larger farmers with the procedures for obtaining credit and because of their ability to obtain from the Government electricity to run the pumps. According to the Farm Mechanisation Survey of 1968, 70 per cent of the tubewells in Pakistan were installed by farmers having more than 25 acres. Only 4 per cent were installed by the size group ranging from 0 to 13 acres—the group that includes more than two-thirds of Pakistan's cultivators.[2]

While the net effects of the seed-fertiliser-tubewell revolution may have been favourable to employment and only moderately unfavourable to income distribution, tractor mechanisation has affected the poorer sections of the rural population, especially tenants, wholly adversely. If mechanisation were to be used mainly to reclaim uncultivable land, it would be land augmenting. However, in its present form, tractor mechanisation in Pakistan is mostly applied to the already cultivable land. The primary function of tractor mechanisation in Pakistan agriculture has been to replace animal or manpower by machine power in the cultivation of land.

The main argument in favour of tractor mechanisation in Pakistan is that it will lead to higher yields per acre. The increased intensity of work permitted by the use of tractors, it is argued, allows the optimal timing of critical operations. By reducing the period between the clearing of one crop and preparation of the ground for the next, it is possible to increase cropping intensity.

However, since water is the limiting factor in the expansion of crop-acreage and output, the provision of a tubewell alone can increase the acreage cropped as well as output per acre. With the complementary inputs

---

[1] Leslie Nulty: *The Green Revolution in Pakistan* (New York, Praeger Publishers, 1972).

[2] Government of Pakistan: *Report of the Farm Mechanisation Committee* (Islamabad, 1970).

of fertiliser and new seeds, this will result both in increased output and in increased demand for labour. The provision of tubewell irrigation is a necessary condition for the increase of cropping intensity. It is claimed, however, that at very high levels of cropping intensity, the harvesting of one crop and ground preparation for the subsequent crop cannot be conducted sufficiently rapidly by the available labour supply without mechanisation. It is thus argued that the full benefits of the tubewell-fertiliser-seed technology cannot be reaped without the aid of the tractor. This has been the main defence of the tractor partisans in Pakistan. It is further claimed that the initial (direct) labour displacement effect of mechanisation is offset by the later (indirect) effect on employment as a result of the expanded work requirement consequent upon an increased crop output.

The preceding arguments in favour of tractor mechanisation have been disputed by a number of authors, C. Gotch and B. Ahmed among them.[1] Ahmed, for instance, claims that tractor mechanisation has not so far led to any increase in yields per acre. Further, he argues that for some crops, notably rice, tractor use actually depresses yields. As regards increases in cropping intensity, he shows that tractorisation is helpful in a rice-wheat rotation of crops by speeding up critical operations, but in a cotton-wheat rotation there is little scope for greater multiple cropping.

Tractor mechanisation in Pakistan has consisted mainly of large four-wheeled tractors of 35-45 h.p., commonly used in Western agriculture, along with a variety of tractor implements. These tractors represent a large and indivisible input and their efficient use requires a large operating area.

There is evidence that mechanisation has led to the growth in the farm size of farmers using tractors. A survey jointly conducted by the World Bank and the Agricultural Development Bank of Pakistan (ADBP) of farmers who received ADBP loans to purchase tractors showed that there was a 142 per cent increase in the average size of such farms, from 45 to 109 acres.[2] Only 10 per cent of the farms did not increase their acreage. The sources of additional land were: previously uncultivated land, 22 per cent; previously rented out land, 42 per cent; newly rented land, 24 per cent; and newly purchased land, 12 per cent.

It is interesting to note that about 80 per cent of the newly acquired land consisted of land already in use. Thus most of the large farmers increased their farm size at the expense of tenants and small farmers. The fact that the second largest source of new acquisitions of land was through newly rented land confirms the apprehension that in the event of legislation against the sale of land obtained as a result of land reforms, the smaller farmers would

---

[1] Carl H. Gotch: "Tractor Mechanisation and Rural Development in Pakistan", in *International Labour Review*, Feb. 1973; B. Ahmed: *Field survey of large farmers in the Pakistan Punjab*, Working Paper No. 7, Project on Rural Development in Pakistan (Cambridge, Mass., Harvard University, June 1972; mimeographed).

[2] IBRD: *The consequences of farm tractors in Pakistan* (Feb. 1975).

lease out their lands to bigger farmers and thus give rise to tenancy in a new and reverse form.

The survey further revealed that the cropping intensity increased from 112 to 119 per cent, the increase being about equal in both seasons. There was some evidence that the increase in intensity was greater on the smaller farms, suggesting that those farms which expanded less in terms of acreage increased their cropping by intensification. There was, however, no convincing evidence of beneficial changes in crop yields associated with tractor use. The increases that were reported can be attributed largely to increased use of fertiliser.

The big-farmer bias of the tractor mechanisation programme in Pakistan has also been noted by Hamza Alavi.[1] He points out that those districts of the Punjab which have above average size holdings are also the districts where tractors are concentrated.

Estimates of employment-displacing effects of tractor mechanisation in Pakistan have differed widely. Bose and Clark report that "interviewing farmers in the Punjab who have mechanised, we received a remarkably consistent response that the labour force per acre had been reduced about 50 per cent from the pre-mechanisation period."[2] The World Bank-ADBP survey found that although the amount of labour used per farm increased for every size group, when allowance is made for the increase in farm size the labour use per cultivated acre decreased by some 40 per cent. Total paid labour input (including both permanent and casual labour) per cropped acre declined by 23 per cent. In addition unpaid family labour input per cropped acre fell by some 47 per cent. Over-all, the total labour use per cropped acre, made up of unpaid family and paid regular and casual workers, dropped by some 40 per cent, implying a net destruction of about five jobs per tractor. The introduction of each tractor, according to the survey, destroys about ten permanent jobs, but this is compensated by the creation of jobs for casual workers, equivalent in income terms to five permanent jobs.

Although the Government's policy has been to encourage the use of tractors, principally by providing credit on easy terms, the number of tractors is not yet very large. In November 1973 the number of tractors in Pakistan was estimated to be approximately 25,000. The report of the Farm Mechanisation Committee stated that at the end of 1968 there were 19,000 tractors. Thus the growth of tractors during those five years was at the rate of about 5 per cent per annum.[3] The survey contained in the Report revealed

---

[1] H. Alavi: "Elite Farmer Strategy and Regional Disparities in the Agricultural Development of Pakistan", in *Economic and Political Weekly*, March 1973.

[2] S. R. Bose and E. H. Clark II: "Some Basic Considerations on Agricultural Mechanisation in West Pakistan", in *Pakistan Development Review* (Karachi), Autumn 1969, pp. 273-308.

[3] Imports of tractors have been further liberalised in recent years and an average of 5,000 tractors per year were imported during the 1970-76 period. More recently the Government has abolished all restrictions on the purchase of tractors and has decided to import 15,000 tractors annually.

that the average size of holding on which a tractor was employed was about 200 acres. The use of this average figure implies that by 1973 about 5 million cultivated acres in Pakistan were affected in some way by mechanical power. However, the total area affected is less than that, because, on the one hand, many large farmers are incompletely mechanised and, on the other, many smaller farmers hire out their surplus tractor capacity for transportation services. If one uses the World Bank-ADBP average figure of five displaced workers per tractor, the total displacement of jobs due to tractors by 1973 would be 125,000. Today the estimated number of tractors in use is 40,000 which, on the same basis, may be causing a total displacement of 200,000 jobs.

Although the present rate of growth of tractors and the consequent displacement effect on employment are not yet great compared to the total labour force in the rural economy, the trend towards greater use of mechanical power and the rural development strategy it implies are causes for concern. As pointed out by Johnston and Cownie, it will lead to a dualistic pattern within agriculture in which increases in productivity and output will be concentrated to a large extent in a subsector of large-scale, capital-intensive farm enterprises, instead of being equitably shared by the majority of farmers.[1]

Although tractor mechanisation has affected mainly tenant farmers whose land has been resumed by landlords for self-cultivation, it may also have affected indirectly small landowners and landless labourers. An interesting hypothesis about the effect of tractorisation on the land of big farmers (i.e. those owning more than 100 acres) and on those with smaller holdings has been advanced by Alavi.[2] A tractor of medium size has a capacity to cultivate 100 acres. Farmers with landholdings below this would be likely to evict all tenants and resume land for self-cultivation. In the case of the owners of large holdings, however, according to Alavi, the sharecroppers are not wholly evicted but only a proportion of the land from all sharecroppers is recovered. This reduces the size of their landholdings below the subsistence minimum and forces them to seek outside employment. In this way the landlord is assured of a source of cheap labour to perform the increased volume of work resulting from higher productivity, especially during periods of a general shortage of labour.

The discussion in this section of the likely trend in agricultural poverty, landlessness and tenurial structure since 1961 does not lead to precise, quantitative conclusions because of the incomplete and fragmentary nature of the empirical evidence. The eventual release of the 1972 censuses of agriculture and population will enable the researcher to quantify these trends. However, some qualitative judgements can be made on the basis of the empirical

---

[1] B. F. Johnston and J. Cownie: "The Seed/Fertiliser Revolution and Labour Force Absorption", in *American Economic Review*, Sep. 1969.

[2] Alavi: "Elite farmer strategy ...", op. cit.

evidence presented above. The increasing pressure on land in the rural areas has not been offset by a technological breakthrough or by land reforms. Ironically, both these developments may have increased the average size of holding and hence reduced the number of farm families which own or rent land. There is thus ample justification for the conjecture, supported by some village surveys,[1] that the number of landless workers is increasing as in the past—the increase was 350 per cent between 1951 and 1961. Since landless agricultural workers, who suffer from a high degree of underemployment, form perhaps the lowest income strata in the rural areas, an increase in their proportion is likely to lead to an increase in the proportion of households living below the poverty line.

Wage trends

Some corroboration or refutation of the likely trends could be obtained by looking at changes in rural wages. Unfortunately, no accurate time series can be assembled to permit the calculation of the trend in real wages in rural Pakistan. All that can be got from the periodic Punjab Wages Surveys are monthly wage rates in Punjab in December 1960, December 1966 and June 1973. These are based on the unweighted averages of wage rates observed in over 1,000 villages in 19 districts of Punjab. The growth rates in these wage rates between December 1960 and December 1966 and between December 1966 and June 1973, along with the corresponding rates of growth in the cost of living index, are summarised in table 9.

It hardly needs to be stressed that the calculation of a trend over a 13-year period cannot be based on three observations over the short period of a month each. As is shown for other countries considered in this volume, there can be quite sharp short-term fluctuations in rural wage rates. Such a possibility is greater in abnormal periods to which the three observations referred to may easily belong. Thus the estimate for December 1960 is probably biased downward since the 1960-61 fiscal year witnessed a 5 per cent decline in food output per head. On the other hand, the 1966 figure is possibly biased upward since during 1966-67 a sharp recovery in output and income was achieved over the preceding year of drought and crop failure. For different reasons the 1973 figure may also be biased upward: June is seasonally a period of high labour demand compared to December. Also in that year agriculture recovered sufficiently from the effects of war and other dislocations to exceed the previous peak output.

It would be wrong, therefore, to attach any great importance to the growth rates shown in table 9, which could easily be overestimates, since

---

[1] For example, J. B. Eckert, op. cit., found that in 1970-71 the proportion of landless workers in Punjab was 12 per cent. This compares with 9 per cent for Pakistan as a whole in 1961 according to the population census. Punjab is believed to have less than the national average land pressure. It is therefore likely that the 1961 figure for Punjab would be lower than the average figure for Pakistan.

Table 9.   Rural wage rates and cost of living in the Punjab
(Percentage increases)

Period	Permanent hired labour	Casual labour
Between December 1960 and December 1966		
Money wages		41.4
Cost of living		25.0
Real wages		13.1
Annual increase in real wages		2.1
Between December 1966 and June 1973		
Money wages	70.6	71.8
Cost of living	44.0	44.0
Real wages	18.5	19.3
Annual increase in real wages	2.6	2.8

Note: The increase in the cost of living has been calculated from M. Ghaffar Chaudhry and M. Anwar Chaudhry: "Cost of Living Indexes for Rural Labourers in Pakistan", in *The Pakistan Development Review*, Spring 1974, the only available source for the period. Note that at least for the period between 1960 and 1966 there is strong reason to suspect an understatement of inflation. Group-specific cost of living indices for rural Pakistan were calculated, showing an increase of 31.7 per cent, 29.2 per cent and 26.2 per cent respectively for the lowest, second lowest and the average of all income groups between 1963-64 and 1966-67.
The calculations do not cover the period before 1963-64 and no alternative rural cost-of-living index is available for the earlier period. A perusal of the various urban cost of living indices suggests an average increase of 6.2 per cent between 1960-61 and 1963-64. If this is used as a conservative estimate for the increase in the rural cost of living during the period, in view of the greater weight of food in rural consumption and higher than average price increases for food, then the increase in the rural cost of living between 1960-61 (of which December 1960 is about the midpoint) and 1966-67 (of which December 1966 is the midpoint) would work out at somewhere between 34 per cent (using the rural index between 1963-64 and 1966-67 for the average of all income groups) and 39.9 per cent (using the rural index for the lowest income group). In either case the increase in money wages is offset more or less completely. For the rural cost of living index see S. M. Naseem: *Rural poverty and landlessness in Pakistan*, op. cit.

1960 was biased downward relative to 1966 and since it is possible that June 1973 was biased upward relative to December 1966.

The other available pieces of information are not of much help in determining trends in real wages. Thus Khan and Bose estimated that modal money wages for unskilled workers in rural Punjab increased from Rs. 2.00 per day in 1960 to Rs. 2.50 per day in 1967.[1] Since the cost of living for those workers increased by at least 25 per cent over the same period there was at best no increase in real wages. For more recent years information is available from Eckert's survey carried out in the autumn of 1971.[2] He found that approximately one-fifth of the money wages reported in 1971 were higher in real terms than those paid five years earlier. Four-fifths showed no change. Of those that reported an increase, the change in money terms was only a little higher than that in the cost of living.

Thus the evidence for Punjab, the most prosperous province, does not provide a firm basis from which to conclude that real wages have increased significantly during the period under consideration. It should, however, be noted that the evidence does not rule out the possibility of some increase in real wages in Punjab. In this context it should also be noted that an increase in real wages is not necessarily inconsistent with the trends in poverty docu-

[1] T. M. Khan and S. R. Bose: *Report on income of agricultural workers in Pakistan* (prepared for the ILO. Karachi, 1968).
[2] J. B. Eckert, op. cit.

mented above. In a period characterised by an increase in the proportion of skilled workers in the labour force induced by changing technology and by the large-scale transformation of tenants into wage earners, an increase in the observed real wage averaged over the entire labour force, which has been undergoing significant change in composition over time, is quite consistent with an increase in the number of the rural population below a poverty line.

REGIONAL DIMENSIONS OF POVERTY

Data on the regional product of the four provinces is not published in Pakistan. An exercise conducted in the late 1960s by a group of economists suggested that inter-province inequality within the then West Pakistan was more acute than the inequality between the then East and West Pakistan. In terms of rural (and indeed combined rural and urban) income per head, Punjab is by far the most prosperous. Sind and North West Frontier Province (NWFP) are respectively second and third. Baluchistan is the poorest province.

The Household Income and Expenditure Surveys present data on an all-Pakistan basis. For 1969-70, however, divisional data on the distribution of household expenditure were obtained. These divisional data were aggregated for each province to give the expenditure distribution for the four provinces.

Using the same methodology and the same poverty lines as shown for Pakistan as a whole in table 6, the percentages of poor households in the four provinces are estimated to be as follows for the year 1969-70:[1]

	Poverty line I	Poverty line II	Poverty line III
Punjab	76	64	57
Sind	69	42	32
NWFP	75	49	29
Baluchistan	100	98	70

The highest proportion is for Baluchistan followed by Punjab. Except for Baluchistan, the order is the reverse, for poverty line III, of what one would expect on the basis of incomes per head. Part of this may be due to the fact that the districts included in the sample are not representative of each province. But the data also show that the incidence of poverty depends not only on the average level of expenditure but also on its distribution. Although Punjab is the most affluent province, it is also the province with the greatest disparities. The distribution of land also is highly uneven in that province.

---

[1] It should be noted that an adequate diet may cost different amounts in different provinces. It is, therefore, not appropriate to use the same poverty line for all four provinces. Unfortunately, enough information on prices to estimate separate poverty lines for each province was not available. On the basis of the incomplete data available, however, it is not thought that the general conclusions would be affected if the construction of separate poverty lines were possible.

CONCLUDING REMARKS

In many ways Pakistan's experience fulfilled the expectations of the development strategists. The country industrialised rapidly and there was a reduction in the share of the labour force engaged in agricultural activities. At the same time agricultural output and income grew at high rates. Indeed, Pakistan often was cited as a model for other countries. This hardly looks like a setting in which mass poverty might be perpetuated. None the less, it appears that this in fact is what has happened.

Admittedly, the data on which the numerical calculations have been based are unsatisfactory. But there is too much direct and indirect evidence which supports the general analysis for this to be dismissed on statistical grounds. During the same period when the rural economy was growing rapidly in aggregate and per capita terms, the proportion of the population and of households who were unable to obtain their minimum dietary requirements continued undiminished at a very high level or even increased. As a consequence, the number of people in acute poverty increased.

The explanation is to be found in the nature of the growth strategy adopted. This strategy included no place for a serious land reform and concentrated on promoting a technology which led to reduced demand for labour, greater land concentration and increased landlessness.

A comparison of the circumstances in the four provinces, based once again on less than satisfactory data, underlines the fact that over-all prosperity measured in terms of output per head is not a major determinant of the level of poverty or lack of it. Thus Punjab, the most prosperous of the provinces, has a proportion of people in poverty which is second only to the poorest province of Baluchistan. This conclusion would almost certainly be strengthened were it possible to take into account the widely recognised phenomenon that the more prosperous the region, the higher is the market cost of a subsistence bundle of goods. Perhaps this merely illustrates another way in which the effects of greater prosperity can be counterbalanced by the effects of an unequal social system. The result is an apparently paradoxical coexistence of general prosperity and mass poverty.

GROWTH AND POVERTY IN THE RURAL AREAS OF THE INDIAN STATE OF PUNJAB, 1960-61 to 1970-71 [1]

3

Indira Rajaraman

Punjab is not only one of the most advanced states in India, but also a very rapidly growing one. During the decade studied its real income per head increased at a rate two-and-a-half times as fast as that of India as a whole.[2] Like the rest of India, Punjab is overwhelmingly rural.[3] During the decade under consideration, the rural economy of the state experienced an improvement in agricultural technology—the Green Revolution—that was quite unprecedented in its spread and in the over-all prosperity it brought to the countryside.

This chapter presents the results of a study aimed at determining the extent to which the benefits of this rapid growth trickled down to the poorer sections of the population. The focus of the study is on the rural sector.

SOURCES OF DATA

There is no systematic collection in India of data from which size distribution of income can directly be derived.[4] Existing computations of the

---

[1] The present chapter makes use of much of the material reported in two working papers published by the Woodrow Wilson School, Princeton University and an article published in the *Journal of Development Studies*. See Indira Rajaraman: *Constructing the poverty line: rural Punjab, 1960-61* (Woodrow Wilson School, Princeton University), Discussion Paper No. 43, Mar. 1974; idem: *Poverty, inequality and economic growth: rural Punjab 1960-61 – 1970-71*, (Woodrow Wilson School, Princeton University), Discussion Paper No. 45, an abridged version of which was published in the *Journal of Development Studies*, July 1975.

[2] An increase of 26.2 per cent at 1960-61 prices as compared to 10.7 per cent for India. See Government of Punjab (Economic Adviser): *The Punjab Statistical Abstract* (Chandigarh, 1972).

[3] According to the 1971 census 10.27 million of the state's 13.47 million people were inhabitants of rural areas, i.e. 76.2 per cent; the corresponding national average is 80.1 per cent. See Registrar General and Census Commissioner: *Census of India 1971*, Series I.

[4] A few income surveys have been conducted, chiefly by the National Council of Applied Economic Research, but not on a systematic basis, so that they yield estimates only for a point in time. Even where a two-point comparison is possible, the years of comparison are limited by the years of the survey. Further, most of the surveys have not had a sample size large enough to permit state-level estimates, with the exception of the 1968-69 survey reported in I. Z. Bhatty: "Inequality and Poverty in Rural India", in T. N. Srinivasan and P. K. Bardhan (eds.): *Poverty and income distribution in India* (Calcutta, Statistical Publishing Society, 1974).

distribution of income are based on consumer expenditure data with arbitrary adjustments for the distribution of saving by level of consumption. Such arbitrary adjustments may at best be meaningless and at worst misleading, especially for a study of changes over time such as this one, where the distribution of saving itself might be expected to change. Thus, inequality was studied here in terms of consumer expenditure alone, the figures including subsistence consumption are evaluated at imputed farm prices, and are therefore comprehensive.

Primary data were obtained from the consumer expenditure surveys of the sixteenth (1960-61), seventeenth (1961-62) and twenty-fifth (1970-71) rounds of the National Sample Survey (NSS).[1] The published reports of the NSS do not process all the information collected in these surveys and are therefore not a satisfactory substitute for the raw data. The most serious omission[2] has to do with the price information collected (implicit in the quantity and value figures recorded for each consumption item). Thus the published figures of consumer expenditure distribution show changes over time only as they have occurred in money terms, which might be quite different from the change in real terms if different groups of the population have faced different price changes. Further, there is no outside source of data from which it may be determined whether or not there has been such a differential price change within each state, and if so, the extent of the difference. An added shortcoming of the published information in the case of Punjab is that the pre-1967 figures are not comparable with those for later years because of the partitioning of the state in that year into the present reduced state of Punjab and the new state of Haryana.

The data for the initial year, 1960-61, were obtained by pooling the schedules from the sixteenth and seventeenth rounds so as to obtain an adequate sample size.[3] The sample size of the twenty-fifth round was sufficiently large so that pooling of rounds was not necessary for the final year of the period. Details with respect to sample design, and with respect to the initial computations done here in order to correct for seasonality, for changes made over the years in the definition of consumption, and for the partitioning of the state, are not given in this chapter.

---

[1] Consumer expenditure surveys have been made for every year from 1950-51 to 1973-74. Starting with the year 1974-75, however, they will be conducted only about every five years.

[2] There are others. The reports do not provide state-level information on the pattern of consumption or the occupational composition of different fractile groups. Further, there have been changes over the years in the definition of consumption and the reports do not adjust for these, nor for the changes made over the years in the geographical definition of many states.

[3] In all, 150 observations were obtained by pooling half the Central sample of the sixteenth and seventeenth rounds together with the entire state sample of the sixteenth round. The other subsamples of the Central sample for these rounds, and the state sample for the seventeenth round, were unavailable.

Table 10.   The distribution of rural consumption in the Punjab in 1960-61 and 1970-71

Decile	Cumulated share in total real consumption	
	1960-61	1970-71
1st	4.34	3.79
2nd	10.40	8.94
3rd	16.83	14.85
4th	23.44	21.29
5th	31.40	29.12
6th	40.58	37.94
7th	50.14	48.23
8th	61.78	60.57
9th	76.84	75.33
10th	100.00	100.00

INCREASING INEQUALITY

The first question to be answered on the basis of the data processed in accordance with the methodology outlined above was whether inequality in the distribution of consumption changed during the decade under review. Lorenz curves, then, were constructed for the two years, after ranking the households by per capita consumption.[1] Laspeyres price indices with 1960-61 as the base year were next constructed for each of three fractile groups of the population—the poorest 30 per cent, a middle group from 30 to 74 per cent, and a third group from 74 per cent upwards. These particular groupings were arrived at by a procedure that was devised to take the place of the more usual and arbitrary division by decile. Clearly there is a trade-off at some point between homogeneity and adequacy of sample size; one might just as well have half-deciles or percentiles in place of deciles. The procedure evolved here was designed to take care of the second requirement without any sacrifice of the first. Thus, the set of households in the base year, 1960-61, were ranked in ascending order by per capita consumption, and a cumulative percentage taken of the ratio of food consumption to total consumption by value, as being the single most important index of homogeneity of consumption pattern. The first significant drop in this percentage occurred at the thirtieth percentile, and the second at the seventy-fourth percentile.

For every commodity group[2] except cereals the price rise faced by the poorest groups was greater than or equal to that faced by the upper fractile.

---

[1] The per capita consumption of each household was obtained by dividing total expenditure by family size.

[2] Prices for each item were obtained by dividing value by quantity for each household, and averaging over all the households falling in each fractile group. For the services and miscellaneous commodity group, however, quantity data were not recorded; prices for these items had to be obtained from other sources.

Figure 3.   Lorenz curves of consumption inequality, 1960-61 and 1970-71

Total consumption

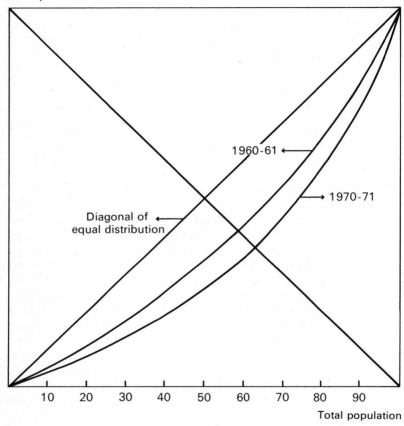

Total population

Indeed, of any pair of substitute items from any non-cereal commodity group, the inferior or cheaper commodity faced the higher price rise. The cereals group was exceptional in that the three most expensive cereals in 1960-61 also rose the most in price. The final values for the price rise faced by the three fractile groups were very similar, indicating slightly more than a doubling for all three;[1] the over-all similarity in price movement was accounted for by the greater weightage for poorer households of cereal consumption. Since the indices do not differ very much, therefore, the distribution constructed for 1970-71 after deflation by the price indices did not differ very much from that constructed before; it was only slightly more unequal.

---

[1] Starting with the poorest group, the values of the indices were 206.96, 206.83 and 206.26.

Table 10 and figure 3 show the distribution of real consumption in the base and final years of the period. The distributions for the two years do not intersect at all; that for 1970-71 lies everywhere below that for 1960-61. The increase in inequality thus was quite unambiguous.[1]

ABSOLUTE DECLINE
IN THE LIVING STANDARDS
OF THE POOR

During the period studied there was a significant rise in the level of average real per capita consumption—from Rs. 25.8 per month in 1960-61 to Rs. 28.5 in 1970-71 at 1960-61 prices. Despite the rise in the average level, the data indicate an absolute decline in consumption levels of the three poorest deciles of the population. Table 11 and figure 4 contain many of the details. The absolute level of consumption marking off each half decile within the poorest 30 per cent of the rural population in 1960-61 is presented in the first column of table 11. The third column indicates the equivalent level of consumption in 1970-71 prices and the final column the percentage of the rural population in 1970-71 that consumed less than this amount. The same information is presented in diagrammatic form in figure 4.

As can be seen, the deterioration in the absolute standard of living was quite widespread. There was a rise, for example, from 20 to 24.95 per cent in the proportion of those living on less than Rs. 16.66 per head at 1960-61 prices. This rise was tested and found to be statistically significant.[2] However, the rise from 25 to 26.9 per cent of those living on less than Rs. 17.13 was found not to be significant. Thus the fall in consumption was confined to those whose level of consumption in 1960-61 prices was equivalent to about Rs. 17. Above that level, living standards did not fall but remained constant in real terms, right up to the thirtieth population percentile.

---

[1] There is no way by which the difference between two Lorenz curves can be directly tested for significance. A non-parametric test, the Kolmogorov-Smirnov two-sample test, was done on the underlying frequency distributions. The two-tailed test indicated that the null hypothesis of similarity could be rejected beyond the 0.001 level. The test, however, is sensitive to any kind of difference in the distributions from which the two samples are drawn – differences in either location or dispersion. Further testing, therefore, was necessary.

    The Lorenz curves of figure 3 were seen to obey the properties peculiar to the two-parametric lognormal distribution and the chi-square test led to the acceptance of the hypothesis of two-parameter lognormality in both cases. In the two-parameter case there is a way by which the difference in dispersion between two Lorenz distributions can be tested for significance. This test confirmed that the two distributions are different at any level of significance. For the steps involved in actual testing see Indira Rajaraman: *Poverty, inequality and economic growth*, op. cit.

[2] The testing of these percentages was done using the normal approximation to the binomial distribution, at the 0.1 level.

Table 11.   Percentages of population lying below selected absolute levels of per capita monthly consumption, 1960-61 and 1970-71

Per capita monthly consumption level, 1960-61 prices (rupees)	Percentage of population in 1960-61	Equivalent consumption level, 1970-71 prices[1] (rupees)	Percentage of population in 1970-71
11.66	5.00	24.14	6.32
14.31	10.00	29.62	12.36
15.72	15.00	32.52	20.52
16.36[2]	18.40	33.86	23.28
16.66	20.00	34.49	24.95
17.13	25.00	35.46	26.90
17.86	30.00	36.97	30.02

[1] The price index of 2.0696 was used uniformly for all consumption levels since the population considered here falls entirely within the poorest fractile group.   [2] The poverty line constructed for the region in the manner described below.

CONSTRUCTING A POVERTY LINE

A poverty line can never be determined solely in terms of objective norms of physical deprivation. Even the food component which, unlike clothing or fuel, does lend itself to objective specification on the basis of norms of nutritional sufficiency, must be constructed subject to cultural constraints on acceptability. It is thus quite meaningless to approach the problem of constructing a poverty line in all-India terms, given the enormous cultural diversity within the country. Yet it was precisely in these terms that the poverty line was first given substance—Rs. 20 per head per month at 1960-61 prices—and it is, correspondingly, the sense in which the poverty line has been conceived of by most contributors to the literature.[1] It is equally meaningless to arrive at regional poverty lines using price indices to "interpret" an all-India poverty line at each different set of prices prevailing in each state. The necessity for constructing poverty lines separately for each region with a distinct cultural identity arises not because of price variations in a common bundle of goods, but because the composition of the appropriate consumption basket itself must differ from region to region.

The first step, then, was to determine an initial set of poor households whose consumption pattern could yield the guidelines needed where objective minima cannot be established or must be modified. The poorest fractile group of the three for which price indices were constructed above provided a useful initial approximation. Beyond this 30 per cent population mark, as

---

[1] The poverty line was the outcome of a study group appointed by the Government of India to go into the matter. The report of the group is reprinted in T. N. Srinivasan and P. K. Bardhan (eds.), op. cit. One notable exception, the only really careful attempt at constructing a poverty line, regionally limited, has been that by Panikar. (See P. G. K. Panikar: "Economics of Nutrition", in *Economic and Political Weekly*, Annual Number, 1972, pp. 413-430.) For some of the problems with that attempt see Indira Rajaraman: *Constructing the poverty line: rural Punjab 1960-61*, op. cit.

Figure 4. Percentage of population lying below selected levels of monthly per capita consumption in 1960-61 and 1970-71

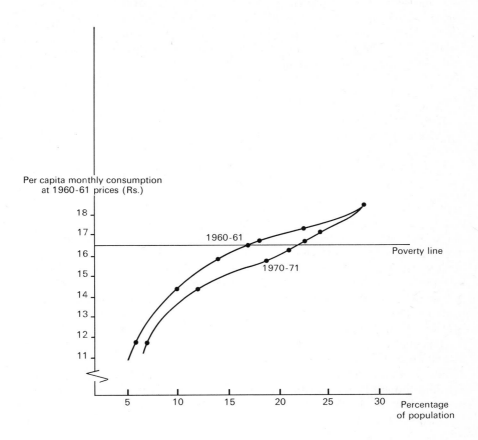

indicated earlier, the non-food component of consumption rose sharply. The procedure thus comes as close as possible to establishing objectively minimal needs for non-food items of consumption. For this group, then, the latter accounted for 20.2 per cent of total consumption (8.2 per cent on clothing, 5.6 per cent on fuel and intoxicants, 6.4 per cent on services and miscellaneous items).

The non-food factor of 20.2 per cent was added to the value of the least-cost diet, calculated on the basis of the nutritional norms established by the Indian Council of Medical Research (ICMR) in 1968.[1] These norms are

---

[1] See Indian Council of Medical Research: *Recommended daily allowances of nutrients and balanced diets* (Hyderabad, 1968).

specified separately for each of three levels of activity. The norms used here were those for moderate activity, and a weighted average was taken of the separate specifications for men, women and children, with the weights derived from the average household composition in the poorest fractile group. The food items taken into account in constructing the diet were limited to those available to and actually consumed by this group; the prices of the items were estimated from the same set of sample households.
The following cost function was minimised:

$$\Sigma_j\, c_j x_j$$

    subject to: $\Sigma_{j} a_{ij} x_j \geq b_i$
    where c_j = cost per unit of jth food;
            x_j = quantity of jth food;
            a_{ij} = amount of ith nutrient per unit of jth food; and
            b_i = amount of ith nutrient required.

The initial calculation of the least-cost diet had to be modified because it included too much maize—for a region where the staple cereal is not maize but wheat—and completely omitted milk and sugar. Lower bounds were therefore introduced into the model on the consumption of milk and unrefined sugar, and an upper bound on maize. Some of the winter vegetables featured prominently in all these solutions because of their low seasonal cost. A summer alternative was therefore obtained after excluding these items from the list of potential foods; here again a modification was required because of the preponderance of Bengal gram, a minor cereal in Punjab.

The final estimate worked out as a simple average of the modified winter and summer diets was Rs. 0.408 per person per day at 1960-61 prices. After adding an allowance for food items such as tea, salt and spices, which are essential though of no nutritional value,[1] and the non-food component, the poverty line at 1960-61 prices for rural Punjab was calculated to be Rs. 0.538 per head per day, or Rs. 16.36 per head per month. At 1970-71 prices the poverty line was Rs. 33.86.

Table 11 indicates that between 1960-61 and 1970-71 the proportion of the population below the poverty line rose from 18.4 per cent to 23.28 per cent. This rise was tested and found significant at the 0.1 level.

Thus, during a decade of rapid growth there was a significant rise in the percentage of those unable to obtain an adequate diet and lift themselves above poverty. In absolute terms, the number of the rural poor increased by 51.6 per cent.

---

[1] These items account for 5 per cent of total food consumption by value.

Table 12.   Occupational composition, 1960-61 and 1970-71

Occupation	Percentage of all households		Percentage of households below poverty line	
	1960-61	1970-71	1960-61	1970-71
Cultivators	53.02	51.17	47.11	31.35
Agricultural labourers	17.45	23.16	22.56	40.51
Other labourers	10.07	9.00	11.83	10.05
Artisans	10.07	3.95	16.78	5.19
Traders	1.34	3.25	0.00	5.41
Other	8.06	9.65	1.73	7.49
Total	100.00	100.00	100.00	100.00

TOWARDS AN UNDERSTANDING OF INCREASING POVERTY

The occupational composition of the population in the two years 1960-61 and 1970-71 was constructed as a first step towards understanding the phenomenon just outlined. This was made possible by the fact that all consumer expenditure surveys of the NSS classify every sample household by major occupation, i.e. that from which the major share of income is derived. The figures, both for all households and for those below the poverty line, are presented in table 12.

There was a significant rise in the number of households which obtained a livelihood from agricultural labour—the proportion rose from 17.45 per cent in 1960-61 to 23.16 per cent in 1970-71. The change was even more startling, however, among those households living below the poverty line, from 22.56 per cent to 40.51 per cent (with a rise *within* the category of those living below the poverty level from 23.67 per cent to 32.90 per cent).

Concurrently with the increased incidence of poverty among agricultural labourers, their monthly mean per capita consumption level rose from Rs. 20.35 to Rs. 23.46. A large sample one-tailed test on this was significant at the 0.1 level. Thus the rise in the incidence of poverty within the occupation group took place *despite* an improvement in the average level of living. The change over the period for this category mirrored the change for the population as a whole—a rise in the mean consumption level, a rise in the incidence of poverty, and a correspondingly larger relative dispersion.

It must be emphasised here that these findings are quite consistent with the possibility of a rise in the average real wage rate of agricultural labourers over the period. Such a rise in real wages would imply (assuming of course no offsetting decline in employment or rise in the average dependency ratio, and no decline in average income from other sources) an improvement in the average level of living, and the figures here do indeed show such an improvement.

Evidence on the movement of real wages in rural Punjab is inconclusive. The studies based on the index of average money wages (IMW) deflated by the Punjab Agricultural Labourers Consumer Price Index (ACPI) indicate there was a modest increase in real wages during the 1960s.[1] The ACPI is not a wholly reliable deflator, however.[2] Moreover, the average IMW conceals many labour market changes, e.g. changes in skill composition. At least one study shows that the rate of increase in real wages, as measured for specific operations such as ploughing and harvesting by dividing money wages by the consumer price index for food, was insignificant over the 15 years ending in 1972.[3]

Whatever the trend in average wages, it is the increased dispersion within the group that holds the key to an understanding of the reasons for increased rural poverty in the Punjab. There is independent evidence that by the late 1960s agricultural labourers in the Punjab had both the highest per capita income and the highest degree of inequality of income of all agricultural labourers in the country.[4]

Unfortunately, there is not enough detailed information available about the rural labour market to permit a conclusive understanding of the phenomenon. There are several possible explanations. The rise in demand for certain types of skills—tractor driving, operating of mechanical equipment—might have, given the initial shortage of such skills, led to a rapid increase in the prices such skills could command. At the same time, the balance beween supply and demand for more traditional types of labour might have become increasingly unfavourable over the years. Another possibility is that there might have been barriers to mobility preventing labour from moving towards those areas with the higher wage rates, though such market imperfections are likely to be more important when the region studied includes many linguistic and cultural groups. Or, there might have been an unequal availability of employment opportunities for secondary earners. The dependency ratio is an important determinant of the level of living of the household, and is closely linked to the availability of employment for women and children. These opportunities might have increased in an unequal regional pattern: the mobility of secondary earners in response to opportunity would be much less than that of the primary earners in the household. Finally, there might have

---

[1] See, for example, Eiswanath Santra: "Trends in Agricultural Wages – Some Indian Evidence", in *Indian Journal of Agricultural Economics*, Conference Number, July-Sep. 1974, pp. 2-16.

[2] The coverage of the data source for the ACPI is not nearly as good as that of the surveys covered here. A comparison, however, of the index for the poorest fractile group with the ACPI for Punjab (which covers Haryana and Delhi) yielded no conclusive indication of the direction of bias in the latter. The rise in food prices was higher than that obtained here, while that for non-food items was lower.

[3] S. S. Grewal and H. S. Bal: "Impact of Green Revolution on Agricultural Wages in the Punjab", in *Indian Journal of Agricultural Economics*, Conference Number, July-Sep. 1974, pp. 40-47.

[4] I. Z. Bhatty, in T. N. Srinivasan and P. K. Bardhan (eds.), op. cit.

taken place over the period a worsening in the distribution of sources of non-labour income, principally land. An attempt is made below to determine whether or not such a worsening in land distribution took place over the period for all households taken together.

Of the other occupation groups, the figures in table 12 for artisans are particularly noteworthy. There was a large, significant fall in the over-all share of the group. Further, whereas in 1960-61 artisans accounted for 16.8 per cent of those below the poverty line, by 1970-71 this had fallen to 5.2 per cent. These figures seem to indicate a decline of the artisan class as a result of growing industrialisation. Prior to the ten-year period studied, there seems to have been a reduction of artisans to a state of poverty by industrial competition. In the ten years covered here these artisans appear to have abandoned their traditional occupations and joined the ranks of agricultural labourers.

The mean consumption level of the cultivator group, not surprisingly, rose significantly over the period, from Rs. 28.13 to Rs. 34.57. Further, the percentage representation below the poverty level of the group fell significantly; since the over-all percentage for cultivators was significantly unchanged, this meant an improvement over the period in the absolute levels of even the poorest among those deriving the major share of their income from cultivation. There is the interesting question of what the Green Revolution did to the relative dispersion within the group (it must be kept in mind that this category includes *only* those deriving the major share of income from cultivation). Lorenz curves for the group are presented in figure 5. The curves intersect. The change seems to have been towards a smaller relative share for the lowest deciles, and a greater equality beyond the sixth decile. The ranking for these curves, as for those in figure 3, was by per capita consumption.

The question of what happened over the period to the distribution of land is an important one. Data for an answer to the question proved to be quite a problem, however. Landholding surveys were conducted by the NSS in the course of the sixteenth, seventeenth and twenty-sixth rounds, but primary data were available for only the latest of these. The data from the earlier rounds were available in tabulated form, but they referred to the pre-partition state and were therefore not strictly comparable. However, an alternative distribution constructed from the consumption surveys indicated that the percentage of households with zero land in 1960-61 was 55.21 per cent; this figure conflicted directly with that obtained from the same source for the percentage share of those households deriving the major share of their income from cultivation (53.02 per cent; see table 12). Since the collection of data on landholding is entirely incidental to a consumer expenditure survey, that they should be inaccurate is not very surprising. The classification of each household by occupation on the other hand is an important part of the survey and is therefore much more carefully done. There was no alternative, therefore, but to compare the Lorenz curve obtained from the twenty-sixth

Figure 5.   Lorenz curves of consumption inequality among the cultivator population,
1960-61 and 1970-71

Total consumption

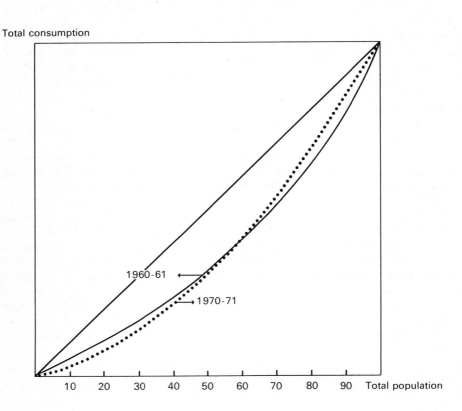

round data with those constructed from the published figures for the earlier
years, despite their vastly different geographical coverage. The ranking for all
three was done by household acreage operated.

The curves are drawn in figure 6. The curves for 1960-61 and 1961-62 lie
everywhere above that for 1971-72. Inequality in landholding thus appears to
have increased unambiguously.[1]

---

[1] Since the underlying distributions have non-zero frequencies at the zero value for
landholding, parametric tests cannot easily be applied. The non-parametric Kolmogorov-Smirnov
two-sample test was done on the cumulated distribution for 1971-72 taken with the distributions
for each of the earlier years in turn. The two-tailed test was significant for both comparisons
beyond the 0.001 level.

Figure 6. Lorenz curves of inequality in landholding, 1960-61, 1961-62 and 1971-72

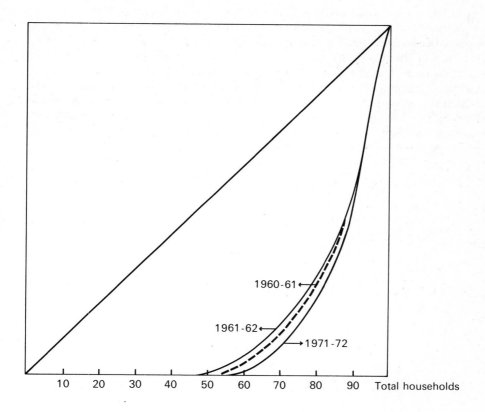

An assessment of the change in the incidence of landlessness was difficult to make as the lowest class of the tabulated frequency distributions for the earlier years (from which the Lorenz curves were constructed) covered 0 to 0.5 acres, thus including more than the strictly landless population. The percentage frequencies of this class, however, were 51.21 per cent and 45.75 per cent for 1960-61 and 1961-62 respectively. Taking a weighted average of these percentages (48.91 per cent), the same percentage of households in 1971-72 operated 0.06 acres per household or less. It seems reasonable to infer from these figures that the percentage incidence of landlessness increased over the period. Since the percentage of households deriving the major share of their income from cultivation remained substantially un-

73

changed, this could only mean a displacement of the marginal cultivator household which derives the major share of its income from activities other than cultivation.

The surveys used for this study did not collect any data on migration so that it was not possible to determine whether rural poverty in Punjab might have been aggravated by immigration from neighbouring states. The investigation of the possibility would have to await detailed probing of the 1971 census data. The sample surveys used here had a survey period spanning the entire agricultural year, so that in order for immigration into Punjab to have been the sole or even principal contributor to the worsening poverty indicated in the data, it would have had to occur on more than just a seasonal or peripheral level. Casual evidence suggests that such a wholesale movement of population into the state did not take place.

WAGES, EMPLOYMENT AND STANDARD OF LIVING OF AGRICULTURAL LABOURERS IN UTTAR PRADESH

4

Rohini Nayyar

The objective of this paper is to examine the economic conditions of agricultural labourers[1] in India's most populous state, Uttar Pradesh,[2] during the post-independence period. This state can be divided into four regions—western, central, eastern and the hill districts. The present study excludes the hill areas because the pattern of work and the life style of the inhabitants of this region are quite different from that of other village communities. For a long time the western region has been economically the most developed part of the state, but in the last few years it has become even more prosperous relative to the other districts because of the widespread impact of the new agricultural technology in this area. On the other hand, the central and eastern regions continue to be comparatively backward and poor. Eastern Uttar Pradesh is especially so, being characterised by subsistence farming and an extremely low rate of industrial development. These inter-regional differences within the state will help to isolate the impact of the so-called Green Revolution on the living conditions of the rural poor.

The data for the post-independence years show an increase in the number and proportion of agricultural labourers for Uttar Pradesh. According to the census estimates, agricultural labourers as a proportion of the total agricultural working population increased from 10.1 per cent in 1951 to 15.0 per cent in 1961 and to 25.7 per cent in 1971.[3] However, these estimates relate only to those whose principal source of livelihood was agricultural labour, i.e. those who either earned more than 50 per cent of their income from it or spent more than half of their total working time on this occupation. In

---

[1] An agricultural labourer is defined as one who works on land owned by someone else for a specific wage payment, either in cash or kind, as his primary or secondary source of income, irrespective of the time spent by him on this occupation. For example, it includes owner-cultivators who also work as labourers on other farms during the course of the year.

[2] In 1971 the population was 88.3 million, 86 per cent of whom lived in rural areas. See *Census of India, 1971*, Series 2, Uttar Pradesh.

[3] Calculated from *Census of India, 1951, 1961 and 1971*, volumes on India and Uttar Pradesh, part II-B: economic tables.

accordance with the definition adopted here (see footnote 1, page 75), the total number of agricultural labourers should include those who follow this vocation to supplement their income from their main occupation. Unfortunately, estimates by secondary means of livelihood are not yet available for 1971 and hence this segment of the agricultural labour force has had to be excluded from our calculation. However, it is noteworthy that between 1951 and 1961 their proportion increased from 1.8 per cent to 6.5 per cent of the agricultural working population.

The dramatic increase in the proportion of agricultural labourers during the decade 1961 to 1971 cannot be attributed solely to demographic factors; whereas the population rose by 20 per cent in Uttar Pradesh, there was a 68 per cent increase in the number of agricultural labourers. A part of this increase is notional—an outcome of definitional changes. The census of 1961 and of 1971 classifies agricultural workers either as cultivators or agricultural labourers. Tenants and sharecroppers are largely recorded in the former category. However, fear of land reforms, together with the enhanced profitability of agricultural production, has frequently resulted in the resumption of land under personal cultivation, leading to a transformation of the erstwhile tenants and sharecroppers into agricultural labourers on an accelerated scale. To the extent that this has happened, the increase in the number of agricultural labourers is not real in the sense that it does not reflect a transformation of erstwhile landowning cultivators into agricultural labourers.

A more detailed analysis of this increase in the proportion of agricultural labourers will show whether it is in any way related to the impact of the "wheat revolution" on the structure of the rural economy. Table 13 contains a breakdown by region of the number of agricultural labourers and the proportion they form of the total agricultural workforce. While there was an increase of 138.9 per cent in the number of agricultural labourers in western Uttar Pradesh between 1961 and 1971, the corresponding increase recorded in central and eastern Uttar Pradesh was only 74 per cent and 45 per cent respectively. The rates of population increase did not differ so much between the regions—22.3, 20.6 and 16.9 per cent respectively.[1] The fact that in western Uttar Pradesh the increase was so much greater tends to suggest that the Green Revolution may have accelerated the process of transformation of erstwhile cultivators into labourers. This aspect needs elaboration.

It has been shown fairly conclusively that the Green Revolution technology is biased in favour of large landowners because it involves the use of scarce and highly priced inputs which are accessible to only a select few.[2] The institutional factors tend to favour the large farmers who have political

---

[1] Calculated from the *Census of India*, op. cit.

[2] See, for example, K. B. Griffin: *The political economy of agrarian change*, op. cit.; W. Ladejinsky: "Ironies of India's Green Revolution", in *Foreign Affairs* (1970), and F. Frankel: *India's Green Revolution – economic gains and political costs* (Princeton, 1971).

Table 13.   Agricultural labourers in Uttar Pradesh, 1961 and 1971

Region	Year	Agricultural labourers (thousands)	Agricultural working population (thousands)	Agricultural labourers as a percentage of agricultural working population
Western	1961	534	4866	10.97
	1971	1275	5790	22.02
Central	1961	778	5883	13.22
	1971	1353	5813	23.28
Eastern	1961	1911	9619	19.87
	1971	2771	8425	32.89

Source: *Census of India 1961 and 1971*, volume on Uttar Pradesh, part II, tables.

influence both at the village level and higher up in the hierarchy and consequently have access to credit and other necessary inputs. This has resulted in unequal gains from the new agricultural technology, widening the gulf between the large farmers and small cultivators. Furthermore, the increasing returns from agricultural production have created an added incentive for the already large landowners to acquire additional land. The natural corollary of this tendency has been the displacement of tenants and small cultivators from their land, and they in turn have joined the ranks of the agricultural labourers. If this process continues there is likely to be a greater polarisation between these classes, with a concomitant reduction in the intermediate groups of tenants, sub-tenants and sharecroppers. At this stage it should be borne in mind that the Green Revolution has so far been confined to wheat production, and hence to a small proportion of the total cultivated area. Neither in the case of rice cultivation nor in coarser grains has there been a substantial breakthrough in yields. Hence the entire issue related to a technological transformation of agriculture is limited to a small area. However, as one of the regions in the state of Uttar Pradesh has experienced the impact of the new technological developments in its wheat-growing districts in the west, its impact deserves consideration in so far as it has a bearing on the structure of the rural society in that area.

The increase in the rural proletariat is itself a disquieting phenomenon. The displacement of households from their land in an economy where 70 per cent of the population is dependent on agriculture for a livelihood portends an explosive situation for the future. Some social scientists consider this process of transformation from peasantry to wage labour to be a serious problem requiring consideration. However, there are economists who argue that if employment opportunities for labour increase and wage rates rise, people could be better off as labourers than they were as cultivators. This necessitates an analysis of changes in the economic conditions of agricultural labourers, and a discussion of trends in wage rates, employment and living standards. The subsequent analysis follows this order.

AGRICULTURAL WAGES

The average daily money wage rates for agricultural labourers have risen considerably between 1953-54 and 1973-74 in Uttar Pradesh as a whole, and in each of its three regions. Table 14 contains the details. There are two series, each computed from a different source. Series A covers the period 1953-54 to 1965-66 only, as data for the subsequent years have not so far been published. Series B begins later, in 1955-56, but the wage rates are more up to date. Analysis is confined to this latter series. Series A is unsuitable for use even if data for subsequent years were available since, given the inadequate coverage of this series, which is based on data collected from two villages in each divisional headquarter district, i.e. six villages per region, the estimates could be regarded as only a very rough indication of the actual situation. Given the wide variation in wage rates as between villages even within a district, at any point of time, such data can be misleading. Moreover, the same two villages are not resurveyed each year, making intertemporal comparisons even more difficult.

The data base of series B is from a larger sample. Until 1966-67 data were collected each month from two villages in each of the 54 districts of the state, as compared to 10 districts covered under series A. In addition, beginning in 1966-67 the sample was enlarged further. A new series has been prepared with estimates of wage rates collected from one village in every development block (administrative unit) within a radius of 8 kilometres from the community development block headquarters, on the first Friday of each month. The simple average of the wages prevailing at each of the selected villages in a district gave the district wage. This procedure is unavoidable as data on employment are not available. However, the average wage rates of the workers at the regional or state level is calculated by weighting the wage rates at the district level by the number of agricultural labourers as given in the census of India of 1951.

Wage data include payments in cash and kind; for example, often during harvesting there is a contractual agreement which determines the wage payment in kind, while for weeding cash payments are usually made. As wage data are available for 1966-67 under both the old and new series, by using the conversion ratio of the new series to the old for the 1966-67 wage rate, series B has been converted in terms of the new series.

The data for real wage rates are presented in table 17. These have been calculated by deflating the money wage rates as shown in series B of table 14 by the consumer price indices for agricultural labourers as given in table 16. Before analysing trends in real wages, it may be useful to explain how the rural consumer price indices are computed. These are based on the prices of 34 commodities. The retail price indices are collected from two villages in each of the districts (with the exception of the hill districts, where data are collected from four villages per district). The villages are chosen through a process of random sampling with probability proportional to size, the latter

Table 14. Money wage rates of agricultural labourers, 1953-74
(Rupees per day)

Year	Western Uttar Pradesh		Central Uttar Pradesh		Eastern Uttar Pradesh		All Uttar Pradesh	
	Series A	Series B	Series A	Series B	Series A	Series B	Series A	Series B
1953-54	1.51	.	0.69	.	0.79	.	0.91	.
1954-55	1.36	.	0.63	.	0.56	.	0.75	.
1955-56	1.24	1.19	0.61	0.88	0.65	0.58	0.76	0.79
1956-57	1.38	1.31	0.75	1.05	0.73	0.78	0.87	1.03
1957-58	1.38	1.28	0.82	1.02	0.74	0.72	0.90	0.95
1958-59	1.70	1.51	0.93	1.09	0.74	0.73	0.99	1.00
1959-60	1.76	1.46	0.88	1.12	0.72	0.70	0.98	0.99
1960-61	1.81	1.54	0.74	1.33	0.75	0.69	0.97	1.03
1961-62	1.80	1.57	0.75	1.14	0.79	0.66	0.98	0.98
1962-63	1.69	1.60	0.88	1.18	0.85	0.75	1.03	1.07
1963-64	1.82	1.62	1.09	1.22	0.86	0.78	1.12	1.09
1964-65	2.31	2.17	1.17	1.47	1.11	1.19	1.37	1.49
1965-66	2.21	2.26	1.44	1.58	1.44	1.41	1.60	1.75
1966-67	.	2.75	.	1.87	.	1.80	.	2.08
1967-68	.	3.31	.	2.25	.	2.05	.	2.38
1968-69	.	3.26	.	2.19	.	1.92	.	2.35
1969-70	.	3.37	.	2.46	.	1.97	.	2.44
1970-71	.	3.47	.	2.40	.	1.96	.	2.45
1971-72	.	—	.	—	.	—	.	—
1972-73	.	4.02	.	2.73	.	2.30	.	2.98
1973-74	.	4.60	.	3.12	.	2.85	.	3.32

Source: Series A: Government of India, Ministry of Food and Agriculture, Department of Economics and Statistics: *Agricultural wages in India*, monthly publication (New Delhi).
Series B: Government of Uttar Pradesh, Directorate of Economics and Statistics: *Monthly/Quarterly Bulletin of Statistics* (Lucknow).

being the rural population according to the 1951 census. Prices of items such as silver, betel nut and matches are collected from district headquarters. The district average price of a commodity is estimated from the village prices in accordance with the sampling procedure. Regional average prices are then calculated by weighting the average price of the district by its rural population in 1951. At the state level, the regional price is weighted by the regional rural population to get the state average. The weights used are indicated in table 15 for each of the three regions and the state as a whole. Given the relative backwardness of the eastern region and the lower wage rates, it is to be expected that a larger percentage of the expenditure of agricultural labourers in that region would be on food items, particularly cereals. However, what is surprising is the greater proportion of consumption of pulses. The weights remained unchanged over time.

A perusal of table 17 reveals that real wages fluctuated throughout the period under consideration in all the three regions. However, over the entire period, the western and central parts of Uttar Pradesh did not experience a significant increase or decrease in the level of real wages. The compound

79

Table 15.   Commodity· weights used in compiling the rural consumer price index

Commodity	Western Uttar Pradesh	Central Uttar Pradesh	Eastern, Uttar Pradesh	Whole state
Food items	76.5	80.0	85.7	81.2
Cereals	44.5	52.9	62.3	53.8
Pulses	5.3	6.9	9.9	7.6
Vegetables	3.5	2.8	3.2	3.2
Milk and fat	14.3	8.6	4.9	9.2
Other foods	8.9	8.8	5.4	7.4
Fuel and light	7.7	8.0	5.8	6.9
Clothing and footwear	7.7	6.7	4.0	5.9
Housing	2.7	1.0	0.2	1.3
Other	5.4	4.3	4.3	4.7

Table 16.   Consumer price indices for agricultural labourers (1957-58 = 100)

Year	Western Uttar Pradesh	Central Uttar Pradesh	Eastern Uttar Pradesh	All Uttar Pradesh
1959-60	110.2	109.1	102.9	106.5
1960-61	115.3	113.2	103.2	108.8
1961-62	116.8	109.2	105.3	109.3
1962-63	119.8	113.1	105.5	111.3
1963-64	135.3	135.2	123.6	129.2
1964-65	177.8	182.2	177.1	176.6
1965-66	178.0	188.8	186.9	182.2
1966-67	229.3	245.0	232.4	233.9
1967-68	257.7	268.5	254.4	256.1
1968-69	215.1	213.6	197.2	204.8
1969-70	227.8	233.0	217.1	222.6
1970-71	214.6	216.8	212.1	212.6
1971-72	n.a.	n.a.	n.a.	n.a.
1972-73	273.0	280.0	261.0	267.0
1973-74	351.8	363.9	346.5	348.2

Source: Government of Uttar Pradesh, Directorate of Economics and Statistics: *Monthly/Quarterly Bulletin of Statistics*, op. cit.

rates of growth of real wages were 0.9 per cent per annum for western Uttar Pradesh and minus 0.7 per cent a year for central Uttar Pradesh, but neither of these was statistically significant. On the other hand, for eastern Uttar Pradesh, there was a 2.4 per cent rate of growth per year significant at the 1 per cent level of probability. For the state as a whole, a 1.2 per cent rate of growth was recorded as significant at the 5 per cent level of probability. The only noteworthy increase in each of the regions was between 1967-68 and 1968-69. Thereafter real wages declined steadily in eastern Uttar Pradesh, while in the western and central regions they rose until 1970-71 and then began to decline.

Table 17.   Real wage rates of agricultural labourers
(Rupees per day at 1957-58 prices)

Year	Western Uttar Pradesh	Central Uttar Pradesh	Eastern Uttar Pradesh	All Uttar Pradesh
1957-58	1.28	1.02	0.72	0.95
1958-59	n.a.	n.a.	n.a.	n.a.
1959-60	1.32	1.03	0.68	0.93
1960-61	1.34	1.17	0.67	0.95
1961-62	1.34	1.04	0.63	0.90
1962-63	1.34	1.04	0.71	0.96
1963-64	1.19	0.90	0.63	0.84
1964-65	1.22	0.81	0.67	0.84
1965-66	1.27	0.84	0.75	0.96
1966-67	1.20	0.76	0.77	0.89
1967-68	1.28	0.84	0.81	0.93
1968-69	1.51	1.03	0.97	1.15
1969-70	1.48	1.06	0.91	1.10
1970-71	1.62	1.11	0.92	1.15
1971-72	n.a.	n.a.	n.a.	n.a.
1972-73	1.47	0.98	0.88	1.12
1973-74	1.31	0.86	0.82	0.95

Source: tables 14 and 16.

The foregoing discussion of trends in money wage rates and real wage rates inevitably leads to the question of whether or not the introduction of the new agricultural technology affected these trends. In recent years there has been some controversy on this issue. Some have argued that consequent on the Green Revolution real wages have risen.[1] Others have tried to establish that real wage rates have either fallen or remained constant.[2] However, no study so far has seriously attempted to separate the Green Revolution areas from the areas that have not felt the impact of the new technology, within individual states. This is clearly necessary if one is to draw meaningful comparisons within areas characterised by the same socio-political environment. For instance, a comparison of Kerala with Uttar Pradesh may not be very conclusive, because it is possible that other factors, such as the existence of a comparatively strong peasant movement, may have helped agricultural labourers to extract a higher wage in Kerala. Again, since agriculture is a "state subject" the state governments may pursue somewhat different policies. Therefore, an attempt will be made to analyse the impact of the new

[1] See, for example, Robert W. Herdt and Edward A. Baker: "Agricultural Wages, Production and the High Yielding Varieties", in *Economic and Political Weekly*, 25 Mar. 1972. The authors have shown that in Punjab, Kerala and Madras, where more than 14 per cent of the area devoted to food grains was under HYV, the real wages were significantly higher in 1968-69 than in the period 1954-61, whereas on other farms real wages had fallen.

[2] See, for instance, P. K. Bardhan: "Agricultural Labourers and the Green Revolution", in *Economic and Political Weekly*, op. cit., p. 1240. The author states that in Punjab and Haryana real wages did not rise between 1960-61 and 1967-68.

high yield variety (HYV) technology on wage rates, by comparing, on the one hand, trends in wages in western Uttar Pradesh, which can be broadly defined as the Green Revolution area, and central and eastern regions, on the other.

This new technology (HYV) was introduced in a significant way in 1966-67, primarily for the cultivation of wheat. It included the adoption of new varieties of seed, with substantial use of chemical fertilisers, on irrigated land. In the case of rice, some new varieties were introduced, but their success in Uttar Pradesh was negligible. Consequently, only the wheat-growing belt of western Uttar Pradesh benefited greatly from the new technology and has continued to do so until the present. In central Uttar Pradesh, which is largely characterised by poor agriculture, the district of Kanpur is an exception, as it is a Green Revolution district. Eastern Uttar Pradesh is primarily rice-growing and agriculturally backward.

In order to analyse the impact of the Green Revolution on real wages it is necessary to divide the time-series on real wages in table 17 into two sub-periods, the period before the Green Revolution (1957-58 to 1965-66) and that after (1966-67 to 1973-74). The trend growth rates (per cent per annum) in real wages were as follows:

Regions	1957-58 to 1965-66	1966-67 to 1973-74	1957-58 to 1973-74
Western	−0.80	1.49	0.85[1]
Central	−3.45[2]	1.79	−0.64
Eastern	−0.04	0.67	2.28[2]
All	−0.82	1.42	1.18[1]

[1] Significant at the 5 per cent level.   [2] Significant at the 1 per cent level.

It is immediately obvious that it is very difficult to make any firm statements about the impact of the Green Revolution on wages. Most of the trend growth rates are not statistically significant,[1] but even if they were the picture remains unclear. In western Uttar Pradesh real wages fell between 1957 and 1966 but increased by 1.5 per cent per annum in the second period. It is tempting to attribute the increase to the effects of the introduction of HYV, but this would be inconsistent with the rest of the evidence. For instance, real wages in central Uttar Pradesh (which was relatively untouched by the Green Revolution) increased faster than in western Uttar Pradesh between 1967 and 1974. Moreover, the "recovery" of wages from the period of decline in 1957 to 1966 was also greater in central Uttar Pradesh than in western Uttar Pradesh.

---

[1] The fit of the trend lines also was very poor (low values of R^2), even in those cases where the growth rates were statistically significant. This leads to odd results like that for eastern Uttar Pradesh where the sub-period growth rates are both substantially lower than that for the period as a whole.

In short, it is difficult to establish any simple causality between the introduction of the HYV technology and trends in real wages. Other factors, such as the availability of alternative employment, the existence of local labour shortages or surpluses, the relative bargaining power of agricultural labour and landowners and the nature of the contractual relations between landowners and labourers, must also have influenced wage rates.

It is also striking that the only region to experience rising real wages in the period between 1957 and 1966 was eastern Uttar Pradesh, and this tendency continued in the following period. The region is the most backward one and, as was seen in table 13, experienced a large reduction in its agricultural working population between 1961 and 1971. Again, it is tempting to link the changes in wages to migratory flows, but there is insufficient evidence to justify this. It would be invalid, for instance, to interpret the changes in table 13 as if they related purely to intra-state movements of agricultural workers. In the absence of additional data on the origins and destinations of migratory flows it is difficult to make firm statements about the effects of migration on changes in wage rates. It could be argued that the higher rates of growth of real wages in eastern Uttar Pradesh over the whole period (1957 to 1974) as compared to the other two regions is due to out-migration. However, it is difficult to establish a link between the Green Revolution in western Uttar Pradesh and the behaviour of wages in eastern Uttar Pradesh. It is true that the rate of increase of wages in eastern Uttar Pradesh was higher in the post Green Revolution period than earlier but, as previously mentioned, the growth rates in these sub-periods are not statistically significant.

So far, we have considered only average wage rates for all agricultural operations taken together. However, these averages conceal wide variations in the wage rates of different farm operations. It is necessary to consider the wage rates for individual occupations because these have a bearing on the next stage of the analysis, which is concerned with the effects of rising labour costs, particularly at peak periods of demand, on the degree of mechanisation. Ploughing, sowing, weeding, harvesting and threshing are the main agricultural operations for landlords heavily dependent on hired labour, and the cost of this labour affects their decisions regarding substitution of capital for labour.

The wage data for particular farm operations are contained in table 18. This refers only to money wage rates. In all regions, the absolute level of money wages is highest for harvesting and threshing, followed by ploughing and sowing and then by weeding. As between regions, the wage rates have been the highest in western Uttar Pradesh followed by central and then eastern Uttar Pradesh, for each of the agricultural operations.

It has been argued that the new agricultural technology has generated additional demand for labour, particularly at peak times, which has created labour shortages for farm operations such as harvesting and ploughing and sowing. This is reflected in the rising wage rates for such activities. An

Table 18.   Money wage rates for agricultural labourers, by farm operations and regions
(Rupees per day)

Region and operation	1964-65	1965-66	1966-67	1967-68	1968-69	1969-70	1970-71	1972-73	1973-74
Western Uttar Pradesh									
Ploughing and sowing	2.06	2.19	2.42	3.00	3.18	3.29	3.34	3.71	4.26
Weeding	1.84	2.01	2.37	2.82	3.06	3.06	3.12	3.61	3.87
Threshing and harvesting	2.76	2.80	3.70	4.30	3.75	4.09	4.25	5.15	6.11
Other	2.02	2.04	2.51	3.10	3.06	3.05	3.17	3.60	4.15
All occupations	2.17	2.26	2.75	3.31	3.26	3.37	3.47	4.02	4.60
Central Uttar Pradesh									
Ploughing and sowing	1.41	1.59	1.79	2.21	2.28	2.37	2.44	2.70	2.87
Weeding	1.19	1.35	1.36	1.76	1.70	1.98	1.96	2.29	2.61
Threshing and harvesting	1.64	1.85	2.24	2.82	2.59	3.02	2.82	3.00	3.92
Other	1.64	1.53	1.92	2.20	2.18	2.46	2.38	2.74	2.83
All occupations	1.47	1.58	1.83	2.25	2.19	2.46	2.40	2.68	3.06
Eastern Uttar Pradesh									
Ploughing and sowing	1.13	1.39	1.65	1.99	1.84	1.89	1.92	2.28	2.71
Weeding	1.01	1.17	1.40	1.82	1.72	1.70	1.67	2.01	2.24
Threshing and harvesting	1.48	1.51	2.35	2.38	2.27	2.35	2.31	2.80	3.65
Other	1.09	1.54	1.81	2.02	1.85	1.93	1.93	2.29	2.78
All occupations	1.18	1.40	1.80	2.05	1.92	1.97	1.96	2.35	2.85
All Uttar Pradesh									
Ploughing and sowing	1.43	1.69	1.90	2.33	2.26	2.32	2.38	2.73	3.14
Weeding	1.36	1.63	1.64	1.89	2.04	2.13	2.14	2.48	2.68
Threshing and harvesting	1.76	2.02	2.76	2.93	2.88	2.97	2.96	3.94	4.27
Other	1.40	1.65	2.02	2.38	2.20	2.34	2.31	2.76	3.19
All occupations	1.49	1.75	2.08	2.38	2.35	2.44	2.45	2.98	3.32

Source: Government of Uttar Pradesh, Directorate of Economics and Statistics: *Quarterly Bulletin of Statistics.*

examination of table 18 reveals that in western Uttar Pradesh the wage rates for harvesting and threshing continued to rise until 1967-68, and then declined in the following year by 55 paisa per day (100 paisa = 1 rupee). However, wage rates in 1972-73 and 1973-74 were higher than in any previous year. It should be noted that these rises were not peculiar to the western region. Both the central and eastern regions recorded similar increases. Moreover, over the period 1964-65 to 1973-74 the average annual rate of growth of money wage rates for harvesting and threshing was similar in all regions, being 10 per cent for the central region, 10.6 per cent for eastern Uttar Pradesh and 9.2 per cent for western Uttar Pradesh. Again, for ploughing and sowing, money wages rose steadily throughout the above period, but in all the regions by about the same amount, viz. 8.4 per cent per annum in western Uttar Pradesh, 10.2 per cent in eastern Uttar Pradesh and 8.2 per cent in central Uttar Pradesh. Hence, it seems rather difficult to establish a correlation between the introduction of the new high-yielding varieties and wage rates for peak season activities.

Some supplementary data which are available for the districts of Aligarh and Muzaffarnagar in western Uttar Pradesh are now analysed to see if these reveal a different picture. In the district of Aligarh it was observed that real wages declined by 6 per cent between 1962-63 and 1967-68.[1] This district was adopted for intensive agricultural development, and it is remarkable that real wages should have fallen there. In Muzaffarnagar, comparable data for nine villages are available for 1954-55 and 1967-68. Table 19 contains data on money wage rates of casual male agricultural labourers and their equivalent in kilogrammes of wheat. In the absence of a consumer price index for the two years and the unavailability of price data for all consumer items, the wheat equivalent can be interpreted as a close approximation to the real wage rate. With the exception of Gagore, all nine villages recorded a fall in real wage rates between 1954-55 and 1967-68 in virtually all farm occupations. In other words, both in Aligarh and Muzaffarnagar there was a decline in real wage rates.

Another observation that can be made from table 19 is the wide variation in money wage rates as between villages in the district at any given point of time. This raises doubts as to the reliability of wage data based on rates prevailing in a few villages only. Clearly, a record of wage rates prevailing in every village is inconceivable. Nevertheless, the present data are far from perfect and should be used with caution when determining trends, formulating policies, evaluating the cost of rural works schemes from published wage data, or fixing minimum wages.

Under the Minimum Wages Act of 1948 the Government fixed minimum wages for all agricultural operations. These were notified and came into effect in 1966. For adult labourers, the daily wage rate was fixed at Rs. 1.50 to Rs. 1.80,[2] which was lower than the wage rate prevailing in western Uttar Pradesh, as is clear from table 14, but little different from rates prevailing in the central and eastern regions. Minimum wages were statutorily increased in 1972 and again in 1973. In December 1973 the Government announced that since farm labour was not sufficiently organised to bargain for higher wages, direct state action was necessary to protect it. The minimum wage for an adult farm worker on farms below 20 acres was to be as follows in each of the three regions: Rs. 3 per day in eastern Uttar Pradesh, Rs. 3.30 per day in central Uttar Pradesh and Rs. 4.25 per day in western Uttar Pradesh. The wages of those employed on farms of more than 20 acres were to be higher, but the rates were not given in the source quoted.[3] The enforcement of minimum wages in rural India is virtually impossible given the structure of the village society and the mode of payment, which is partly in kind and

---

[1] *Modernising Indian agriculture*, Fourth Report on India Agricultural Development Plan (IADP) (1960-68), Vol. II, p. 218.

[2] Government of India, Department of Labour and Employment, Labour Bureau: *Agricultural labour in India: a compendium of basic facts* (Simla, 1969), pp. 56-57.

[3] *Economic Times* (Bombay), 7 Dec. 1973.

Table 19.   Wage rates for casual male agricultural labourers in nine villages in Muzaffarnagar

Village	Period	Ploughing		Sowing		Weeding and hoeing	
		Rupees per day	Kg of wheat equivalent per day	Rupees per day	Kg of wheat equivalent per day	Rupees per day	Kg of wheat equivalent per day
Biralsi	1954-55	1.30	3.46	1.25	3.32	1.39	3.70
	1967-68	3.00	2.81	2.85	2.67	3.50	3.27
Khanpur	1954-55	1.50	3.95	1.50	3.95	1.00	2.63
	1967-68	2.95	2.93	2.70	2.68	2.60	2.58
Bhuma	1954-55	1.41	3.84	1.41	3.84	1.60	4.36
	1967-68	2.60	2.31	2.90	2.57	3.20	2.84
Salanpur	1954-55	1.30	3.47	1.31	3.49	1.33	3.55
	1967-68	2.50	2.25	2.70	2.43	2.70	2.43
Sisoli	1954-55	1.44	3.72	1.55	4.01	1.33	3.44
	1967-68	3.90	3.83	3.00	2.94	3.40	3.34
Datiyana	1954-55	1.23	3.19	1.31	3.40	1.12	2.91
	1967-68	3.00	2.92	3.00	2.92	2.62	2.55
Gagore	1954-55	0.94	2.51	0.92	2.45	0.89	2.37
	1967-68	3.00	2.75	3.00	2.75	3.62	3.32
Sikri	1954-55	1.15	3.07	1.25	3.34	1.41	3.77
	1967-68	2.50	2.38	2.50	2.38	2.50	2.38
Khandroli	1954-55	2.50	6.58	2.51	6.61	2.22	5.84
	1967-68	3.15	3.12	2.75	2.64	2.80	2.69

Note: Daily wage rates have been converted into kilogrammes of wheat equivalent by using the prices prevailing in each village at that point in time, given in the same source.

Source: Government of India, Directorate of Economics and Statistics: *Studies in the economics of farm management, Uttar Pradesh*, 1954-55 and 1966-67, 1967-68.

often in the form of a meal. Actual wage rates are affected by the relationship between landowners and agricultural labourers, which varies in every situation.

So far the analysis has been concerned with the question of wage rates and the changes in their level over time, without reference to the employment that is available at different wage rates. Earnings of an agricultural labourer depend on the employment he is able to secure at given wages. In other words, wage rates are a necessary but not a sufficient index of the economic condition of agricultural labourers. The employment aspect will, therefore, now be examined with focus on the effects of the Green Revolution on employment. This is followed by an examination of poverty and living standards of agricultural labourers.

EMPLOYMENT

In a labour-abundant economy such as that of India there exists substantial underemployment and even unemployment in the rural sector. However,

Table 20. Wage-paid employment of adult male agricultural labourers, casual and attached, for Uttar Pradesh in 1956-57
(Days per year)

Category	Agricultural employment	Non-agricultural employment	Total
Casual labour	*141.74*	*38.91*	*180.65*
with land	120.31	35.82	156.13
without land	163.50	42.11	205.61
Attached labour	*224.97*	*33.87*	*258.84*
with land	205.32	39.45	244.77
without land	271.31	20.67	291.98
All	173.80	36.95	210.75

Source: Government of India, Ministry of Labour and Employment: *Agricultural labour in India, Report of the Second Inquiry, 1956-57*, Vol. XII: Uttar Pradesh (Simla, 1962), p. 22.

attempts at estimating the extent of this underemployment have not been very successful. Unless a country-wide survey is carried out which measures the daily employment of individuals, no accurate estimate can be made of the nature and magnitude of the rural employment problem. Given the nature of the agrarian structure and the pattern of family relationships, the underemployment often does not manifest itself as open unemployment. Most persons seem occupied, whereas it is likely that many are not fully employed either in terms of man-hours per day or of effort. To begin with, the available evidence on the extent of underutilisation of labour will be considered. This will be followed by a discussion of the impact of the new agricultural technology on employment in two situations: (i) where the new inputs are used but the techniques remain traditional and (ii) where mechanical power is used instead of human labour and animal power. Finally, certain implications of the new technology, as it is being applied, will be considered.

The paucity of data is a serious problem, but the general discussion will be substantiated wherever possible by the available estimates. The years 1950-51 and 1956-57 are those for which comprehensive estimates of the average number of days for which an agricultural labourer is employed are available. This is so because in each of these two years a detailed survey was carried out with a view to studying the economic conditions of agricultural labourers.

Table 20 contains the estimates for the average number of days for which an agricultural labourer was able to secure employment during 1956-57 in Uttar Pradesh. Paid employment, i.e. excluding self-employment, for all households averaged 211 days in 1956-57 compared to 289 days in 1950-51. This decline has been attributed to *(a)* the substitution of family labour for hired labour between 1950-51 and 1956-57; *(b)* an increase from 32 days in 1950-51 to 49 days in 1956-57 on account of self-employment, i.e. greater self-employment, e.g. on one's own farm, at the cost of a decline in wage employment; *(c)* changes in the method of data collection between the two inquiries, notably a switch from work to income as the criterion for determining occupational categories. This change in the criterion could lead to an underestimation of employment (i) by excluding unpaid family workers and (ii) by treating incorrectly those who were cultivators-cum-labourers on the margin. Clearly neither the landless nor those who were primarily cultivators would be affected, as they would be employed for more than 50 per cent of their time on their respective occupations and would also derive more than 50 per cent of their income from it. However, given the fact that between 1950-51 and 1956-57 there was an increase in the price of agricultural commodities, it follows that money income accruing from cultivation will have been higher in 1956-57 for some of those who were previously recorded as agricultural labourers. Some of those whose income from cultivation was less than 50 per cent of their total income in 1950-51 qualified in the later year as cultivators because more than 50 per cent of their total income was from cultivation, and thus they were excluded from the employment survey.

The fact that those without land were able to find greater wage employment during the year than those with land can be seen in table 20. This may be due to the greater mobility of the landless compared to those with land, who are in a sense tied to it. In addition, the landless may have been motivated to a greater extent by the need to seek employment urgently. However, considering only the casual male agricultural labourers, it appears that while in 1950-51 they received 317 days of employment (including self-employment), in 1956-57 the number of days worked had declined to 241. Assuming that 300 working days per year represents full labour utilisation, it follows that in 1956-57 there was considerable underutilisation. This may have been due to an increase in the number seeking employment during that year.

A similar conclusion was obtained from the results of a study of eight sample villages in five districts of western Uttar Pradesh. As shown in table 21, in all eight villages there was a decline in the number of days for which employment was available for casual workers. In Sohalpur village of Saharanpur district and in Zahidpur-Mohammadpur village of Bulandshahr district the decline was marginal. On the other hand, in the other villages of Saharanpur the decline was significant and has been attributed to an increase in the female participation rate. The only other explanation for the decline in the number of days employed per person per year is that the number of agricultural labourers seeking employment increased at a faster rate than the demand for labour. This does not seem to be applicable in the case of Kalinjan in the Agra district and Gati in the Etawah district, where there was a decline in the number of labourers and yet employment was available for only half the number of days. In any case, with the exception of Katra Rahmat Khan in Farrukhabad district, the number of days for which employment was available varied between 54 and 151, indicating a considerable degree of underutilisation, which became worse over the four- to five-year period.

Table 21.   Employment of casual agricultural labourers in selected villages of Uttar Pradesh, 1955-56 to 1957-58 and 1958-59 to 1961-62

District	Village	Number of labourers		Average man-days	
		1955-56 to 1957-58	1958-59 to 1961-62	1955-56 to 1957-58	1958-59 to 1961-62
Saharanpur	Sohalpur	11	18	139	137
	Chiana	26	51	151	132
	Sanoli	24	39	118	66
Bulandshahr	Zahidpur-Mohammadpur	16	38	118	114
Agra	Gazmalpur	8	12	143	73
	Kalinjan	32	22	108	54
Etawah	Gati	21	17	114	63
Farrukhabad	Katra Rahmat Khan	134	169	224	192

Note: In each of the villages data were collected in different years; the terminal years at either end varied from village to village, but in each case it was in one of the three years mentioned. For details see Saini and Sharma, below, p. 1.

Source: G. R. Saini and E. K. Sharma: *Impact of economic development on agricultural labour, case studies of 15 selected villages in Punjab and Uttar Pradesh* (Agricultural Economics Research Centre, University of Delhi, 1962), p. 76.

These estimates refer to western Utter Pradesh alone. There is only one study which attempts to compare the availability of employment in a western and an eastern district. This study compares Meerut, a Green Revolution district, and Deoria for the year 1970.[1] However, as the study is based on data for only one village in each of the districts, the basis for such a comparison is very weak. Assuming that these villages are representative of the two regions, certain inferences can be made. On average, employment per person in both villages was approximately the same—240 days per year in Meerut and 237 in Deoria. That is, the employment situation was the same in the Green Revolution district as in the backward subsistence farming district. It would be hazardous to project the experience of these two villages to the respective regions in which they are located, but the study does throw a little light on the question of employment in different parts of the state.

Another study of 100 villages in Meerut district[2] revealed that in 1965 casual agricultural labourers were employed for 244 days, and if attached workers are included, they were employed for 283 days. In the 1970 survey no distinction was made between casual and permanent attached labourers. Even if employment of only casual labourers in 1965 was compared with the estimate for 1970, the situation remains unchanged. In other words, in this Green Revolution district, there seems to have been no increase in the aver-

[1] Planning, Research and Action Division, State Planning Institute: *Income level of the underemployed, additional work desired by them, and terms and conditions on which their labour will be available (A diagnostic case study of two village communities in Uttar Pradesh)* (Lucknow, 1971).

[2] R. C. Saxena: *Agricultural labour: wages and living conditions in Meerut* (Research Programmes Committee, Planning Commission, New Delhi, 1964), p. 110. (Also published in Elite Publications, New Delhi, 1969.)

age number of days per year for which a labourer was able to secure employment. This certainly contradicts the contention that the Green Revolution has generated an increased demand for labour. However, this apparent lack of a relationship between the new technology and employment cannot be considered conclusive on the basis of such fragmentary evidence. A much more detailed analysis is necessary, which is now made.

The new agricultural technology consists of a package of inputs—high-yielding varieties of seeds, chemical fertilisers and irrigation facilities. However, it does not necessarily imply the use of mechanical devices. It can be satisfactorily implemented using traditional techniques based on human and animal power. There is little doubt that a shift from traditional technology to the HYV technology leads to an increase in labour requirements per hectare, provided tractorisation is avoided. This follows logically from the impact of the new inputs on the pattern of cultivation. The new varieties require a careful preparation of the seedbeds; a shift from dependence on rainfall to irrigation schemes requires more timely delivery of water together with an increased demand for labour during the course of construction of these schemes; higher yields imply a greater amount to be harvested and threshed. All these create an additional demand for labour. Other agricultural operations such as weeding, application of fertilisers, pesticides, insecticides, etc., also require more labour inputs. This argument can be substantiated with the data available from surveys for Uttar Pradesh:

1. Table 22 shows that a shift from local varieties to the HYV technology resulted in an increase of 58 per cent in labour input per hectare on wheat farms in Aligarh. Each of the farm operations required a higher labour input under the new technology than they did with traditional agriculture. However, the table gives the total labour input including both hired and family labour. If only the hired labour component is considered, when the total demand for labour increased, the increase in the demand for hired labour was proportionately less than the increase in the family labour input. In other words, while the demand for hired labour increased from 23.4 days per hectare to 31.8 days per hectare consequent on the adoption of the new varieties, family labour increased dramatically from 49.33 days per hectare to 82.74 days per hectare.[1]

2. A more recent analysis for Budrun district in western Uttar Pradesh, based on a linear programming model, showed that for Bisanli block the total amount of labour employed in crop production increased by 30-50 per cent between 1967-68 and 1972-73.[2] In this model the new technology was defined as a package of new strains of seed, irrigation by pumping sets and chemical fertilisers. However, from this exercise it is not possible to isolate the impact on hired labour. One can only infer that the increase in total

---

[1] R. S. Dixit and P. P. Singh, op. cit.

[2] National Council of Applied Economic Research: *Impact of mechanisation in agriculture on employment* (New Delhi, 1973).

Table 22.   Labour input on 12 irrigated wheat farms in Aligarh district, 1967-68, using HYV but with traditional techniques (Man-days per hectare)

Operations	High-yielding varieties	Local varieties	Percentage difference
Ploughing	25.9	19.7	31.5
Sowing	9.2	5.0	84.0
Manuring	12.1	4.2	188.1
Irrigation	17.4	13.6	27.9
Harvesting	22.1	14.4	53.5
Threshing-winnowing	28.0	15.8	77.2
All	114.7	72.7	57.8

Source: R. S. Dixit and P. P. Singh: "Impact of High Yielding Varieties on Human Labour Input", in Government of India: *Agricultural situation in India* (New Delhi, 1970), table 6, p. 1085.

labour input is bound to have had some favourable effects on the demand for hired labour.

3. The most detailed estimates of labour requirements available are for six villages in Muzaffarnagar district situated in western Uttar Pradesh.[1] Employment estimates have been made at four levels of mechanisation. To begin with, the effect of a shift from non-mechanisation to tubewell irrigation on small and medium farms, defined as farms of 0-4 hectares and 4-12 hectares respectively, is considered. The evidence indicates that when a shift was made to tubewell irrigation, employment of labour in crop culture increased from 178.5 man-days per hectare to 269.3 man-days per hectare on small farms and from 128.4 man-days per hectare to 161.1 man-days per hectare on medium farms. The impact on hired labour alone, both casual and permanent, can be seen in table 23.

It appears that permanent farm labour tended to gain at the expense of casual labour. This may be attributable either to real shortages of labour at peak seasons or to a fear of such bottlenecks, which made it more rational for farmers to employ farm labour on an annual basis.

A more detailed breakdown of labour utilisation by farm occupations is included in table 24; this table refers to hired labour only. From the table, it is clear that when a shift was made to tubewell irrigation, there was an increase in labour input per hectare in all operations with the exception of inter-culture on small farms. One thing which is notable, however, is the decline in labour input as one moves from small to medium farms. This reflects a greater intensity of cultivation on smaller farms. Indeed, the non-mechanised small farms are more labour-intensive than even the tubewell-irrigated medium farms. This argument would certainly hold if total labour input were considered. But what is curious in the above case is that the input of wage labour is much higher on small as compared to medium farms.

[1] National Council of Applied Economic Research: *Impact of mechanisation in agriculture on employment*, op. cit.

Table 23. Wage employment in different types of farms in six villages in Muzaffarnagar, 1971
(Man-days per hectare)

Type of labour	Non-mechanised		Tubewell-irrigated	
	Small	Medium	Small	Medium
Permanent	28.9	4.7	75.7	15.1
Casual	59.8	19.4	42.6	32.7

Source: National Council of Applied Economic Research: *Impact of mechanisation in agriculture on employment*, op. cit., p. 32.

Table 24. Hired male labour for different crop operations on small and medium farms, without tractor but with tubewell irrigation, in Muzaffarnagar, 1971
(Man-days per hectare)

Operation	Non-Mechanised		Tubewell-irrigated	
	Small	Medium	Small	Medium
Ploughing	10.1	1.4	19.7	4.3
Manuring	1.6	0.2	3.2	1.1
Sowing	5.5	0.8	7.4	4.5
Fertilisation	0.2	—	0.4	—
Irrigation	8.8	1.6	13.4	6.3
Inter-culture	21.0	6.2	14.7	8.8
Harvesting	28.3	12.6	37.2	14.3
Threshing	9.4	1.1	13.9	6.4
Winnowing	—	—	0.6	—
Transportation	3.8	0.2	7.8	0.9
Other	—	—	—	—
Total	88.7	24.1	118.3	46.6

Source: National Council of Applied Economic Research: *Impact of mechanisation in agriculture on employment*, op. cit., p. 32.

The evidence presented so far seems to indicate that the introduction of the new technology, consisting of improved seeds, chemical fertilisers and irrigation, leads to an increase in labour inputs per hectare. But no account has been taken of a possible change in technique involving a switch in the source of energy from animal and human power to mechanical power. However, the Green Revolution has brought in its wake a shift from traditional techniques to mechanical devices, and this has serious implications in a labour-abundant, capital-scarce economy. The data on this issue to enable an assessment of the dimensions of the problem are, unfortunately, scarce.

Only two surveys are available on Uttar Pradesh. Therefore, some examples from the experience of the Punjab are included in support of the argument that mechanisation is leading to a displacement of labour. Since the economic characteristics of western Uttar Pradesh and the Punjab are much the same, and both have experienced a breakthrough in wheat cultivation, it

Table 25. Wage employment of permanent and casual labour on small and medium holdings on tubewell-irrigated and tractorised farms, 1971 (Man-days per hectare per year)

Type of labour	Tubewell-irrigated		Tubewells and tractors	
	Small holdings	Medium holdings	Small holdings	Medium holdings
Permanent	75.7	15.1	—	13.6
Casual	42.6	32.7	72.6	16.6

Source: National Council of Applied Economic Research: *Impact of mechanisation in agriculture*, op. cit., p. 32.

is reasonable to assume that the trends that have occurred in the Punjab are also representative of Uttar Pradesh:

1. The study of Muzaffarnagar discussed above revealed that although the transition from non-mechanised to tubewell irrigation led to an increase in *total* labour input per hectare, the introduction of tractors led to a fall in total labour input. On small farms this decline was 32.6 per cent, and on medium farms it was 32.9 per cent. The same phenomenon was observed in the case of *hired* labour, details of which are set out in table 25. On medium farms permanent plus casual labour input declined by 36.8 per cent when a transition was made to tractors. In other words, while a move to irrigation, which under the definition adopted here is a shift to HYV technology, generated additional demand for labour, the replacement of traditional techniques by mechanical power in the form of tractors displaced most of the additional labour utilised.

2. A study covering 242 "progressive" and 161 "less progressive" farmers in north-west Uttar Pradesh[1] provided the data for a subsequent analysis of the effects of mechanisation on labour requirements.[2] In the study, a progressive farmer was one who fulfilled three of the following criteria: (i) 30 per cent of sown area irrigated; (ii) 20 per cent of the sown area under HYV seeds; (iii) 20 per cent of the sown area under chemical fertilisers; (iv) independent irrigation facilities; (v) ownership of a tractor or a power thresher, except in the case of small farms. On the assumption that most of the labour demand is concentrated on large and medium farms, only such farms were selected and thus small farms were excluded. The selected farms were grouped into "tractor farms", i.e. those using tractors and threshers, and "typical farms", which were synonymous with farms using traditional techniques.

---

[1] *Changing agriculture and rural life in a part of northern India – socio-economic behaviour of progressive farmers in north-west Uttar Pradesh* (Uttar Pradesh Agricultural University, Pantnagar and the Rockefeller Foundation Cooperative Project, Pantnagar, 1969).

[2] S. L. Shah and C. R. Singh: "The Impact of the New Agricultural Technology on Rural Employment in North-West Uttar Pradesh", in *Indian Journal of Agricultural Economics*, July-Sep. 1970, pp. 29-33. The authors used the data contained in *Changing agriculture and rural life...*, op. cit.

Expenditure on labour was used as the index of employment. In all cases there was a decline in expenditure on labour when one moved from a typical to a tractor farm, implying a fall in employment per acre with increased mechanisation. The difference in expenditure on labour per acre between typical and tractor farms was Rs. 22.7 for medium progressive farms, Rs. 65 for medium non-progressive farms, Rs. 4.5 for large progressive farms and Rs. 32 per acre for large non-progressive farms.

3. A study of irrigated wheat farms in the Punjab showed that the introduction of the new technology led to substantial increases in labour input per hectare provided cultivation occurred with the use of traditional techniques.[1] A shift to mechanisation more than counteracted this increase, so that there was a 24 per cent decline in labour input per hectare when compared to the traditional technology-cum-technique situation.

4. A similar conclusion emerged from another study of Punjab for the year 1968-69.[2] A shift from the conventional technology employing traditional techniques to a mechanised HYV technology resulted in a 5.5 per cent decline in demand for labour. However, in this study, it is calculated that by 1983-84 total demand for human energy will be down by 17.4 per cent. The basic assumptions underlying the calculation are that *(a)* 100 per cent of the wheat is threshed mechanically; *(b)* 20 per cent of the gross cropped area is tilled by tractors; *(c)* 50 per cent of the wheat crop is mechanically reaped and *(d)* 60 per cent of the area is irrigated by pump sets and tubewells.

5. A survey of four districts in the Punjab showed that tractor cultivation was labour-displacing. Taking all agricultural operations together, 8.8 tractor hours for every acre saved 52 hours of male labour per acre.[3]

The evidence thus indicates that the adoption of mechanised techniques has been successful in substituting capital for labour. Unfortunately, only certain of the studies isolate the impact of mechanisation on hired labour, while others are concerned only with total labour input. Nevertheless, studies of the impact of mechanisation on labour input provide an indication of its effects on the input of hired labour, particularly since mechanisation is often the result of labour shortages, notably at peak seasons. It can be argued that even though the labour input per unit area may have declined because of a

---

[1] William H. Bartsch: *Employment and technology choice in Asian agriculture* (New York, Praeger, 1977), pp. 34-36. He defines technology as "the application of knowledge involving the use of combinations of material inputs of a biological-chemical nature in conjunction with particular cultivation practices typically associated with such inputs", while techniques relate to "the methods of delivery of these inputs and implementation of these practices in association with different sources of power (human, animal, mechanical) and corresponding equipment"; he identifies three types of technology—traditional, improved, and modern or high-yield variety—and three types of techniques—traditional, intermediate, and mechanised (pp. 4-5).

[2] Martin Billings and Arjan Singh: *Farm mechanisation and the Green Revolution, 1968-84 – the Punjab case* (USAID, New Delhi, 1972).

[3] B. Singh: "Economics of Tractor Utilisation – A Case Study", in *Indian Journal of Agricultural Economics*, Jan.-Mar. 1968, p. 85.

more capital-intensive cultivation of the land, the total demand for labour, over the whole year, and taking multiple cropping into account, may in fact rise. If this were so, mechanisation would generate some additional demand for labour. Unfortunately, absence of data makes it impossible to resolve this debate. But even if there were some increase in employment as a result of the adoption of mechanical devices, mechanisation could only be justified if it led to increases in output which could not be achieved otherwise, and if these increases were sufficient relative to the costs in terms of scarce capital.[1]

STANDARD OF LIVING

In recent years there has been a lengthy debate in India about the concept and measurement of absolute poverty. The controversy has centred around the definition of a minimum level of living, the use of statistical data and the method of estimating the number of those who live below the poverty line. The lack of consensus is reflected in widely divergent estimates of poverty. Clearly in a country such as India the notion of poverty must be based on some minimum diet necessary for subsistence. This requires a cost evaluation of the diet which provides the essential nutrients to an individual. The quantity of essential nutrients and hence this total cost is different for males, females and children and depends also on the nature of work and climatic conditions. In 1962 a group appointed by the Government of India specified the minimum level of living at Rs. 20 per head per month at 1960-61 prices, but it did not specify the nutritional norms used nor the items included in its computation. Nevertheless, this minimum was accepted by the Planning Commission and was subsequently used by several economists in their estimation of rural poverty.

In the following analysis an estimate is made of the magnitude of rural poverty in Uttar Pradesh using two alternative methods. First, the yardstick advocated by the Planning Commission will be adopted as the poverty line. Secondly, the extent of poverty will be estimated on the basis of the minimum nutritional requirements as recommended by the Indian Council of Medical Research.

1. Given that prices in rural areas are somewhat lower than in urban areas, the minimum consumption expenditure should in those areas be lower than the Rs. 20 per head per month referred to above. A conservative estimate of the rural minimum may be taken as Rs. 15 for India as a whole. However, it has been shown that in Uttar Pradesh the same basket of goods costs somewhat less than the average for India. Assuming the latter to be 100, the average price of a given composition of commodities was 96.4 for the rural poor in Uttar Pradesh during 1960-61.[2] Consequently, in Uttar

---

[1] See K. N. Raj: "Mechanisation of Agriculture in India and Sri Lanka", in *Mechanisation and employment in agriculture: case studies of four continents* (Geneva, ILO, 1973).

[2] P. K. Bardhan: "On the Incidence of Poverty in Rural India", in *Economic and Political Weekly*, Feb. 1973, pp. 245-254.

Table 26. Distribution of rural population by per capita expenditure classes in Uttar Pradesh for 1960-61 and 1970-71
(Percentages)

Monthly per capita expenditure class in rupees (1)	1960-61 (2)	1970-71 (3)
0- 8	6.5	0.4
8-11	12.7	2.2
11-13	12.8	2.9
13-15	9.6	5.3
15-18	15.2	11.7
18-21	10.3	14.8
21-24	8.3	14.3
24-28	6.8	12.0
28-34	8.0	15.8
34-43	5.7	9.6
43-55	3.0	7.5
55 and above	1.1	3.5

Notes: (i) The data for 1960-61, as given in the source, were collected as part of the *National Sample Survey, Sixteenth Round*; (ii) the data for 1970-71 are presented in two sets, each drawing upon a sample of different villages. In one sample 1,309 households were surveyed and in the other 1,653. The estimates given in the table are weighted averages of the two samples. The weights are the total number of rural people surveyed under each sample.

Source: column (2): Government of Uttar Pradesh, Directorate of Economics and Statistics: *Consumer expenditure in Uttar Pradesh*, Bulletin No. 98, July 1960-June 1961, p. 67; column (3): Government of India, National Sample Survey Organisation; *National Sample Survey, Twenty-fifth Round*, July 1970-June 1971, Tables on Consumer Expenditure, Indebtedness and Other Economic Aspects in Rural Areas, State: Uttar Pradesh, July 1973.

Pradesh Rs. 14.50 would buy the same quantity of goods as Rs. 15 elsewhere. All consumers who spent less than Rs. 14.50 in rural Uttar Pradesh in 1960-61 may be assumed to be living below the poverty line.

Table 26 contains data on the percentage of the rural population by expenditure class in Uttar Pradesh for the years 1960-61 and 1970-71. From this table it is clear that about 41.6 per cent of the rural population in Uttar Pradesh appear to have been below the poverty line in 1960-61. This includes the expenditure classes from 0-8 to 13-15, which is the closest approximation to those falling below Rs. 14.50. Therefore, to this extent, 41.6 per cent is a slight overestimate.

Between 1960-61 and 1970-71 the consumer price index for agricultural labourers increased in Uttar Pradesh by 95.4 per cent. Opinion has been divided about the suitability of the consumer price index for agricultural labourers as a deflator. There are some who argue that in the absence of a consumer price index for the rural poor this is the most appropriate index, while others favour the national income deflator. Those who use the latter assume implicitly that price changes are felt uniformly by all sections of the rural population, and that there is no inequality in the pattern of their consumption expenditures. Clearly, this is not justifiable. For the poor, a large part of total expenditure is on food grains, and the fact that the price of food grains rose faster than the prices of other consumer goods would have affected the poorer sections more adversely. Moreover, even in the case of cereals, it has been shown that the price paid by the lowest 10 per cent of the rural population rose at a faster rate than that paid by the top 10 per cent. The consumer price index for agricultural labourers has therefore been used as a deflator, rather than the national income deflator.

On this basis, the basket of consumption goods which cost Rs. 14.50 in 1960-61 cost Rs. 28 in 1970-71. From table 26 it follows that in 1970-71 63.6 per cent of the rural population in Uttar Pradesh were below the "minimum" standard. In other words, while in 1960-61, 26.7 million in rural Uttar Pradesh lived below the "poverty line", in 1970 their number had risen to 48.3 million. Over the decade there was a 50 per cent increase in the proportion of rural inhabitants who lived below the defined minimum in Uttar Pradesh.

2. As explained earlier, this method of estimating rural poverty may not be a satisfactory one, unless the stipulated minimum can provide the rural poor with a sufficient intake of food to meet their nutritional requirements. According to the Indian Council of Medical Research, an average adult person engaged in moderate activity requires 2,700 calories and 55 grams of protein per day. In addition, it has prescribed the minimum necessary intake of other nutrients including calcium, iron, phosphorus, vitamins, thiamine, nicotinic acid and riboflavin. In order to meet these nutritional requirements, a balanced diet has been suggested by the Council. This is presented in table 27. This table also contains information on the price per unit weight of each of the commodities in the rural areas of Uttar Pradesh in 1960-61. Given the price and the quantity of each food item that should be consumed the monthly cost of the recommended diet for a vegetarian adult male in Uttar Pradesh engaged in moderate activity has been worked out.

The total cost of the recommended diet is Rs. 16.74 for an adult male at 1960-61 prices. An average person is taken as 0.81 adult units, so that the cost per person on average would be Rs. 13.56. But this does not allow for other necessary consumption expenses which would be incurred even by the rural poor. In 1960-61 the items included in table 27 accounted for 73 per cent of the total consumption expenditure of agricultural labourers.[1] The remaining expenditure was distributed as follows: (i) other food items, 7.0 per cent; (ii) fuel and lighting, 7.9 per cent; (iii) clothing and shoes, 6.2 per cent; (iv) housing, medicine, ceremonial expenses, services and other miscellaneous items, 5.9 per cent. Therefore, if to the cost of the recommended diet, an amount equivalent to 27 per cent of total consumption is added for expenditure on the items listed above, an average person would have required a minimum of Rs. 18.58 in 1960-61 for subsistence. In terms of 1970-71 prices the same basket of food and non-food items would cost Rs. 36.31 per month per person.

---

[1] Government of Uttar Pradesh: *Monthly Bulletin of Statistics*, op. cit.

Table 27. Cost of recommended diet in Uttar Pradesh in 1960-61

Commodity	Recommended intake in grams per capita per day	Average rural retail price in rupees per seer[1]	Cost of recommended diet in rupees per month
Cereals	475	0.36	5.50
Pulses	80	0.48	1.23
Vegetables and fruits	330	0.30	3.18
Sugar	40	0.46	3.28
Milk	200	0.31	0.59
Oils and fats	40	2.32	2.96

[1] 1 seer = approx. 933 grams.

Notes: (i) The price of each commodity is a simple average of the monthly prices during July 1960 to June 1961 in the rural areas of the state of Uttar Pradesh.   (ii) In the case of cereals the price of wheat, rice and "other cereals" has been weighted by the proportion of each item consumed by agricultural labourers in 1960-61. Similarly, for pulses, the weighted average of the different varieties is used.

Sources: column (2): P. G. K. Panikar: "Economics of Nutrition", op. cit.;   column (3): Government of Uttar Pradesh, Directorate of Economics and Statistics: *Monthly Bulletin of Statistics*, numbers published in 1960-61.

From the data contained in table 26 it can be seen that on the basis of the above evaluation of a minimum consumption expenditure, over 57 per cent of the rural population in Uttar Pradesh lived below the poverty line in 1960-61. This proportion increased over the decade to such an extent that well over 80 per cent of the rural population was below the poverty line in 1970-71. However, it has been argued that the diet recommended by the Medical Research Council is too generous, and that it would be possible to provide the basic nutrients to an individual by changing the composition of the "balanced diet" in favour of cheaper cereals, roots and vegetables. To test this view would require a detailed analysis of the availability of various food items in the area under consideration, the eating habits of the population and the cost of non-food items. However, the paucity of data makes such an evaluation beyond the scope of the present chapter. In any case, it is clear that a large proportion of the rural population in Uttar Pradesh lives under conditions of abject poverty, undernourishment and malnutrition. Furthermore, there is little doubt that their numbers have increased over time, both absolutely and relatively.

Agricultural labourers account for a substantial part of the rural poor. Using the data collected by the National Council of Applied Economic Research, Bhatty has estimated the proportion of the rural population and the proportion of agricultural labourers living below the poverty line, defined in terms of Sen's measure of poverty, in Uttar Pradesh in 1968-69.[1] The details are as follows:

---

[1] I. Z. Bhatty: "Inequality and Poverty in Rural India", in T. N. Srinavasan and P. K. Bardhan (eds.): *Poverty and income distribution in India*, op. cit. Sen's measure uses rank order weights in a way that is sensitive to the gaps in the income of the poor. It attaches greater weight per unit to lower incomes the wider the gap in such incomes. See A. K. Sen: "Poverty, Inequality and Unemployment. Some Conceptual Issues in Measurement", ibid.

	Poverty line (rupees per head per year)				
	180	240	300	360	420
Proportion of rural population living below the poverty line	29.32	46.08	56.96	67.18	74.94
Proportion of agricultural labourers living below the poverty line	39.76	67.89	78.38	89.28	92.82

Given the fact that Rs. 180-240 was the minimum per head required to maintain a person at subsistence level in 1960-61, approximately Rs. 300-360 would have been the equivalent minimum in 1968-69, allowing for the inflation in the interim period. On that basis, while 57-67 per cent of the rural population in Uttar Pradesh lived below the poverty line in 1968-69, 78-89 per cent of the agricultural labour households were "poor". From this it is obvious that the conditions of agricultural labourers are deplorable and their struggle for survival a constant and hard one.

So far no consideration has been given to other aspects of poverty such as educational and medical facilities, which are items of social consumption. Even if these are services performed by the State without cost to the individual, there arises the question of access and whether the poor derive any benefit from these social services. Furthermore, there are the problems of specific groups such as expectant mothers, babies and children who need extra medical care and nourishment. But these issues can only be resolved once the basic minimum is provided to each human being.

In short, it is undeniable that the number of those living below the poverty line, however defined, increased during the 1960s and that those poor form a substantial proportion of the rural population. Moreover, agricultural labour households must form the core of this poverty group. Despite the problems of quantification and the controversies centred on this issue, it is evident that the magnitude of rural poverty is staggering.

SUMMARY AND CONCLUSIONS

It has been shown that in Uttar Pradesh there has been a sharp rise in the proportion of agricultural labourers in rural areas. Presumably there has been a correponding rise in landlessness and near-landlessness. The data, although not entirely reliable, indicate there has been virtually no tendency for real wage rates to increase during the period from 1953 to 1974.

Information about the number of days worked by agricultural labourers is sparse. The evidence, however, does not suggest that there has been an increase in employment per man per year. On the contrary, in those areas where tractors and other mechanical devices have been introduced it is likely that the demand for labour per hectare of wheat has fallen.

There is no doubt that the problem of poverty has assumed serious dimensions. Despite differences in the definition of a "poverty line", all the evidence suggests there has been an increase in the number and proportion of the rural poor. The most conservative estimate is that during the decade of the 1960s the proportion of the rural population living below the poverty line increased from 41.6 per cent to 63.6 per cent. In other words, the number of the rural poor increased from slightly less than 27 million to slightly more than 48 million.

The policy implications of this phenomenon are far-reaching.

Agricultural labourers have been the object of government interest since independence. In the early 1950s two inquiries were conducted to study the economic conditions of agricultural labourers. As a first measure, an Act was passed abolishing *zamindari* (large landed proprietors) and providing security of tenure to erstwhile tenants. The Act also contained provision for a future redistribution of land, but it did not include a policy of redistribution of existing landholdings on a more egalitarian basis. In 1961 a second Act imposed a ceiling on rural landholdings, with the specific aim of achieving greater equality in the landholdings of individual cultivators. However, the existence of legal loopholes, coupled with ineffective enforcement, resulted in a complete failure of this Act to achieve its objective. In 1971 the land reform issue was reopened, but so far has remained unresolved.

During the 1960s a series of programmes aimed at creating greater rural employment was launched by the Government. These were largely rural works programmes and none achieved much success. In some cases the employment generated was not commensurate with the expenditure on the programme, while in others no productive assets were created. The reasons for the failure of the schemes were many, and varied from project to project, but in broad terms they can be ascribed to faulty planning and poor implementation.

In other words, the employment-oriented schemes devised to raise agricultural labourers from poverty met with little success. It has become clear that without a redistribution of land on a more equal basis, employment will not be generated on a sufficient scale to alleviate the problem of rural underemployment and poverty in Uttar Pradesh, or indeed, in India as a whole.

POVERTY AND INEQUALITY IN RURAL BIHAR

5

Rohini Nayyar

Bihar, with a population of 56.4 million, is the second most populous state in India. Geographically it can be divided into three regions—the North Bihar plains, the South Bihar plains and the Chotanagpur plateau. The river Ganges provides a natural boundary separating the north and south plains. The Chotanagpur plateau region is rich in minerals and almost half of India's coal output is mined there. The plateau region is sparsely populated and within the region population is concentrated in the district of Dhanbad, which contains the main mining area. The density of population in the plains, however, is high, namely 489 persons per square kilometre in the North Bihar plains and 392 per square kilometre in the South Bihar plains,[1] and it is in the plains where most of the agricultural activity occurs.

The state of Bihar is commonly regarded as one of the most backward in India. According to the Ministry of Finance income per head in Bihar in 1968-69 was the lowest in the country: Rs. 375.50 in current prices, compared to the average for India of Rs. 557.10.[2] Moreover, there has been little tendency for living standards in the state to improve. Indeed, during the period examined here, 1961-62 to 1970-71, there was no clearly discernible trend. Output per head remained roughly constant throughout the first half and was abnormally depressed by drought during all but the final year of the second half.

The state is one of the least urbanised of India. About 90 per cent of the population live in rural areas and 82 per cent cent of the labour force are classified as cultivators or agricultural labourers;[3] 51 per cent of the state's income originates in agriculture and allied activities.

Paradoxically, however, Bihar is not a backward state in terms of the standard of living of its rural population. In fact in 1968-69 it ranked fourth

---

[1] *Census of India, 1971*, op. cit.

[2] Government of India, Ministry of Finance: *India: pocket book of economic information 1973 and 1974* (Delhi, 1975).

[3] The corresponding figures for India as a whole are 80 and 70 per cent, respectively.

PHILLIPS MEMORIAL
LIBRARY
PROVIDENCE COLLEGE

of 14 states as regards the average level of per capita income in rural areas.[1] The per capita income of agricultural labourers in Bihar was the second highest in India and that of cultivators was the fifth highest.[2] Inequality, moreover, is less in Bihar than in most other states. The Gini coefficient of the distribution of per capita income and of per capita consumption in rural areas is reported to be the fourth lowest in India.[3]

The performance of the agricultural sector, however, has been poor. The per capita net output of food grains in 1970-71 was noticeably lower than a decade earlier, viz 130.2 kg per person per year as compared to 150.9 kg in 1960-61.[4]

As was the case with total state output per head, there was no clear trend in agricultural production. Output was stagnant during the first half of the 1960s and then fell by more than 50 per cent during the famine of 1966-67; output failed to recover fully during the next three years and exceeded the previous peak only in 1970-71. Meanwhile, population continued to expand, so per capita agricultural output showed a marked tendency to decline.

POVERTY AND INEQUALITY

In the absence of reliable data on rural incomes, use is made of consumer expenditure data obtained from various rounds of the National Sample Survey (NSS) in analysing trends in poverty and inequality. The distribution of consumer expenditure by decile groups of the rural population is first examined in an attempt to learn something about relative poverty and the way it has changed over time. This is followed by estimates of the proportion of the rural population which lives below the poverty line. Lastly, the distribution of the most important rural asset, land, is analysed.

Distribution of consumption

Between 1961-62 and 1970-71 there was apparently very little change in the distribution by decile groups of total consumption expenditure when it is valued in current prices. Thus it would seem at first glance that there was little change in the distribution of income in rural areas during this period.

---

[1] Bhatty, op. cit., table 2, p. 302. Bihar's relative standing as regards average per capita income and its relative position as regards rural consumption and income per head are based on data from independent sources. It is not clear if the two can be satisfactorily reconciled. This would be possible only if non-agricultural incomes in the states that rank below Bihar in terms of per capita rural income and above it in terms of per capita income over-all are significantly higher than in Bihar and account for a higher proportion of state income.

[2] Bhatty, op. cit.

[3] ibid., table 1, p. 302 and table 3, p. 305.

[4] Government of Bihar, State Planning Board: *Selected plan statistics* (Bihar, 1976), p. 228.

This sort of comparison, however, is subject to three important limitations. First, as in all household surveys of this type, it is highly likely that the consumption of the top decile groups is underestimated. The reasons for this are obvious and well known, and lead to an understatement of the degree of inequality at any point in time. The problem is further compounded in Bihar, however, because the extent of underestimation of the consumption of the rich is likely to have increased over time as a result of the growing political tension in the state. This bias in the household data may partly account for the fact that in recent years there is a growing discrepancy between the macro-economic information (which shows a rise in agricultural production and in state income per head in 1970-71) and the sample survey data (which show a fall in average consumption in rural areas in that year).

Second, an examination of trends in the level and distribution of consumption may be an inaccurate indication of trends in income. This could occur, for example, if the lowest income groups attempted to maintain their consumption, despite falling incomes, by increasing their indebtedness. Under these circumstances, inequality in the distribution of consumption could remain broadly the same while the distribution of income worsened. Since the standard of living in rural areas did indeed decline, it is quite possible that borrowing was used in an attempt to reduce the impact of falling incomes on consumption.

Similarly, after a series of bad years, household savings in a good year, such as 1970-71, might rise very rapidly. This could occur because households would take advantage of a bountiful harvest to rebuild their stocks of grain and increase the number of livestock (which might have been slaughtered during the preceding years of drought). Behaviour such as this also would account for part of the discrepancy between macro-economic estimates of income and micro-economic estimates of consumption.

Third, the consumption expenditure data derived from the NSS are in current prices and thus provide a misleading picture of changes in relative real consumption if different groups or deciles purchased different baskets of goods and if relative prices changed during the period. For exemple, it has been shown that, for India as a whole, the lowest 10 per cent of the rural population paid higher prices for food than the top 10 per cent.[1] Similarly, for Bihar it is known that during the 1960s the wholesale price of cereals rose much faster than the over-all consumer price index for agricultural labourers. Given that the lowest income groups spend about 70 per cent of their incomes on cereals and cereal substitutes and the highest income groups about 30-40 per cent, there is a strong presumption that the cost of living of the poor rose more rapidly than that of the rich.

Table 28 contains data on real per capita consumption expenditure of the rural population by decile groups. Four years are included in the table: 1961-62, 1963-64, 1964-65 and 1970-71. The original information was obtained

---

[1] P. K. Bardhan: "On the Incidence of Poverty in Rural India of the Sixties", op. cit.

from the National Sample Survey, seventeenth, eighteenth, nineteenth and twenty-fifth rounds. No adjustment has been made to the data to try to compensate for the first two sources of bias mentioned above. An attempt has been made, however, to take into account changes in relative prices.

This was done by constructing a crude approximation to the decile-specific cost-of-living indices for each year. The implicit deflator for gross state product was used as the point of departure. This was then corrected by introducing the appropriate weights for cereals corresponding to each decile.

Knowing the gross state product deflator, the price series for cereals and the average proportion of expenditure devoted to cereals and non-cereals, it was possible to estimate the price index of all non-cereal items of consumption by using the following equation:

$$D = w_c \, (P_c) + (1 - w_c) \, (P_n),$$

where D = gross state product deflator,
P_c = price of cereals,
w_c = average weights attached to cereals,
$(1 - w_c)$ = average weight attached to non-cereals, and
P_n = the price of non-cereals.

Once the two commodity price series were available (for cereals and non-cereals), a calculation can be made of the decile-specific cost-of-living index number for any given year (I_i) by inserting the decile-specific weight for cereals (obtained from the NSS) into the following equation:

$$I_i = w_{ci} \, (P_c) + (1 - w_{ci}) \, P_n$$

This equation is based on an implicit assumption that P_n and P_c are the same for all income groups, an assumption that almost certainly is not correct, and perhaps a source of relative understatement of the deflator for the poor.

These index numbers were used to deflate the uncorrected NSS data to obtain the estimates of real consumption expenditure reported in table 28. This rather simple adjustment for changes in relative prices makes a noticeable difference to the results that would have been obtained if the current value data had been uniformly deflated by some standard price index. For example, between 1961-62 and 1970-71 it is estimated that the range of the increase in the cost of living was between 80 per cent (for people in the top decile) and 100 per cent (for people in the third decile). The increase in the cost of living for the poorer half of the population was much the same, regardless of the specific decile in which they happened to be, but the increase in the cost of living of those in the top two deciles was significantly lower. The differences would probably have been even greater if proper group-specific indices had been available.

Some interesting facts and puzzles are raised by the data in table 28. During the early 1960s (i.e. between 1961-62 and 1964-65) the distribution of expenditure became worse and the lower decile groups experienced a signifi-

Table 28. Monthly real consumption expenditure per head in 1961-62 prices

Decile group	1961-62	1963-64	1964-65	1970-71
1	8.10	6.73	7.06	5.91
2	10.22	9.34	9.72	8.25
3	12.09	11.02	11.32	9.55
4	13.91	12.72	13.44	11.03
5	15.37	13.58	15.15	12.62
6	17.35	16.27	15.95	14.49
7	19.49	17.83	19.40	15.98
8	21.64	20.34	21.77	19.01
9	28.12	25.00	27.14	22.59
10	43.95	44.21	48.91	34.86
Average	19.02	17.70	18.99	15.43
Gini coefficient	0.27	0.29	0.31	0.28

Source: National Sample Survey, seventeenth, eighteenth, nineteenth and twenty-fifth rounds.

cant reduction in real income. In 1963-64 the average expenditure of the bottom 60 per cent of the population at 1961-62 prices was Rs. 11.61, i.e. about 10 per cent below the 1961-62 level of Rs. 12.84. Over the same period real expenditure by the top 40 per cent of the population increased by 4 per cent. The comparison between 1970-71 and the earlier years is more problematical. Once again, the real per capita expenditure of the lower income groups is lower than in earlier years. But so is the per capita expenditure of the higher income groups. The distribution of expenditure, as measured by the Gini coefficient, is marginally better than in 1964-65 but no better than in the earlier years.

The fact that, according to the NSS data, real consumption per capita in 1970-71 was nearly 19 per cent lower than in 1964-65 is itself a matter that deserves to be examined closely. Per capita state domestic product and per capita agricultural output are estimated to have actually increased over the same period. Movements in income and expenditure can of course diverge in different directions over short periods and such a divergence may have been quite pronounced in 1970-71. In that year agricultural output recovered to previous levels for the first time after four bad years and it is quite likely that rural households saved at a high rate to make up for the dissaving and lack of investment in the preceding years. But the extent of divergence is too big in the present case to be explained away in this way.

It is possible that the macro-economic estimates of state product have been improving over time. This possibility is suggested by the fact that, at current prices, per capita expenditure from the NSS in the early 1960s is significantly *higher* than the macro estimates of per capita state domestic product. The ratio of per capita expenditure to state product per capita declines steadily over the years until in 1970-71 the NSS estimate of per capita expenditure falls below per capita state domestic product by about 15 per cent.

However, it is also possible that the 1970-71 NSS understated per capita expenditure. Indeed, it seems probable that this understatement was concentrated in the estimates for the upper decile groups. There is no direct evidence to support this assertion, but an examination of the composition of expenditure by the richer groups leads to such a suspicion. Thus in 1970-71 the percentage of expenditure on food by the top quintile is much higher compared to that in the past and to that elsewhere in the developing world. The difference is too great to be credible and leads one to suspect that the non-food (and hence aggregate) consumption by the richer groups was understated. It is easy to imagine that the motivation for such under-reporting would be stronger among the higher income groups.

While uncertainty must remain about the estimates for 1970-71 it may be stated with some confidence that any probable under-reporting would be concentrated among the richer groups and, on any plausible set of assumptions, the real per capita expenditure of the poor would appear to have declined sharply. If the estimates are accepted as true the real incomes of the poor would again appear to have declined sharply from the early 1960s.

An estimate of rural poverty

In recent years there has been considerable debate on the concept and measurement of poverty. This has led to somewhat differing estimates of the number of rural poor in India. The different studies in which attempts have been made to estimate rural poverty in India are not summarised here as this has been done elsewhere.[1]

The estimate of rural poverty in Bihar is based upon the rather arbitrary poverty line of Rs. 20 per capita per month at 1960-61 prices recommended by a group of experts appointed by the government (see Chapter 4). The specification of Rs. 20 per capita per month as proposed by the experts was for the entire country, including both the urban and the rural population. Given that prices are lower in the rural areas, let it be assumed that Rs. 15 per capita per month would be the minimum level of income for an "average" rural area.[2] This takes into account disparities in prices between urban and rural areas, but it fails to take into account the fact that prices also vary as between regions in India. It has been shown that a basket of goods that cost Rs. 100, on an average, for India in 1960-61, cost Rs. 105.50 in Bihar.[3]

---

[1] See P. K. Bardhan: *The pattern of income distribution in India: a review* (Development Research Centre, World Bank, Washington, 1973; mimeographed); D. Kumar: "Changes in Income Distribution and Poverty in India: A Review of Literature", in *World Development*, Jan. 1974.

[2] This figure has also been used as the rural minimum by Bardhan and Dandekar and Rath in their respective studies. See P. K. Bardhan: "On the Minimum Level of Living and the Rural Poor", in *Indian Economic Review*, Apr. 1970; V. M. Dandekar and N. Rath: "Poverty in India: Dimensions and Trends", in *Economic and Political Weekly*, 2 Jan. 1971.

[3] P. K. Bardhan: "On the Incidence of Rural Poverty in India", op. cit.

Table 29. Percentage distribution of rural population by per capita expenditure classes in Bihar

Monthly per capita expenditure class in rupees	Percentage distribution of rural population			
	1960-61	1963-64	1964-65	1970-71
0- 8	4.20	4.31	1.71	0.39
8-11	12.92	8.62	4.19	1.78
11-13	13.38	9.50	6.30	2.35
13-15	7.14	11.13	6.61	2.86
15-18	12.99	16.19	11.76	7.47
18-21	7.92	13.43	12.23	9.29
21-24	8.47	10.40	11.28	9.50
24-28	6.52	7.83	12.89	12.04
28-34	7.07	8.36	13.75	17.13
34-43	9.01	4.41	9.32	16.30
43-55	0.84	3.16	5.47	10.89
55-75	} 9.54	{ 1.53	2.89	7.01
75 and above		1.13	1.60	2.29

Source: National Sample Survey, sixteenth, eighteenth, nineteenth and twenty-fifth rounds.

Thus, the minimum income required to stay above the poverty line in rural Bihar, at 1960-61 prices, would be Rs. 15.83 per capita per month.

Table 29 contains data on the distribution of the rural population in Bihar by expenditure classes for the years 1960-61, 1963-64, 1964-65 and 1970-71.

By simple linear interpolation it is estimated that, in 1960-61, about 41 per cent of the rural population of Bihar, or 17.5 million people, lived under conditions of abject poverty.

Given the increase in prices during the 1960s, the consumption basket that cost Rs. 15.83 in 1960-61 would have cost more in 1963-64, 1964-65 and in 1970-71. It would be ideal if there were a consumer price index for the rural poor which could be used to estimate the cost of the basket of goods consumed by them. In its absence use is made of the consumer price index for agricultural labourers.

The consummer price index for agricultural labourers increased from 100 in 1960-61 to 120 in 1963-64, to 149 in 1964-65 and to 206 in 1970-71 in Bihar. This implies that the basket of goods worth Rs. 15.83 in 1960-61 prices cost Rs. 19.00 in 1963-64, Rs. 23.59 in 1964-65 and Rs. 32.61 in 1970-71.

From table 29 it follows that in 1963-64 the entire rural population in the expenditure classes Rs. 0-8 to Rs. 15-18 was living below the poverty line. In addition, 4.48 per cent of the rural population in expenditure class Rs. 18-21 was poor. Thus, about 54 per cent of the rural population was living below the recommended minimum in 1963-64. Following a similar procedure, it is estimated that the proportion living in poverty declined slightly to 52.5 per cent in 1964-65 and then rose again to nearly 59 per cent in 1970-71. That is, over the entire period, the combination of population increase and growing impoverishment resulted in a rise in the number of rural poor to 29.8 million people.

In other words, within a period of only one decade the number of rural poor increased by 12.3 million, the proportion of the poor rose by more than two-fifths and the average level of consumption of the poor declined by as much as 20 per cent.

The distribution of land

At the time of independence the Government appointed an Agrarian Reforms Committee to study the problems that existed with respect to the structure of the rural economy and to suggest measures for its reorganisation. The Bihar Land Reforms Act, 1950, which was afterwards passed, was concerned with the abolition of *zamindari*, the elimination of intermediaries and the vesting of ownership rights with the actual cultivators. Its implementation, however, was deficient, even after two amendments were passed to eliminate loopholes, and the poor got very little benefit from it. Indeed the author of a recent study has concluded that "nowhere in any of this land reform legislation were the interests of the landless labourers or sharecroppers considered."[1]

In 1961 additional legislation was passed, viz. the Bihar Land Reforms (Fixation of Ceiling Area and Acquisition of Surplus Land) Act. Again, a series of loopholes virtually nullified the redistributive effects presumably intended by the legislators. As a result, the improvement in the distribution of landownership has been only marginal. For example, in 1954-55 the poorest 50 per cent of the rural population owned 3.41 per cent of the land. The percentage fell fractionally to 3.24 in 1960-61 and then rose to 3.92 in 1971-72. These variations clearly were not sufficient to make any noticeable difference in the extent of poverty.

Table 30 contains information on the Gini coefficients of the distribution of land owned and operated. It can be seen that the coefficient of landownership has varied only slightly while the coefficient of the area operated has remained constant.

In summary, a large proportion of the rural population of Bihar has limited access to the principal means of production, namely land. The rural population consists of a large number of small farmers and landless workers on the one hand, and a small number of big landowners on the other, who control a high proportion of the total cropped area. In 1970-71 for instance, the smallest farmers, i.e. those in the size class 0-1 hectares, accounted for

---

[1] Thomasson Januzzi: *Agrarian crisis in India: the case of Bihar* (Delhi, 1974), p. 28.

Table 30.   Gini coefficients of the distribution of land owned and operated in Bihar

Year	Area owned	Area operated
1954-55	0.70	n.a.
1960-61	0.71	0.65
1971-72	0.69	0.65

Source: National Sample Survey, twenty-sixth round.

64 per cent of the holdings in Bihar but only 15.3 per cent of the area.[1] In addition, as is shown in the next section, there was a large and rapidly growing number of agricultural labourers.

AGRICULTURAL LABOURERS

In the last quarter of a century there has been a marked increase in the number of agricultural labourers and in the proportion of agricultural labourers in the total agricultural labour force. The official census figures for 1951, 1961 and 1971 are reported in table 31. It can be seen that the number of agricultural labourers apparently doubled over the two decades and their proportion in the labour force increased from 25 per cent in 1951 to 30 per cent in 1961 and 48 per cent in 1971.

It is to be noted that, according to the census, the agricultural labour force remained essentially constant between 1961 and 1971 while the number of agricultural labourers increased by over 50 per cent. If these figures are accepted at face value it is evident that there must have been an enormous transformation of former cultivators (tenants, sharecroppers and small land-owners) into agricultural labourers. Undoubtedly something of the sort did occur, but the figures from Bihar are perhaps too dramatic to be credible. In India as a whole, for example, the proportion of agricultural labourers in the total agricultural working population actually declined from 27.8 per cent in 1951 to 24 per cent in 1961; the proportion then rose substantially to 37.5 per cent in 1971. Thus the general tendency in Bihar is broadly consistent with the rest of the country although the specific figures may somewhat overstate reality.

The economic well-being of agricultural labourers is largely a function of the prevailing wage rates and the amount of employment they can secure. Table 32 contains data on both money and real wage rates. The time trend in real wages, estimated on the basis of 15 annual observations, gives the following fit:

$$\log W = 0.099 + 0.011t; \; R^2 = 0.18$$
$$(0.050) \quad (0.007)$$

---

[1] *Agricultural census of Bihar, 1970-71.* The details of land distribution according to size class are contained in the appendix to the census.

Table 31. Agricultural labourers in Bihar

Year	Agricultural labourers (millions)	Total agricultural workers (millions)	Labourers as a percentage of all agricultural workers
1951	3.17	12.50	25.4
1961	4.42	14.78	29.9
1971	6.87	14.45	47.5

Source: *Census of India*, 1951, 1961, 1971.

Thus the estimated trend rate of growth is not significantly different from zero at the 5 per cent level. The low proportion of explained variation is a reflection of unsystematic fluctuations over time.

Even the above estimates are strongly influenced by the consideration that the time series ends immediately before a sharp upward rise in the cost of living. As is known on the basis of the evidence for the other Indian states (e.g. Uttar Pradesh, as reported in Chapter 4), the consumer price indices in India rose sharply beginning in 1972-73. Money wages failed to keep up with the rise in the cost of living and, as a consequence, real wages fell. From the available, though fragmentary, evidence it appears that Bihar was not an exception to the trends observed elsewhere in India, including the neighbouring states. If data were available for more recent years, the above estimate of an insignificant trend rate of increase in real wages would almost certainly have turned out to be unrealistically optimistic.

Nevertheless, it must be recognised that the series of money wages reproduced in table 32 is unreliable. The series is based on data collected from two villages only in each of the original 17 districts of the state, for the years up to 1966-67. Thereafter the coverage was further reduced to ten districts. In view of the wide variation in wage rates from one village to another, the size of the sample evidently is too small to permit generalisations about trends in money wage rates throughout the state. Clearly, more accurate information is sorely needed.

To compound the difficulties, data on agricultural employment in Bihar is almost non-existent and it is impossible to assess whether the average number of days of employment has increased in the last 10 or 15 years. There are a few studies in which attempts have been made to measure the extent of unemployment and underemployment, but these have been based on a small sample and hence cannot be relied upon. Thus what exactly has been happening to real wages is uncertain and trends in employment are unknown.

SUMMARY AND CONCLUSIONS

Despite the fact that Bihar contains an important mining sector and a few major industrial centres, the state has been viewed as relatively underdevel-

Table 32.   Daily money and real wage rates of agricultural labourers in Bihar

Year	Money wage rates (rupees)	Real wage rates (rupees at 1960-61 prices)
1957-58	1.20	1.18
1958-59	1.21	1.16
1959-60	1.08	1.06
1960-61	1.06	1.06
1961-62	1.30	1.27
1962-63	1.37	1.28
1963-64	1.51	1.26
1964-65	1.80	1.21
1965-66	2.31	1.29
1966-67	2.46	1.07
1967-68	2.32	0.93
1968-69	2.41	1.29
1969-70	2.73	1.35
1970-71	2.94	1.43
1971-72	2.87	1.39

Note: Money wages have been deflated by the consumer price index for agricultural labourers in Bihar published regularly in Central Statistical Organisation: *Monthly Abstract of Statistics*. Access to this index for years before 1959-60 was not possible. For the two years in the late 1950s the trend from the cost of living index for the workers in nearby urban centres was spliced. Since the cost of living had been falling gently over this period the error due to this step is unlikely to be significant. Money wage rates are from Ministry of Agriculture, Directorate of Economics and Statistics: *Agricultural Wages in India* (monthly).

oped with a low level of per capita income. It is true that the extent of urbanisation is low: about 90 per cent of the population lives in rural areas. Yet within the rural areas the level of income of the population may be relatively high by Indian standards and its distribution somewhat less inegalitarian than in many other states.

During the 1960s the economy performed poorly. Aggregate income and agricultural income fell sharply during the second half of the decade. It was not before 1970-71 that per capita income and output recovered to the pre-famine levels of 1965-66. During the 1960s the proportion of the rural population living below an acceptable minimum standard increased sharply. Adjusting the widely used poverty line of Rs. 20 per capita per month for India at 1960-61 prices for the specific circumstances in Bihar, it was found that the poor as a percentage of the rural population increased from 41 per cent in 1961-62 to 59 per cent in 1970-71.

Despite attempts at land reform, the distribution of landownership and of the amount of land operated continues to be very unequal in Bihar. There is a large mass of agricultural labourers, increasing both numerically and as a proportion of the agricultural working population at a very fast pace. Data on the real wages of agricultural labourers are unreliable, but there appears to have been no tendency for real wages to rise. Unfortunately, there are almost no data on trends in rural employment in Bihar. There is little doubt, however, that since nearly 60 per cent of the rural population lives in poverty, a very large proportion of the agricultural labourers must be classified as poor.

The Government, claiming an awareness of the problems of the rural economy, has taken some steps intended to increase output and employment. The two most important examples are the Kosi and Gandak River Projects designed to control floods and increase the amount of land under irrigation. Rural works programmes and institutions such as the Small Farmers Development Agency and the Marginal Farmers and Agricultural Labourers Development Agency have also been promoted for the explicit purpose of generating additional employment and income in the rural sector.

The measures have encountered little success, however. Studies of the impact of the Kosi River Project have indicated that there is a growing differentiation among the peasantry in this area and have attributed this to the inequality in the distribution of land. Increases in output arising from the various government schemes accrue largely to the bigger peasant farmers and to large landowners who have access to credit and material inputs. Thus such development as has occurred has tended to generate further inequalities in the distribution of income in rural areas.[1] Perhaps as a result of this, rural discontent in Bihar has noticeably increased in recent years.[2] The political implications of increasing poverty are clear even if the substantiating economic data are incomplete.

---

[1] See, for example, P. S. Appu: "Unequal Benefits from Kosi Development," in *Economic and Political Weekly*, 16 June 1973; G. B. Rodgers: "Effects of Public Works on Rural Poverty," in ibid., Feb., 1973; Geoff Wood: *The process of differentiation among the peasantry in Desipur, North Bihar, India*, Discussion Paper No. 24 (Institute of Development Studies, University of Sussex).

[2] See P. H. Prasad: "Agrarian Unrest and Economic Change in Rural Bihar," in *Economic and Political Weekly*, 14 June 1975; "Adivasis on Warpath", in ibid., Special Number, July 1968; A. N. Das: "Bihar: Struggle of Workers and Tribal Peasants in Chotanagpur", in ibid., 1 Mar. 1975.

RURAL POVERTY IN
TAMIL NADU

6

C. T. Kurien

Tamil Nadu, with a 1971 population of 41.2 million and an area of 130,000 square kilometres, is the seventh largest state in India in terms of population and the eleventh in terms of area. It is also one of the most industrialised states, ranking third behind Maharashtra and West Bengal. About 30 per cent of the state's population live in urban areas.

RURAL TAMIL NADU

Rural Tamil Nadu, naturally, is predominantly agricultural. According to the 1971 census, about 80 per cent of the rural workforce was engaged in agriculture (over 40 per cent as cultivators and the rest as agricultural labourers), as compared with only around 72 per cent in 1961. The non-agricultural occupations in the census are further divided into several categories: mining and quarrying; household industry; manufacturing; construction; trade and commerce; transport; storage and communication; and other services. Of these, household industry, manufacturing, trade and commerce, and other services are the more important ones in the rural areas and account for approximately 80 per cent of non-agricultural occupations.

There are no estimates of the usual indicators—per capita income or per capita consumption—used to study levels of living in rural areas. However, the National Sample Survey Organisation of the Department of Statistics, Government of India, has conducted sample surveys about expenditure patterns separately in rural and urban areas in Tamil Nadu as well as in other parts of the country. How close the NSS estimates of consumption expenditure are to the actual figures is debatable. In any case, the NSS data on consumption expenditure are the only source of information at present available for a systematic discussion of rural levels of living. These figures for rural Tamil Nadu, for selected years in the 1960s, are as follows:

Year	Per capita consumption expenditure (in rupees)	
	In current prices	In 1960-61 prices
1960-61	222.84	222.84
1961-62	260.28	249.36
1963-64	280.68	252.00
1964-65	294.60	226.08
1968-69	343.56	195.72
1969-70	394.20	215.28

The deflator used here is the rural price index reproduced in table 33. Over the decade there has been a decline in the level of per capita consumption expenditure after an initial increase from Rs. 223 in 1960-61 to Rs. 252 in 1963-64.

The great advantage of the NSS data is that they contain a detailed breakdown which permits a study both of the composition and the distribution of expenditure among different size classes. Table 34 shows the distribution of average monthly per capita expenditure on major items of consumption in rural Tamil Nadu. This shows that around 70 per cent of the total expenditure is on food items and that in the latter half of the period it is higher—over 72 per cent in 1964-65, about 78 per cent in 1968-69 and close to 77 per cent in 1969-70. The absolute figures of consumption show

Table 33.   Rural price index
            (Base 1936=100)

Year	Index number
1955	375
1956	417
1957	440
1958	459
1959	491
1960	502
1961	524
1962	538
1963	559
1964	654
1965	700
1966	806
1967	894
1968	881
1969	919
1970	993

Note: The index numbers of rural prices have been compiled and published by the Department of Statistics, Government of Tamil Nadu, "to represent the movement of prices relevant to villages in rural areas". The index is measured for eight representative villages pertaining to the five zones in the state. For the purpose of this study, a simple average of the eight indices has been computed to represent the general rural price index of Tamil Nadu.

how desperately low the consumption standards are. In fact, a detailed examination of consumption patterns undertaken by the Indian Council of Medical Research (ICMR) revealed that in terms of nutritional standards Tamil Nadu has the lowest level of consumption among all the states in the country.[1] Indeed, except for cereals, the intake of all other foods, particularly pulses, milk and leafy vegetables, is much lower than the levels recommended by the ICMR.

What has been described above is the average consumption pattern in the rural areas of the state. The NSS data on consumer expenditure divide the consumers into 12 (13 since 1961-62) expenditure classes beginning with those spending less than Rs. 8 per capita per month going on to those above Rs. 55 (above Rs. 75 since 1961-62). In 1960-61, for example, in the lowest expenditure groups (the lowest three income classes) food items account for 80 per cent or more of the total expenditure. The percentage falls to between 70 and 75 in the case of the next five classes and to between 60 and 68 in the case of the next three. The share of expenditure on food falls sharply to 48.97 in the highest class. The pattern of expenditure seen here is as one would expect. Moreover, within food items cereals account for over 70 per cent in the lowest three classes and then steadily decline to just above 20 per cent in the highest class.

Whether the disparities in the levels of consumption are being reduced over time is also relevant. The earliest period for which data are available is 1957-58 and the latest for which comparable information can be obtained is 1964-65. Thus the period covered does not coincide with the period included later in this chapter when trends in rural poverty are analysed. The Lorenz curve for 1964-65 shows an unambiguous shift towards the diagonal as compared to that for 1957-58,[2] indicating that inequalities were reduced over this period.

It is now recognised, however, that the NSS data are likely to underestimate the expenditure of the upper expenditure classes who, for various reasons, considerably understate their true expenditure when replying to interviewers. A time series study of the expenditures of the different size classes brings out inconsistencies which lend support to this. For example, the results indicate that in real terms the upper expenditure classes enjoyed rising incomes, yet total expenditure decreased and the proportion of expenditure on food increased very sharply. Expenditure on non-food items of the top group in 1964-65 was 30 per cent of what it was in 1957-58. It is difficult to imagine that during a period of rising prosperity and increased availability of non-food consumer goods, especially consumer durables, the top expenditure

---

[1] Reported in Rajammal Devadas: *Nutrition in Tamil Nadu* (Madras, Sangam Publishers, 1972), p. 12.

[2] A diagrammatic representation of the Lorenz curves is given in C. T. Kurien: *Rural poverty in Tamil Nadu, India* (Geneva, ILO, 1976; mimeographed World Employment Programme research working paper; restricted).

Table 34. Distribution of monthly per capita expenditure on major items of consumption in rural areas of Tamil Nadu, 1960-61 to 1969-70 (in current prices)

(In rupees and as percentage of total expenditure)

Item	1960-61		1961-62		1963-64		1964-65		1968-69		1969-70	
	Rupees	Per cent	Rupees	Per cent	Rupees	Per cent	Rupees	Per cent	Rupees	Per cent	Rupees	Per cent
Cereals, grams, and substitutes	7.81	42.06	9.03	41.63	8.75	37.41	10.65	43.38	14.59	50.96	15.47	47.09
Pulses and their products	0.57	3.07	0.73	3.37	0.93	3.98	1.03	4.20				
Milk and milk products	0.53	2.85	0.59	2.72	0.75	3.20	0.75	3.05	1.09	3.81	1.46	4.44
Other food items, including oil, meat, eggs, fish and vegetables	3.97	21.38	4.74	21.85	5.19	22.19	5.34	21.75	6.69	23.37	8.29	25.24
All food items	12.88	69.36	15.09	69.57	15.62	66.78	17.77	72.38	22.37	78.13	25.22	76.77
Fuel and light	1.13	6.09	1.49	6.87	1.68	7.18	1.80	7.33	1.98	6.91	2.18	6.64
Clothing	1.53	8.23	1.37	6.32	1.96	8.38	1.45	5.91	1.03	3.60	1.38	4.20
Other non-food items	3.03	16.32	3.74	17.24	4.13	17.66	3.53	14.38	3.25	11.35	4.07	12.39
All non-food items	5.69	30.64	6.60	30.43	7.77	33.22	6.78	27.62	6.26	21.87	7.63	23.23
Total consumer expenditure	18.57	100.00	21.69	100.00	23.39	100.00	24.55	100.00	28.63	100.00	32.85	100.00

Source: various rounds of the National Sample Survey.

groups in fact reduced their absolute expenditure on non-food items so sharply.[1]

POVERTY IN RURAL TAMIL NADU

Recent studies on poverty in India have evolved two widely accepted, though by no means undisputed, norms for the identification of the poverty line.[2] The first is the nutrition standard recommended by the ICMR. The Council estimated various levels of nutritional requirements for the population depending on age, sex and conditions of work. For adults they range from 1,900 calories per day for women engaged in sedentary work to 3,900 in the case of men doing heavy manual work. When identifiying the poverty line, however, what is normally accepted as the minimum requirement is a daily intake of 2,400 calories (and 44 grams of protein). Based on the consumption habits in the state it has been estimated that this minimum requirement would cost 51 paisa in 1960-61 prices, or around Rs. 15 per month.[3] With a norm of this kind the NSS data on consumer expenditure could be used to calculate the percentage of the population below the poverty line. But price variations must be taken into account and the cost of the nutritionally adequate diet for each year estimated. The rural price index has been used for this purpose. But a mechanical correction procedure of this kind is not adequate to deal with the problem caused by price variations. For instance, the differential impact of prices on the poor will depend on how they earn their incomes and to what extent they depend on the market to satisfy their consumption. Unfortunately, however, it is not possible to take this into account so a crude statistical correction for price variations has been made to arrive at the monetary indicators of the nutritionally adequate diet for different years and these have been used as cut off points to make estimates of those below the poverty line.

Column (3) of table 35 gives the estimate of the percentage of population below the poverty line so arrived at. Thus at the beginning of the period slightly over 50 per cent of the rural population, and at the end slightly below 50 per cent, are classified as coming below the line. More interesting is the fact that there was a tendency for the incidence of poverty to decline from the mid 1950s to the early years of the 1960s, with 1961-62 showing the lowest figure of 36.04 per cent. Since then, however, the percentage of the

---

[1] For a documentation of the evidence see Kurien, op. cit.

[2] For a critical review of the literature see P. K. Bardhan: *The pattern of income distribution in India: a review*, op. cit.; T. N. Srinivasan and P. K. Bardhan (eds.): *Poverty and income distribution in India*, op. cit.

[3] M. Ramamurthy: *Poverty and supply of wage goods in Tamil Nadu* (Madras, Sangam Publishers, 1974). The estimate is based on what is known to be the standard consumption pattern in Tamil Nadu and cannot claim to represent the least cost diet to provide the minimum nutritional requirement.

Table 35.   Estimates of rural population below the poverty line

Year	Nutritionally adequate diet (norm: 2400 calories per day)		Minimum levels of living (norm: Rs. 21 per month in 1960-61 prices)	
	Cost per month in current prices (rupees)	Percentage of population below the poverty line	Cost per month in current prices (rupees)	Percentage of population below the poverty line
(1)	(2)	(3)	(4)	(5)
1957-58	13.37	53.10	18.48	74.10
1959-60	14.92	53.79	20.62	79.21
1960-61	15.30	47.89	21.11	69.82
1961-62	15.90	36.04	22.00	66.49
1963-64	16.99	38.98	23.47	64.36
1964-65	19.88	45.81	27.46	72.45
1969-70	27.93	48.63	38.58	73.98

population below the poverty line has been steadily increasing, reaching 48.63 per cent in 1969-70.

The second norm used by Indian scholars for identifying poverty is a minimum level of living which includes items such as clothing and housing as well as food requirements. An expert committee set up by the Government of India in July 1962 put the nationally desirable minimum level of consumer expenditure at Rs. 20 per capita per month at 1960-61 prices (excluding expenditure on health and education, both of which "are expected to be provided by the State according to the Constitution and in the light of other commitments"). The basis of this calculation is not clear but it has become a sort of magic number in' writings on poverty in the country. What is a reasonable figure for minimum levels of living in the rural areas of Tamil Nadu? Table 34 has shown that in 1961-62 monthly per capita expenditure on food was Rs. 15.09, which, when combined with an expenditure of Rs. 6.60 on non-food items, gives a total per capita monthly consumer expenditure of Rs. 21.69. On this basis it is reasonable to say that if the cost of a nutritionally adequate diet is Rs. 15 per month, the cost of a minimum level of living is between Rs. 21 and Rs. 22. Using this as the norm, the percentage of the population below the poverty line increases substantially, as can be seen from column (5) of table 35. The poor represented over 74 per cent of the rural population in 1957-58, rising to nearly 80 per cent towards the end of the 1950s and then steadily declining to 64 per cent in the mid-1960s. But as in the case of the nutritional norm, according to the income norm the percentage of the population below the poverty line also rises in the late 1960s, reaching in 1969-70 almost the same figure as in 1957-58.

The picture that emerges, then, is one of a fall and then a rise in the proportion of the population below the poverty line. The maximum reduction in the proportion of the poor was reached in the early 1960s; thereafter poverty increased steadily, even dramatically. Between 1961-62 and 1969-70 the percentage of the rural population with a nutritionally inadequate diet increased from 36 to nearly 49 per cent. Admittedly this proportion was lower than in the late 1950s, but there was alarming retrogression throughout the 1960s. Using the more generous norm of Rs. 21 per month (in 1960-61 prices), the same general pattern is seen. Indeed, the proportion of the rural population living below this poverty line was virtually the same in 1969-70 as in 1957-58. Given the increase in the size of the rural population in the intervening years, the absolute numbers of poor people increased substantially.

Some dissatisfaction has been expressed in recent discussions of poverty with a mere "counting of heads" to identify and quantify the extent of poverty. In particular it has been suggested that the amounts by which the incomes of the poor fall short of the specified level must also be taken into account.[1]

Elaborate computations are required for such a quantification of poverty. But it is possible to gain a better understanding of the problem of poverty by studying the distribution of the population *below* the poverty line over a period of time. This approach can give some indication of the "intensity" of poverty. In table 36 the population below the poverty line is divided into three groups—borderline poverty, acute poverty and extreme poverty—and trace the distribution of the poor among these groups from 1957-58 to 1969-70. In terms of the nutritional norm, in 1957-58 about 24 per cent of the poor belonged to the borderline poverty group, 37 per cent to the acute poverty group and 39 per cent to the extreme poverty group. By 1969-70 the proportion in extreme poverty had declined to 23 per cent. The proportionate share of the other two groups increased, however—their shares rising to 42 per cent in the case of acute poverty and to 35 per cent in the case of borderline poverty. A similar pattern occurs when the minimum levels of living norm is used. Extreme poverty declines from 54 per cent at the beginning of the period to 43 per cent at the end, while the shares of acute poverty and borderline poverty increase.

There are a few other observations that can be made by comparing tables 35 and 36. From table 35 it is seen that the percentage of the population below the poverty line increased during the 1960s. But both extreme poverty and borderline poverty tended to fall. Hence in terms of the nutritional norm there was a bulging of poverty in the intermediate group of acute poverty. The percentage of the population below the poverty line in terms of the minimum level of living norm also increased during the 1960s. But the distribution of the poor into the three groups shows a different pattern. In the 1960s (starting from 1963-64) both borderline poverty and acute poverty fell while extreme poverty increased. Since the difference between the two norms consists in the inclusion of expenditure on non-food

---

[1] See A. K. Sen: "Poverty, Inequality and Unemployment: Some Conceptual Issues in Measurement", in T. N. Srinivasan and P. K. Bardhan (eds.): *Poverty and income distribution in India*, op. cit.

Table 36. Percentage distribution of those below the poverty line in rural Tamil Nadu by monthly per capita expenditure groups, 1957-70

Per capita expenditure groups [1]		1957-58	1959-60	1960-61	1961-62	1963-64	1964-65	1969-70
Extreme poverty	*(a)*	39.08	31.66	34.86	29.51	24.16	25.28	22.80
	(b)	54.38	43.00	52.17	40.67	37.04	41.12	42.73
Acute poverty	*(a)*	36.59	36.91	41.37	45.58	37.01	39.74	42.40
	(b)	30.02	36.18	28.79	29.11	38.25	34.97	36.74
Borderline poverty	*(a)*	24.33	31.43	23.77	24.91	38.83	34.98	34.80
	(b)	15.60	20.82	19.04	30.22	24.71	23.91	20.53

[1] *(a) Nutritionally adequate diet as norm:* Extreme poverty below Rs. 8 per month; acute poverty between Rs. 8 and Rs. 11; borderline poverty between Rs. 11 and Rs. 15.

(b) Minimum level of living as norm: Extreme poverty below Rs. 11 per month; acute poverty between Rs. 11 and Rs. 15; borderline poverty between Rs. 15 and Rs. 21.

items in the minimum levels norm, it may be surmised that during the late 1960s non-food items became increasingly unavailable to the extremely poor.

IDENTIFICATION OF THE POOR

The figures in the above section have given some idea of the extent of poverty in Tamil Nadu. But they do not convey much about the nature of poverty. Mass poverty of the kind that exists in the state has two visible aspects.[1] The first, as already noted, is the inadequate availability of essential goods to those who are poor. But such deprivation constitutes only one side of the problem of poverty. A second, and in the long run a more important aspect of poverty, is the tremendous waste of human potential not only as a consequence, but as a cause of poverty. Mass poverty exists because the mass of the people do not and, under certain kinds of institutional patterns, cannot contribute to productive activity and hence have become a drain on the economy by existing as consumption agents to the extent that they do consume. The nature of poverty can, therefore, be more properly understood by identifying the poor mainly in terms of their occupational characteristics. It has been noted that the workforce in rural areas is usually divided into three categories, cultivators, agricultural labourers (i.e. those who earn a living primarily by working for others) and the residual group "other workers". An attempt will be made to identify the poor in terms of these occupational categories.

A major handicap in the identification procedure is that data are available only from different sources which are not always comparable. Hence all that can be claimed is that the calculations made show the order of magnitude of the different occupational groups that come below the poverty line.

---

[1] This theme has been developed by C. T. Kurien in his contribution to: M. S. Adiseshiah (ed.): *Techniques of perspective planning* (Madras Institute of Development Studies, 1972).

Cultivators

To estimate the percentage of cultivators who should be classed as being below the poverty line, information is required on size of holdings, yield per hectare, prices and costs to arrive at net income, and size of family to calculate per capita earnings. In Tamil Nadu it is also important to know whether the land is dry or wet.

Take first the size of holdings. The recent census[1] has, for the first time, made a complete enumeration of operational holdings in the state for 1970-71. Operational holding is defined as "land operated as one technical unit by one person alone or with others without regard to title, legal form, site or location". In using operational holding as the unit for calculation of earnings per cultivator, therefore, it is assumed that the returns from an operational unit go entirely to the operator. This is not correct. Land is leased, and consequently the earnings from an operational unit can be more or less than what the operator could otherwise claim to be his own. However, there is no easy way of taking into account rents paid out and rents received, which vary considerably according to tenurial conditions and location. Farmers also may have earnings from other sources, such as payments received for working for other farmers and non-farm incomes. Earnings calculated from operational holdings can, therefore, be treated only as approximations to the earning power of the farmers of the relevant size classes.

The size distribution of operational holdings in the state is given in table 37 separately for wholly irrigated, unirrigated and partially irrigated units. This forms the basis of the calculations. There have been recent estimates of net earnings per hectare for different crops. For paddy an estimate for Chingleput district (one of the well irrigated districts) shows a figure of Rs. 2,347.50 as the annual net earnings per hectare.[2] Another figure for North Arcot (a dry district) gives a figure of Rs. 1,255.26.[3] For dry crops, estimates of net earnings for best varieties of *cholam* per hectare is Rs. 545.00; of *cumbu*, Rs. 640.00, of *ragi*, Rs. 470.00; and groundnuts, Rs. 495.00.[4] With all the limitations it imposes an average of these (i.e. Rs. 537.50) is taken as indicative of net earnings per hectare from dry land.

According to the writer's estimates the amount required in 1970-71 for minimum levels of living was Rs. 500 a year per head; for a family of four members the total income required to assure minimum levels of living thus would be Rs. 2,000 and for a family of five Rs. 2,500. On this basis approximately 1 hectare of wet land and 3 hectares of dry land would be necessary

[1] Government of Tamil Nadu (Director of Agricultural Census): *World Agricultural Census 1970-71, Tamil Nadu* (1974).

[2] Joan P. Mencher: "Conflicts and Contradictions in the Green Revolution: The Case of Tamil Nadu", in *Economic and Political Weekly*, Feb. 1974.

[3] N. B. Chinnappa: *Farmers in the North Arcot survey* (mimeographed; 1974).

[4] R. K. Sampath and J. Ganesan: *Economics of dry farming in Tamil Nadu* (Madras, Sangam Publishers, 1972). Apart from groundnuts, the crops in question are varieties of millet.

Table 37.   Size distribution of operational holdings in terms of irrigated and
unirrigated holdings

Size class (hectares)	Percentage of number of operational holdings				
	Total holdings	Wholly irrigated	Unirrigated	Partly irrigated	Unreported
0-0.5	35.01	18.10	10.68	2.51	3.72
0.5-1	22.15	8.38	8.09	4.27	1.41
1-2	21.55	5.92	7.69	6.80	1.14
2-3	9.21	1.94	2.94	3.97	0.36
3-4	4.47	0.76	1.30	2.28	0.13
4-5	2.52	0.38	0.68	1.38	0.08
5-10	3.92	0.50	0.92	2.41	0.09
10-20	0.98	0.09	0.19	0.66	0.04
20-30	0.13	0.01	0.02	0.09	0.01
30-40	0.04	0.003	0.01	0.02	0.007
40-50	0.01	0.001	0.001	0.007	0.001
50 and above	0.01	0.001	0.001	0.007	0.001
	100.00	36.085	32.522	24.404	6.989

Source: *World Agricultural Census, 1970-71, Tamil Nadu*, op. cit.

to ensure the minimum level of living of a cultivator family. The land distribution table shows that 26.48 per cent of operational holdings is below 1 hectare of wet land and 29.42 per cent is below 3 hectares of dry land. Thus close to 56 per cent of operational holdings would yield net earnings hardly sufficient to provide minimum levels of living for cultivator families.[1]

Agricultural labourers

It has already been seen that agricultural labourers—who either do not own any land at all or have so little that their main source of income is working for others—are as numerous as the "cultivators" of operational holdings. According to the all-India studies on poverty, the landless agricultural workers constitute the biggest single component of those who are regarded as poor in the rural areas.

To estimate the percentage of agricultural labourers living below the poverty line, information is needed about the number of days worked in a year and wage rates. A series on the wage rate of agricultural labourers compiled by the Labour Bureau of the Government of India is available for the period from 1956-57 to 1971-72. The Bureau also publishes a consumer price index for agricultural labourers in the state. Using these two it is possible to construct a real wage index for agricultural labourers. The relevant figures are given in table 38 and show that (taking 1956-57 as the base) the real wage rate was below the base with two exceptions (1962-63 and

---

[1] These calculations do not include farmers having partly irrigated land and unreported categories.

Table 38. Money wage rates, consumer price index numbers and real wage rates of agricultural labourers in Tamil Nadu, 1956-57 to 1971-72

Year	Money wage rates in paisa per day	Consumer price index numbers of agricultural labourers	Real wage rates in paisa per day	Indices of real wage rates
1956-57	132	98	135	100
1958-59	130	99	131	97
1959-60	135	105	129	96
1961-62	143	113	127	94
1962-63	148	104	142	105
1964-65	185	138	134	99
1965-66	187	143	131	97
1966-67	210	175	120	90
1967-68	225	172	131	97
1968-69	241	177	136	101
1969-70	247	190	130	96
1970-71	256	174	147	109
1971-72	287	187	153	113

Source: original data from Directorate of Statistics of the Ministry of Agriculture: *Agricultural wages in India.*

1968-69) up to 1969-70. Since then real wages have begun to rise. These results must, however, be interpreted with the limitations of the data relating to the cost of living in mind. It is widely believed that the consumer price index underestimates the true wage deflator. Even when compared to the rural price index in table 33 the consumer price index shows a considerably lower rate of increase.

Nothing can be said about the situation of agricultural labourers with reference to the poverty line on the basis of figures of real wages alone. Fortunately, information on wage rates in agricultural operations, man-days worked and earnings from other sources for 1950-51 and 1956-57 is available from the reports of the Agricultural Labour Enquiry.[1] Similar information for 1964-65 can be obtained from another report.[2] For a more recent period relevant data are available from the twenty-fifth round (1970-71) of the National Sample Survey. Table 39 brings together information on man-days worked and wage rates per day for the years referred to above. It will be seen that, for male workers, there was an increase in the average number of days worked in the early 1950s. Thereafter the figures remained unchanged for men until the mid-1960s. For women the number of days worked in 1964-65 was lower than in 1950-51. There was little change in the amount of employment per child between the middle of the 1950s and that of the 1960s.

[1] Ministry of Labour and Employment, Labour Bureau: *Agricultural labour in India: Report on the Second Enquiry (1956-57)* (1960).

[2] Government of India, Ministry of Labour and Employment, Labour Bureau: *All-India rural labour enquiry, 1964-65.*

Table 39. Average number of full days of wage-paid employment per year of agricultural labour households and their average earnings per day

Years	Workers	Agricultural employment		Non-agricultural employment		Total man-days worked in a year
		Number of man-days worked in a year	Average earnings per day	Number of man-days worked in a year	Average earnings per day	
1950-51	Males	168	0.97	17	1.03	185
	Females	148	0.59	7	0.44	155
	Children	—	0.59	—	0.33	—
1956-57	Males	193	0.84	20	0.91	213
	Females	135	0.44	7	0.48	142
	Children	199	0.39	26	0.55	225
1964-65	Males	194	1.39	14	1.53	208
	Females	146	0.85	3	1.18	149
	Children	209	0.70	10	0.74	219
1970-71	Males	147	2.38	48	3.52	195
	Females	81	1.50	14	2.02	95
	Children	16	1.04	7	0.85	23

Sources: *Agricultural Labour in India: Report on the Second Enquiry, 1956-57* (1950-51 and 1956-57); *All-India rural labour enquiry, 1964-65*, op. cit. (1964-65); *National Sample Survey*, Twenty-fifth Round, July 1970 – June 1971 (1970-71).

For 1970-71 the average number of full days of wage-paid employment has been estimated from the NSS, twenty-fifth round. It is difficult to say whether these are strictly comparable with the earlier figures. The figures for employment in agriculture are lower than in the mid-1960s in the case of all three groups, strikingly so in the case of females and children. Using the employment and wage rate figures shown in table 39 estimates have been made of annual earnings of agricultural labourers at current prices and are given in table 40.

The Agricultural Labour Enquiry and the Rural Labour Enquiry have also examined the earnings of agricultural labour households from various sources. The estimates of average annual earnings of agricultural labour households for 1950-51, 1956-57 and 1964-65 are given in table 41. From these sources there is also information on the average size of the agricultural labour households: 4.1 persons in 1956-57 and 4.0 in 1964-65. On this basis the per capita annual income for agricultural labour in Tamil Nadu was Rs. 88.30 in 1950-51, Rs. 91.52 in 1956-57 and Rs. 165.00 in 1964-65. On the other hand the cost of the minimum level of living was Rs. 210 per annum in 1956-57 and Rs. 329 in 1964-65. Thus in both these years the average earnings of agricultural labourers were well below the poverty line.

No figures are available for subsequent periods on earnings of agricultural labour households. An estimate can, however, be made for 1970-71 based on employment and wage rate figures given in the NSS twenty-fifth round (see table 40) supplemented by information on the number of earners

Table 40.   Average annual earnings per head of agricultural labourers from agricultural and non-agricultural occupations
(In current rupees)

Year	Workers	Agriculture	Non-agriculture	Total
1950-51	Male	162.96	17.51	180.47
	Female	87.32	3.08	90.40
	Children	81.42	5.94	87.36
1956-57	Male	145.32	18.20	263.52
	Female	66.15	3.36	69.51
	Children	77.61	14.30	91.91
1964-65	Male	269.66	21.42	291.08
	Female	124.10	3.54	127.64
	Children	146.30	7.40	153.70
1970-71	Male	349.86	170.26	520.12
	Female	121.95	28.28	150.23
	Children	16.64	5.95	22.59

Source: table 39.

per family. The Labour Enquiries have shown that there were slightly more than one male earner per family and slightly less than one female. It seems reasonable, therefore, to assume that there was one male earner and one female earner per household for calculating household earnings for 1970-71. On this basis, and relying on the NSS information, the annual wage earnings from agriculture and non-agriculture of an agricultural labour household would work out at Rs. 670. An upward revision of this figure would be required to arrive at the total earnings of the agricultural labour households because, as seen in table 41, these households also have some income from "other sources". For the three years shown in table 41 income from other sources (which for 1964-65 is shown under three separate categories in the table) can be seen to have increased from 8 per cent in 1950-51 to nearly 15 per cent in 1964-65. Based on this trend a liberal assumption can be made that from other sources agricultural labour households earned 25 per cent of their total income in 1970-71. Total earnings of a household in 1970-71 would thus become Rs. 893 (Rs. 670 from agricultural and non-agricultural employment, Rs. 223 from other sources). The NSS twenty-fifth round showed the size of the family to be 4.5. Hence per capita earnings in 1970-71 would turn out to be Rs. 198. The cost of the minimum level of living in 1970-71 was Rs. 500 per annum. Once again it is seen that the earnings of agricultural labourers were well below the poverty norm.

The earnings of agricultural labourers arrived at in the above calculations are average figures. But even within this group there are considerable variations in earnings. Information is not available about the distribution of earning patterns. However, the sources referred to above (the Labour Enquiries and NSS) give information on the percentage distribution of the estima-

Table 41. Average annual income of agricultural labour households from different sources
(In current rupees)

Average income of household from:	1950-51 (1)	1956-57 (2)	1964-65 (3)
Cultivation of land	83.85 (22.6)[1]	10.69 (2.85)	19.45 (3.52)
Agricultural labour	230.02 (62.0)	312.64 (83.31)	424.44 (76.76)
Non-agricultural labour	27.08 (7.3)	18.92 (5.04)	28.81 (5.21)
Occupations other than farming	—	—	17.82 (3.22)
Non-manual labour (wages and perquisites)	—	—	5.78 (1.05)
Other sources	30.05 (8.1)	33.01 (8.80)	56.63 (10.24)
Total	371.00 (100.00)	375.26 (100.00)	552.93 (100.00)

[1] Figures in brackets are percentages of total income.

Sources: cols. (1) and (2): *Agricultural labour in India: Report on the Second Enquiry*, op. cit.; col. (3): *All-India rural labour enquiry, 1964-65*, op. cit.

ted number of agricultural labour households by annual expenditure class for 1956-57, 1963-64 and 1970-71. Using these distributions, a calculation has been made of the percentage of agricultural labour households living below the poverty line in terms of minimum levels of living. This shows that 88.56 per cent of agricultural labourers in 1956-57, 67.37 per cent in 1963-64 and 87.36 per cent in 1970-71 came under the poverty line. It must be repeated that these estimates are based on different sources of data which are not really comparable and their accuracy, especially intertemporal consistency, cannot easily be verified.

Other workers

As regards "other workers" the data problems become even more pronounced. There is some scattered material available on the wage rates in some occupations (handloom workers, carpenters, blacksmiths, cobblers, etc.). But it is virtually impossible to get any figures on duration of work, and consequently on total earnings, of any of these categories. Hence the extent of poverty in this sector can be estimated only indirectly. According to table 35 about 74 per cent of the rural population was below the poverty line in terms of the minimum levels of living norm in 1969-70. It will be assumed that there was no change in this proportion in 1970-71. It has already been noted that, according to the 1971 census, approximately 40 per cent of the rural labour force consisted of cultivators and another 40 per cent of agricultural labourers. It has already been estimated that around 56 per cent of cultivators and 87 per cent of agricultural labourers came below the poverty line in 1970-71. It must therefore follow that 85 per cent of "other workers" were below the line in that year.[1]

When the problem of poverty is viewed not in terms of consumer units but in terms of producer groups, the dimensions of poverty take on a different meaning. The poor are not only those who do not get enough to meet their consumption requirements but those whose levels of productivity and earnings are also extremely low. The problem of poverty, therefore, is related to the total production and distribution aspects of the economy and can be understood only with reference to them. An examination of rural poverty in Tamil Nadu is therefore made in the light of the total economic process in the state during the past two decades.

RURAL POVERTY: AN ANALYSIS

Mass poverty of the kind seen in rural Tamil Nadu and elsewhere cannot be viewed as a "pocket phenomenon" or as a mere aberration of the system. It is a reflection of the total malfunctioning of the economic order, closely related to production processes, the manner in which resources are owned and utilised, and policy measures. Hence any attempt to analyse the problem in terms of one or two variables such as low capital formation or absence of policy measures to ensure adequate distribution of income must be viewed with suspicion. On the other hand it is not easy to comprehend the totality of the system or to place the poverty problem within it. There is no comprehensive theory which details the working of an economy such as that of Tamil Nadu. But in what follows an attempt is made to examine how the mass poverty in rural Tamil Nadu can be related to the different aspects and operations of the economy.

Table 42 shows that net state domestic product has grown at an annual average rate (linear) of 5.3 per cent per annum, with considerable variations from year to year. The performance during the 1950s was somewhat better than that during the 1960s. Since 1968-69 the rate of growth has picked up again. Not unexpectedly, these movements in net domestic product are closely associated with the performance of agriculture, which accounted for over 50 per cent of total output in the early 1950s and over 40 per cent in the early 1970s. The growth performance of the major agricultural commodities is shown in table 43. Since rice is the leading crop the pattern is best illustrated with reference to it. Production showed an annual rate of growth of 10.5 per cent in the early 1950s, slightly over 4 per cent in the late 1950s, a negative

---

[1] See C. T. Kurien: *Rural poverty in Tamil Nadu, India*, op. cit., for a discussion of the limitations of this estimate and for an alternative method which nevertheless gives a result which is very close to it.

127

Table 42.   The net state domestic product between 1950-51 and 1970-71 in constant (1960-61) prices

Year (1)	Net state domestic product (in millions of rupees) (2)	Year-to-year percentage variation in net state domestic product (3)	Per capita income (in rupees) (4)
1950-51	7749	—	257.3
1951-52	8137	5.0	—
1952-53	7980	− 1.9	—
1953-54	8628	8.1	—
1954-55	9313	7.9	—
1955-56	9635	3.5	302.0 (3.5)[1]
1956-57	10047	4.3	—
1957-58	10357	3.1	—
1958-59	10538	1.7	—
1959-60	11065	5.0	—
1960-61	11296	2.1	335.0 (2.2)
1961-62	11845	4.9	—
1962-63	12128	2.4	—
1963-64	12452	2.7	—
1964-65	12756	2.4	—
1965-66	12884	1.0	346.0 (0.7)
1966-67	13477	4.6	—
1967-68	13542	0.5	—
1968-69	14342	5.9	—
1969-70	15138	5.6	—
1970-71	15988	5.6	389.0 (2.5)

[1] Figures in brackets in column (4) show annual growth rates over the preceding five years.

Source: (i) from 1950-51 to 1959-60: K. S. Sonachalam: *Land reforms in Tamil Nadu* (New Delhi, Oxford and IBM Publishing Company, 1970), p. 29; (ii) from 1960-61 to 1970-71: Government of Tamil Nadu, Finance Dept.: *Tamil Nadu: an economic appraisal* (1972), Part II, p. 8.

rate of 0.58 per cent in the early 1960s and close to 8 per cent growth in the late 1960s. Millets, which also account for a substantial part of the area under cultivation, though not of output, show a different pattern. The annual rate of increase was 0.8 per cent in the early 1950s, 3.2 per cent in the late 1950s, and then became negative—very markedly so—towards the end of the period. The pattern of change in the growth performance of cereals, particularly rice, is very important in understanding the general economic situation in the rural areas.

Before turning to a discussion of the relationship between agricultural change and rural poverty, a few more aspects of economic transformation in the state which have a bearing on the problem may be touched upon. Agriculture and allied activities constituted a little over 50 per cent of the net state domestic product throughout the 1950s. But in the 1960s the share declined substantially, reaching 42 per cent in 1970-71. This can be explained both in terms of the stagnation of agriculture in the early 1960s as well as the rapid growth of industries in the state during that decade. The share of

Table 43. Production of major agricultural commodities, including food grains over-all, and growth rates
(In thousands of tonnes)

Year	Food grains	Rice	Millets[1]	Groundnuts	Sugar cane	Cotton
1951-52	3 607	2 129	1 031	782	332	292
	—	—	—	—	—	—
1956-57	4 870	3 247	1 072	884	332	339
	(7.0)[2]	(10.5)	(0.8)	(2.6)	(0.0)	(3.2)
1961-62	5 703	3 907	1 245	1 082	632	384
	(3.4)	(4.06)	(3.2)	(4.5)	(18.1)	(2.7)
1966-67	5 458	3 791	1 185	883	831	335
	(-0.9)	(-0.58)	(-0.9)	(-3.7)	(6.3)	(-2.6)
1971-72	6 884	5 302	1 052	1 253	1 076	423
	(5.2)	(8.0)	(-2.2)	(8.4)	(5.9)	(5.3)

[1] Millets include *cholam, cumbu* and *ragi*. [2] Figures in brackets show annual growth rates over the preceding five years.

Source: Government of Tamil Nadu, Finance Dept.: *Tamil Nadu: an economic appraisal*, op. cit., annual issues for 1971 and 1975.

mining and manufacturing in the net state domestic product was slightly over 12 per cent in 1950-51, rose to above 17 per cent in 1960-61 and to 24 per cent in 1970-71. However, this should not be taken as evidence of a major structural transformation of the economy in favour of industry since the reduction in the share of the primary sector (and an increase in the share of the secondary sector) in the net state domestic product was accompanied by an *increase* in the share of the workforce in the primary sector, with the share of the secondary sector remaining fairly stable. The primary sector claimed 63.33 per cent of the workforce in the state in 1961, and this rose to 64.79 per cent in 1971. In fact the chances are that the primary sector absorbed a larger proportion of the labour force in 1971 than indicated by these figures as the change in the definition of "workers" in the census of 1971 would have affected the agricultural sector more adversely than the industrial sector.

Within the labour force there was a change in the division of agricultural workers into cultivators and agricultural labourers. In 1961, 51 per cent of agricultural workers were cultivators and 22 per cent agricultural labourers (with the rest being "other workers"). In 1971 the proportion of cultivators declined to 40 per cent and that of agricultural labourers went up to over 38 per cent. These figures, derived from the census reports of the two years, cannot be compared directly because of the changes that occurred in the definition of "workers" and in the procedure of classifying agricultural workers into "cultivators" and "non-cultivators". A detailed examination has shown, however, that the changes in the proportions of cultivators and agricultural labourers cannot be explained away in terms of differences in the census definition.[1] A big increase in the number and proportion of labourers

---

[1] For a detailed discussion of this point see C. T. Kurien and J. Joseph: *Economic change in Tamil Nadu: a regionally and functionally disaggregated analysis* (forthcoming).

in the total of workers in agriculture must be accepted as one of the main structural changes in the rural sector of the state during the past decades.

With an awareness of these structural changes table 42 may be examined again for a further analysis of the growth process in the state during the 1950s and 1960s. The second half of the 1950s was a period of high growth which steadily declined, reaching the very low performance of the mid-1960s, followed by a recovery in the late 1960s and early 1970s. Reference to table 43 will show that this pattern is closely related to the performance of agriculture, particularly rice. This phenomenon is examined more carefully as it is crucial to the understanding of the time profile and characteristics of rural poverty noted above.

Some details of the pattern of change in agriculture during these two periods is necessary in order to understand the process adequately. The total geographical area of Tamil Nadu is 13 million hectares. In 1950-51 about 5.4 million hectares (around 40 per cent) constituted the net sown area. This rose to nearly 6 million hectares (46 per cent) in 1960-61 and remained at the same level even in 1966-67. There was a marginal increase in the net area, to 6.2 million hectares in 1970-71. That the extensive cultivation of the 1950s was caused by an increase in irrigation can be seen from the fact that the total net irrigated area, which was 1.9 million hectares in 1950-51, rose to 2.5 million hectares in 1960-61 and remained at this level in 1966-67. With irrigation becoming available, the area sown more than once increased from 0.93 million hectares in 1951-52 to 1.32 million in 1960-61, but declined somewhat by 1966-67.

Table 43 shows that the extensive cultivation of the 1950s resulted in a considerable increase in the output of all major crops, but particularly of food grains. What is more important is that during this period output per hectare of all crops increased. The extensive cultivation of the 1950s, therefore, differed from the usual case of less fertile land being brought under the plough, resulting in an increase in total output but with a decrease in production per hectare. It was essentially a case of more dry land being converted into wet land through irrigation (although there was some increase in net area sown also), thus demonstrating the fundamental importance of water in the agricultural situation in the state.

The nature of the irrigation that enabled the extensive cultivation of the 1950s is also important to the understanding of the effect of that process on agriculture and the rural scene in general. Increasing irrigation facilities had received highest priority in state policy from the beginning of the planning process in the state in 1951. A number of large river irrigation projects were undertaken during the First and Second Five Year Plans, the last continuing during the Third Plan. Under these major irrigation schemes public irrigation facilities (government canals and tanks) increased substantially in the state, the area irrigated by then rising from 1.36 million hectares in 1952-53 to 1.87 million hectares in 1962-65. Since then no major irrigation scheme has been started and the official view is that there is no scope for a further increase in major or even medium irrigation projects in the state.

The main features of the agricultural change and economic growth of the first phase (from the early 1950s to the mid-1960s) can now be summed up. It was a period of extensive cultivation made possible by an increase in public irrigation facilities which led to big increases in agricultural production and productivity. Because food production had increased from 3.6 million tonnes in 1951-52 (the beginning of the First Five Year Plan) to 5.3 million tonnes in 1960-61 (end of the Second Plan) a 7 million tonnes target was set for the Third Plan. But after rising to 5.7 million tonnes in 1962-63 food production tended to stagnate. It touched a low figure of 4.9 million in the drought year of 1965-66 and just managed to return to the 1960-61 level the following year.

The year 1966-67 marks the beginning of the second phase of economic growth in the state, with agriculture reviving and the economy picking up generally. The strategy of growth of the second phase was very different from that of the first. As compared to the extensive and general improvement of agriculture during the first phase, the second period witnessed a strategy of intensive and selective growth. This was dictated partly by the physical circumstances resulting from the alleged inability further to increase public irrigation, and the virtual necessity, therefore, to subsidise private irrigation schemes, particularly wells and tubewells to ensure an increase in the production of food. But the new strategy was based essentially on a new philosophy of growth. It was argued that the surest way to increase output (in all sectors of the economy, but especially in agriculture) was to make crucial inputs available to a few well selected agents who had both the motivation and facilities to take advantage of them. Since in Tamil Nadu the critical input in agriculture was water, and water could be provided only by farmers who could install their own wells, the new agricultural strategy was to concentrate on the "efficient farmers" by making available to them electricity (to activate pump sets for irrigation), high-yielding varieties of seeds, fertilisers and other inputs and credit, all at highly subsidised rates. This was the background thinking that gave rise to the Green Revolution in the state and which formed the main plank of the new strategy of development of the second half of the 1960s.

In the form of the high-yielding varieties (HYV) programme, the Green Revolution was inaugurated in the state in 1966-67, and almost immediately reversed the downward trend in the production of rice. Rice output rose from 3.5 million tonnes in 1965-66 to 3.8 million tonnes in 1966-67, then to 4.0 million tonnes in 1969-70 (after a dip in 1968-69 because of severe drought) and to 5.0 million tonnes in 1970-71. Official sources claimed also that, by that year, almost 70 per cent of the total area under paddy had come under the HYV programme. But to see the main thrust of the new agricultural strategy and the strategy of growth some of the details must be examined. While, as noted, area covered by public irrigation reached 1.87 million hectares in 1962-63, it declined to 1.76 million hectares in 1970-71; the area irrigated by private sources, however, rose from 0.42 million hectares in

1952-53 to 0.69 million hectares in 1962-63 and to 0.78 million hectares in the beginning of the 1970s. The increase in private sources of irrigation was achieved essentially by what is coming to be called the "pump-set revolution" in Tamil Nadu. The total number of pump sets in use in the state in 1956 was 62,000. By 1966 it had increased to 257,000 and by 1970 to 471,000. By that time the state had achieved first place in the country in terms of the number of pump sets in use, claiming over 40 per cent of the pumps connected with electricity in the whole country. It has been shown that the pump-set revolution gave special benefits to the bigger farmers.[1]

It was not only the irrigation policy of the state that came to have a bias in favour of the bigger farmers. Its financial assistance to the agricultural sector mainly benefited them also, and they had better access to fertilisers and other inputs, especially when those were in short supply. All this had an impact on the HYV programme as well. The technology of the HYV programme is now generally conceded to be size-neutral, but the accessibility to it increases considerably with size. This aspect has not been as adequately studied in Tamil Nadu as in some of the other states. Two recent studies have shown, however, that the adoption rate of the HYV programme has been considerably influenced by the size of operations and asset structure of farmers although it is not confined to large farmers alone.[2] It may, therefore, be concluded that the agricultural strategy of the late 1960s was to increase output, particularly rice, relying mainly on the large farmers by making available to them at subsidised rates electricity (and thereby water), credit, high-yielding seeds and the complementary inputs required to boost production. Under its impact, there certainly was a subtantial increase in output.

How the two phases of growth in the state affected the poverty situation must now be discussed. First it must be recorded that continuing mass poverty in the state is not the result of lack of growth. During the 1950s and 1960s the Tamil Nadu economy registered a rate of growth which was better than that of the country as a whole and quite commendable by international standards. Secondly it may be noted also that the economic growth was not neutralised by the growth of population. During the two decades, particularly in the 1950s, the growth of population in the state was much lower than in the country as a whole, namely 1.85 per cent per annum, and this permitted significant increases in per capita income.

In spite of this, the evidence is that the poverty situation in the early 1970s was not much better than in the mid-1950s and was worse than in the early to mid-1960s. There is a striking coincidence between the time profile of poverty seen at the end of the section on poverty in rural Tamil Nadu and the two phases of growth discussed above. During the first phase of

---

[1] Kurien and Joseph, op. cit.

[2] N. B. Chinnappa: *Adoption of the new technology for paddy cultivation in the survey area: North Arcot District* (mimeographed, 1974), and C. Muthiah: "The Green Revolution—Participation by Small Versus Large Farmers", in *Indian Journal of Agricultural Economics*, Jan.-Mar. 1971.

growth the extent of poverty declined, but with the new strategy of growth the proportion of the population below the poverty line again increased almost to the level of the 1950s. Is this a mere coincidence, or can it be explained in terms of the differential impact of the two kinds of growth? The pattern of growth of the late 1950s could be considered to be more size neutral than the strategy of growth of a decade later. The new agricultural strategy of the 1960s, it has been noted, provided special benefits to the larger farmers. There were, during the late 1960s and early 1970s, special programmes of assistance to small farmers also, but the nature of assistance and of the system itself were such that only those with reasonable command over resources could respond effectively to the many schemes of subsidisation offered by the state. The strategy of growth thus resulted in its primary benefits being confined to a selected few. It probably also had something of a percolation effect but the process itself was selective, by-passing many segments of society. Two concrete instances can be cited. The supply of pump sets, electricity and credit at subsidised rates would have enabled the larger farmers to convert their dry lands into wet lands and to shift from the cultivation of millets to that of the more profitable rice or sugar cane. In that process employment and incomes of some agricultural labourers might also have gone up. But the small farmers, who out of necessity continue to produce millets, are likely to be left out of this pump-set revolution. Similarly, the increased availability of electricity in the rural areas may lead to more electrically operated rice mills which may provide regular employment at higher wage rates to some but may throw out of employment many others. These are not merely conjectures. It has been noted that in the late 1960s, when the extent of poverty increased, the proportion of acute poverty also increased. It is reasonable to assume that the acute poverty group consisted of the small dry farmers and many groups of rural artisans. There is also independent evidence that the small farmers are a very vulnerable group. The NSS twenty-fifth round reported that only 22.6 per cent of small farmers felt that their employment and earnings (in 1970-71) were adequate and that a sizable proportion of small farmers (over three-quarters) expressed a willingness to take up other work in their own villages or even outside. The selective and intensive strategy of growth thus confers benefits on a few, but it also pushes down many to the ranks of the poor.

This is not to suggest that there must be a return to the growth strategy of the 1950s. For growth, after all, is not a mechanical process of which the rythm can be changed at will. It is essentially a social phenomenon reflecting the basic structure of society with its property relationships and the distribution of economic power. From this point of view the growth strategies of the 1950s and the 1960s were simply minor variations of the same basic social structure, represented by the ownership and distribution of resources in the economy. In a predominantly agrarian rural economy the main resource is obviously land. Even a casual examination of the ownership patterns of land in rural Tamil Nadu will reveal the basis of mass poverty. According to the

Table 44. Distribution of ownership of land: rural Tamil Nadu

Size of household holding (hectares)	Cumulative percentage					
	Households			Area owned		
	1954-55	1960-61	1971-72	1954-55	1960-61	1971-72
Below 1.0	62.74	60.42	60.53	3.08	3.43	4.45
Up to 2.49	76.56	77.51	78.40	13.03	17.19	20.23
Up to 4.99	86.88	88.84	89.79	29.36	36.92	42.07
Up to 7.49	92.60	93.38	94.55	44.47	50.42	58.02
Up to 9.99	95.49	95.94	96.54	55.37	61.15	67.28
Up to 14.99	97.52	97.82	98.55	66.03	72.24	80.27
Up to 19.99	98.42	99.02	99.27	72.73	81.88	87.00
Up to 24.99	98.87	99.36	99.54	77.21	85.44	90.25
Up to 29.99	99.21	99.56	99.69	81.21	88.21	92.97
Up to 49.99	99.71	99.83	99.91	89.09	93.21	96.95
All sizes	100.00	100.00	100.00	100.00	100.00	100.00

Source: National Sample Survey, eighth, sixteenth and twenty-sixth rounds.

latest available information (from the twenty-sixth round of the NSS for 1971-72) 17 per cent of rural households in Tamil Nadu are without any land at all—the highest proportion among all the states in India. Some 60 per cent of the households own less than 1 acre of land and account for less than 5 per cent of the land. This pattern has remained more or less the same during the past two decades, as can be seen from table 44. The heavy concentration of land ownership remains practically unaltered in spite of the many radical legislative measures adopted, particularly in the 1960s, setting very low ceilings on such ownership.[1] It must be evident that rural poverty is closely associated with the fact that a large proportion of the population has little or no claims on resources—their livelihood, therefore, depending precariously on how those who own resources utilise them. *The World Agricultural Census, Tamil Nadu* has now documented what was always suspected to be the case—that those who own resources in large quantities do not make the best use of them. Gross cropped area as a percentage of total operated area declines sharply as the size of holding increases, falling from 100 per cent in the case of very small holdings to less than 50 per cent in the case of holdings above 50 hectares. This is one aspect of the problem. The second and related aspect is that with such an unequal distribution of resources, and hence of incomes and economic power, the choice of products and of techniques tends to be dictated by the wants of the few rather than the needs of the many. Growth of a kind may take place under these circumstances, and may even

[1] For details of land reforms in Tamil Nadu, see K. S. Sonachalam: *Land reforms in Tamil Nadu*, op. cit., and G. Venkataramani: *Land reforms in Tamil Nadu* (Madras, Sangam Publishers, 1973). In an official review of the progress of land reform in Tamil Nadu, especially with reference to land ceilings, it was conceded that less than 1 per cent of the estimated surplus land had been taken over and actually distributed.

be quantitatively impressive, but the natural proclivity of the system is to direct resources towards the growing wants of a few who happen to have ownership and control over resources. The system, therefore, cannot provide for the elementary needs of those who have no resources at their command with which to influence its working in their favour. What, for instance, can ensure that when industries in the state are becoming diversified and sophisticated the cloth that the poor require or the kerosene that they use is available to them? This is the basic explanation of mass poverty such as exists in rural Tamil Nadu. Poverty, therefore, is not a matter of arithmetic, even economic arithmetic. It must be seen as the result of certain economic and social processes without reference to which it cannot be properly understood and analysed.

POVERTY AND INEQUALITY
IN RURAL BANGLADESH

7

Azizur Rahman Khan

Bangladesh is the eighth most populous country in the world. But only four countries (viz., China, India, Indonesia and the USSR) have a larger rural population and only three—China, India and Indonesia—have larger numbers directly dependent on agriculture for a living. While in terms of absolute numbers Bangladesh is the fourth largest agricultural society in the world, in relative terms (i.e. in terms of the proportion of the population living in rural areas and directly dependent on agricultural activities for living) it is overwhelmingly more rural than the three larger agricultural economies. Of the country's estimated population of nearly 79 million in 1975, nearly 72 million were inhabitants of rural areas and about 58 million were directly dependent on agriculture for their livelihood. Thus 91 per cent of the population of Bangladesh live in rural areas, as compared to about 80 per cent in India, probably about 85 per cent in China and about 82 per cent in Indonesia.

The share of Bangladesh in the world's rural poor is even greater than its share of the world's rural population. The combination of a very unfavourable average resource endowment (only 0.3 acres of cultivable land per rural person and only 0.4 acres per member of an average agricultural household) and a high degree of inequality has resulted in an unprecedented concentration of extreme poverty in rural Bangladesh today.

The purpose of this chapter is to quantify the direction and magnitude of change in rural poverty in Bangladesh in recent times. The time period for the present study is the last quarter of a century although the quantification of many variables will not cover the entire period. A brief description is first given of the "anatomy" of rural poverty in a benchmark year. This is done because the measurement of change, without a description of the benchmark conditions, would be totally inadequate in promoting an understanding of the gravity of the problem.

Next, an attempt is made to quantify the change in the incidence of poverty over the entire period, using the benchmark year as a point of reference. This will be done both by estimating the proportions of the rural population at various levels of poverty at different points of time and the change in the real earnings of specific groups of the rural population. Finally, some of the "causative" factors are investigated in an attempt to understand the observed trends in the extent of poverty.

The analysis is based on statistics collected by various official agencies. Their quality is somewhat uncertain and uneven and they have sometimes been manipulated for the purposes of this chapter by employing arbitrary but hopefully plausible assumptions. In such a situation no single estimate can be interpreted as quantitatively precise but an effort has been made to ensure that major conclusions are derived from several alternative sources of numerical evidence and that the evidence is of such numerical magnitude as to be trusted as an indicator of the broad direction of change even after allowance is made for the likelihood of significant errors in measurement.

POVERTY

The year 1963-64 has been used as the benchmark, primarily because of the relatively abundant statistical information in that year. The household income and expenditure survey[1] for this year is the most detailed available in published form. The only completed nutrition survey (carried out between March 1962 and January 1964) covers most of this fiscal year.[2] The sixth round of the *Master Survey of Agriculture*[3] includes information for this year. The year also satisfies other standard criteria for selection: it was not a year of drought or flood of unusual magnitude and, if anything, the natural conditions were better than average and output per head higher than in the adjacent years. Being close to the mid-point of the period under survey, the year must also have been fairly typical with respect to such dynamic factors as tastes and preferences of consumers and the technology of producers.

The definition of a poverty line is essentially arbitrary. To determine such a line and make it useful for purposes of analysis, one must take into account the general living standard in the economy and the minimum consumption that can realistically be provided for everyone within the constraints of available resources and production. On the basis of such criteria the income level corresponding to a poverty line for Bangladesh must be defined very conservatively because of the very low levels of average income and the poor resource endowment of the country.

All those families who have levels of income inadequate to ensure a minimum diet are defined as poor. Adequate diet is not easy to define, however. A number of attempts have been made to define such diets for the

---

[1] Central Statistical Office of Pakistan: *Quarterly Survey of Current Economic Conditions* (Karachi, 1967); hereafter in the text this publication is referred to as the "QSCEC".

[2] United States Department of Health, Education and Welfare: *Nutrition survey of East Pakistan* (May 1966).

[3] Bangladesh Bureau of Statistics: *Master Survey of Agriculture* (Dacca, 1966).

poor nations of south-east Asia.[1] These have been presented in the appendix to this chapter after slight adjustments to reflect conditions in Bangladesh, e.g. dividing cereals into rice and wheat according to the local consumption pattern.

Although these diets are indeed minimum standards that even the poorest societies should attempt to achieve in the near future, they represent unrealistically high levels for a minimum income for Bangladesh. At 1963-64 prices the "Sukhatme diet" would cost about Tk. 24 per person per month, which was the expenditure on food incurred by a household with a per capita income of Tk. 37 per month. In that year nearly 96 per cent of the rural households, accounting for 88 per cent of the rural population, were below such an income level. The diet recommended by FAO would cost only slightly less and be within the reach of only a few more families. There is also some doubt that even if a family had enough income in 1963-64 to buy the diet, it would, in fact, do so. The evidence of actual consumer preferences as revealed by the household expenditure survey suggests that families would consume more cereals and less milk, pulses and fat than recommended in the Sukhatme-FAO diets.

The reason Sukhatme-FAO diets are so expensive is that they provide a balanced diet for an average person, with adequate calories, protein (both animal and vegetable) and vitamins. Clearly, few Bengalis can hope for the "luxury" of such a diet. The minimum needs of a society as poor as Bangladesh must be based on a more modest dietary standard. This standard could be one that merely provides enough calories without ensuring the adequacy of other forms of nutrients (e.g. protein, vitamins, etc.). The estimated FAO requirement for calories for the population of Bangladesh (based on height, weight, age, sex and environmental temperature) is about 2,150 per person per day.[2]

In order to find the minimum income level corresponding to the poverty line the question to be asked is what is the income that would ensure the intake by a family, faced with 1963-64 prices, of a bundle of food that would provide the specified per capita calorie level? The 1963-64 QSCEC data show the following relationship between per capita calorie intake (measured in 100 units by Y) and per capita family income (measured by X at 1963-64 prices):

$Y = -1.4255 + 15.1309 \log X$; $R^2 = 0.98$ (with 11 observations based on
  (1.0761) (0.6920)   grouped data)

---

[1] See P. V. Sukhatme: *Feeding India's growing millions*, op. cit., and FAO: *Monthly Bulletin of Agricultural Economics and Statistics*, op. cit., Jan. 1973.

[2] See United States Department of Health, Education and Welfare: *Nutritional survey of East Pakistan*, op. cit., p. 79. Note that the Sukhatme diet would provide 2,350 calories, nearly 10 per cent more than this recommended level. The calorie value of the FAO diet recommended for south-east Asia is close to that of the Sukhatme diet and is higher than the FAO recommendation of calorie intake for Bangladesh.

Table 45.   Definition of poverty lines for 1963-64

Levels of poverty	Corresponding per capita income (taka)	Per capita calorie intake by the family at corresponding income level	Calories in col. (2) as percentage of recommended intake	Percentage below poverty line in 1963-64 of:	
				House-holds	Popula-tion
	(1)	(2)	(3)	(4)	
Absolute poverty	23.61	1 935	90	51.7	40.2
Extreme poverty	17.02	1 720	80	9.8	5.2

—from which it results that a per capita family income of Tk. 32.75 per month would ensure an intake of adequate calories. Once again a very high proportion of the households—85 per cent, accounting for 76 per cent of the population—was below this level of income. The standards used have, therefore, been lowered further and poverty lines defined as in table 45. The absolute poverty level has been defined as a figure so low that, at the income corresponding to this poverty level, only 90 per cent of the calorie needs are satisfied. There are two possible ways to explain the choice of such a low level. The first is to refer to the widely held belief that there are significant components of self-consumption which are not caught by the usual kind of household income and expenditure surveys. While it is impossible to take a final position with respect to this argument it is thought to be unlikely to apply to the estimates used because several upward adjustments have been made in the consumption data shown in the QSCEC especially in the category of vegetables and fruits.

Moreover, the Nutrition Survey, in which a special effort was made to catch all items of self-consumption, estimates the calorie intake from all non-cereal sources to be no higher than the estimates here.[1] The inclination of the author of this chapter is therefore to take the alternative view that the low level of income corresponding to the poverty line is justified because of the widespread incidence of extreme poverty and the resulting situation in which a family with an adequate level of calorie intake is, in relative terms, a highly privileged one.

The comparison of a single statistic of the proportion of the population below some given poverty line at different points of time will sometimes be misleading in that the distribution below the line may change. Ideally, one should look at the entire distribution below such a poverty line to find out the amounts by which the incomes of the various groups of poor fall short of the specified level.[2] This has been done whenever there are enough data to

---

[1] Note, however, that the Nutrition Survey estimates per capita cereal consumption to be significantly higher than does the QSCEC. There is no need for the two surveys to give identical measurements as their time periods are different. However, on the basis of a good deal of evidence, it is concluded that the Nutrition Survey estimates are biased upwards because of the difference in methodology and possible concentration on seasonal observations. The QSCEC data are consistent with other aggregate and time series estimates.

[2] See A. K. Sen: *On economic inequality* (Oxford, Clarendon Press, 1973), for an account of the issues involved.

Figure 7.

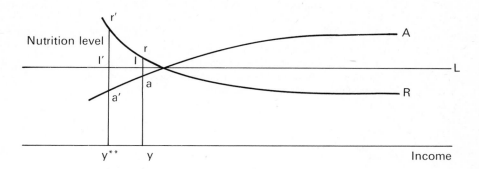

conduct such an exercise. The use of an extreme poverty line is a convenient additional statistic for revealing a characteristic of the distribution below the absolute poverty line.

Table 45 indicates the numbers below the absolute and extreme poverty lines in 1963-64. About 52 per cent of the households, accounting for 40 per cent of the rural population, were absolutely poor (in the sense of having 90 per cent of the recommended calorie intake or less) and about 10 per cent of the households, accounting for 5 per cent of the rural population, were extremely poor (in the sense of having no more than 80 per cent of the recommended calorie intake) in that year.

The data in table 45 understate the magnitude of the problem, however, because the distance of poor households from adequate levels of nutrition is a great deal more than such measurements, literally interpreted, indicate. The reason for this is that the amount of calories required is not invariant with respect to income. A simple diagrammatic explanation may be useful. In figure 7 per capita income is represented along the X axis while nutrition is shown along the Y axis. The line *L*, representing the poverty line, implies that the nutritional requirement is invariant with respect to the level of income. It is well known, however, that the lower the level of income of the recipient, the more likely he is to be engaged in physical labour harder than the average. Moreover, such an association is stronger in a poorer country with a lower level of technology than in a richer country. Thus a line which correctly indicates nutritional requirements should be a curve such as *R* which at first falls rather sharply as incomes rise and then levels off as one approaches an income range in which sedentary work predominates. The relationship between actual nutritional intake and income is represented by a curve such as *A* which increases at a diminishing rate.

At the marginal level of absolute poverty a household is only 10 per cent below the line *L* but it is below the requirement level *R* by a much wider margin. The shortfall in calorie intake at that level of income is not the distance *al* but *ar* in the diagram.

Table 46.   Per capita consumption of cereals in rural Bangladesh by occupational group, and by size of farm household for agricultural operators (Average of all rural population=100)

Occupational group	Index
Agricultural operators	104
Large farm household (above 7.5 acres)	116
Medium farm household (between 2.5 and 7.5 acres)	106
Small farm household (below 2.5 acres)	97
Craftsmen	97
Fishermen	91
Agricultural labourers	90
Transport workers	78
Beggars	71

Source: Bangladesh Bureau of Statistics: *Master Survey of Agriculture* (Dacca, 1968), 7th Round, Phase-I.

To illustrate the importance of this phenomenon, take information for rural Bangladesh as summarised in table 46. Various types of households have been arranged in descending order of cereal consumption.

Since cereals account for 87 per cent of the calorie intake for the lower income groups and a progressively but only slightly lower proportion for the higher income groups, these statistics somewhat understate the differences in calorie intake between various types of households. Yet it is well known that the calorie requirements for transport workers, agricultural labourers and fishermen are far higher than those for farm managers and indeed for the average member of the rural population. There are no direct estimates of the calorie requirements of the different occupational groups shown in table 46, but some idea of orders of magnitude can be obtained from estimates made by the Indian Nutrition Advisory Committee for the Indian "reference man and woman" (table 47). Thus, agricultural labourers, transport workers and fishermen (each of whom is engaged in at least eight hours of heavy labour during work seasons) probably require at least 40 per cent more calories than the operators of the larger farms (who are unlikely to perform more than the equivalent of eight hours of industrial work). Thus, while the energy consumption of the agricultural worker is only about 22 per cent below that of the larger farmer according to the information in table 46, the ratio of energy availability to energy requirements for the agricultural worker is lower than that of the larger farmers by a greater margin.[1] Indeed, most agricultural and

---

[1] The calculation of the ratio of calorie availability to requirements for the two groups would require more information than that available. To illustrate, however, consider that an average member of a larger farmer's family requires 2,150 calories and gets 2,300 calories per day. Assume that a fourth of the members of an average family of an agricultural labourer work as labourers and hence require 3,880 calories. Let the remaining members of such a family require 2,150 calories per capita per day. On the basis of these assumptions the per capita calorie requirements of an average labourer's family would be 2,583 and the per capita calorie availability would be 1,794 (78 per cent of that of the larger farmers). Thus an average member of a larger farmer's family would have 1.07 times the calorie requirement while that of a labourer's family would have 0.69 times the requirement.

Table 47. Daily calorie requirements of Indians in various types of work

Activity		Calorie requirement	
		Men	Women
A	Eight hours in bed	460	354
B	Eight hours off work	1 220	826
C_1	Eight hours of sedentary work	750	610
C_2	Eight hours of light or industrial work	1 100	900
C_3	Eight hours of heavy work	2 200	1 800
	$A + B + C_1$	2 430	1 790
	$A + B + C_2$	2 780	2 080
	$A + B + C_3$	3 880	2 980

Source: P. V. Sukhatme: *Feeding India's growing millions*, op. cit., p. 36.

transport workers and fishermen in Bangladesh work as hard during the peak seasons as the rickshaw-pullers whose daily calorie requirement has been estimated to be 4,880,[1] more than twice the amount required by those engaged in sedentary work. "Men engaged in exceptionally heavy work, such as harvesting, without mechanical help... have reached levels of 5,000 calories a day over a few days."[2] Even this is not the whole story since the requirements in table 47 refer to adequately nourished and healthy people. An FAO study concludes that the "amount of food needed for the full rehabilitation of individuals who have subsisted for long periods on a diet low in calories, or who have suffered acute starvation, is in excess of that needed to maintain such individuals in health when rehabilitation has taken place."[3]

The above is a frequently neglected aspect of the problem of income distribution. In most studies no allowances are made for differences in calorie requirements. In order to make income or welfare estimates of different groups comparable, calorie requirements should be subtracted from gross incomes in the same way that other current inputs and depreciation are subtracted in estimating net income. Nor are energy requirements the only such items that should be taken into account; the same applies to clothes (which get dirty more frequently in low income jobs) and many other items of consumption.

It is clear from the above discussion that those called absolutely poor are severely undernourished and those called extremely poor are in a state of acute malnutrition for much of the year. Protein deficiency is even more serious. Using data from the nutrition survey, protein consumption of the

---

[1] J. V. Durnin and R. Passmore: *Energy, work and leisure* (London, Heinemann, 1967).

[2] ibid., p. 48.

[3] FAO: *Calorie requirements*, FAO Nutritional Studies No. 15 (Rome, 1957).

absolutely poor is estimated to be 48 grams or less per person per day and no more than 43 grams for the extremely poor families. The former is only 78 per cent of the FAO recommended dose of 61.5 grams for an average Bengali while the latter is less than 70 per cent of the recommended level. There is little doubt that the expectation of life at birth for the absolutely and extremely poor population was lower than the 48 years estimated for an average Bengali during the 1960s. Similarly, the infant mortality rates for these poor groups must have been substantially higher than the 140 per thousand estimated for Bangladesh for the same period.

Since food and calorie consumption varies less than proportionately as income changes, a comparison of food and nutrition levels of different groups presents an inadequate picture of how badly off the poor are in relation to the average. For example, while the annual per capita consumption of textiles in rural Bangladesh in 1963-64 was the equivalent of 8.8 square yards of coarse cloth, the consumption of the absolutely poor and the extremely poor was no more than 7.3 and 5.7 square yards respectively. Information on the distribution of basic services, e.g. health and education, is not available. But there is virtually a complete absence of public health services and the average person in rural Bangladesh spent only 5 taka (Tk.) on medical services and medicines (i.e. two days' wages for an unskilled rural labourer) during 1963-64. A member of an absolutely poor household spent no more than Tk. 2.12 on such services. Per capita expenditure on education by an average rural household amounted to Tk. 2.93 per year. For the absolutely and extremely poor households such expenditures were no more than Tk. 0.89 and Tk. 0.43 respectively. While no direct information is available about the educational levels for different income groups, the 1968 *Master Survey of Agriculture* shows that 89 per cent of the agricultural labourers were completely illiterate as compared to the average of 73 per cent for the rural population (10 years of age and above) as a whole.

THE INCIDENCE OF POVERTY IN LATER YEARS

A description has been given of the living standards of the rural poor in 1963-64, the benchmark year. The next task is to determine to what extent there has been a change over time in the proportion of the rural population below the absolute and extreme poverty lines, i.e. below per capita incomes of Tk. 23.61 and 17.02 per month at 1963-64 prices. Since income estimates are available only at current prices an appropriate deflator is needed, a cost-of-living index with 1963-64 as the base.

This index has been constructed on the basis of price movements for 16 categories of food, clothing, fuel and services. One important item of expenditure that has been left out of the cost-of-living index is housing, an item which accounts for up to 9 per cent of total expenditure. Housing has been omitted because of the lack of any information on prices for this service. For the poorer households this does not appear to be of great significance since their houses are almost invariably self-produced and purchased current inputs amount to a small proportion of total cost. Indeed, the imputation of a rental value to such self-produced items would be highly arbitrary.

The most crucial problem in constructing a cost-of-living index is to determine the weights. These should refer to the actual consumption proportions of the group whose income is to be deflated by the index. Three different sets of weights have been used for the low, middle and high income groups, respectively. The weights for the low income group have been derived from the actual consumption of the second-lowest income group (between Tk. 50 and 100 per *family* per month) from the 1963-64 QSCEC. The weights for the middle income group have been derived from the actual consumption of the group with a monthly family income of between Tk. 250 and 300. This is the median income group in the 1963-64 QSCEC. For the high income group the weights have been derived from the actual consumption of the second-highest income group in the 1963-64 QSCEC (Tk. 700 to 900 per month per household).

Services are an important category of expenditure for the middle and high income groups. Unlike other items of consumption there is no readily available time series on the price of services and it is not easy to prepare one. Use has been made of the time series on rural money wages as the price series for these services. The main justification is that a very high proportion of them is accounted for by "domestic help" whose price probably moved in line with rural wages. Furthermore, the remaining categories of services are dominated by activities (e.g. barbers and tailors) in which wages are the major component of total cost. In the case of the low income group personal services are an insignificant element in their expenditure budget and have been assigned a zero weight.

The three price indices are shown in the appendix to this chapter (table 56). It should be noted that the rise in the index for the low income group, especially during the more recent years when the rate of inflation accelerated, has been considerably greater than the rise in the indices for the higher income groups. The reason for this is that the rise in the prices of the goods which have a heavier weight in the budget of the low income groups has been greater than average. While there is no *a priori* reason why this should occur, the phenomenon has been observed rather widely elsewhere[1] and implies that studies which compare income distributions over time should give careful attention to changes in relative prices.

In this chapter the cost-of-living index is used, first, to determine the poverty lines in years other than the base year and, second, to convert money wages into real wages. For such purposes the relevant index is that for the low income group. Most of the absolutely poor and a fairly high proportion

---

[1] See, for example, "The Pattern of Income Distribution in India: A Review", in Srinivasan and Bardhan (eds.): *Poverty and income distribution in India*, op. cit.

of the extremely poor in 1963-64 belonged to the income group whose consumption pattern has been used to derive weights for this index. Moreover,
in 1963-64 the household of an agricultural labourer would be within the
income range of the group that has supplied weights for this index. Unless
otherwise specified, the cost-of-living index in this chapter will refer to the
index for the low income group.

It has sometimes been argued that an index such as this may overstate the
rise in the cost of living in years subsequent to the base year. The argument is
that in a situation of generally rising prices expenditure will shift in favour of
the commodities whose prices have been rising at a lower rate than the
average. Thus by defining constant real income as the money income that
would be sufficient to buy the benchmark bundle of goods, the required
adjustment in money income may be overstated.

While the general validity of the argument is undeniable, the actual magnitude of the phenomenon is determined by specific circumstances, notably
the availability of substitutes, and in the specific case of Bangladesh the
effect is likely to have been minimal. The major commodity whose price rose
faster than average is rice. It would have been possible to maintain food
consumption for a lower increase in money expenditures than that implied
by the cost-of-living index only if it had been possible to shift to other cereals
whose price increased less rapidly. Unlike the rest of the subcontinent,
however, Bangladesh is characterised by an undiversified supply of cereals.
Rice and wheat together account for nearly the entire supply. Moreover,
wheat is largely imported and consumed in the urban areas. In 1963-64
wheat accounted for only 6.6 per cent of the consumption of cereals in
Bangladesh, but its share rose to 12.6 per cent in 1973-74. This increase,
however, was concentrated in urban areas where statutory rationing of imported wheat was introduced. In the rural areas the free market for wheat
was insignificant and the small quantities distributed through a "modified
rationing" scheme probably never accounted for more than 5 per cent of
total cereal consumption in those areas. It is likely that for the lower income
groups the increase in the share of wheat was more significant because the
income elasticity of demand for wheat by the higher income groups is very
low. It is, however, clearly untrue that there was a massive shift in favour of
wheat for the vast majority of the poor. In summary, there may have been a
shift in consumption patterns of the poor such that an adjustment in money
income in proportion to the rise in the Laspeyre cost-of-living index would
overcompensate for price increases, but this effect must have been slight
because of the limited possibility of substituting other cereals for rice. The
possible minor bias in the cost-of-living index need not be a source of worry
because, as shown below, the results derived from its use are of such a
magnitude as not to be affected by small differences in the rate of change of
the deflator.

For the post-independence period comparable information is available on
household incomes for the fiscal year 1973-74 and for the first quarter of the

Table 48.   Incidence of poverty in rural Bangladesh
(Percentages)

Year	Absolutely poor		Extremely poor	
	Households	Population	Households	Population
1963-64	51.7	40.2	9.8	5.2
1968-69	84.1	76.0	34.6	25.1
1973-74	86.7	78.5	54.1	42.1
1975 (first quarter)	70.3	61.8	50.5	41.0

calendar year 1975. The information for 1973-74 is available from the House-hold Expenditure Survey (HES), the successor of the QSCEC, while the information about the distribution of households according to income for the first quarter of 1975 is available from the Fuel Consumption Report based on the HES.[1] One problem about the information for 1975 is that income data represent the average for a quarter rather than the whole year. We cannot ascertain the possible direction of bias due to this factor.

We also have some data for 1968-69, a year for which the QSCEC has not been published but for which some information has been made available. Unfortunately, this information was not enough to enable us to interpolate and, therefore, we have introduced numerical assumptions from other sources (e.g. other QSCECs).[2]

Table 48 summarises the situation in the four years. The outstanding feature indicated in the table is the sharp increase in poverty in the decade since the early 1960s. The increase in the proportion of the extremely poor is truly remarkable. While only 5 per cent of the rural population in Bangladesh could be categorised as extremely poor in 1963-64, the proportion rose to over 40 per cent in the 1970s.

Figure 8 shows the entire distribution of income for the four periods. Compared to the benchmark year the incomes of all the groups seem to have been lower in 1968-69 and as a result a much higher proportion of the population was pushed below poverty lines.[3]

---

[1] Bangladesh Bureau of Statistics: *Report on household consumption of fuels in Bangladesh* (July 1975).

[2] For an account of such statistical operations see A. R. Khan: *Poverty and inequality in rural Bangladesh* (Geneva, ILO, 1976; mimeographed World Employment Programme research working paper; restricted).

[3] As previously mentioned, access to the 1968-69 QSCEC was limited to a few tables and the document remains unpublished to date. As a result, a number of numerical assumptions had to be introduced to fill in gaps. Some of the features of the survey appear a little inconsistent with alternative sources of information. From figure 8 it should be clear that, according to the survey, per capita real income in rural Bangladesh fell sharply between 1963-64 and 1968-69. Indeed some of the sources have quoted the survey to claim that income per household remained static in monetary terms so that the decline in real terms would be about 27 per cent. The GDP estimates and the estimates of agricultural output from the Central Statistical Office and other sources do not suggest such a drastic fall. This and the non-availability of the complete survey suggests that caution should be exercised when interpreting the results for 1968-69.

Poverty and landlessness in rural Asia

Figure 8.

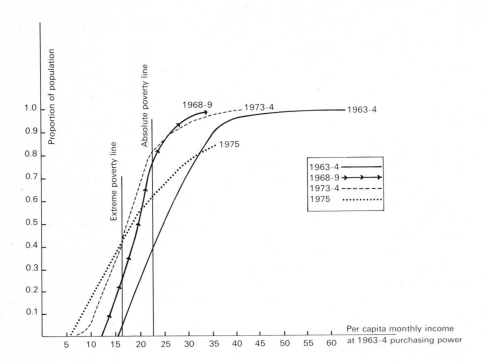

The comparison between any other pair of years reveals a number of interesting features. First, take 1968-69 and 1973-74. The proportion of the absolutely poor population increased a little while the proportion of extremely poor population increased sharply. A significant proportion of the rural population (perhaps about 15 per cent) in 1973-74 had higher real incomes than the corresponding proportion at the top in 1968-69. The lower down along the income scale the greater is the vertical distance between the curves representing the distribution for the two years.

Next, let us consider the distribution for 1975. One important thing to note is that the incidence of absolute poverty is significantly below that in the preceding year but the incidence of extreme poverty is only marginally lower. Whether the lower incidence of poverty in 1975 as compared to that in 1973-74 is explained by a short-term improvement or seasonality of quarterly data for 1975 or a combination of both is not possible to ascertain on the basis of the available information. It should, however, be noted that in 1975 over 40 per cent of the population at the bottom end of the income scale had lower real income than the corresponding proportion in 1973-74.

The comparison between the distribution for 1975 and that for the other years has to be heavily qualified due to the seasonality of the former. And yet a few features of such comparison deserve emphasis. Nearly 20 per cent of the people at the top of the income scale had higher real income than the corresponding proportion during any other period, while approximately 40 per cent of the people at the bottom of the scale had lower real income than the corresponding proportion during any other period under review.

REAL WAGES

Other evidence on trends in living standards of the rural poor is now examined to see whether it is consistent with the previous findings. The variable that merits close examination is the real wage of agricultural labourers. A typical agricultural labourer belongs to the category of rural poor according to the criteria used here. In 1963-64 the monthly per capita income of an average agricultural labourer's household entirely dependent on wage income was Tk. 14.55. This estimate is based on the following assumptions: 259 days of employment per year, 1.2 earners per household, and 4.45 persons per household.[1] Such a family would be classified as among the extreme poor. If it also had significant non-wage income (e.g. from the ownership of land) then it would fall into the category of the absolute poor. Only those agricultural labourers' families (with the same earner/dependant ratio as above) which derived at least 40 per cent of their income from non-wage sources would be above the absolute poverty line.

Table 49 contains information about the numbers who were completely or very significantly dependent on wages as their source of income during the mid-1960s. As is shown later, the number of wage earners has almost certainly increased over the years. But even in the mid-1960s nearly a sixth of the agriculturally active population depended entirely on wages as a source of income and about a quarter of the rural population depended on wages as their major source of income. Thus movements in real wages were the main determinant of movements in real income of a fairly high proportion of the agricultural households.

Agricultural wages, compiled by the Directorate of Agriculture, are reported on a monthly basis for each of the districts of Bangladesh. The district averages are in turn based on the information collected in subdivisional centres within the districts. The information presumably refers to the cash value of wages. Whether this means that the information reflects only those cases in which payment is entirely in cash or whether payments in kind

---

[1] These assumptions are taken from the following sources: days of employment from S. R. Bose: "Trend of Real Income of the Rural Poor in East Pakistan", in *Pakistan Development Review* (Autumn 1968), pp. 452-488; earners per household from the second lowest income group in the QSCEC and the household size from the *Master Survey of Agriculture*, op. cit., Seventh Round, Phase-I.

Table 49.   Different categories of wage earners as a percentage of all cultivators

Category	Percentage of cultivators in:	
	1963-64	1964-65
Landless wage earners	11.5	10.5
Landless wage-earners-cum-sharecroppers	1.0	1.3
Cultivating domestic servants	3.3	3.6
Wage earners owning some land	6.1	6.2
Wage-earners-cum-sharecroppers owning some land	2.9	3.8
Total of five categories	24.8	25.4

Source: *Master Survey of Agriculture*, op. cit., Sixth Round.

have been converted into cash equivalents is not known. But this seems to be a minor difficulty in that both the labourers and the employers are likely to behave so as to ensure that the value of the wage payment is the same whether or not it is entirely in the form of cash. The information on wage rates is available, with only a few exceptions, for all years since 1949.

There are several limitations of the wage rates series used. Perhaps the most serious is due to its being an unweighted average of wages in various centres and for various months of a year. Ideally weighted averages should be used, each month's average being compiled by weighting the rates in individual centres by employment in those centres and the annual average compiled by weighting the monthly averages by monthly employment.

The lack of weighting would seriously affect measurements of change if wage rates in individual centres moved very differently and if the share of various regions in employment changed sharply. From available statistics it is possible to ascertain that wage rates in individual centres moved roughly in line with one another. While it is not known to what extent the shares of the various districts and subdivisions in agricultural employment changed, it is likely that only modest shifts took place over time, apart from occasional sharp, short-term fluctuations.

Table 50 contains the data on money wage rates and real wage rates for the period between 1949 and the first half of 1975. Real wages, obtained by deflating money wages by the 1963-64 based cost-of-living index, represent wages at constant 1963-64 purchasing power. Figure 9 illustrates the movement of real wages.

While it is impossible to find any trend over the entire period a few phases can be distinctly identified: *(a)* during the late 1940s and early 1950s real wages declined sharply; *(b)* for about a decade thereafter there was a steady rise; *(c)* after 1964 real wages started to decline again. Since 1964, despite some short-term fluctuations, there has been a pronounced downward trend. In the early 1970s the rate of decline accelerated sharply and real

Table 50.   Agricultural wages in Bangladesh
             (Taka per person per day)

Year	Money wage (taka) (1)	Index of cost of living (1963-64 = 100) (2)	Real wage [(1) ÷ (2)] × 100 (3)
1949	1.92	81.4	2.36
1950	1.62	76.2	2.13
1951	1.56	78.2	2.00
1952	1.52	77.2	1.97
1953	1.38	80.6	1.71
1954	n.a.	75.4	n.a.
1955	1.32	68.6	1.92
1956	n.a.	80.7	n.a.
1957	1.70	85.4	1.99
1958	1.85	96.1	1.93
1959	1.85	95.5	1.94
1960	1.95	94.9	2.06
1961	2.18	95.9	2.27
1962	2.25	102.0	2.21
1963	2.41	102.2	2.36
1964	2.65	99.7	2.66
1965	2.34	105.4	2.22
1966	2.40	126.1	1.90
1967	2.60	135.3	1.92
1968	2.75	134.6	2.04
1969	3.12	140.3	2.22
1970	2.98	132.8	2.24
1971	3.15	n.a.	n.a.
1972	3.93	246.4	1.60
1973	5.59	351.5	1.59
1974	8.04	565.2	1.42
1975 (first half)	9.43	735.6	1.28

Note: n.a. = not available.   Sources have been described in the text.

wages reached a lower level in the first half of 1975 than in any period during the preceding two decades.

The above findings are consistent with the earlier studies of real wages of agricultural labour carried out by Bose for the period up to 1966.[1] Indeed wage data used here are the same as those of Bose, but the cost-of-living indices are different. The method used to obtain the weights of our index was described above. Bose's weights were obtained from a local rural consumption survey in Rajshahi. The main difference between the two sets is that rice has a much greater weight in Bose's index than in that used here. Had his

---

[1] Bose: "Trend of Real Income of the Rural Poor in East Pakistan", op. cit.

Figure 9.   Real wages in rural Bangladesh

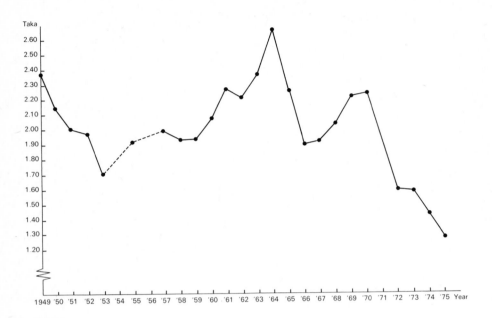

weights been used the rise in the cost-of-living index would have been much greater in recent years and the fall in real wages consequently sharper.[1]

The movement in real wages is also consistent with the findings of a growing incidence of poverty. The average of real wages in 1968 and 1969 was 15 per cent below the average in 1963 and 1964. This must be the major explanation for the dramatic increase in the numbers of the extreme poor in the later years.

Although a complete and detailed analysis of the movement of real wages over time has deliberately been omitted from this chapter, some understanding of the cyclical movement of wages is necessary. The phenomenon that most requires an explanation is the steady rise in real wages in the decade after 1953. This rise can best be seen as little more than a recovery to the level of the late 1940s and early 1950s. Real wages declined sharply from 1949 to 1953 in part as a consequence of the sharp decline in the terms of

---

[1] Unfortunately, this expectation is not consistent with the updated version of Bose's study; see S. R. Bose: "Agricultural Wage Rates in Bangladesh" in A. Mitra (ed.): *Economic theory and planning* (1974). Although the general trend of real wages in more recent years reported in that version is similar to estimates given here, he finds that real wages declined by less in the early 1970s than is indicated here. The difference is due to a smaller rise in his cost-of-living index in the early 1970s. The writer of the present paper is unable to account for the inconsistency between his own expectation and the findings of Bose's updated study.

trade for agriculture brought about by the ending of the commodity boom of the Korean war. The rise in the decade after 1953 represented essentially a process of returning to the level of the late 1940s. In fact, in no year except 1964 were real wages higher than in 1949. Circumstances during the decade after 1953 were conducive to a recovery of real wages to previous levels. The terms of trade for agriculture improved[1] although agriculture still continued to be subjected to severe discrimination; industrial employment grew quite fast and absorbed some labour from rural areas.

The decline after 1964 has been dramatic. While the sharp fall in the early 1970s must be due in part to the absolute decline in agricultural output in recent years, a significant downward trend would have been present in any case given the worsening demographic conditions in relation to the expansion of non-agricultural employment and the absence of compensating redistributive policies. As figure 9 indicates, real incomes of the top 20 per cent of the rural population were higher in early 1975 than in the base year. Thus substantial adverse changes in the distribution of income have been associated with declining real wages. Evidently, the effects of lower output were not distributed equally among all income groups: a minority improved their standard of living while the great majority became even further impoverished.

THE PROCESS OF INCREASING IMPOVERISHMENT

Several points have now been established.

(1) The living standards of the vast majority of the rural population in Bangladesh declined in absolute terms during recent decades. The real wages of agricultural labourers fell. These phenomena have been particularly pronounced in recent years. Comparing the decline in recent years with the already dreadful poverty in the benchmark year, it is clear that the vast majority of the rural population today must be suffering from severe undernutrition and starvation in various degrees. It seems highly likely that mortality rates have increased and that the expectation of life has declined from the already unfavourable levels mentioned earlier.[2]

(2) Per capita rural income and output fell in recent decades, especially during the last five years.[3] Average income thus moved in the same direction as the incomes of the vast majority. It is, however, not true that the incomes

---

[1] For an account of the movement in sectoral terms of trade, see S. R. Lewis and S. M. Hussain: *Relative price changes and industrialisation* (Pakistan Institute of Development Economics, 1967).

[2] No proof of this is available. It is noteworthy, however, that the population aggregates estimated by the 1974 census are significantly below the level suggested by the growth rates estimated in the 1960s even after taking into account underenumeration indicated by a follow-up survey and the unusual loss of lives in the 1970 cyclone and the 1971 war. This cannot be explained by a decline in the birth rate. Indeed the birth rate probably rose if for no other reason than the breakdown of family planning programmes after 1969.

[3] For statistics on output see the relevant issues of the monthly *Economic Indicators of Bangladesh* published by the Bangladesh Bureau of Statistics.

Table 51.   Share of agriculture and related activities in total employment

Year	Agricultural labour as % of total labour force (12 years of age and over) (1)	Farmers, fishermen, hunters and loggers as a percentage of:	
		Total labour force (2)	Rural labour force (3)
1951	83	—	—
1961	85	—	—
1963-64	—	76	80
1966-67	—	78	81
1967-68	—	80	83

Sources: col. (1): population censuses; cols. (2) and (3): labour force surveys of the Pakistan Central Statistical Office.

of all groups fell. A very significant proportion of the households at the top of the scale obtained increases in real incomes. This was quite pronounced in recent years, i.e. precisely in the years when the real incomes of the poor declined precipitously.

The remainder of the chapter is devoted to trying to determine who moved down the income scale and how, and what were the forces operating in the reverse direction, raising the incomes of those at the top of the scale.

The first important fact to note is that the growth in non-agricultural employment was not fast enough to absorb the increase in the labour force. Agriculture, being the residual source of employment, thus accumulated labour at a higher rate than the expansion in demand for labour consequent upon changes in output. The sluggish growth in non-agricultural employment was due partly to the failure of the non-agricultural activities to expand fast and partly to the use of inappropriate technology in these activities.[1] Although it is impossible to quantify long-term trends, it is well known that even within the rural areas the volume of traditional non-agricultural activities (e.g. the handloom and other cottage industries' products) declined in absolute terms. The share of the manufacturing sector (both modern and traditional) in total employment declined from 5.81 per cent in the benchmark year to 5.39 per cent in 1967-68, the most recent year for which a labour force survey is available on a comparable basis.[2] A recent manpower survey estimated the share of "industry" in total *employed manpower* to be only 3.69 per cent in August 1974.[3] Despite differences in definition and methodology this almost certainly indicates a further drop from the levels of earlier years.

---

[1] See A. R. Khan: *Capital-labour ratios and labour requirements in Pakistan* (Karachi, Pakistan Institute of Development Economics, 1970).

[2] Pakistan Central Statistical Office: *Twenty-five years of Pakistan in statistics* (Karachi, 1972).

[3] Bangladesh Bureau of Statistics: *Manpower in Bangladesh* (provisional figures for July-December 1974), (Dacca, Apr. 1975; mimeographed).

Table 52.   Landlessness in rural Bangladesh

Year	Landless labourers as a percentage of total cultivators (1)	Number of landless labourers in millions (2)
1951	14.3	1.51
1961	17.5	2.47
1963-64	17.8	2.71
1964-65	17.5	2.75
1967-68	19.8	3.40

As a consequence, the share of agriculture in total employment increased steadily. Table 51 contains some of the available information. The census definition of the agricultural labour force (including plantation workers, animal husbandry workers, etc.) is somewhat wider than the definition employed by the labour force surveys. The figures in column (1) are, therefore, not comparable with those in column (3). It is, however, clear from the table that the share of agriculture in both total employment and employment in rural areas has been increasing. The labour supply in agriculture has, therefore, been increasing faster than the population (the participation rate being relatively stable). According to all available evidence the demand for labour increased at a slower rate than output, which itself increased at a rate lower than that of the population. Thus the gap between the supply and demand for labour in agriculture has been widening.

The widening gap led to the decline in real wages already analysed. The absence of workers' organisations in agriculture helped this process of adjustment. The extent of unemployment and underemployment probably increased too during the period, resulting in fewer days of employment per year.[1] Thus real earnings of agricultural labourers declined even more than is indicated by the fall in daily real wages.

The main changes that resulted in an increase in the number of the poor in rural Bangladesh were the following. First, the number of landless labourers increased both absolutely and as a proportion of the agricultural population. This process of increased proletarianisation was brought about by the conversion of families owning small amounts of land into households of landless workers. Second, the distribution of land among the remaining landowners became less equal. An increasing proportion of landowners joined the category of small or "below subsistence" cultivators.

---

[1] For Bangladesh no direct quantitative measurement is available of this phenomenon. For the 1960s, when Bangladesh was part of Pakistan, some information is available for Pakistan as a whole to show that the intensity of employment per agricultural worker declined. Thus in 1967-68 about 37 per cent of the agricultural workers had on the average less than 40 hours of work per week as compared to 25 per cent in 1963-64. Since the balance between supply and demand totals in West Pakistan agriculture over the period under review was far more favourable than in Bangladesh (then East Pakistan) these figures largely reflect the worsening situation in the latter. The relevant data are reported in *Twenty-five years of Pakistan in statistics*, op. cit.

It is very difficult to construct a time series of the number of landless labourers and the figures in table 52 must be treated as approximate. Unfortunately, the definitions changed from one survey to another. The decennial censuses of 1951 and 1961 enumerated the landless agricultural labourers as a distinct category. But the various rounds of the Master Survey of Agriculture used different and usually more detailed categories. The estimates in table 52 have been built up from these categories as carefully as possible in the absence of a detailed explanation of some of the important terms. Moreover, the methodology employed was designed to ensure that, if anything, the estimates for the later years understate the extent of landlessness in rural Bangladesh.[1]

The rise in landlessness cannot be explained by demographic factors alone. As a proportion of cultivators the landless labourers increased substantially. The increase in the absolute number of landless labourers was staggering; in one-and-a-half decades since 1951 they increased by two-and-a-quarter times, an annual compound rate of growth of 5¼ per cent.

Table 53 contains some information on the distribution of land holdings in 1960 and in 1967-68, the most recent year for which information is available. Unfortunately, the data refer to the size distribution of operational holdings, not of ownership units. Thus in this table farm size refers to the amount of land owned plus the net amount of land obtained under sharecropping and other forms of rental arrangements. It is a great pity that the important global surveys made little effort to obtain information on the distribution of land ownership. A number of smaller surveys collected such information[2] and their experience indicates that it is not difficult to collect reasonably accurate data on this subject.

From these smaller surveys it can be ascertained that the ownership distribution is much more unequal than the distribution of operational holdings.[3] The very small farms have smaller ownership units than operational units whereas for the bigger farmers the operational units are smaller than the ownership units. This indicates that the larger farmers rent some of their land to smaller farmers. The ratio of ownership units to operational units increases with size.

---

[1] For a description of the methodology, see A. R. Khan: *Poverty and inequality in rural Bangladesh*, op. cit.

[2] See, for example, Registrar of Co-operative Societies: *Agricultural credit in East Pakistan, January 1966* (Dacca, 1967), and Agro-economic Research, Ministry of Agriculture, Bangladesh: *Survey of sale of land and other assets* (1975, unpublished tables).

[3] Using the grouped data from the recent survey on land sales (which is the only source that provides all relevant information) the following relation was found between the ratio of ownership to operating unit (Y) and the size of the operating unit (X): $Y = 0.905 + 0.477 \log X$. Applying this to the 1967-68 data (which is perhaps not quite an admissible procedure in deriving the ownership pattern in that year, since the land sales data refer to the early 1970s) and scaling down the resulting estimates uniformly to ensure consistency with aggregate acreage, it was found that the "ownership distribution" thus estimated was far more unequal than the distribution of holdings shown in table 53. For example, the farmers with less than 1 acre of land owned 33 per cent less land than they farmed while farmers with over 25 acres owned 38 per cent more land than they farmed.

Table 53.   Size distribution of land holdings

Size groups in acres	1960 agricultural census		1967-68 Master Survey of Agriculture	
	Percentage of holdings	Percentage of land	Percentage of holdings	Percentage of land
Less than 0.5	13.1	0.9	12.3	1.2
0.5 to 1.0	11.2	2.3	12.7	3.1
1.0 to 2.5	27.3	13.0	31.6	17.1
2.5 to 5.0	26.3	26.4	26.3	30.0
5.0 to 7.5	11.4	19.3	9.2	17.8
7.5 to 12.5	7.2	19.1	5.2	15.5
12.5 to 25.0	3.1	14.1	2.2	11.0
25.0 and above	0.4	4.8	0.5	4.5

It would, therefore, be inappropriate to formulate judgements on changes in the distribution of land *ownership* from the information in table 53. It could be argued that the operational holdings determine access to productive resources and hence their distribution is the relevant consideration for an analysis of income distribution. But this argument would be valid only on the assumption of unchanged shares of owned and rented land in the total for each size group. An improvement in the distribution of holdings despite a worsening of the distribution of ownership units is possible if the smaller farmers are able to rent larger amounts of land from the bigger farmers on a sharecropping or other basis. Such a change, however, would not result in an improvement in the distribution of income or output for the simple reason that a very high proportion of the output of the rented land would accrue to the owners.

It is impossible to ascertain what actually happened in Bangladesh with respect to the distribution of rented land. The total acreage cultivated by the tenant and tenant-cum-owner farmers declined slightly from 46 per cent of the total in 1960 to 42 per cent in 1967-68 (according to the Master Survey of Agriculture) but it is not known whether this was due to a decline in the acreage owned by these categories of farmers or to a reduction in the amount of renting. The 1961 census showed that 29 per cent of the agricultural holdings were partly or fully rented.[1] The proportion rose in 1967-68 to 34 per cent, although no information is available on the average amount rented by the farmers.

It is, however, important to note that even if it is assumed that the ownership distribution moved in the same direction and to the same extent as the distribution of holdings, this does not imply that there was an improvement in the distribution of land ownership. Taking somewhat gener-

---

[1] This estimate was obtained indirectly by first estimating the number of holdings (by excluding landless labourers and unpaid family help from the total number of cultivators) and then by using this estimate to divide the number of all those farmers who rented land.

ously and arbitrarily the 2.5 acre limit as the line below which farms are considered to be "small", there was a significant increase in the proportion of small farmers between 1960 and 1967-68. There was also an increase in the proportion of land held by them; but, allowing for the absolute increase in their numbers, the average size of their farms declined. On the other hand, the decline in the number and average size of farms at the other end of the spectrum was less than what one would expect from demographic factors alone.

While no information is available about the pattern of land ownership after 1967-68, it is almost certain that it worsened significantly, perhaps dramatically. This conclusion is based on both *a priori* reasoning and on information obtained about the pattern of land sales from the recent survey.

In recent years per capita agricultural production remained below the levels of the late 1960s. The terms of trade for agriculture improved, largely as a result of the sharp relative rise in the price of food. Real wages of agricultural labourers, as has been seen, declined sharply. So too did the income of the "deficit farmers", i.e. of those whose farms were too small to ensure self-sufficiency in food consumption. This is because that portion of the income of "deficit farmers" which was obtained from wage employment declined in real terms partly because the real wage rate fell and partly because the number of days employed also probably fell.

The improvement in the sectoral terms of trade for agriculture was due mainly to a sharp rise in the relative price of rice. Within agriculture the rise in the price of rice was much higher than that of jute, the competing cash crop. This had important effects on the level of employment and wages. Labour input per acre is much higher for jute than for rice.[1] There was a sharp shift in acreage away from jute and in favour of rice which resulted in a lower aggregate demand for labour. For the year as a whole jute acreage is small (about 7 per cent of the total) but in the mid-monsoon *(aus)* season it is nearly a quarter of the total. Thus, while the over-all demand for labour for the year as a whole may have declined only modestly, the effect on employment and wages in the mid-monsoon season must have been very significant.

In order to survive most of the small farmers (perhaps up to 50 per cent of the total if 2 acres is accepted as the limit for self-sufficiency) must have been forced to borrow and to sell assets. Since most of them already were heavily indebted, distress sales of assets (including land) must have occurred very frequently.

Some of these trends have been detected by the recent land sales survey organised by the Agro-economic Research section of the Ministry of Agriculture. Table 54 summarises some of the information on land sales obtained through sample surveys in 14 districts, each supplying one sample area. The

---

[1] It has been claimed that labour input into jute is 92 per cent higher than that in traditional rice. See Planning Commission, Government of Bangladesh: *The First Five-Year Plan* (1973), p. 186.

Table 54. Sale of land by various size groups

Holding size group in ascending order	Average amount of land owned (acres)	Percentage of owned land sold in 1969-70	Percentage of owned land sold in 1972-73
1	0.53	53	60
2	1.66	16	18
3	3.48	14	16
4	7.46	7	8
5	19.58	4	4

table dramatically illustrates the process of increasing landlessness in rural Bangladesh. Those who own less than 1 acre (accounting for about a quarter of the farmers) sold well over half of their remaining land in each year. The bigger farmers, in contrast, sold progressively less. The small proportion of land sold by the farmers with the largest farms probably represents little more than an attempt to rationalise and consolidate their holdings.

Unfortunately, the survey does not provide comparable information on purchases of land. Had it done so, the pattern of change in land distribution could have been shown even more clearly. There is little doubt, however, that the pattern of land purchase reinforced the tendency to greater landlessness and poverty.

Appendix

Table 55. Normative minimum dietary patterns
(lb. per person per day)

Food	Sukhatme based [1]	FAO based [1]
Rice	0.807	0.791
Wheat	0.081	0.079
Pulses	0.229	0.165
Gur and sugar	0.110	0.077
Milk	0.443	0.216
Meat	0.015	0.079
Fish and eggs	0.041	0.059
Fruits, vegetables and roots	0.403	0.848
Oil and fat	0.039	0.035
Cost in takas per day [2]	0.79	0.78

[1] The Sukhatme and FAO diets have been regrouped and their cereal category divided into rice and wheat to reflect consumption patterns in Bangladesh. [2] As far as possible the prices in rural centres have been used.

Table 56.   Cost-of-living indices for low-, middle- and high-income groups
(Base: fiscal year 1963-64=100)

Year	Low income	Middle income	High income
1949	81.4	80.8	80.1
1950	76.2	75.3	74.4
1951	78.2	76.3	74.9
1952	77.2	74.0	71.7
1953	80.6	77.3	75.4
1954	75.4	73.1	72.1
1955	68.6	65.4	65.2
1956	80.7	75.8	73.6
1957	85.4	82.5	81.7
1958[1]	96.1	92.4	88.6
1959[1]	95.5	92.3	88.9
1960[1]	94.9	92.8	90.5
1961[1]	95.9	94.6	93.0
1962	102.0	101.0	98.9
1963	102.2	101.5	99.6
1964	99.7	101.3	103.1
1965	105.4	104.9	102.4
1966	126.1	122.5	115.7
1967	135.3	130.4	122.9
1968	134.6	132.0	125.7
1968-69[2]	137.9	136.4	130.6
1969	140.3	138.8	133.4
1970	132.8	132.5	127.4
1972	246.4	233.5	221.5
1973	351.5	339.0	321.1
1974	565.2	532.2	488.1
1975[3]	735.6	687.8	608.2

[1] Averages of the adjacent fiscal years. For these years price information was not readily available on a calendar year basis.
[2] Fiscal year (July to June).   [3] January-June.

RURAL POVERTY IN SRI LANKA, 1963-73

8

E. L. H. Lee

In this chapter an attempt is made to establish trends in the level of rural incomes in Sri Lanka, with particular emphasis on the incomes of the poorest 20 per cent of the rural population, between 1963 and 1973. The principal sources of data are the Central Bank of Sri Lanka's *Surveys of Ceylon's consumer finances* for 1963 and 1973. Although a similar survey is available for 1953, it was not possible to extend the analysis to this earlier date. In the 1953 survey figures are available for the rural and urban areas separately but, unlike the two later surveys, the estate sector is not distinguished from paddy cultivation. Since it is in the estate sector where the principal concentration of rural poverty is thought to occur and since the estate sector is institutionally distinct from the rest of the rural economy,[1] it was decided to focus on the period in which it was possible to make this crucial breakdown between the estate sector and the rest of the rural economy.[2]

CHANGES IN THE LEVEL AND DISTRIBUTION OF INCOMES, 1963-73

The most striking feature of the change in income distribution, according to the survey data for 1963 and 1973, is the sharp reduction in the degree of inequality between these two years. The Gini coefficient for all incomes fell from 0.49 in 1963 to 0.40 in 1973. This reduction in inequality occurred in both the rural and urban sectors. If the estate sector is examined separately, however, it is apparent that it constituted a striking exception in that there was a sharp increase in inequality in that sector. In both, the decrease in

---

[1] The labour force of the estate sector is made up predominantly of Indian Tamils who are ethnically distinct, largely without voting rights and locked into a captive labour market. Indian Tamils comprised 9.5 per cent of the total population of Sri Lanka in 1970 and 86.3 per cent of them lived in the estate sector where they comprised 78.4 per cent of the population.

[2] The term "rural sector" in this chapter thus refers to the rural economy outside the estate sector. In practice, this essentially means the paddy sector.

Table 57.   Mean income per income receiver by quintiles, 1963 and 1973
(Sri Lanka rupees per month)

Sectors and quintiles	1963	1973	1973 at 1963 prices	Col. (3) ÷ Col. (1)
	(1)	(2)	(3)	(4)
Rural sector				
0-20	22.9	59.6	38.4	1.68
20-40	55.6	129.3	83.2	1.50
40-60	90.0	189.0	121.7	1.35
60-80	140.2	260.8	167.9	1.20
80-100	326.3	476.2	306.6	0.94
Whole sector	127	223	143.6	1.13
Estate sector				
0-20	27.6	44.7	28.8	1.04
20-40	45.9	69.8	44.9	0.98
40-60	56.3	88.7	57.1	1.01
60-80	69.6	122.9	79.1	1.14
80-100	123.2	269.0	173.2	1.41
Whole sector	64.5	119.0	76.6	1.19
Urban sector				
0-20	41.9	85.4	55.0	1.31
20-40	93.8	170.2	109.6	1.17
40-60	151.1	255.7	164.7	1.09
60-80	241.7	355.4	228.9	0.95
80-100	746.4	718.3	462.6	0.62
Whole sector	255	317	204.1	0.80

Notes: (1) An income receiver is defined as a "person who has received an income during the six months immediately prior to the survey". (2) Column 3 was derived by deflating column 2 with the Colombo cost-of-living index (1963 = 100). (3) The pattern of change remains the same as that shown above, when the income unit used is "spending unit" instead of "income receiver". A "spending unit" is defined "to consist of one or more persons who are members of the same household, and share major items of expenditure".

Source: Central Bank of Ceylon: *Survey of Ceylon's consumer finances*, 1963 and 1973 (Colombo).

relative inequality appears to have been brought about by a highly progress-ive change in the income levels of rich and poor. The increase in mean income was highest for the bottom quintile of income receivers and the margin of increase diminished steadily for successively higher quintiles. In the rural areas the mean income of the top quintile declined while in the urban areas that of the top 40 per cent fell (see table 57).

Given this pattern of change in the intra-sectoral income distribution, it is not surprising that there was also a narrowing of the rural-urban income differential and the degree of regional inequality. As can be seen in table 58, the ratio of mean income in urban areas to that in rural areas declined from 2:1 in 1963 to 1.4:1 in 1973. There was also a similar narrowing of income differentials between the urban and the estate sector, but the ratio of rural sector to estate sector incomes declined only very slightly.

Table 58.   Inter-sectoral income differentials, 1963 and 1973

Sector	Average two-monthly income per income receiver (rupees at current prices)	
	1963	1973
(1) Rural	254	446
(2) Urban	510	633
(3) Estate	129	237
(4) [(2) ÷ (1)]	2.01	1.42
(5) [(2) ÷ (3)]	3.95	2.66
(6) [(1) ÷ (3)]	1.97	1.87

Source: Central Bank of Ceylon: *Survey of Ceylon's consumer finances*, op. cit.

The survey data also permit separation into four zones which broadly correspond to ecological regions. Taking these zones as a proxy for regions, it is found that inter-regional inequality has also narrowed slightly. The range in the mean incomes of the richest and poorest regions declined from 1.62 in 1963 to 1.48 in 1973 while the Kuznets index of inter-regional inequality also declined from 21.5 to 19.1 between these two years.

An important exception to this general picture of narrowing inequalities is revealed when the data are broken down by race (see table 60). The mean incomes of the Singhalese, the majority of the population, increased significantly while those of other racial groups, with the minor exception of Malays, either stagnated or declined. This trend emerges even more clearly when the comparison is made in terms of the per capita income of each racial group. The per capita income of Kandyan and low country Singhalese increased by 24 and 18 per cent respectively while that of Ceylon Tamils and Indian Tamils fell by 28 and 1 per cent respectively. In the case of the Ceylon Tamils, the fall in their mean incomes probably represents a movement toward greater equity, since their average income was slightly higher than that of the Kandyan Singhalese and one-third higher than that of the low country Singhalese in 1953. The developments since then have resulted in a reversal in the income ranking of Ceylon Tamils and low country Singhalese and also have considerably reduced the income disparity between Ceylon Tamils and Kandyan Singhalese. The case of Indian Tamils is, however, entirely different. They were the poorest group in 1963 and had an average income per income receiver half that of the low country Singhalese. The fall in their per capita incomes, albeit slight, is inequitable and this inequity is even more serious given the substantial income gains experienced by the Singhalese majority.

CHANGES IN THE LEVEL OF CONSUMPTION AND REAL WAGES

The income data analysed in the preceding section suggest that the pattern of economic change in Sri Lanka between 1963 and 1973 has been

163

Table 59.   Inter-regional income differences, 1963 and 1973

Region	Average two-monthly income per income receiver (rupees at current prices)	
	1963	1973
I. Colombo, Kalutara, Galle and Matara	333	525
II. Hambantota, Moneragala, Amparai, Polonnaruwa, Arunadhapura and Puttalam	279	525
III. Jaffna, Mannar, Vavuniya,Trincomalee and Batticaloa	315	547
IV. Kandy, Matale, Nuwara Eliya, Badutta, Ratnapura, Kegalle and Kurunegala	206	357
All island	267	455
Kuznets index of inter-regional inequality	21.46	19.07

Note: The Kuznets index is a weighted sum of absolute differences between relative income in each region and unity, the weight being the share of the region in total population.

Source: Central Bank of Ceylon: *Survey of Ceylon's consumer finances*, op. cit.

impressive. The substantial reduction in income inequality occurred in the context of a growing economy; gross domestic product (GDP) in real terms increased by 4.1 per cent per annum while per capita GDP grew 1.9 per cent per annum. Such a conjunction of growth and changes in income distribution is extremely rare in a developing economy. Other studies have shown that inequality tends to widen in the initial stages of development and even that the absolute incomes of the poorest 40 per cent of households tends to fall,[1] but the direct opposite appears to have occurred in Sri Lanka.

It is very important, therefore, to examine this pattern of change closely and to identify the factors which have brought it about. A prior task, however, is to ascertain from other data the plausibility of the changes suggested by the Central Bank Survey data on incomes.

The most obvious alternative source of data is that relating to consumption. Where a reduction in income inequality of the magnitude described has occurred, data on changes in consumption levels should show a parallel change. Apart from serving as a cross-check on income data, it could be claimed that under some circumstances consumption data might be a more reliable indicator of changes in economic welfare than income data. It has been argued that consumption is less subject to transitory influences than is income (*vide* the Permanent Income Hypothesis), and hence data on consumption are more reliable. Moreover, if data on consumption were available in terms of quantities consumed, they would have the further advantage of circumventing some of the problems of estimating a change in real income, especially in situations where inflation has been significant. In Sri

---

[1] See for example I. Adelman and C. T. Morris: *Economic growth and social equity in developing countries* (Stanford, California, Stanford University Press, 1973) and other chapters in this volume.

Table 60.   Inter-racial income differentials, 1963 and 1973

Racial group	Average real income per income receiver (rupees per 2 months at 1963 prices)		
	1963 (1)	1973 (2)	Ratio of cols. (2):(1)
Kandyan Singhalese	219	277	1.27
Low country Singhalese	292	342	1.17
Ceylon Tamils	327	309	0.94
Indian Tamils	148	148	1.00
Moors and Malays	414	441	1.065
Others	819	646	0.788
	Per capita income (rupees per 2 months at 1963 prices)		
	1963 (1)	1973 (2)	Ratio of cols. (2):(1)
Kandyan Singhalese	53.0	65.5	1.24
Low country Singhalese	71.4	84.5	1.18
Ceylon Tamils	105.9	75.8	0.72
Indian Tamils	67.2	66.3	0.987
Moors and Malays	107.2	n.a.	n.a.
Others	273.1	n.a.	n.a.

Note: The racial composition of Sri Lanka in 1963 was as follows: Kandyan Singhalese 28.8 per cent, low country Singhalese 42.2 per cent, Ceylon Tamils 11.1 per cent, Indian Tamils 10.6 per cent, Moors and Malays 6.7 per cent and others 0.6 per cent.

Source: Central Bank of Ceylon: *Survey of Ceylon's consumer finances,* op. cit.

Lanka the rate of inflation was high between 1963 and 1973,[1] and therefore the available data on changes in consumption in real as well as in value terms will be used.

It can be seen in table 61 that total consumption expenditure increased by 7 per cent between 1963 and 1973 but, unlike income, consumption became less equally distributed. The divergence between the trends suggested by the data on income and those on consumption becomes even clearer when one examines the change in average consumption expenditure per spending unit by quintiles. Indeed, the consumption of the bottom quintile decreased while that of the top quintile increased more than any other. Consistent with this pattern of change in consumption expenditures is the fact that expenditure on consumer durables, a category of expenditure associated with the rich, increased very sharply over this period. The share of total expenditure devoted to consumer durables increased from under 0.5 per cent in 1963 to 6 per cent in 1973. Those changes cannot be easily reconciled with the data in table 57 which showed that the mean income of the top quintile of income receivers in urban areas fell by 40 per cent.

These observations remain true when the data are broken down by sectors. Both total consumption expenditure and expenditure on food became more unequally distributed in all three sectors. Thus even in the rural sector,

---

[1] The Colombo price index increased by 52 per cent between 1963 and 1973.

Table 61.   Average consumption expenditure by quintiles, 1963 and 1973
(Rupees per 2 months per spending unit)

Percentage of spending units	1963 (1)	1973 (at 1963 prices) (2)	Ratio of cols. (2): (1)
0-20	191.3	163.8	0.856
20-40	248.7	276.4	1.075
40-60	334.7	337.8	1.009
60-80	430.4	440.2	1.023
80-100	717.3	829.2	1.156
Average	382.6	409.5	1.070

Note: The data on consumption were obtained by recording, for each respondent, the consumption over seven consecutive days. The shortness of this reference period is not necessarily a factor making for greater unreliability in the data; it is an empirical question whether, in a household survey, questions about consumption based on a short reference period would necessarily elicit less accurate answers. In any case, the reference period of seven days was the same in both the 1963 and 1973 surveys and thus comparisons would not be affected by this factor. Moreover, the period of enumeration was in the same quarterly period in both surveys and there were no abnormalities in consumption patterns during these months due to harvests or festivals.
Source: Central Bank of Ceylon: *Survey of Ceylon's consumer finances*, op. cit.

Table 62.   Per capita consumption of rice, all island, 1963 and 1973
(Measures of rice per 2 months)

Income class (rupees)	1963	1973
0-50	18.2	8.7
51-100	18.3	11.0
101-200	18.7	12.7
201-400	19.3	15.2
401-800	18.6	15.9
801-1600	18.0	16.9
1601-2000	19.0	17.9
2001-3000	18.9	17.6
Above 3000	13.2	18.2

Source: Central Bank of Ceylon: *Survey of Ceylon's consumer finances*, op. cit.

where one might have expected otherwise, there has been a regressive change in consumption levels.

The fact that an adverse change occurred in the pattern of consumption can be confirmed by examining data on the quantities of major food items consumed, as opposed to monetary expenditure data. The per capita consumption of rice per two months in the rural sector fell from 19.05 measures in 1963 to 16.18 measures in 1973, while in the estate sector it fell from 20.9 measures to 16.5 measures. To some extent, this was compensated by increased consumption of wheat flour, but for the country as a whole per capita expenditure on food fell by 1.4 per cent at a time when mean income, as conventionally measured, is reported to have increased by 12 per cent.[1]

---

[1] Central Bank of Ceylon: *Survey of Ceylon's consumer finances, 1973*, op. cit., table 93, p. 108.

Table 63.   Central Bank real wage index
(1952=100)

Year	Agriculture	Industry and commerce	Wage Boards trades	All central Government	Government school teachers
1963	104.2	120.3	105.9	116.5	107.9
1964	103.5	118.4	105.0	112.9	104.6
1965	103.4	118.0	105.0	112.6	104.4
1966	103.5	118.6	105.1	112.8	104.6
1967	104.9	121.0	106.4	114.4	104.0
1968	114.3	133.1	116.3	125.7	106.7
1969	106.3	123.1	108.2	120.4	101.5
1970	101.5	120.2	103.4	124.0	102.1
1971	99.8	124.2	102.3	120.8	99.5
1972	98.4	120.3	100.7	113.8	93.6
1973	101.5	120.7	102.7	108.8	87.3

Notes: "Agriculture" refers to estate agriculture only. The figures in the first three columns refer to minimum wages set by Wages Boards, while those in the last two columns refer to initial wages of government employees. There were 31 Wages Boards and they were set up to encourage collective bargaining procedures. Wage fixing is done by surveying actual wages and proposing increases to the actual wage paid. The minimum wages are thus actual minima and not statutory minima which bear no relation to market wages.

Source: Central Bank of Ceylon: *Annual Report for 1974*, tables 58 and 59.

Even more significant are the figures on the change in per capita consumption of rice by income class (see table 62). It can be seen that the fall is overwhelmingly concentrated among the lowest income classes and that the extent of the fall in consumption was very slight for those with incomes of 800 to 3,000 rupees. For those with incomes above 3,000 rupees, on the other hand, there was a substantial increase in consumption. A similar pattern occurred in the case of consumption of wheat flour but not in the case of sugar, where consumption fell sharply for all income classes. Although the figures refer to income classes unadjusted for price changes, it is clear, at least as regards rice consumption, that regardless of how the adjustment is made to arrive at real income classes there was a clear downward trend in the per capita consumption of rice.

There was thus a strong contradiction between the trends revealed by the income data and those of the data on consumption. The two types of data from the consumer finance surveys are internally inconsistent. Examination of independent data on trends in real wages casts further doubt on the picture presented by the income data.

It will be recalled from table 57 that the incomes of the bottom two quintiles of income receivers in both the rural and urban sectors showed a substantial increase between 1963 and 1973. With such a pattern of change in the income distribution one would expect that real wages would also have been increasing by similar margins over this period, especially in the urban sector where there must be a significant overlap between unskilled workers and the poorest 40 per cent of income receivers. The average earnings of an unskilled worker in the urban sector was 65 rupees per month in 1963, while the mean incomes of the bottom two quintiles of urban income receivers from the 1963 consumer finance survey were 42 and 94 rupees per month respectively. The latter source also shows that 64 per cent of urban income receivers were "employees". The data in table 63, except for the column headed "Agriculture", relate to wages in urban employment. Contrary to expectation, all employee categories experienced a fall in real wages, except for workers in commerce and industry where real wages remained constant.

REDUCTION IN INCOME INEQUALITY: A REALITY?

The facts, therefore, show a basic conflict on what actually happened to income distribution in Sri Lanka between 1963 and 1973. There is thus little justification for choosing one or the other set of data unless there is strong supporting empirical evidence or an explanation which could convincingly resolve the contradiction between the two sets of data. Nevertheless, it is frequently claimed that a favourable change in income distribution has occurred between 1963 and 1973.[1] The claims are based exclusively on the income data from the consumer finance surveys; all accept at face value the trends revealed therein, and all proceed to "explain" the favourable change by relating it to the redistributive measures undertaken by the Government.

It is clear that there is a large element of circularity in this procedure. It is invalid to start from uncertain "facts" and then to argue that, since there were policies with a redistributive purpose introduced during this period, these provide both a confirmation of the facts and an explanation of why the redistribution in income occurred. All this can only be accepted as true after evidence has been provided confirming the truth of the initial "facts". Thus the quantitative impact of the redistributive policies must be evaluated in order to determine whether they could have brought about the changes in income distribution that has been assumed to have occurred.

Unfortunately, however, this has not been how the issue has been tackled. The inadequacy of such explanations can be shown by looking at that offered by a senior civil servant.[2] This explanation has not only influenced ministerial pronouncements[3] but has also figured as one of the case studies in an recent IBRD volume on income distribution and economic growth. The Jayawardena essay claims that the improvement in the size distribution of incomes in Sri Lanka is attributable to the fact that growth rates have been highest in activities which generate income for the small-scale producer and unskilled worker and that "most paddy incomes accrue to households in the income range of the bottom 40 per cent of the population,

---

[1] See, for example, Felix R. Dias Bandaranaike: *Budget Speech 1976*; L. Jayawardena: "Case Study on Sri Lanka" in H. Chenery, et al.: *Redistribution with growth* (Oxford University Press, 1974); H. N. S. Karunatilake: "Changes in Income Distribution in Sri Lanka", in *Central Bank Staff Studies*, Apr. 1974.

[2] Jayawardena, op. cit.

[3] See Felix R. Dias Bandaranaike, op. cit., p. 18.

as does most income from subsidiary crops and small industries".[1] Such a claim, however, will not stand up to close scrutiny; it is based almost entirely on the notion that since 95 per cent of paddy holdings are below 5 acres in size, most paddy incomes accrue to the poor. This ignores the fact that the size distribution of holdings is not the same thing as the distribution of land-ownership. Of the total paddy area 25 per cent was in holdings of more than 5 acres and about 35 per cent of the total area under paddy cultivation was under some form of tenancy[2] in 1964. Thus, given the possibility of owner-ship of multiple holdings by landlords and the existence of owner-operators of large holdings, it does not follow that "most paddy incomes accrue to the poor". Moreover, the 1958 legislation regulating tenancy shares and the subsequent amendments have been ineffective. There is, therefore, no reason to assume that the gains from increased paddy output and higher prices have been distributed even proportionately to tenants.[3]

The Jayawardena study also claims that the reduction in income inequality has been partly brought about by an "increase in income from property accruing to the lower income groups". This claim is based, first, on the fact that the non-monetary income of the poor increased and, second, on the assumption that this increase in non-monetary income (mainly the value of home-grown produce and the net rental value of owner-occupied houses) is "linked to net accretions to property".[4] This explanation is also unsatisfactory; the rise in non-monetary income was due almost entirely to a sharp increase in the price of rice and other food crops and this had nothing to do with the accretion of property by the poor. The fact that the increase in non-monetary income was proportionately greater for the poor was simply a reflection of the fact that a far greater proportion of their income was in the form of home-grown produce. This cannot be interpreted as an indication that property had become more evenly distributed over this period.

The inadequacy of this particular explanation does not, of course, exhaust all possibilities along this line of enquiry. It is possible that a more thorough analysis of the redistributive policies in this period might yield results that satisfy the standards of proof that were set out at the beginning of this section. A closer look is therefore taken at the impact of the major policies which affected income distribution during this period. These are the land reform of 1972 and the import substitution policies which favoured food production in the rural sector.

The Land Reform Law of 1972 imposed a ceiling on individual owner-ship of 25 acres on paddy land and 50 acres on land under other crops. Land held by public companies was, however, exempt. The "nationalised" land was to be converted into individual holdings yielding an income of not less

---

[1] Jayawardena, op. cit., p. 275.

[2] P. Richards and E. Stoutjesdijk: *Agriculture in Ceylon until 1975* (Paris, OECD, 1970), p. 48.

[3] In similar circumstances in paddy growing areas in Malaysia the gains from large productivity increases in paddy land have gone largely to landlords.

[4] Jayawardena, op. cit., p. 275, footnote.

than 300 rupees per month, with preference being given to residents in the administrative district in which the expropriated land was located. There were, however, "no specific provisions to hand over to the tillers of the soil, whether they be tenants, lessees or labourers on vested land".[1] By 1974, 375,000 acres (or 17 per cent of the total acreage cultivated under the three principal crops of tea, rubber and paddy) had been vested with the Land Reform Commission. Of this, 215,000 acres had been alienated, with 60 per cent of it distributed to state plantations and co-operatives. The policy was to preserve existing estates in export crop production and to transform them into state or co-operative ownership. The remaining 90,000 acres were turned over to individual farmers on the basis of payments in instalments. The alienated units were 2 acres for irrigated paddy land, and 1½ to 2 acres for other crops.

It can be seen from the above figures that the land reform is unlikely to have a major impact on rural incomes. This is especially true in the case of paddy, the predominant crop in peasant agriculture, where only 25,000 acres or 2.3 per cent of the "asswedumised"[2] paddy area is expected to be turned over to the Land Commission. Thus the reform is "likely to be a corrective of tenancy conditions on only about 5 per cent of tenanted paddy land".[3] This limited impact springs directly from the fact that the ceiling of 25 acres on paddy land was very high in relation to the existing size distribution of holdings of paddy land.

While, therefore, the land reform could have had some effect in raising the incomes of the poorest groups in the rural sector, it could not by itself have brought about the reported dramatic change in the intra-rural distribution of income. Indirectly, however, it could have helped to exaggerate the true extent of the redistribution of incomes in rural areas. The uncertainty that undoubtedly was created by the promulgation of the 1972 Act would have created an incentive for landowners to understate their incomes when enumerated in official household income surveys. The introduction of an income ceiling of 2,000 rupees in 1972, noted below, would also have reinforced this incentive to understate incomes. There is, however, no way in which this suspicion that incomes were understated can be verified.

Another possible explanation is that, independently of the land reform, there has been a redistribution of land towards the smallest farmers such as to involve a reduction of inequality in the size distribution of paddy holdings. The available evidence, however, does not support this view. The data in table 64 in fact suggest that the opposite has occurred: the percentage of paddy holdings of less than 1 acre in size increased from 43 to 65 between 1962 and 1970. Using an alternative measure, it is found that the Gini

---

[1] Nirmal Sanderatne: "Agricultural Productivity Consideration of Land Reform Law of 1972", in *Cental Bank Staff Studies*, op. cit., Apr. 1974.

[2] "Asswedumised" paddy area refers to paddy land that has been bunded and ridged, preparatory to cultivation. It is equivalent, in practice, to the net area under paddy cultivation.

[3] Sanderatne, op. cit., p. 71.

Table 64.   Size distribution of paddy holdings, 1962 and 1970

Size group (acres)	1962			1970		
	Percentage of:		Average size (acres)	Percentage of:		Average size (acres)
	Holdings	Area		Holdings	Area	
0-1	43	17	0.79	65.0	21.0	0.49
1-5	51	59	2.3	31.8	54.4	2.60
5-10	5	16	4.2	2.7	15.2	8.61
More than 10	1	8	15.9	0.5	9.4	27.2

Note: "Holdings" refer to operating units. Whereas in 1962 there were 570,000 such holdings, with an average size of 1.99 acres, covering a total area of 1,135,000 acres, by 1970 there were 863,200 holdings, with an average size of 1.52 acres, covering a total area of 1,272,900 acres.

Sources: P. Richards and E. Stoutjesdijk, op. cit., table 21, p. 47; IBRD, South Asian Department: *Recent economic developments and current prospects for Sri Lanka* (1974), table 7.7 of Statistical Appendix.

coefficient of the size distribution of holdings increased from 0.35 in 1962 to 0.41 in 1970.

Such a trend is consistent with what one would expect given the relationship between population growth and the increase in cultivated acreage in Sri Lanka. The rural population increased by about 20 per cent while the area under paddy cultivation increased by only 12 per cent. Even more striking is the increase in the number of paddy holdings over the same period by 42 per cent and a decline in the average size of a holding from 2 acres to 1.5 acres. It might be argued that these figures refer to the situation before the land reform of 1972 and that the figures for 1973, had they been available, would have shown a different situation. The contents of table 64 will be sufficient to dispel such a belief. The maximum impact of the land reform, as mentioned, would be confined to a redistribution of 25,000 acres or 2.3 per cent of the total area under paddy cultivation. Even if all this land were to be distributed to paddy farmers with holdings smaller than 1 acre, it would only raise the share of the total paddy acreage farmed by this group from 21 to 23.3 per cent and hence make no significant difference to the size distribution of holdings.

Similarly, there is little basis for believing that the expansion of dry zone colonisation schemes has had any significant impact in improving the size distribution of paddy holdings. Between 1962 and 1970 the area under paddy cultivation increased by 138,000 acres (or 12 per cent). Assuming that the entire increase was due to the expansion of land colonisation schemes, this would imply, given the fact that land on colonisation schemes was parcelled out in 3-acre units, that 46,000 new holdings were created. This accounts for only 17 per cent of the increase in the number of holdings over the same period, and thus the creation of most of the new holdings must have been due to fragmentation of existing land in response to demographic pressure.

The other possible source of increase in the incomes of the poorest rural groups is the increase in the output and price of minor food crops such as potatoes, onions and chillies under the programme of import substitution. Given the small initial production of these items, however, the impact on rural incomes necessarily was quite limited. Between 1963 and 1970 the increase in the value of output of potatoes, onions and chillies amounted to only 2.7 per cent of total rural income in 1973, as estimated by the consumer finance survey. Moreover, the foremost consideration under the import substitution drive was to increase output, not improve the distribution of income; commercial production of these crops was encouraged through preferential treatment in land alienation and through tax incentives.[1] At the same time there is no evidence that paddy land was diverted into chilli cultivation. This is hardly surprising given imperfect substitutability of land between these two alternative uses.[2] Thus the growth in production of subsidiary crops might have had some effect on encouraging a fuller utilisation of land and labour in peasant agriculture, but the quantitative impact on peasant incomes is unlikely to have been very great.

In 1972 an income ceiling of 2,000 rupees per month was introduced, but this did not directly affect the data under consideration since the surveys relate to pre-tax income. Indirectly, however, it could have increased the inducement for the rich to understate their incomes in the 1973 survey. It is interesting, none the less, to complete this review of redistributive policies by looking at what effect this income ceiling could have had on the post-tax distribution of incomes.

The impact of the income ceiling depends directly on the degree to which it was enforced. Unfortunately, enforcement does not appear to have been very rigorous. As pointed out in an IBRD report, "in order to provide incentives for particular activities, such as non-traditional exports, hotel investments, etc., the incomes from these activities have been excluded from the base to which the maximum is applied. The ultimate net effects upon income distribution are likely to be different from that in the minds of the authors of the legislation".[3] Moreover, in 1973 income from the sale of paddy to the Paddy Marketing Board (the principal legal trading agency for rice) was exempted from income tax (including the income ceiling). This latter exemption, given the importance of paddy income to the rural areas, would have removed most of the potential redistributive impact of the income ceiling on rural incomes.

Even assuming complete enforcement, however, the tax would have covered less than 1 per cent of the total number of income receivers, according to the 1963 survey figures. Although this group earned 10.5 per cent of total income, the excess or taxable income would clearly be a smaller proportion of total income. Assuming all income in excess of 2,000 rupees to have

---

[1] P. C. Bansil: *Ceylon agriculture: a perspective* (Oxford and IBH Publishing Company, Calcutta, 1971) p. 77; L. C. de Silva; "A Critical Evaluation of Agricultural Policy 1960-68", in *Central Bank Staff Studies*, op. cit., Apr. 1971, p. 97.

[2] K. S. E. Jayatillake and M. U. A. Tennakoon: "Competitiveness of Chilli and Paddy Cultivation: An Examination of Data from Anuradhapura District", in *Central Bank Staff Studies*, op. cit., Apr. 1975, p. 193.

[3] IBRD: *Recent economic developments and current prospects for Sri Lanka*, op. cit., Technical Note to Chapter 2, p. 9.

been taxed, the amount realised would be only 5 per cent of total income. This would, however, amount to a reduction of 9 per cent in the total income accruing to the top quintile of income receivers. As in the case of land reform, therefore, the introduction of the income ceiling could have contributed to some extent to an actual reduction in the incomes of the rich but also to the possible understatement of top incomes.

NON-POLICY INFLUENCES ON THE DISTRIBUTION OF INCOMES

In the previous section government policies were analysed in order to ascertain whether they could confirm the trends suggested by the income data from the consumer finance surveys, and some of the explanations for the apparent improvement in the distribution of incomes were found not to be very convincing. Economic policies are not, however, the only determinants of changes in the distribution of incomes. Other factors must be examined to complete this line of inquiry. The test applied remains the same. Assuming that the trends described by the income data are true, can corroborative evidence for it be found that would also explain why these changes have occurred?

Broadly, the data suggest that there has been a substantial reduction in income differentials between the non-estate rural areas and the urban areas. That this has in fact occurred can be verified from independent data. Since 1970 the internal terms of trade have turned sharply in favour of agriculture through a combination of import substitution policies in food products and the sharp upturn in food grain prices in the early 1970s.[1] In addition to the rise in prices, the output of paddy (the predominant peasant crop) and production of other food crops such as potatoes, chillies and onions increased significantly faster than the population. Both yields and the area under cultivation of these crops rose steadily between 1963 and 1973.

In contrast to these indications of rising incomes in the rural areas, real wages in both the estate and urban sectors, apart from those of a few groups of workers, fell or at best remained constant. Thus, if it is assumed that the income gains in the rural sector were widely diffused, it follows that this configuration of income changes is broadly consistent with the trend toward narrowing inter-sectoral income differentials as suggested by the survey data.

However, the situation is less clear when one moves away from this broad generalisation and examines the details of intra-sectoral shifts in the size distribution of income. As noted earlier in this chapter, the narrowing of over-all inequality occurred not only because inter-sectoral inequalities diminished, but also, very significantly, because intra-sectoral inequalities diminished markedly.

---

[1] P. J. Richards: *A note on wage policies in Sri Lanka, 1968-73* (Geneva, ILO, 1975; mimeographed World Employment Programme research working paper; restricted); L. Jayawardena: "Case Study on Sri Lanka", in H. Chenery et al.: *Redistribution with growth*, op. cit., p. 275.

What then brought about the highly favourable redistribution of incomes that is suggested by the survey data?

A priori, one would expect a shift in the internal terms of trade, or increased productivity in the peasant agricultural sector, either to leave the intra-rural size distribution of income unchanged or to increase inequalities, since the larger farmers would have a greater capacity to respond to the new income-raising opportunities. Similarly in the urban areas, the decline in real wages in the context of a moderately rapid increase in productivity in secondary industry should have led to a rising share of profit and hence an increase in inequality. In fact, however, the opposite appears to have occurred and some specific explanations are necessary.

A search for explanations for the change in income distribution involves an examinination of why incomes of the bottom quintiles are reported to have increased so significantly and also why the incomes of the top quintile fell in absolute terms.

One factor likely to have influenced the behaviour of the incomes of the top quintile of income receivers was the decline in the profitability of the export sector. The Central Bank share index fell 37 per cent between 1963 and 1972 for "all equities", with the heaviest falls in tea and tea-cum-rubber shares (60 per cent and 45 per cent respectively). The only exception to this general fall in share prices was shares of coconut plantations, which increased by about 1 per cent. The value of government securities also declined significantly over this period. It should be noted, moreover, that the above decline in share prices was calculated in nominal terms. If the 52 per cent increase in the retail price index over this period is taken into account, then the fall in share prices in real terms would have been even more pronounced. This fall in share values is also reflected in the National Accounts, which show that income from "interest and dividends" fell by 22 per cent between 1963 and 1970. Furthermore, the return to power of a coalition Government led by the Sri Lanka Freedom Party in 1970 resulted in a rapid expansion of state enterprises, especially in the large-scale manufacturing sector.

Although there is substantial foreign ownership in the export sector, the Central Bank share index refers to the share prices of "rupee companies", i.e. those which are locally incorporated. The shares are locally traded and the majority of shareholders are local residents. The data from the 1963 consumer finance survey show that about 10 per cent of the income of those earning more than 1,000 rupees per month came from dividends. Thus a fall in share prices of the magnitude described above would have reduced the income from dividends of the rich. Hence this would explain, in part, the observed fall in the mean income of the top quintile of income receivers.

There is also some confirmation of this cause of a fall in the mean incomes of the rich in the data from the two consumer finance surveys. Table 65 contains a breakdown of income by source for each income class in 1963 and 1973. It will be observed that for all income classes there has been a fall in the share of total income from rents and from dividends and that this

Table 65.   Proportion of income from main occupation, rent and dividends, 1963 and 1973
(Percentages)

Income class (rupees per 2 months)	Main occupation		Rent		Dividends	
	1963	1973	1963	1973	1963	1973
0-51	80.4	76.5	7.9	0.05	—	—
51-100	67.0	85.4	11.9	1.5	—	—
101-200	80.2	86.6	5.2	2.0	—	—
201-400	77.1	62.2	6.5	4.8	—	—
401-800	76.7	62.7	6.1	5.5	—	—
801-1600	72.9	66.1	8.5	5.8	—	—
1601-2000	80.4	61.9	8.5	6.8	0.8	6.7
2001-3000	59.7	66.9	18.4	5.4	10.4	5.4
Above 3000	62.9	63.1	21.0	7.1	8.7	2.7

Source: Central Bank of Ceylon: *Survey of Ceylon's consumer finances*, 1963 and 1973, op. cit.

fall has been very marked for the top income classes. For those earning between 2,000 and 3,000 rupees per month, the share of total income from rent fell from 18 to 5 per cent, while for those earning more than 3,000 rupees the fall was from 21 per cent to 7 per cent. A similar sharp fall also was evident in the share of total income derived from dividends for these two groups. This fall in the proportion of income from rent (which was also a fall in absolute terms, given the fall in the mean incomes of the topmost income groups) is of great relevance to the change in the size distribution of rural incomes. It is tempting to link this phenomenon to the effects of the Paddy Land Act of 1958 and the land reform of 1972, but there is very little evidence on the matter. It is generally believed that the Paddy Lands Act has been ineffective[1] and despite a tightening up of the legislation in 1972 it is probably still true that "the higher (illegal) rent of 50 per cent of the crop continues to be paid in most areas".[2] The land reform, as mentioned earlier, has not as yet had a major impact in improving the lot of the poorest peasants and landless labourers. Yet it is still plausible that these legislative measures did have some effect in reducing rental income. Although the Rent Control Act may not have effected a general fall in the level of rents, it is likely to have acted as a restraining influence on the tendency for rents to increase—a tendency that would have been quite strong given the substantial increase in productivity that occurred on paddy lands as a result of the introduction of high-yielding varieties and increased double-cropping. In addition, the rental incomes of some of the larger absentee landlords must have fallen when the 215,000 acres were expropriated under the land reform.

---

[1] Nirmal Sanderatne: "Tenancy on Ceylon's Paddy Lands: The 1958 Reform", in *South Asian Review*, op. cit., Jan. 1972, pp. 117-136; L. C. Arulpragasam: "Land Reform", Paper for ILO Comprehensive Employment Mission to Ceylon 1971.

[2] ibid., p. 10.

These factors explain, to some extent, the fall in the mean incomes of the topmost income receivers. They do not, however, explain why average incomes increased more towards the lower income quintiles. Thus changes in productivity and incomes in the rural areas must be examined to see whether they could provide an explanation.

There were two sources of productivity increase in paddy cultivation during this period: a continued expansion of double-cropping made possible by the spread of irrigation and the introduction of high-yielding varieties. There is, however, no information available on the distribution of these productivity increases among farms of different size groups. For both of these sources of productivity increase to have contributed significantly to a reduction in inequality, they would have had to be concentrated very heavily on the smallest farmers. This appears, however, to have been highly unlikely: irrigation works are specific to localities and cannot discriminate between small and large farms, while problems of access to supplementary inputs tend to favour larger farms in the adoption of high-yielding varieties.

There is, however, one other factor which could provide a partial explanation of the sharp reduction of inequality in the distribution of rural income. The shift in the terms of trade between agriculture and industry has already been discussed, but there was also a shift in relative prices within agriculture itself. The price of export crops, tea and rubber, stagnated between 1963 and the beginning of 1973, while the price of paddy and other import-substitutes increased sharply. There was thus a redistribution away from smallholder producers of export crops towards producers of import substitutes. The smallholding sector is relatively small as regards tea production (17.4 per cent of total tea acreage in 1969) and somewhat larger in rubber (31 per cent of total rubber acreage in 1969), but smallholdings are quite significant in terms of employment. In 1969 there were 112,000 tea and 150,000 rubber holdings under 10 acres in size.[1] Thus, assuming that there was only one person employed per holding, these two crops would account for 17 per cent of total agricultural employment. There were also another 8,300 holdings of between 10 and 100 acres in size, but the owners of these holdings would be included among the richest income classes in the rural areas. In contrast, the smallholding group with holdings of under 10 acres in size contains some of the poorer rural inhabitants, particularly when the smallholding is the sole source of income. The average size of rubber holdings in the bottom category was just under 1 acre, while in tea cultivation it was 1.2 acres. Nevertheless, at the prices prevailing in 1963 the return per acre was higher in tea and rubber cultivation than in paddy cultivation.[2] Thus a smallholder cultivating an export crop would have been higher on the income scale than a peasant cultivating an equivalent sized holding of paddy.

---

[1] Arulpragasam, op. cit., Annex 4, p. 71.

[2] ibid.

The relative price changes between paddy and export crops between 1963 and 1973 would therefore have contributed to a narrowing of income differentials among the majority of low-income peasants. It was also another contributing factor to the fall in the mean incomes of the top quintile of income receivers.

It should be noted, however, that the foregoing discussion has referred to peasant cultivators only and not to landless labourers employed in rice cultivation or the smallholder section of export crop cultivation. No time series data exist on the wages of landless labourers outside the estate sector, but it appears that they are similar to wages on the estates,[1] and these, as will be seen below, fell in real terms between 1963 and 1973. There is thus no reason to suppose that the increase in paddy yields and price led to significant increases in the real wages of landless labourers or that this was an important factor explaining the reduction in income inequalities. Any increases that might have occurred would have been merely in the form of a higher imputed value being placed on payments received in kind because of the increase in prices of food crops.

AN ALTERNATIVE EXPLANATION

The previous two sections assumed that the trends revealed by the income data were correct and then went on to attempt to confirm and explain these trends. This was done not because it was believed that the income data were inherently more plausible than the consumption and real wage data, but simply because this had been the procedure adopted by previous studies. It was, therefore, necessary to evaluate the types of arguments, either explicitly contained in or implied by these studies before attempting to offer an alternative explanation for the discrepancy between the two sets of evidence and an evaluation of which of the two is the more reliable.

While there does not appear to have been any convincing supporting evidence for the trends revealed by the income data, this does not necessarily imply that they are, *ipso facto*, false. It simply means that alternative explanations might be available either for the changes implied by the income data (if they are correct) or for why the figures are misleading (if they are incorrect).

It is believed that a large part of the discrepancy between the two sets of evidence can be explained away by deficiencies in the methodology of estimating changes in real income that have been adopted. Because of this deficiency, the true situation is closer to that suggested by the consumption data and therefore to the thesis that inequality did not decrease by the margins suggested by the income data.

---

[1] United Kingdom Department of Trade: *Sri Lanka tea estates* (Her Majesty's Stationery Office, London, 1975), p. 32.

177

The crux of the problem lies in the fact that the period spanned by the consumer finance surveys was one of rapid inflation and in which, in particular, the price of the staple food, rice, increased sharply relative to other commodities. Compared to one where both the general price level and relative prices remain constant, this situation poses severe problems for the estimation of a change in real incomes. Moreover, the problem is particularly acute when one is attempting to establish changes in the distribution of real incomes.

The estimates of the change in real incomes between 1963 and 1973 were derived by deflating money income with the Colombo cost-of-living index. Using National Accounts data and the implicit deflators therein, Peter Richards has shown that this cost-of-living index significantly understates the true extent of inflation between 1968 and 1973.[1] Adjusting for this factor would not, of course, alter the fact that inequality has narrowed, but it does reduce the extent of the real income gains experienced by the poorest income earners.

A related but more fundamental point concerns the appropriateness of the method of estimating the change in real incomes that has been used. Quite apart from the underestimation of inflation, the Colombo cost-of-living index does not take into account the large differences in consumption patterns between rich and poor and the consequences of this for the estimation of real incomes in a period when the relative prices of staples and other consumption items changed sharply. Specifically, the price of rice and other domestically produced food items rose by far more than the price of non-food items. Rice constituted 70 per cent of the value of total consumption of the poorest income class in the rural sector but only 1.3 per cent of the total consumption of the richest income class (see table 66). This difference in consumption patterns tends to "overstate" the extent of the real income gains of the poor relative to the rich in the case of families which produce and consume their own rice. Since the price of rice rose sharply[2] and since the imputed value of self-consumption of rice is a predominant part of the consumption of the poor, this component has a far bigger impact on raising the *money* incomes of the poor than that of the rich. The situation in this case is analogous to a revaluation of assets; rice is the "asset" held proportionately more by the poor and a rise in its price relative to other goods causes a greater proportionate increase in their incomes. Their real consumption of rice need not have risen and, indeed, if they had no marketable surplus and their tastes were rigid, there need not have been any increase in their real consumption generally.

For those with a marketable surplus, the increase in their money income would be as great as the increase in the imputed value of the income of the

---

[1] Richards, op. cit.

[2] Data show that the retail price of rice increased by 2.6 times between 1963 and 1973 (see Central Bank of Ceylon: *Survey of Ceylon's consumer finances, 1973*, op. cit., tables 89 and 93).

Table 66.   Rural sector: expenditure on rice as a proportion of mean income by
            income group, 1963
            (Per spending unit per 2 months)

Income class (rupees)	Mean income (rupees) (1)	Expenditure on rice (rupees) (2)	Col. (2) ÷ col. (1)
0-50	33.33	23.40	0.70
51-100	76.75	30.52	0.40
101-200	153.25	34.32	0.22
201-400	291.38	43.37	0.15
401-800	539.10	50.65	0.09
801-1600	1 053.64	61.48	0.06
1601-2000	1 786.37	88.75	0.05
2001-3000	2 476.83	54.22	0.02
Above 3000	5 362.62	68.46	0.01

Source: Central Bank of Ceylon: *Survey of Ceylon's consumer finances, 1963*, op. cit., table 2.00, p. 276 of Statistical Appendix.

poor without any marketable surplus, if they derived the same or a greater proportion of their income from the sale of rice. For those with a greater extent of non-rice income, however, the rise in money income would be smaller. The rise in their real income would, in fact, be understated since the marketable surplus would command a larger quantity of other commodities. In general, therefore, any given rise in money income would imply a greater increase in real income, appropriately deflated by disaggregated price indices, for those with a larger marketable surplus. Thus, measured in terms of real consumption, the reduction of income differentials has been overstated; the change in relative prices exaggerates the increase in the real incomes of the poor, while the reverse is true of the real incomes of the rich. This can be seen by inspecting the data in table 67.

In fact, a more general point can be made about biases of this type and the interpretation of changes in the distribution of incomes. The size distribution of money incomes is strongly influenced by the relative price of "wage goods" and other items of consumption. In comparing two distributions of money incomes at different points in time, a sharp increase in the relative price of "wage goods" would bring about a reduction in the estimated degree of inequality, actual consumption bundles remaining equal. The Gini coefficient in the latter year, for instance, would be lower. This false impression of a reduction in inequality would still remain if the comparison was made in terms of "real incomes" arrived at by the procedure of deflating the money incomes in the later year by an over-all consumer price index (i.e. an index that uses weights from average consumption of all income groups). The reduction in the value of the Gini coefficient here would be the same as that for money incomes. Neither of these measures of a change in the distribution of incomes, however, would be an accurate reflection of the change in the distribution of real incomes. The correct procedure would be to use income-group-specific cost-of-living indices or to look at actual quantities consumed.

Table 67. Disaggregated cost-of-living index for lowest and highest income classes, 1963 to 1973

Consumption item	Weight in total consumption expenditure in 1963		Price index (1963 = 100) in 1973
	Lowest income group (0-50 rupees for 2 months)	Highest income group (more than 3000 rupees for 2 months)	
Food	0.6598	0.2895	145.82
Clothing	0.0445	0.0730	145.01
Fuel and light	0.0454	0.0429	145.05
Rent	0.0632	0.1382	108.18
Miscellaneous	0.1871	0.4564	133.97

Increase in price index for lowest income
 class based on their consumption weights = 141.16

Increase in price index for highest income
 class based on their consumption weights = 135.11

Source: Central Bank of Ceylon: *Annual Report 1974*, table 53; idem: *Survey of Ceylon's consumer finances*, 1963 and 1973, op. cit.

The use of money incomes or "real incomes" derived via an over-all consumer price index can be misleading for two reasons. First, rising prices of food have an asymmetrical effect on money incomes among peasant cultivators as a result of the practice of imputing the value of self-consumption that has just been discussed. Secondly, even in the non-agricultural sectors a similar bias is likely to operate. A rise in the relative price of wage goods will lead to increasing money wages where workers are able to resist sharp falls in real incomes. However, even if money wages are increased in the same proportion as the rise in a general consumer price index (i.e. an *average* index for all income groups), this would still leave workers with a lower real income. This is because wage goods have a much heavier weight in their consumption basket than in that of higher income groups and the rise in their cost of living would be understated by an average index for all income groups. Thus the money income data would exaggerate the real income gains of the poor and understate those of the rich, giving a spurious impression of a narrowing in inequality in the distribution of money incomes as well as in "real incomes" that are inappropriately derived.[1]

Specifically, the fall in real wages in the modern sector in Sri Lanka that was described earlier is understated and thus the fall in real consumption has in fact been greater than the wage data imply. The fall in real wages, properly measured, is likely to have been more in line with that suggested by the consumption data. Thus the more plausible conclusion is that inequality

---

[1] This argument has been used by Wilfred Beckerman to cast doubt on the validity of cross-section studies of income distribution where the ratio of food prices to total income varies across countries. It is obvious that the argument is equally valid when applied to comparisons of income distributions at two points of time in a single country (see W. Beckerman: *Economic development and the distribution of income in developing countries*, mimeographed, 1976).

Table 68.   Change in the per capita consumption of rationed rice
(Measures of rice per 2 months per spending unit)

Income class (rupees per 2 months)	1963	1973
0-50	13.87	5.94
51-100	19.30	8.48
101-200	14.75	10.23
201-400	14.55	12.28
401-800	12.86	12.26
801-1600	11.67	12.01
1601-2000	11.00	9.29
2001-3000	11.49	8.11
Above 3000	7.02	6.06
Total	13.84	11.96

Source: Central Bank of Ceylon: *Survey of Ceylon's consumer finances*, 1963 and 1973, op. cit.

increased in the urban and estate sectors. This would be so because the fall in real consumption is consistent with the sharp rise in food prices for these wage earners and with the fall in the amount of food subsidies received (see table 68).

It is therefore argued that the money income data are misleading in that they would show a spurious reduction in the degree of inequality in the size distribution of incomes. The procedure for estimating the money incomes of those having subsistence production as part of their income leads to a distortion in the figures on money incomes. Furthermore, the use of an average consumer price index to convert money incomes into real incomes compounds this distortion in the case of both peasant incomes and the incomes of wage earners in the non-rural sectors.

These inadequacies in the estimation procedure are sufficient to explain the discrepancy between the income data and the consumption and wage data without having to resort to theoretical arguments about the relative merits of income versus consumption data. It is worth noting, however, that consumption data, especially when expressed in terms of physical volume rather than in value terms, are likely to be more reliable than income data. Apart from the argument that consumption data, unlike income data, are less sensitive to transitory influences, an analysis based on data on quantities of consumption avoids most of the pitfalls of estimating real incomes in situations where relative prices change significantly. However, physical consumption data (not measured by value but in absolute terms) would be difficult to collect.

In conclusion, Occam's razor is invoked and it is asserted that the simple explanation suffices and thus obviates the need for more complicated explanations. The discrepancy between the two sets of data is resolved, and it can be stated with some degree of confidence that real consumption fell for the poor and that real income, appropriately measured, is unlikely to have become more equally distributed. The discussion in the previous two sections has shown that the changes that occurred in economic policy or in the pattern of economic growth do not contradict this interpretation. Indeed, plausible explanations are available for the trends suggested. The fall in real wages is partly a result of government policy, since there is government regulation of minimum wages in the private sector and since it controls public sector wages. The fall in real wages is also consistent with the rise in open unemployment (over the already high levels of 1963) between 1963 and 1973, while the fall in the consumption of staple foods can be directly linked to the reduction in the real levels of government subsidy between 1963 and 1973.

THE ESTATE SECTOR

Concentration so far has been on the non-estate rural sector where the majority of the population lives. It has been argued that any claims that a substantial rise has occurred in living standards there are highly debatable. In the case of the estate sector, however, there is no doubt that this section of the population experienced a continuous fall in their real standard of living.

The data from the surveys of consumer finances indicate that the mean income per income receiver in the estate sector increased by 18 per cent in real terms between 1963 and 1973, but this increase is almost entirely due to the inclusion of supervisory and managerial staff in the coverage of the 1973 survey.[1] The effects of this can be seen clearly in table 57, which shows that virtually the entire increase in mean income was concentrated in the top two quintiles, whereas for the bottom three quintiles real incomes either fell or increased insignificantly. When the fact that the retail price index understated the extent of inflation is allowed for, it is clear that the vast majority of the estate labourers suffered a fall in their real living standards. This would be especially apparent if a separate deflator appropriate to the income levels of estate labour were available. Such a deflator would capture the effect of the sharp increase in the price of rice on the income of a group which did not produce it but for whom it was a major item of consumption.

The contention that the living standards in the estate sector have fallen is supported by other available data. For instance, it was shown earlier that the per capita income of Indian Tamils, who are virtually synonymous with the working population of the estate sector, fell slightly between 1963 and 1973. Moreover, it will be recalled that the Indian Tamils were already the poorest ethnic group in 1963 and earlier. The Central Bank real wage index for agricultural labourers (with 1952 as the base year) fell from 104.2 to 101.5 between 1963 and 1973, while the average earnings per day of male workers

---

[1] Central Bank of Ceylon: *Survey of Ceylon's consumer finances, 1973*, op. cit., p. 68.

on tea plantations in 1973 was 6.5 per cent lower than in 1963 (see table 69). Although for the period as a whole the trend is of stagnation in earnings per worker, other pieces of evidence in the survey data show that earnings per family fell. For instance, the per capita input of labour in the estate sector fell by 9.6 per cent (from 5.24 months per worker to 4.79 months), and the rate of unemployment increased from 7.5 per cent to 12 per cent between 1963 and 1973.[1] This deteriorating employment situation in the estate sector also can be easily inferred from other available data. Between 1960 and 1971 employment on tea, rubber and coconut estates fell by almost 23 per cent,[2] while the population of Indian Tamils grew by 2 per cent per annum,[3] despite some repatriation of labourers to India under the Sirimao-Shastri Pact of 1964. Given the fact that the Tamils are locked into the estate economy with little prospect of finding alternative employment, the rise in unemployment and underemployment is easily understood.

The recent British Board of Trade investigation into conditions on British-owned estates provides further evidence of the declining standards of living in the plantation sector. Real wages fell by 16 per cent between 1970 and 1974 and the level of wage income in 1974, even on the generous Assumption that both husband and wife worked 25 days a month, was insufficient even to purchase rationed foods.[4] As a result, malnutrition was widespread and there was a marked increase in the death rate attributable to this malnutrition.

Finally, there is little prospect of improving living conditions in the estate sector. The profitability of the estates has apparently fallen and even if the plantations were prepared to pay higher wages the special problems concerning the Indian Tamil minority would have to be solved. "The government frowned upon any suggestion that plantation wages should be increased, as this would create problems in other agricultural sectors. Other agricultural workers were little if any better off in money terms and any suggestion that Tamil workers should receive increased wages would give rise to a demand for a round of increased wages in other sectors."[5] The operative phrase in the above quotation is "in money terms"; the daily wage rate in the non-plantation agricultural sector may have been no higher but there were more opportunities for these labourers to receive income in the form of rice and there was also better access to government rations than on the estates.[6] In any case, even if other agricultural workers were actually no better off, the

---

[1] Central Bank of Ceylon: *Survey of Ceylon's consumer finances, 1963*, op. cit., table 30, p. 53 and table 31, p. 55; idem: *Survey of Ceylon's consumer finances, 1973*, op. cit., table 34, p. 47 and table 35, p. 48.

[2] *Ceylon: Census of Population*, 1963 and 1971.

[3] ILO: *Matching employment opportunities and expectations: a programme of action for Ceylon* (Geneva, 1971).

[4] United Kingdom Department of Trade: *Sri Lanka tea estates*, op. cit., p. 11.

[5] ibid.

[6] ibid. The report quotes instances where rations were not available on the estates because of a combination of government indifference and neglect by the management.

Table 69.   Earnings per day on tea plantations (Rupees)

Year	Money wage		Real wage	
	Male	Female	Male	Female
1963	2.75	2.35	2.75	2.35
1964	2.80	2.32	2.66	2.20
1965	2.86	2.36	2.72	2.24
1966	2.84	2.32	2.70	2.24
1967	2.88	2.41	2.68	2.16
1968	3.31	2.73	3.08	2.24
1969	3.31	2.75	2.91	2.40
1970	3.40	2.74	2.78	2.21
1971	3.47	3.38	2.68	2.61
1972	4.24	3.00	3.00	2.12
1973	3.91	3.58	2.57	2.35

Note: The figures are an average of earnings per day in March and September of each year.
Source: ILO: *Bulletin of Labour Statistics* (Geneva), various issues.

condition of plantation workers demonstrates that the problems of absolute poverty in the rural areas are still widespread despite claims of substantial improvements in real incomes that have been put forward.

CONCLUSION

The principal conclusion to emerge from this study is that considerable doubt must be attached to the claims, based on the Central Bank survey data, that there has been a dramatic reduction in income inequality in Sri Lanka and that the situation of the rural poor has improved substantially. These doubts are based on the statistical problems involved in measuring a change in real income and on the absence of a convincing explanation for the reported changes in the distribution of income. Moreover, the data on consumption and real wages point strongly to the fact that there has been an increase in inequality and even a reduction in the levels of real consumption of the poor.

The experience of Sri Lanka in the period after 1963 does not, therefore, demonstrate the possibility of improving the distribution of income relatively painlessly, without having to resort to fundamental structural changes. A redistribution of incomes achieved through turning the terms of trade in favour of agriculture is likely, at best, to improve living conditions of one poverty group at the expense of others and does not represent an unambiguous redistribution from rich to poor. Moreover, a redistribution achieved in this way is unlikely to persist in the long run. It can be reversed by successful defensive action by groups which are adversely affected (such as urban workers) or by subsequent changes in relative world or domestic prices.

RURAL POVERTY IN WEST MALAYSIA, 1957-70

9

E. L. H. Lee

The economic performance of West Malaysia between 1957 and 1970 is instructive and exceptionally interesting in that a large proportion of the rural population became absolutely poorer despite the sustained growth of agricultural output and the rapid growth of national income that occurred during the period. The increasing poverty and inequality that can be observed in Malaysia may surprise many in view of the fact that rural development received high priority in the development plans of the period.

Rural poverty became recognised as a serious economic problem in the years immediately prior to independence, and the configuration of communal politics in Malaysia ensured that the Government had a strong political motive to improve standards of living in rural areas. The majority of the Malay population were employed in the peasant agricultural sector, and they formed the power base of the Alliance Government. However, despite this favourable political circumstance and the resulting large proportion of development expenditure that has been channelled to rural development, the incomes of the poorest 40 per cent of the rural population have fallen.

The agricultural sector of Malaysia comprises an estate sector, which accounted for about 20 per cent of agricultural employment in 1967, and a peasant sector, which accounted for the remainder. About 77 per cent of the peasant farmers are engaged primarily in the cultivation of two crops, paddy and rubber. In paddy farming 97 per cent of the farms in 1960 were less than 10 acres in size. In rubber planting, however, the official definition of a "smallholding" includes farms of up to 100 acres; in 1960, 25 per cent of these holdings were larger than 10 acres and many of these belonged to non-Malay absentee owners. Thus the non-estate rubber sector includes many medium-sized holdings which do not strictly belong to the peasant sector. Apart from this, however, the non-estate rubber sector is similar to the paddy sector in consisting mostly of small farms.

When surveying trends in rural incomes, it is necessary to make a distinction between estate labour and peasant farmers. The former are wage employees who are highly unionised, and their real wages rose steadily between

1957 and 1970 despite falling rubber prices. Yields per acre as well as physical productivity per worker on rubber estates doubled between 1957 and 1970; this was a much faster rate of increase than in the smallholding sector. Wages increased by almost 40 per cent, significantly higher than the 23 per cent increase in the value of output per worker; employment, however, fell by 18 per cent. This contraction in employment was due not to the introduction of labour-saving innovations but rather to a contraction of estate acreage; there was no significant change in acreage per man in the plantation sector. The reduction of employment on the estates during this period was a continuation of a trend which began in the early 1950s whereby foreign-owned estates were subdivided and sold mainly to Chinese and Indian absentee landlords and speculators.[1] This process involved the breaking up of whole estates, mainly those on the margins of profitability, and hence involved the discharge of the entire labour force of these estates. The welfare implications of such a pattern of reduction in estate employment are more serious than they would have been had the fall in employment been evenly spread over the estate sector in the form of a reduction in the number of workers per family. Some of the dismissed labour force obtained employment in the subdivided holdings, but the majority found no alternative employment. This is reflected in the data on unemployment by race which shows that Indians, who comprise the majority of the estate labour force, had the highest rate of unemployment.

Estate labour is very heavily unionised and the National Union of Plantation Workers is the largest trade union in the country. Those who remained in employment enjoyed rising real wages, even though rubber prices had fallen, as a result of successful trade union pressure.[2] Therefore one must distinguish between the one-fifth of the 1957 estate labour force who lost their jobs and those who remained in employment. Those who lost their jobs suffered a sharp fall in income while those who kept their jobs enjoyed rising incomes. Similarly, there is a clear contrast between the fortunes of this last group and the majority of those employed in the peasant agricultural sector.

CHANGES IN THE DISTRIBUTION OF INCOME

Between 1957 and 1970 GDP at current prices grew at 5 per cent per annum (see table 70). There is no time series for GDP at constant prices covering the whole of this period, but this was a period of remarkable price stability. The retail price index increased by only 10 per cent over this 13-year period and hence the growth rate of real GDP could not have been much lower than the figure for GDP at current prices. Population growth, however, continued at the high rate of 3 per cent per annum, leaving a

---

[1] U. A. Aziz: *Subdivision of estates in Malaya, 1951-60* (University of Malaya, Department of Economics, 1962).

[2] E. L. H. Lee: *Income distribution in a developing economy: a case study of West Malaysia* (D. Phil. thesis, Oxford, 1975), Ch. VI.

Table 70.   Trend rates of growth, 1957-70

	Growth (per cent per annum)
Gross domestic product	4.99
Agricultural output	1.36
Population	2.96
GDP per capita	2.01

Note: The figures used in calculating trends in GDP and agricultural output for 1957-59 are at constant 1959 prices while those for 1960 onwards are at current prices. The retail price index increased by just under 10 per cent between 1959 and 1970.

Sources: *National Accounts of the Federation of Malaya*, 1955-60; *National Accounts of West Malaysia*, 1960-68; *Monthly Bulletin of Statistics*, various issues.

growth rate of 2 per cent per annum for per capita GDP at current prices. After making a rough correction for inflation[1] a growth rate of real per capita GDP of 1.25 per cent per annum remains.

The rate of growth of the agricultural sector revealed by the National Accounts data was substantially lower than that for GDP, being only 1.4 per cent per annum at current prices. This relatively low growth rate is, however, largely a reflection of the declining trend in rubber prices and belies the substantial increases that occurred in the physical output of rubber and paddy during this period.

These aggregate figures give few grounds for suspecting that rural poverty increased absolutely. Yet this is what is implied by the figures on the size distribution of household incomes presented in table 71. Between 1957 and 1970 the Gini concentration ratio for all households increased sharply from 0.41 to 0.51, while for rural households alone the increase was from 0.37 to 0.47. This sharp increase in inequality is in itself disturbing, but the figures on mean income by quintile group are even more so. The data in table 72 show that the average income of the bottom 40 per cent of households fell significantly and that this was concentrated among rural households. The bottom 20 per cent of rural households experienced a fall of over 40 per cent in their average income while the next 20 per cent of households experienced a fall of 16 per cent. In contrast, the top 20 per cent of rural households experienced a 21 per cent increase in their mean incomes over the period.

Two immediate objections might be raised against the conclusions reached in the previous paragraph, namely that the survey data on household income are unreliable and that one cannot interpolate a trend between two widely separated estimates.

No conclusive proof can, of course, be provided to refute the first objection, but careful cross-checking of the data, and of the underlying concepts and definitions of income used in the surveys, provides no basis for rejection of the figures as unreliable.

---

[1] This was done by deflating the 1970 GDP by the retail price index (1957 = 100) and then taking the compound growth rate of the increase in per capita GDP between 1957 and 1970.

Table 71.   Gini concentration ratios, 1957 and 1970

	1957 (1)	1970 (2)
All households	0.408	0.513
Rural households	0.366	0.470
Urban households	0.420	0.499

Sources: Column (1) was calculated from the figures as presented in the *Household Budget Survey of the Federation of Malaya 1957-58* (Department of Statistics, Kuala Lumpur), p. 39. The figures were adjusted to allow for the exclusion of households with incomes of more than $1,000 per month from the Household Budget Survey. This adjustment was made on the basis of data on assessments for personal income tax obtained from *The Annual Report of the Department of Inland Revenue, 1958,* Abstract F, p. 16. Column (2) was calculated from figures from the Post Enumeration Survey, 1970, published in the *Mid-term review of the Second Malaysia Plan, 1971-75* (Government Printer, Kuala Lumpur), tables I-1 and I-2, pp. 3 and 4. The same data, with a larger number of class intervals, also is reproduced in D. R. Snodgrass: *Trends and patterns in Malaysian income distribution, 1957-1970* (Development Discussion Paper No. 2, Sep. 1974, Harvard Institute for International Development), tables A16 to A19 and tables A24 and A25.

Both surveys were conducted by the same agency, the Statistics Department of Malaysia. There is thus a basic consistency in some of the central concepts used. "Household" was uniformly defined in all three surveys as "a group of people living together and having a common budget for food and other essential living".[1] "Urban" areas were commonly defined as settlements with a population of 10,000 or more, with the residual being treated as "rural" areas. Both surveys were two-stage stratified random sample surveys with the stratification being done by rural and urban areas.

The 1957 and 1970 surveys have a uniformly broad definition of "income". The 1957 survey was primarily a household expenditure survey and the income estimates were carefully checked against the expenditure estimates. The definition of income in this survey must have been a comprehensive one since the only items which were excluded from income were loans and gifts.[2] The 1970 survey defined income as including "wages and salaries, business and property income, remittances and transfers in both cash and kind". A money value was also imputed to consumption of own production and to owner-occupied housing.[3]

In both surveys the data collected were of monthly household income. The 1957 data were collected on the basis of daily visits to the surveyed households for a period of one month. The fact that the 1957 survey was conducted over a 12-month period and that the 1970 data refer to an "average month" shows that the problem of seasonal variations in income, especially rural incomes, has been taken into account. In both the surveys there was considerable probing of the replies on income and there can thus be reasonable confidence that there are no serious biases arising out of seasonal variation.

One defect common to both the 1957 and 1970 surveys is that no details are given of the prices used to arrive at the imputed value of consumption of

---

[1] Department of Statistics: *Post enumeration survey* (Kuala Lumpur), p. 6.

[2] *Household Budget Survey*, op. cit., 1957-58, p. 3.

[3] *Post enumeration survey*, op. cit., 1970, form 3.

Table 72. Mean household income by sector and by quintiles, 1957 and 1970
(In constant 1957 prices, Malayan dollars per month)

Sectors and quintiles	1957[1]	1970[2]	1970 ÷ 1957
Whole economy	215.4	244.5	1.14
0-20	61.2	40.2	0.66
20-40	110.4	96.4	0.87
40-60	156.4	152.7	0.98
60-80	225.4	243.1	1.08
80-100	523.7	680.5	1.30
Rural	172.6	184.5	1.07
0-20	55.8	32.7	0.59
20-40	97.4	81.8	0.84
40-60	132.2	130.2	0.98
60-80	189.1	201.7	1.07
80-100	388.6	471.6	1.21
Urban	319.3	395.5	1.24
0-20	92.9	79.3	0.85
20-40	154.9	156.7	1.01
40-60	217.2	244.9	1.13
60-80	321.1	374.1	1.17
80-100	810.2	1 110.8	1.37

[1] The 1957 figures are calculated from the household budget figures referred to in table 71.   [2] The 1970 figures have been corrected for price changes between 1957 and 1970.
Source: as for table 71.

own produce or the rental value of owner-occupied houses. It is thus not known if the prices used to estimate the former were ex-farm or market prices and whether a consistent concept was used in both surveys.

A crucial test of the reliability of the data on income distribution lies in a comparison of the total income derived from the survey with an alternative estimate of this magnitude from National Accounts data.[1]

The estimates of total income yielded by the survey data are not inconsistent with the estimates of personal income from National Accounts data. Moreover, the increases in average income per capita revealed by the surveys also are compatible with National Accounts estimates. While it must be admitted that National Accounts data are by no means an infallible yardstick, other investigators have used these data in conducting their analyses and found them to be reliable.

[1] It should be noted that the National Accounts data are not entirely independent of the budget survey. Estimates of consumption are obtained from extrapolations based on per capita consumption figures derived from the survey, supplemented by data on net imports of consumption goods. Estimates of farmers' own consumption of their produce are also based on the survey data. It should also be noted that, in principle, the test of agreement with National Accounts data is only a necessary but not a sufficient condition for the reliability of the data.

Figure 10.   GDP at market prices, 1947-1970
(1,000 million dollars at current prices)

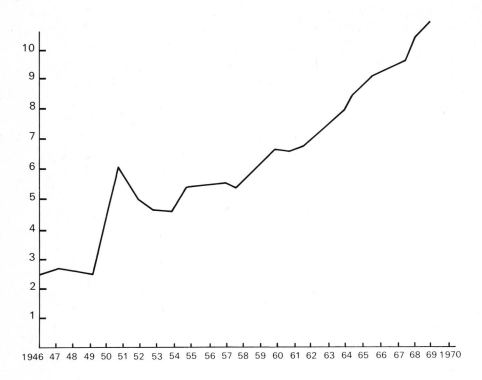

Notes: (1) Figures for 1947-59 are at constant 1959 prices while those from 1960 onwards are at current prices; the retail price index increased by less than 10 per cent between 1959 and 1970.   (2) Trend equations:
(i) Linear: $Y = 2300.3 + 278.6\ T$ where: $Y = $ GDP
  (269.3) (18.347) $T = $ time
    $R^2 = 0.9085$
(ii) Log: Log $Y = 7.9528 + 0.05139\ T$
    (0.05975) (0.00410)
    $R^2 = 0.8728$

Sources: Lim Chong-Yah: *The economic development of modern Malaya* (Oxford University Press, Kuala Lumpur, 1967), table I.1, p. 7; *National Accounts of the Federation of Malaya*, 1955-60; *National Accounts of West Malaysia*, 1968-71.

The second objection can be dealt with more readily because it is possible to provide independent corroboration of the income trends suggested by the household budget survey data. The main thrust of the second objection is that short-term influences could lead to biases in the trends inferred from merely two sets of survey data.[1] From figure 10, however, it can be seen that

---

[1] For a detailed discussion of this and other aspects of the reliability of the survey data see Lee, op. cit., Ch. II.

1957 and 1970 were essentially "normal" years. Neither was a year of abnormal boom conditions nor a year of serious depression.

TRENDS IN INCOMES IN PEASANT AGRICULTURE

The reliability of the trends suggested by the survey data may be checked by examining the trends in incomes in peasant agriculture. This will be done below.

The value of total output as well as physical productivity per worker increased sharply in both paddy and smallholding rubber. Between 1957 and 1967 physical productivity per worker increased by 62 per cent in paddy cultivation and by 26 per cent in smallholding rubber. These productivity increases were due to the extensive spread of double-cropping and of high-yielding varieties in paddy cultivation and to replanting as well as substantial new planting with high-yielding clones in the case of rubber smallholdings. As shown in table 73, in 1957 less than 1 per cent of paddy land was double-cropped, whereas by 1970 this had increased to almost one-third of paddy land. High-yielding varieties had also been introduced on 50 per cent of paddy acreage by 1970. In the case of smallholding rubber, over 500,000 acres of virgin land was brought under cultivation on government land development schemes, representing an increase of 31 per cent over the 1957 acreage. All of the new planting was with high-yielding clones and together with replanting of low-yielding holdings and the subdivision of estates, this raised the proportion of high-yielding land in total smallholding acreage from 12 per cent in 1957 to 60 per cent in 1970.

In the case of paddy the increases in physical productivity were reflected in increases in the gross value of output per worker because the guaranteed minimum price of paddy increased marginally in nominal terms between 1957 and 1970. The reverse was true, however, in the case of smallholding rubber, where declining prices negated the increases in physical productivity: the gross value of output per worker in fact fell by 20 per cent. These two parts of the peasant sector, taken together, therefore showed only a modest increase of 7 per cent in real terms in the value of output per worker, despite the large increases in physical productivity. (It is interesting to note that the household budget survey data also indicate the average income per household rose only 7 per cent over the same period.)

It is evident, therefore, that the average figures for the peasant sector as a whole conceal an important difference between the peasants dependent on paddy cultivation and those dependent on rubber; there were rising average incomes for the former group and steadily falling income for the latter.

The increase in yields per acre in paddy that occurred at the same time as rubber prices were falling might suggest that the large increase in rubber acreage was a perverse reaction to the change in the relative profitability of these two crops. This, however, was not so. The net return per acre from rubber has always been substantially higher than that from paddy, even at

191

Table 73.   Progress in double-cropping, adoption of high-yielding varieties and increase in cultivated area by state

State	Percentage under second crop in 1970	Percentage under high-yielding varieties in 1970	Percentage increase in cultivated area 1957-70
Perlis	53.0	75.8	13.8
Kedah	30.0	60.2	1.4
Kelantan	15.2	17.2	—6.5
Selangor	67.3	99.8	13.9
Pahang[1]	9.4	8.4	29.3
Negri Sembilan	31.2	33.1	3.2
Trengganu[1]	12.3	20.0	40.4
Province Wellesley	95.0	86.7	2.6
Perak	66.0	77.6	6.1
Malacca	12.9	15.3	3.3
Johore	54.5	81.1	3.8
West Malaysia	35.7	50.7	5.9

[1] The two states with very large percentage increases in acreage, Pahang and Trengganu, accounted for only 10.5 per cent of paddy acreage in 1957.

Sources: *Monthly Statistical Bulletin*, West Malaysia, various issues. I. Palmer: *The new rice in monsoon Asia* (UNRISD, Geneva, 1974), Part II, table 17.6, p. 239.

the very low rubber prices prevailing at the trough of the depression in the 1930s.[1] Paddy cultivation had to be artificially sustained by a combination of support prices above world market prices and restrictions on the conversion of paddy land to other crops.[2] It should also be noted that not all land is suitable for substitution between the two crops. To convert land already planted with rubber involves destroying an asset with years of productive life left and the decision is thus more complicated than in the case of a substitution between two non-perennial crops. Moreover, most of the new planting in rubber was carried out by the Government under its land development schemes and was not the result of the investment decisions of individual peasants. The new planting was also with high-yielding clones which yield a substantially higher return than old rubber land.

It might appear at first sight that this change in the relative price of rubber and rice brought about a desirable redistributive change. Such a view, however, assumes a degree of homogeneity within each group of peasants that does not exist in reality. There are considerable inequalities in the size distribution of farms in both paddy and rubber cultivation, as can be seen in table 74, and a significant degree of poverty exists among those engaged in

[1] P. T. Bauer: *The rubber industry: a study in competition and monopoly* (Cambridge (Mass.), Harvard University Press, 1948), table 1.

[2] M. Rudner: *The state and peasant innovation in rural development: the case of Malayan rubber* (The Hebrew University of Jerusalem, May 1969); W. R. Roff: *The origins of Malay nationalism* (Yale University Press, New Haven, 1967), pp. 25, 26, 138-140.

Table 74.   Size distribution of rice and rubber farms, 1960

Size group (acres)	Percentage of farms	
	Wet rice	Rubber
Less than 1	9.9	1.9
1-1.99	23.2	7.9
2-2.99	21.3	14.1
3-3.99	14.3	12.2
4-4.99	9.7	10.3
5-9.99	18.6	30.0
10-39.9	3.0	19.6
Above 40	0.0	4.0

Note: "Farms" refer to operating units and not to ownership units. The 1960 *Census of agriculture* shows that 62 per cent of paddy farms were under tenancy and another 6 per cent were operated by owner-cum-tenants. The distribution of land ownership is thus more highly unequal than the distribution of farms. For instance, a survey of a major rice growing area, Krian, showed that nine of the largest landowners accounted for two-thirds of the total cultivated area while the largest two landowners owned half of the total area. See T. B. Wilson: *The Economics of padi production in North Malaya* (Ministry of Agriculture, Federation of Malaya, 1958), part I, p. 20. Tenancy is less widespread on rubber smallholdings, where 80 per cent of farms are owner-operated.

Source: *Census of agriculture*, 1960, Report No. 3, table 34, and Report No. 8, table 56.

the cultivation of both crops.[1] The poverty group in both cases is composed of owner-cultivators and tenants on extremely small plots of land as well as contract labourers. An optimistic view of the course of rural development in Malaysia can only be justified if it can be shown that the benefits of the observed growth in the average incomes of paddy cultivators has been evenly shared and that the observed fall in incomes among rubber smallholders has not been concentrated on the poorest farmers. It will be shown below that there is no basis for holding such an optimistic view.

There is abundant evidence that the great majority of rubber smallholders, especially the poorest among them who were unable to replant with high-yielding clones, experienced a sharp fall in income. As shown in table 75, the 40 per cent fall in rubber prices during this period caused a fall of about 50 per cent in real incomes for those who had already replanted with high-yielding clones by 1957, and also for those who had not made such a transition, during the period 1957-70.[2] This latter group constitutes the poorest elements in the smallholding sector, who could not afford to replant in spite of the subsidised replanting scheme. They comprised more than 35 per cent of those employed in the rubber smallholding sector. Over-all, less than 25 per cent of the number of smallholders experienced an increase in their

---

[1] A survey of farm incomes on rubber smallholdings in 1964 showed that average earnings per worker on low-yielding holdings was $239. This was lower than average earnings per worker in paddy farming as revealed in a series of farm surveys in 1968. See Lim Saw Ching: *Land development schemes in West Malaysia: a study of costs and benefits* (Ph. D. thesis, Australian National University, 1972), p. 199.

[2] The fall in real incomes exceeds the fall in rubber prices because of domestic inflation over this period.

Table 75.   Price of rubber and income per acre of rubber smallholders
(In US dollars)

Year	Low-yielding holdings			High-yielding holdings	
	Rubber price[1] (cts/lb)	Revenue per acre[2]	Net income per acre[2]	Revenue per acre[2]	Net income per acre[2]
1957	75.2	386.5	356.2	816.7	730.9
1958	69.0	354.7	324.4	749.3	663.5
1959	83.8	430.7	400.4	910.1	824.3
1960	85.6	439.9	409.6	929.6	843.8
1961	68.7	353.1	322.8	746.1	660.3
1962	65.2	335.1	304.8	708.1	622.3
1963	60.5	310.9	280.6	657.0	571.2
1964	57.5	295.6	265.3	624.5	538.7
1965	58.6	301.2	270.9	636.4	550.2
1966	54.8	281.7	251.4	595.1	509.3
1967	44.1	226.7	196.4	478.9	393.1
1968	42.9	219.5	189.2	465.9	380.1
1969	57.4	295.0	264.7	623.4	537.6
1970	45.2	232.3	202.0	490.9	405.1
1971	34.9	179.4	149.1	379.0	293.2

[1] The price data are an average of the annual average prices quoted by rubber dealers for smallholding rubber in five major towns.
[2] In calculating revenue and net income per acre on low-yielding holdings it was assumed that yields were 514 lbs per acre and non-labour operating costs were $30.3 per acre. On the high-yielding holdings it was assumed that yields were 1,086 lbs per acre and non-labour operating costs were $85.8 per acre. The figures for yield per acre and for non-labour operating costs were obtained from a national survey of rubber smallholdings carried out by the Rubber Research Institute of Malaysia in 1963/64. See Colin Barlow and Chan Chee Kheong: *Towards an optimum size of rubber holding* (Natural Rubber Conference, 1968, Kuala Lumpur, reprint), tables 19-24, pp. 19-23. Non-labour operating costs consist of processing charges, cost of equipment and materials, and quit rents. These cost items are invariant with respect to the price of rubber. There is no evidence on how these costs behaved during the period 1957 to 1970, but there is certainly no basis for believing that they would have decreased. Hence, the assumption of unchanged costs in this period is a conservative one in respect to the estimates of the net income of rubber smallholders. The assumption of constant yields per acre over the period does not conflict with the observation of rising average yields per acre of rubber smallholdings as a whole. The rising average yields are the result of replanting and new planting with high-yielding clones, but there are significant subgroups among rubber smallholders for whom the assumption of constant yields per acre is an accurate one.
Source: *Monthly Statistical Bulletin* (Statistics Department, Kuala Lumpur), various issues.

real incomes in this period,[1] and most of them were the fortunate minority who were settled on government land development schemes. This latter group, the "prosperous peasantry", the creation of which was the avowed aim of rural development policy, experienced a substantial rise in income. In contrast, the weakest elements, the owners of smallholdings planted with low-yielding clones and the crop-sharing labourers, saw their real incomes halved.

Apart from this dramatic illustration of the effects of declining commodity prices on a major section of the peasantry, there is also considerable evidence that even in the paddy sector, where the value of output per worker has risen steadily, a substantial number of peasants experienced falling real

---

[1] For the derivation of the size of the various sub-groups of rubber smallholders see E. L. H. Lee: *Rural poverty in West Malaysia, 1957 to 1970* (Geneva, ILO, 1976; mimeographed World Employment Programme research working paper; restricted), pp. 27-29.

incomes. As in the case of smallholding rubber, the observed increase in productivity in paddy cultivation was unevenly spread, with the result that inequality widened as a minority enjoyed large income gains while the rest saw their incomes either stagnate or fall. Most of the productivity increase is due to the spread of double-cropping made possible by public investments in irrigation works and, to a lesser extent, to the introduction of high-yielding varieties. As shown in table 73, almost half of the total paddy land did not benefit from either of these innovations. Significantly, the poorest paddy growing areas of Kelantan, Trengganu and Malacca benefited least from these developments.

Since most of the observed increase in output is due to double-cropping and the introduction of high-yielding varieties, it is safe to infer that productivity did not increase in the "unaffected" paddy land. Indeed, in the least affected state, Kelantan, yields per acre actually fell by 15 per cent between 1956 and 1968. Price, therefore, becomes the crucial determinant of incomes for farmers in these areas. The guaranteed minimum price of rice did not keep pace with inflation but fell by 4 per cent in real terms between 1957 and 1970. At the same time the costs of inputs[1] as well as rents increased[2] and this had the effect of squeezing incomes. As shown in table 76, in the states which benefited relatively more from double-cropping and the introduction of high-yielding varieties, increases in rents were lower than the increases in productivity, but in Kelantan and Province Wellesley the reverse was true. This is particularly serious in Kelantan where, as indicated, yields per acre actually fell by 15 per cent while average rental levels rose by more than 80 per cent.

In addition to these factors, there is the distinct possibility that the pecuniary externalities generated by the farmers who received large income gains would have bid up the prices of variable inputs. The behaviour of rentals over this period is one indication of this phenomenon: the Green Revolution has been accompanied by increased mechanisation[3] while double-cropping is unlikely to have increased the demand for hired labour. There is considerable underutilisation of family labour even in fully double-cropped areas such as Province Wellesley,[4] and the spread of double-cropping would thus provide an opportunity for the reduction of this underutilisation of family labour. Given the considerable scope for the substitution of leisure and off-farm employment for on-farm work, it is unlikely that the increased labour requirements generated by the introduction of double-cropping would imply

---

[1] C. P. Brown: "Rice Price Stabilisation and Support in Malaysia", in *The Developing Economies*, June 1973, p. 164.

[2] Yukon Huang: *The economies of paddy production in Malaysia* (unpublished Ph. D. thesis, Princeton University, 1971), table 3a, p. 101.

[3] I. Palmer: *The new rice in monsoon Asia*, op. cit.

[4] I. M. D. Little and D. G. Tipping: *A cost benefit analysis of the Kulai oil palm estate, West Malaysia* (OECD, Paris, 1972), p. 64.

Table 76.   Percentage change in total paddy output per acre and in land rents

State	Output per acre (average 1956-58 to average 1966-68)	Rent (1957 to 1965-68)	
		In cash	In kind
Perlis	51.5	7.7	22.9
Kedah	43.3	29.2	1.6
Province Wellesley	43.0	44.3	104.5
Kelantan	—15.1	17.9	83.6
Perak	38.9	n.a.	20.3
West Malaysia	26.9	n.a.	n.a.

Sources: Output per acre: *Monthly Statistical Bulletin*, various issues. Rents: Y. Huang: *The economics of paddy production in Malaya*, op. cit., table 3a.

an increase in the demand for hired labour. Thus the benefits from the spread of double-cropping were confined strictly to those families which actually began to grow a second crop; there was little or no spill-over to landless labourers or families which could not grow a second crop. Thus, given the fact that at least half of the total paddy average was still growing only one crop in 1970, the benefits from double-cropping could not have been evenly shared by all paddy farmers; the aggregate figures conceal a very sharp difference between subgroups.

It should also be noted that neither non-farm income opportunities nor rates of remuneration in them could have been expected to increase during this period. Firstly rural unemployment and underemployment had been increasing (see table 77). Secondly, the sharp fall in the demand for labour on rubber estates would have reduced the opportunities for casual work there. Thirdly, those who were engaged in off-farm employment in the small-holding sector would have experienced a fall in earnings. The predominant form of labour contract there is crop-sharing, and earnings would have fallen proportionately with the fall in revenue productivity. Moreover, the total incomes of those engaged in mixed farming of rubber and paddy would also have been adversely affected by the fall in rubber prices.

Thus in each of these two main sectors of the peasant economy there were specific factors causing a reduction in the income levels of at least a substantial minority. There was, in addition, the basic factor of demographic pressure on the land. This would appear to be a surprising assertion to make in view of the common belief that Malaya is still a land-abundant country. This paradox can be explained by a combination of three factors: the sharp rise in the growth rate of the rural population since 1947, the existence of administrative constraints to land alienation and the wide inter-regional differences in population density.

Between 1960 and 1970 the area of cultivated land increased by 12 per cent while the rural population increased by 27 per cent. The figures on land/man ratios in paddy cultivation and smallholding rubber show a marginal increase between 1957 and 1970 (3 per cent and 6 per cent respectively).

Table 77. Trends in unemployment and underemployment, 1957 to 1970

Population group	1957	1962	1967	1970
(1) Economically active population	2 149 000	2 453 000	2 727 000	3 150 000
(2) Number of "actively unemployed" according to 1957 census definition	38 600	76 700	113 600	152 000
(3) Percentage unemployed, i.e. (2) ÷ (1)	1.79	3.2	4.2	4.8
(4) Percentage of actively unemployed according to *Labour force survey* definition	n.a.	6.0	6.8	8.0
(5) Number working less than 25 hours per week	n.a.	146 800	267 300	n.a.
(6) Number willing to work a normal day	n.a.	53 900	184 100	n.a.
(7) Percentage actively unemployed in rural areas according to *Labour force survey* definition	n.a.	5.0	5.5	n.a.
(8) Percentage actively unemployed in "metropolitan towns" according to *Labour force survey* definition	n.a.	9.6	10.1	n.a.
(9) Percentage actively unemployed in "other urban areas" according to *Labour force survey* definition	n.a.	8.1	10.0	n.a.

Notes: The 1957 *Census of population* defined the unemployed as "persons who have been in employment for less than 4 of the preceding 12 months, but who have been actively looking for work for at least 6 of the 12 months". The labour force surveys defined the unemployed as "a person not gainfully employed on any employment during the week preceding enumeration, but actively seeking employment and capable of taking a job if offered it". The census definition is clearly a more restrictive one and tends to give a lower number of unemployed persons than the labour force surveys. The labour force surveys, however, do contain data on the distribution of the unemployed by the length of time for which they have been out of work. The number who have been out of work for 8 months or more, prior to the enumeration data, would thus give an estimate of the number of unemployed that is consistent with the census definition. The figures in row (3) thus represent the trend in unemployment on a consistent definition.
The problem of seasonal variations has been taken care of by the reference period of one year in the census and by the use of two sub-rounds of enumeration in the 1962 survey and three sub-rounds in the 1967 survey. The survey figures are averages obtained from the sub-rounds of enumeration.
The figure for 1970 was obtained from the *Second Malaysia Plan*, table 7-1, p. 102. From the comparisons with unemployment in 1965 and from the discussion in the text it is clear that this refers to unemployment according to the labour force definition. To obtain an estimate of the number of unemployed in 1970 that is consistent with the census definition, the 1967 proportion of the unemployed who had been out of work for 8 months or more has been applied.
Sources: *Census of population*, 1957, Report No. 14, table 10, page 97; Federation of Malaya: *Report on employment, unemployment and underemployment*, 1962; *Socio-economic sample survey of households – Malaysia, 1967-68: employment and unemployment*.

These aggregate figures are not, however, inconsistent with declining land/man ratios in certain areas. In the paddy sector the marginal improvement in land/man ratios is due to a fall in the number employed in paddy cultivation as well as a slight increase in cultivated area. The increase in acreage was heavily concentrated in two states, Pahang and Trengganu, which between then accounted for only 10 per cent of total cultivated acreage in 1957. On the other hand, in Kelantan, the second-most important rice growing state and the state which had the most unfavourable land/man ratio in 1957, there was a decrease in cultivated acreage. The decrease in employment could be due simply to increased mechanisation in the double-cropped areas while land/man ratios fell in the unaffected areas. Similarly, on rubber smallholdings, the increase in the land/man ratio is a reflection of the continued subdivision of estates and the creation of government land development schemes. Both these processes created farms which were significantly larger than the prevailing average of 6.4 acres shown in the 1960 *Census of agriculture*.[1] Since the labour-intensity on these new holdings is much lower than on smaller holdings,[2] the employment figures suggest a significant decline of the land/man ratio in holdings of less than 10 acres, notwithstanding the increase in the aggregate land/man ratio.

Apart from this broad indication, no detailed data are available on trends in land/man ratios in peasant agriculture. However, several studies of the peasant economy, especially local case studies, have documented the effects of demographic pressure on land/man ratios. Increased pressure on the land has been reflected, as is usual, in subdivision into very small plots and the fragmentation of holdings. This process has been shown to have occurred in both paddy and rubber growing areas.[3] There is also clear evidence of considerable land hunger among the peasantry from the backlog of applications at land offices throughout the country.[4] Given this information, it seems clear that demographic pressure continued to operate between 1957 and 1970. This was offset only in part by the movement of the rural population into urban areas and land development schemes. Even after taking migration into account, a large increase in the population still had to be supported on pre-existing land. This demographic pressure and increasing poverty in the stagnant peasant sector of the economy has provided the rationale for the Government's emphasis on rural development ever since independence in 1957.[5] The investments in rural development were not very substantial between 1957 and 1960 but, thereafter, they increased to 25 per cent of public investment or to an average of 2.1 per cent of GDP between 1966 and 1970. The strategy can be characterised as one of operating on the intensive margin in paddy growing as well as on the extensive margin in export crop cultivation. In paddy cultivation the income gains were expected to flow from rising output per acre due to double-cropping and the introduction of high-yielding

---

[1] The holdings on federal land development schemes were 10 acres in size while the average size of subdivided holdings, as revealed by a survey in 1960, was also 10 acres. The survey also showed that less than 10 per cent of subdivided holdings were owner-operated and that 95 per cent of the holdings had been bought by non-Malays. This latter statistic highlights the fact that the subdivision of estates did little to enhance the incomes of Malay smallholders, the poorest group in the smallholding sector. See U. A. Aziz: *The sub-division of estates in Malaya, 1951-60*, op. cit.

[2] The cultivated area per worker on holdings was 1.3 acres for farms of less than 3 acres, and this increases steadily to 7.1 acres for holdings of more than 10 acres in size. See Colin Barlow and Chan Chee Kheong, op. cit., table 9, p. 8.

[3] T. B. Wilson: *The economics of padi production in North Malaya*, op. cit.; E. K. Fisk: "Productivity and Income from Rubber in an Established Malay Reservation", in *Malayan Economic Review*, Apr. 1961.

[4] See *Annual Report of the Federal Land Development Authority*, 1963, pp. 45, 54.

[5] See K. Fisk: "Features of the Rural Economy", in T. H. Silcock and K. Fisk (eds.): *The political economy of independent Malaya* (Berkeley, University of California Press, 1963). Fisk shows that between 1950 and 1958 average rural incomes fell significantly.

varieties. In rubber it was to come from replanting as well as new planting on land development schemes. Significantly, there was no talk of land reform or structural changes in the rural economy; land development was seen as the painless solution, with yield increases on existing land simultaneously spreading rural prosperity.

THE LIMITATIONS OF RURAL DEVELOPMENT POLICIES

It is obvious from the preceding discussion that there were serious omissions in this strategy. First, it was clearly a growth-orientated strategy which paid no attention to the needs of the poorest sections of the rural population. This was reflected in the concentration of irrigation investments in the relatively more prosperous "rice bowl" areas and in the choice of 10 acres as the farm size to be parcelled out on land development schemes.[1] It was also reflected in the administration of the rubber replanting schemes, where there was no special provision to help those with very small holdings who could least afford to wait out the 7-year gestation period between planting and maturity.[2] The policy statements of this period give the impression that the rural population (in effect the rural Malay population) was seen as a homogenous group of peasants engaged low-productivity agriculture who had to be lifted out of poverty. This tendency thus to view the Malay peasantry was accompanied by what might be characterised as a "frontier mentality" among the political leadership. There was a belief that Malaysia had abundant untapped resources, especially of arable land. This belief was reflected in the official attitude towards population control during the early post-independence period[3] and it also accounts in part for the policy decision to allocate alienated land in plots which were much larger than the prevailing average farm sizes in peasant agriculture. Within this broad orientation of rural development policy, it is easy to see how it was possible for the poverty of the poorest 40 per cent of the rural population to increase.

It will be recalled that those who suffered a fall in their income belonged to precisely the weakest segment of the peasantry who either did not receive, or could not respond to, the opportunities for raising incomes that were generated by the investments in rural development. Those who were most

---

[1] According to the 1960 census of agriculture, 97 per cent of rice farms and 76 per cent of rubber smallholdings were under 10 acres in size, while 78 per cent and 46.4 per cent respectively were under 5 acres in size (see table 74).

[2] The need to replant arises from the fact that the rubber tree's productive life extends from the seventh to the thirty-third years. Replanting is thus required to maintain productivity as much as to increase it through replanting with high-yielding clones. Those on larger holdings could replant in stages while maintaining a sufficient income from the rest of their holding. Such an alternative was not open to those with very small holdings and near-subsistence incomes. For this latter group the replanting grants, although covering the direct costs of replanting, were insufficient, in the absence of loans, to tide them over the gestation period.

[3] See T. E. Smith (ed.): *The politics of family planning in the Third World* (London, George Allen & Unwin, 1973), Ch. 8.

affected were the farmers outside the "rice bowl" areas where irrigation schemes were concentrated and the rubber smallholders who worked small plots of low-yielding land.

It might be argued that the role of non-selective rural development policies in the increasing impoverishment of the rural population has been exaggerated. Clearly an important factor was the exogenous one of declining rubber prices. Indeed, it has been shown that this declining price, together with some domestic inflation, brought about a halving of the real incomes of substantial numbers of rubber smallholders. It remains true, however, that the incidence of this income loss fell most heavily on those who were least able to take compensatory action through replanting. The domestic distributional impact was thus highly adverse; those who replanted avoided a fall in income, as did the fortunate minority who were settled on land development schemes, while the poorest suffered a sharp fall in income.

The land development policy can also be seen as a highly disequalising influence. On the one hand it created, quite consciously, a small minority of prosperous peasants with incomes several times higher than that of the average peasant household.[1] On the other hand the high incomes given to this minority placed a severe restriction on the poverty-reducing effect of public investment on rural development. As shown in table 78 the number of beneficiaries from these investments amounted to only one-quarter of the increase in the number of households between 1957 and 1970 or to only 11 per cent of the number of households in 1957. This high concentration of the benefits meant not only that relative inequality was bound to increase but also, as an "externality" associated with this policy, that absolute poverty would increase as well. This latter contention rests on the view that the decline in the income of the rural poor is inversely related to the number of beneficiaries from these investments. The greater the number of beneficiaries, the smaller the pressure of population on land and hence the weaker would have been the income-reducing tendencies. This argument can in fact be extended to the whole of rural development expenditure, where the income gains were obtained by only a minority while the position of the rest deteriorated.

This argument, of course, rests on the assumption that most of the increases in income that can be obtained from the peasant sector derive from public investments. This assumption is considered to be an accurate reflection of reality because of the history of stagnation and even deterioration in the peasant economy prior to the injection of public investment. Such an injection should not be seen in terms of the breaking of bottlenecks or the quick dissemination of critical inputs which spread productivity increases throughout the rural economy. Rather, public investment has turned out to

---

[1] According to a 1968 farm income survey, the incomes of settlers on these land development schemes were ten times as high as the mean income of the poorest quintile of households in 1970 and 24 times higher than the income of the poorest 10 per cent of paddy farmers in Kelantan. (S. Selvadurai and A. Arope: *Socio-economic survey of paddy farmers in the Kumbu area of Kelantan* (Ministry of Agriculture, Kuala Lumpur, 1969)).

Table 78. Number of households benefiting from public investments in land development and irrigation, 1957 to 1970

(1) Federal land development schemes	20 700
(2) State, government and other land development schemes	20 000
(3) Double-cropping of paddy land	61 000
(4) Number of rural households in 1957	858 000
(5) Number of rural households in 1970	1 250 000

Notes: The figure in line (1) was obtained from the *Second Malaysia Plan*, p. 125, while that in line (2) was inferred from the figures on the acreage of land development by agencies other than the FLDA in *Second Malaysia Plan*, table 9-2, p. 125. The figure in line (3) was estimated on the basis of the data on the change in acreage under double-cropping in table 73. This showed that 35 per cent of paddy land was under a second crop in 1970, whereas the corresponding figure for 1957 was 0.8 per cent. We assumed that the proportion of persons engaged in paddy cultivation who had benefited from double-cropping by 1970 was the same as that of the total area double-cropped. This is probably an overestimate since the double-cropping had occurred mainly in Kedah, Perlis, Province Wellesley and Selangor, which all had larger average farm sizes than the remaining states. See Wilson, op. cit., table 75, p. 79.

be highly localised and to result in a piecemeal distribution of higher income opportunities. Irrigation works and land development are perfect illustrations of this: the income-generating effects are specific to the location of the project and have no effect on rural incomes elsewhere. In contrast, the instruments which could have ensured a more complete diffusion of benefits— such as land reform, the manipulation of relative prices, the provision of extension services, and the spread of high-yielding varieties—either were not contemplated or were not pushed vigorously enough.

The actual pattern of rural development thus created a queue for higher income opportunities, while the limited number of beneficiaries created by the high cost[1] land development schemes meant that the movement of the queue was very slow. Thus, while this strategy was successful in raising output, it did not have the desired distributive consequences.

It could be argued, however, that the chosen strategy, by its very nature, involved long time-lags and hence it is unfair to judge the success or failure of these policies in a relatively short period of 13 years. Two rebuttals immediately spring to mind. First, there is the question of intertemporal equity, of the fact that an entire generation of peasants would have no prospect of improving their living standards because of the slow movement of the queue. Secondly, there is the question of how much faster the queue could be made to move, if at all. In the case of land development it is unlikely, given the rate of growth of the rural population and the available supplies of virgin land, that the ideal of 10 acres per family is a feasible long-term goal. In paddy cultivation the process cannot accelerate because the target of self-sufficiency was nearly fulfilled by 1970 and, since Malaysia is a high-cost producer of rice, the immediate propects of those farmers who have not so far benefited from the productivity increase are bleak. In smallholding rubber almost

---

[1] See Syed Hussein Wafa: "Land Development Strategies in Malaysia: An Empirical Study", in *Kajian Ekonomi Malaysia*, Dec. 1973.

1 million acres remained to be replanted in 1970 and it is here that a big "push" is feasible. Replanting alone, however, will not be sufficient. The income levels of those with very small rubber holdings will depend crucially on the movement of the world market price of rubber. The vulnerability of this group was starkly demonstrated at the end of 1974 when a combination of high domestic inflation and low export prices reduced many to extreme poverty.

CONCLUSION

The evolution of the rural economy in Malaysia between 1957 and 1970 illustrates the limitations inherent in the conventional approach to development. A strategy of leaving the pattern of land ownership unchanged while concentrating on investments in infrastructure and land development has been shown to be inadequate. Because the process did not touch many of the rural poor, the drift into poverty continued and inequality increased sharply. Moreover, even if the diffusion of benefits had, miraculously, been universal and the incomes of all had increased proportionately, the process would still have left the original inequalities in income distribution on the "old" land unchanged. Since the target farm size on land development schemes was unrealistically high, and its development has been capital intensive, the prospects of creating a large prosperous peasantry through operating only on the margin of new land must remain slim.

A severe limitation of policy in this period was its lack of focus on specific groups. The situation of the marginal paddy farmers outside the "rice bowl" areas was overlooked, as was the special predicament of the rubber smallholders with very small plots of old, low-yielding trees. Apart from this lack of focus, there was also a lack of awareness of the dimensions of the poverty problem. This deficiency is seen most clearly in the case of land development policies. The settlers were selected on the correct principles of equity, with preference being given to the landless, but there was little discussion of the enormous imbalance between the number eligible for settlement and the number of settlers who could be accommodated on these schemes. This "blind spot" also characterised the research work in this area: the main preoccupation was with cost/benefit ratios of specific schemes. These cost/benefit analyses were standard applications of the Little-Mirlees method and no attempt was made to include income-distribution considerations in the calculations.[1]

Thus, while these specific cost/benefit ratios were often shown to be acceptable, the wider implications of a strategy based on such schemes were not.

---

[1] See, for example, I. M. D. Little and D. G. Tipping, op. cit.; Lim Sow Ching: *Land development schemes in West Malaysia: a study of costs and benefits*, op. cit.; and Syed Hussein Wafa, op. cit.

One explanation of this choice of rural development strategy is that the Government was well intentioned but unwittingly failed to adopt a more effective policy. Such an explanation, however, ignores important dimensions of the political economy of Malaysia. Although the ruling party is dependent on the political support of the predominantly Malay rural population, it is not a populist agrarian-based political movement.[1] Given the political and economic background, it is clear that alternative policies involving fundamental changes in agrarian structure were never seriously entertained. In contrast, the chosen strategy of land development not only avoided any confrontation with vested interests but had the additional advantage that it could be used as an instrument of patronage, since the state exercised direct control over the selection of settlers.[2] Thus the land development schemes created not only a prosperous peasant élite with an economic stake in the system but also a group that was politically committed to the particular ruling party. It also had the advantage of being seen as an important part of the redistribution of income and wealth in favour of Malays, to which the Government is heavily committed.

The erosion of political support for the United Malay National Organisation (UMNO) in some rural constituencies in the 1969 general elections and the subsequent outbreak of anti-Chinese riots led to the promulgation of the New Economic Policy. There was, however, little that was fundamentally "new" in it. The policy was a response to a challenge to UMNO's political power from the Islamic party (PMIP) and consisted of stronger pro-Malay measures. The new policy promised a larger redistribution, but within the existing economic framework. The rural development strategy remained unchanged except for an increase in public investment in land development. However, the emphasis in the redistribution policies shifted to the question of access of Malays to modern sector employment, to a higher education and to the ownership of modern sector assets.[3] These latter policies, even more so than the rural development strategy, will tend to increase income inequality within the Malay community. The primary beneficiaries will be a narrow group of Malay businessmen, plus those Malays obtaining university degrees and professional qualifications, and not the majority of the rural population.

---

[1] O. Tilman: "Policy Formulation, Policy Execution and the Political Elite Structure of Contemporary Malaya", in Wang Gangwu: *Malaysia: a survey* (London, Pall Mall Press, 1964).

[2] Syed Hussein Wafa, op. cit., p. 26; G. P. Means: *Malaysian politics* (University of London Press, 1970), p. 413.

[3] See Lee, op. cit., Ch. IX.

RURAL POVERTY IN INDONESIA, WITH SPECIAL REFERENCE TO JAVA

10

Ingrid Palmer

In spite of its long-established and large civil service, Indonesia's statistics are woefully deficient and it is not possible to analyse trends in rural poverty using the usual information on income distribution or real wages. Yet developments in this fifth most populous country, which is listed amongst the poorest in the world, warrant a study of rural poverty. In order to gain an insight into trends in poverty, changes in the volume of mass-based rural production, and in particular per capita production, as well as reports of the impact of the new rice technology on rural employment in Java, will be examined. Results of the four household expenditure and consumption surveys undertaken during the 1960s, i.e. the Survey Social Ekonomi Nasional (SUSENAS), will be examined against the background of contemporaneous economic changes.

The study will be divided into three periods: 1950 to 1960, 1961 to 1968 and 1969 onwards. The reason for this is twofold. First, they delineate, roughly, periods which were, respectively, distinctive for their relative prosperity, turbulence, and aggressive promotion of economic growth. The impact of each period on poverty deserves to be separately assessed. Second, trends in poverty can most usefully be observed over many years in order to take into account the effects of long-term shifts in resource allocation. In the case of Indonesia this is of special significance since there is a danger that recent events under the present administration will be viewed solely against the immediately preceding turbulent years of the mid-1960s, without establishing the continuity of basic structures before and after that period.

The subject is introduced with a summary view of the intensity and distribution of poverty in Indonesia.

INDICATORS OF POVERTY

The statistical and interpretative problems presented by an inflation rate which varied greatly in the 1950s complicate the measurement of any poverty

Table 79.   Per capita daily consumption of calories and proteins for Indonesia and Yogyakarta District, certain dates

Region and period	Calories	Protein (grams)	Animal protein (grams)
Indonesia			
Requirements[1]	1 950	48	12
Prewar[2] (Java only)	1 800	37	5
Central Bureau of Statistics around 1963	1 650	34	4
Yogyakarta District			
1951	1 345	22.7	
1955	1 303	20.1	
1960	1 284	21.4	
1964	1 012	16.4	
1965	1019	15.9	
1966	1 160	19.9	
1967	1 091	18.6	
1968	1 179	19.8	
1969	1 080	18.5	

[1] This refers to Indonesians of average weight. It cannot be seen as an ideal calorie intake.   [2] This would probably pertain, like most similar data, to the years immediately preceding the Japanese occupation.

Sources: Indonesia (including "Requirements") data used in the National Nutrition Seminar (1963) quoted by B. Napitupulu: "Hunger in Indonesia", in *Bulletin of Indonesian Economic Studies*, Feb. 1968, pp. 63 and 65; Yogyakarta data: Mubyarto: "Economic Developments in D.I. Yogyakarta", ibid., Nov. 1970, p. 16.

line defined in monetary terms. The rate rose to 845 per cent in 1965[1] and, after falling to a negligible amount in 1971, rose again to 47 per cent per annum in 1973. Moreover, differences between urban and rural prices were heightened by the fact that Indonesia is an archipelago, so that at a given time the price of rice in one place could be twice that in another.

Aggregate data place the country's per capita Gross National Product in 1974 at $150 compared with neighbouring Malaysia's $600, the Philippines' $310 and India's $130. But it is difficult to believe that Malaysia's average standard of living could be described as four times that of Indonesia's. Moreover, those who have observed living standards in both India and Indonesia believe that poverty is clearly more acute in the former.[2] The problems presented by chronic inflation, and the difficulties the country's statisticians face in measuring the total population of the archipelago and in assessing a wide range of rates of population change, are such that Indonesia's per capita GNP data possibly are amongst the most erroneous.

Nevertheless, nobody has disputed the presence of widespread and severe poverty on the island of Java ever since the poverty studies undertaken at the turn of the century were discussed in a shocked Dutch Parliament. Any

[1] According to the Jakarta 62 commodities cost-of-living index.

[2] This point is also made by H. W. Arndt: "Development and Equality: The Indonesian Case", in *World Development*, Feb.-Mar. 1975, p. 77.

"poverty map" of the archipelago would reveal that the worst mass poverty is centred on this crowded island. For this reason special reference will be made to Java.

In the last few decades there have been reports suggesting that not only is malnutrition widespread but that death induced by starvation is a commonplace in certain parts of Java. Official data reveal that there has been a continuous decline in food intake since the prewar period, and that this trend accelerated in the early 1960s. Table 79 provides data on national average consumption of calories and proteins for the prewar era and for around 1963, and then illustrates the postwar trend in the reputedly poorest area in the country, the district of Yogyakarta in Central Java. The calorie intake recorded for the Yogyakarta District from 1964 onwards is scarcely credible as it would signify starvation, but the data have been reproduced here as they were published. It is possible that some items of consumption have not been fully represented in the final calorie count, but if this source of error can be assumed to have remained proportionately constant then the figures are adequate to demonstrate a strong downward trend in food intake.

Although consumption of both calories and proteins has risen since 1965 it appears that they have not regained the levels achieved in the 1950s.

Food consumption is a common indicator of the level of poverty in rural Java. The survey Sosial Ekonomi Nasional, relating food sufficiency to income sufficiency, took 240 kg of rice equivalents per person per year as the "poverty line". Penny and Singarimbun[1] use the same quantity of food as the Javanese peasant's own definition of poverty. They use the term *cukupan* (to have enough) and state that this is traditionally seen as 120 kg of rice per person per year consumed, plus a surplus of another 120 kg for sale. For a family of five, *cukupan* then means an income equivalent of 1,200 kg of rice. (A point to be noted here is that the peasant himself sees an actual intake of about 330 grams a day as *cukupan*. This is the same as 120 kg per year.)

Indonesian economists and sociologists use food production as a rough indicator of rural income, because there are few sources of income other than food production. Using the SUSENAS income poverty line of 240 kg of rice plus maize per person per year, the data on per capita food production shown in table 80 provide some idea of average trends in poverty in Java over a 40-year period.

The average production for 1965-69 is little more than is necessary for daily requirements. It should also be borne in mind that these figures are averages and so do not reveal the distribution amongst the rural population. That is, it is not known what proportion of the population is below the poverty line, let alone the proportion below what might be called the "bodily functioning line".

---

[1] D. H. Penny and M. Singarimbun: *Population and poverty in rural Java: some economic arithmetic from Sriharjo* (Ithaca, New York, 1973), Cornell International Agricultural Development Mimeograph No. 41.

Table 80. Per capita average annual food production (less seed requirements) on Java during certain periods
(Kilograms)

Food	1925-28	1936-39	1956-59	1965-69
Rice	83	85	84	82
Maize	47	43	27	25
Rice + maize	130	128	111	107
Cassava + sweet potatoes	71	76	64	47
Total rice equivalents [1]	201	204	175	154
Peanuts	3.3	3.6	2.9	2.3
Soybeans	2.4	5.6	5.6	3.7
Peanuts + soybeans	5.7	9.2	8.5	6.0

[1] The use of "rice equivalents" to evaluate the nutritional value of non-rice staples must be treated with caution since not all forms of protein (especially that in maize) are easily digested by humans. Nor are the different amino-acid components of protein of equal nutritional value.

Source: Sajogyo: *Usaha Perbaikan Gizi Keluarga 1973*, Lembaga Penelitian Sosiologi Pedesaan (Institut Pertanian Bogor, Bogor), p. 67.

Food intake data from SUSENAS IV, 1969-70, and a 1973 UNICEF-supported evaluation study differ substantially, with the latter showing the lower figure. The differences are so great that they must largely be put down to sampling differences. But both are presented in table 81 as a source of information on provincial variation in average levels and on dependence on different foods.

As indicated, the UNICEF-supported survey data do not correspond closely with the SUSENAS data, even by order of magnitude. It is doubtful whether the difference in years can account for this, although the severe drought of 1972 no doubt affected already low incomes. The former survey also included estimates of calories and proteins but there appeared to be major discrepancies in conversion coefficients applied to each region, so these have not been reproduced here.

There are three main points to note when trying to interpret table 81. First, the geographical variation is so great that poverty cannot be seen as uniform. (The two islands of Java and Sumatra represent the range of island averages.) Second, in the better-off West Java and Sumatra provinces consumption is greater than production while in the poorer Central and East Java provinces production is greater than consumption. Third, there is marked seasonal variation in consumption.

This evidence of inadequate nutritional standards is supported by disturbing demographic information. The results of the 1971 population census showed that (widely diverging) rates of population increase exhibited perfect rank correlation with per capita income by province. The estimated annual average rate of increase since the 1961 population census was 1.94 per cent for the whole country, 1.8 per cent for Java, and 2.7 per cent for Sumatra.[1] Within Java, West Java's rate was 2.0 per cent, Central Java's 1.7 per cent

---

[1] P. McDonald: "Fewer Indonesians?", in *Bulletin of Indonesian Economic Studies*, Mar. 1972, p. 75.

Table 81.   Daily per capita consumption of staple foods[1] (1969-70 and 1973), and daily per capita production of staple foods[1] (1969-70) (Grams)

Source of data	West Java	Central Java	Yogyakarta	East Java	Total Java	Sumatra
SUSENAS (1969-70)						
Rice:						
Production	310	229	168	208	229	377
Consumption I[2]	389	213	184	198	262	403
Consumption II[2]	397	214	185	175	256	408
Rice + maize						
Production	331	320	214	399	308	393
Consumption I	397	311	190	304	329	408
Consumption II	415	338	268	348	359	411
Rice + maize + tubers:						
Production	441	455	334	476	429	449
Consumption I	441	381	369	365	390	471
Consumption II	452	384	369	406	406	444
Evaluation study (1973)						
Rice consumption	n.a.	n.a.	n.a.	n.a.	198	376
Rice + maize consumption	359	227	218	169	257	377
Rice + maize + tubers consumption	362	284	303	244	286	382

[1] These include rice and the rice equivalents of maize, cassava and sweet potatoes.   [2] Consumption I was between October and December 1969; consumption II between January and April 1970.

Source: Sajogyo, op. cit., pp. 55-57, and 59.

and East Java's 1.4 per cent. The poorest areas of all, the District of Yogyakarta, recorded 1.0 per cent. It has been suggested that Indonesia's age distribution was not stable during the 1960s; that there was a real deficiency of persons aged 10 to 19 years in 1961 resulting in a lower birth rate in the 1960s. It is certainly true that the 1940s were a most unsettling period for would-be parents, and Widjojo Nitisastro estimated the birth rate for 1966 to 1971 to be 39 per 1,000, compared with estimates for the 1950s ranging between 42 and 52.[1] But this does not explain the association of population growth with income levels.[2] How this occurs, whether by differential mortality rates or by migration, is not known.

Poverty has, for good reasons, frequently been defined in terms of lack of access to the means of production. In rural societies this can be taken to mean lack of access to land. Two writers[3] have done much to press home the

[1] McDonald, op. cit., pp. 77-78.

[2] There is some evidence that within rural Java there has been migration from areas of poor soils to areas of good soils, and that this represents a shift in population from southern to northern districts, but this should not affect statistics on a province level. The urban drift is substantial only in the cases of Jakarta and Surabaya. See R. D. Montgomery: "Migration, Employment and Unemployment in Java", in *Asian Survey*, Mar. 1975, p. 224.

[3] D. H. Penny and M. Singarimbun, op. cit.

point that Javanese themselves quite clearly see poverty in this way. Farmers interviewed stressed again and again to the writers that an annual output of 1,200 kg of rice was enough to maintain a household of five. If the land yielded as much as 3.5 tons of (milled) rice per hectare[1] a year land requirements would be only 0.34 hectare per household (assuming this is net of input costs). But this net yield is far above the average. Since land quality is so variable in Java, it is not very helpful to state one figure for farm size below which the household is in dire poverty. Without more information on annual yield fluctuations and output net of input costs it is not possible to determine the minimum necessary size of farm. Although Penny's figure of 0.7 hectare of good irrigated rice land *(sawah)* as necessary for a contented household is probably too high, 0.5 hectare cannot easily be dismissed as an excessively high farm size measure of a "poverty line". One writer[2] claims that 0.25 hectare of first class *sawah* under high yielding varieties will support a family of five.

According to the 1971 population census the Western Province of Java carried 440 persons per square kilometre, the Central Province 634 and the Eastern Province 539. With such population pressure landlessness can be expected to be extensive. Unfortunately, however, the data on Java's landlessness are patchy.

According to the 1971 population census, of Java's 62.3 million rural residents, 21 million were defined as economically active and they were divided into: 7.8 million unpaid family workers; 7.5 million farm operators; and 5.7 million farm labourers. Thus, according to these figures, the landless represent about 20 per cent of the rural labour force. An immediate problem of interpreting these figures is one of the occupational categorisation, arising from the variety of employment, of the rural households that do not have enough land for self-sufficiency. Thus many people are family workers part of the time and labourers at other times.

More substantial circumstantial data on Java's landless come from data on farm size distribution. With total farming land of 10.1 million hectares, or 0.16 hectare per rural resident (by 1975) an egalitarian distribution of land would lead to operating household plots averaging well under 1 hectare, even if a percentage of the rural residential households were not farming. Clearly, if farming has remained profitable it must be because there has been resistance to fragmentation beyond a certain level. This is borne out by the data. A 1903 poverty survey described 45 per cent of farms as having less than 0.5 hectare, whereas the 1963 agricultural census specified only a slightly

---

[1] This was taken as a generalised yield figure for high-yielding varieties on good irrigated land, seen in the agro-economic surveys.

[2] J. Hickson: "Rural Development and Class Contradictions on Java", in *Journal of Contemporary Asia*, 5 (3), 1975, p. 331. (Hickson quotes R. Franke's unpublished Harvard Ph.D. thesis: *The Green Revolution in a Javanese village*).

higher figure: 52 per cent.[1] Moreover, over the same period the proportion of farms greater than 1 hectare changed only from 21 to 22 per cent. Yet over that 60-year period Java's population rose from 29 to 66 million. There has been little migration to urban areas, except to Jakarta and Surabaya, and transmigration to the other islands has been insignificant. Some more land was brought under cultivation and the decline of the sugar plantations also put more land under staple food crops. But the last significant extensions of cultivated land were made prior to 1920. On the evidence so far, then, between 1903 and 1961 something between 24 and 28 million rural residents (80 per cent of a 30-to-35-million population increase) have been added to the category of landless households.

Further data come directly in the form of numbers of landless households. Of the 9.4 million farming households in 1970 the bottom 20 per cent of all farming households averaged less than 0.1 hectare, while the bottom 60 per cent averaged 0.2 hectare.[2] Thus in 1970 an estimated 1.9 million households (20 per cent of 9.4 million) operated farms too small to be included in any census (which only considers farms larger than 0.1 hectare). These households can be regarded as virtually landless.

Unfortunately the figure for the absolutely landless in 1970 is not available, but according to the 1963 agricultural census they amounted to 21 per cent of all rural households. Combining the 1963 census and the 1970 survey, it can be said that in 1970 at least 41 per cent of rural households had no land or less than 0.1 hectare. The results of the 1973 agricultural census are not yet available, but in the absence of effective land reform and in view of the impact of the rice intensification programme in recent years (which is described later), it would not be far wrong to say that by 1973 almost half of Java's rural households were, or were virtually, landless. In terms of the figure of 62.3 million rural residents in 1971, and assuming household size does not vary by state of access to land, then 31.2 million people belong to virtually landless households in Java. This number does not include those (unknown) numbers of tenants and their families operating farms more than 0.1 hectare, but who have been reduced to *de facto* landless labourers through the modernisation of rice production.

The 1963 agricultural census (see table 82) revealed that 54 per cent of households operating more than 0.1 hectare were within the "0.1 to 0.5 hectare" category. It is unlikely that this percentage has declined since then. If the idea of an adequate farm size were to be extended to 0.5 hectare of any

---

[1] All censuses record only farms of at least 0.1 hectares. It is not known what the 1903 poverty survey defined as a farm.

[2] Sajogyo: *Modernisation without development* (Bogor Agricultural University, Bogor). Another report (W. Brand: "Some Statistical Data on Indonesia", in *Bijdragen tot de Taal –, Land –, en Volkenkunde* [Contributions to linguistics, geography and ethnography], 125, No. 3-1969, pp. 307, 309, quoted by Margo L. Lyon: *Bases of conflict in rural Java* (Center for South and Southeast Asia Studies, Berkeley, California), Research Monograph No. 3, p. 16) stated that 2.2 million households in Java cultivated less than 0.1 hectares.

Table 82. Numbers of operational farms (over 0.1 hectares) by size and area, Java, 1963

Farm size (hectares)	Jakarta	West Java	Central Java	East Java	Yogyakarta	Total
0.10-0.49	14640	1205857	1378675	1358650	194612	4152434
0.50-0.99	4130	525412	731946	813603	82617	2157708
1.00-1.49	1970	216462	276163	335062	28830	858487
1.50-1.99	960	83567	113844	140627	11891	350889
2.00-2.99	860	74409	79289	112531	6824	273913
3.00-3.99	300	23034	25314	38230	1758	88636
4.00-4.99	140	10714	10092	14583	454	35983
5.0 and over	120	11929	8020	13147	651	33867
Total	23120	2151384	2623343	2826433	327637	7951917

Source: Sie Kwat Soen: *Prospects for agricultural development in Indonesia* (Centre for Agricultural Publishing and Documentation, Wageningen, 1968), p. 59. Also Central Bureau of Statistics: *Results of the Agricultural Census, 1963*, p. 1.

land, not necessarily of *sawah*, the conclusion could be drawn that something in the vicinity of 75 per cent (almost 50 per cent "landless" plus 54 per cent of the remaining "non-landless") of Java's rural households clearly do not have land enough to meet the farmer's own idea of the "poverty line", and that the true percentage might be much more. Again using the 1971 estimate of rural residents, at least 46.7 million rural Javanese are below their own idea of a "poverty line".

Thus aggregate per capita food production data reveal a poor and worsening standard of nutrition. Demographic data hint at a situation in which extreme poverty is having a downward effect on net population increases. But it was only information on land distribution and calculations on likely proportions of the rural population which is landless that provided evidence that poverty must be very unequally distributed.

THE POST-INDEPENDENCE PERIOD, 1950-60

Upon gaining independence the Government began the task of rehabilitation from eight years of Japanese occupation and the physical struggle against the Dutch. It was only well into the 1950s that prewar production levels of food crops were regained. The primary agricultural exports of the outer islands, rubber and copra, were encouraged, as were tea and coffee on Java's foreign-owned plantations and smallholdings. The peasant staple food sector received periodic attention culminating in the costly, but largely unsuccessful, Three Year Rice Plan, 1959-61. The small scale and cottage industries were aided by several schemes to raise their productivity, in particular the (very)[1] first Five Year Plan, 1956-60, which promoted small-scale indus-

[1] Not to be confused with the later First Five Year Plan, 1969-74.

Table 83.   Indonesia: area, production and average yield of major export crops: 1955, 1960 and 1965

Crop and year	Smallholder			Estates		
	Area (1,000 hectares)	Production (1,000 metric tons)	Yield (quintals per hectare)	Area (1,000 hectares)	Production (1,000 metric tons)	Yield (quintals per hectare)
Rubber						
1955	1430	507	3.54	491	266	5.42
1960	1430	404	2.82	506	216	4.26
1965	1609	504	3.13	507	220	4.32
Dry copra						
1955	1514	1039	6.86	23.2	16.2	6.98
1960	1610	1239	7.70	18.8	8.8	4.68
1965	1540	1235	8.02	16.6	6.6	3.98
Coffee						
1955	148.6	47.3	3.18	48.3	16.1	3.39
1960	230.7	77.9	3.38	47.1	18.3	3.89
1965	265.8	120.7	4.54	40.4	19.8	4.90
Tea						
1955	64.6	21.9	3.39	80.3	39.3	4.89
1960	64.4	37.3	5.79	72.9	41.9	5.75
1965	55.1	35.0	6.35	74.3	44.8	6.03
Tobacco[1]						
1955	100.5	35.0	3.48	11.4	7.0	6.14
1960	140.3	49.5	3.53	11.0	6.5	5.91
1965	140.5	55.5	3.95	3.7	4.8	13.21

[1] People's tobacco for smallholders; all varieties for estates.
Source: Central Bureau of Statistics, Jakarta.

tries in rural and semi-rural areas. Contrary to what many of his critics maintain, President Sukarno did have an ideology of economic development, but his faith in transmigration to the outer islands led to a hostile attitude towards family planning.

When Dutch estate managers and technical advisers were expelled in 1957-58 the fortunes of the estate export sector and the peasant sector began to diverge, with the latter holding its own production levels and even raising them. Inflation, always subject to strong annual fluctuations, began an upward trend by rising to 50 per cent per annum in 1958 and 65 per cent in 1959. But, as can be seen from table 83,[1] the complaints about Sukarno's mismanagement of the economy were largely to do with trends in the estate sector whose former and remaining foreign owners were more vocal than smallholders.

---

[1] The figures for 1965 are also introduced to show the later impact of a continuation of these influences.

Table 84. Java and Madura: population and volume of production of principal farm food crops (Index: 1960=100)

Year	Population (millions)	Irrigated paddy	Non-irrigated paddy	Total paddy	Maize	Cassava	Sweet potatoes	Peanuts	Soybeans
1940	77.5	116	92	106		97	101	91	75
1955	90.0	68	91	82		75	72	82	78
1956	91.8	96	58	94	80	74	107	83	80
1957	93.7	95	66	94	73	82	114	89	77
1958	95.8	99	73	98	112	93	125	89	97
1959	97.9	101	79	100	82	105	106	92	96
1960	**100.0**	**100**	**100**	**100**	**100**	**100**	**100**	**100**	**100**
1961	101.9	94	117	95	95	97	87	94	96
1962	104.4	99	164	102	137	93	142	94	86
1963	106.8	87[1]	114	88[1]	98	100	112	85	76
1964	109.4	85[1]	120	87[1]	161	105	163	93	84
1965	112.0	97	120	98	95	112	103	90	88
1966	114.5	101	148	103	155	95	91	99	92
1967	117.4	97	136	98	94	96	80	88	92
1968	120.2	112	141	113	126	99	91	102	81
1969	123.3	116	120	116	89	95	77	90	87
1970	126.0	137	123	136	117	92	76	102	110
1971	128.9	144	131	143	106	84	67	101	104
1960 volume (100 tons)		*93009*	*4225*	*97234*	*17927*	*86881*	*14033*	*2161*	*3905*

[1] Drought, floods and rat infestation.

Source: Calculated on the basis of data taken from *Statistical Pocketbook of Indonesia 1968 and 1969*, p. 128; and ibid., *1970 and 1971*, p. 112.

The progress of peasant food production during the 1950s followed roughly the path of smallholders' export crops. It was 1954 before rehabilitation of food land in Java allowed harvested areas to return to their 1940 levels, after which, for reasons of limited land supply, the rate of increase of the area under cultivation tapered off. Increases in production then had to come from yield improvements, unlike in the other islands where land extension continued. The struggle to raise food production to its prewar level on land-hungry Java is reflected in the slow rise in output from 1955 to 1960 (table 84). Over that period there was a 10 per cent increase in paddy output entirely due to irrigated land. But in per capita terms only soybean production returned to prewar levels by 1960.

In the whole country rice production kept pace with population increases between 1955 and 1960 — postwar rehabilitation of land, if not of productivity, having been achieved. But in the outer islands, in contrast to Java, production of non-irrigated rice rose faster during the 1950s than production of irrigated rice. The explanation lies in the extension of land under cultivation.

Thus the first decade of independence, as far as it affected the mass-based economy, can be described as a period of sober and rational progress. Smallholders' production for export did well in spite of chronic inflation. The major weakness lay in the inability to find new land and irrigation resources on Java to enable that island to regain former nutritional levels. There were areas of economic policy which were irresponsible and the estate sector certainly suffered badly, but in the light of what has happened since in Indonesia and in many other developing countries the detractors of Sukarno have grossly underestimated the relative prosperity he secured for the poor during this period. It is also important to appreciate the level of achievement reached by 1960 when reviewing production changes after 1965.

THE PERIOD OF INSTABILITY, 1961-68

It is difficult to point to one year during this period which could be termed normal from an economist's viewpoint. The 1960s began with the campaign to wrest West New Guinea from the Dutch, followed by confrontation with Malaysia. The effect was twofold. The military budget rose rapidly and caused the money supply to pass totally out of the Bank of Indonesia's control. British estate managers were also expelled and the continued decline in estate production took its toll of foreign earnings. Debt servicing in 1966 alone was estimated to be $530 million, compared with average annual export earnings over the period 1962 to 1965 of less than $550 million.

The violent upheaval of September 1965 gradually ushered in a new administration which then performed a *volte face* on economic policy, placing great reliance on market forces. Export bonuses (increasing percentages of foreign earnings which could be exchanged by exporters at virtually free

Table 85. Volume of main traditional exports, Indonesia
(Index: 1961 = 100)

Export item	1938	1961	1965	1966	1967	1968	1969	1970	1971	1972	1973	1974
Rubber	45	100	109	104	100	117	130	121	121	121	134	118
Copra	139	100	74	71	68	128	93	110	46	21	25	—
Copra cakes[1]	—	—	—	—	—	—	100	109	140	164	137	109
Coffee	103	100	159	143	235	125	187	152	110	141	148	162
Tobacco	n.a.	100	80	72	118	63	34	65	109	146	184	150
Palm oil	188	100	112	158	118	136	158	142	187	207	230	216
Palm kernels	n.a.	100	101	97	119	112	131	130	149	147	122	67
Pepper	n.a.	100	66	111	200	132	89	14	130	132	132	99
Timber	—	—	—	—	—	—	100	216	289	385	524	458
Tea	200	100	114	98	77	106	94	108	117	123	100	122

[1] A new arrival; 1969 = 100.

Sources: Calculated on the basis of data collected from: *Indonesian Financial Statistics*, VI (11), Nov. 1973, p. 122; VII (11), Nov. 1974, p. 128; VII (1), Jan. 1974, p. 114; VIII (1) Jan. 1975, pp. 136, 138; and *Bank Indonesia Report 1966-67*, p. 99; and S. Grenville: "Survey of Recent Developments", in *Bulletin of Indonesian Economic Studies*, Mar. 1974, p. 15; and (1938) *Statistical Pocketbook of Indonesia 1963*.

market rates) helped to rehabilitate and advance further some primary exports (see table 85); but as has already been seen, the smallholder sector (largely in the outer islands) had been expanding steadily all the time anyway.

In rural Java the chief feature of the post-1965 administration was its promotion of higher yields in the rice industry. Rice was the one large item on the import bill that could be reduced (by applying the latest technology) and the Government encouraged a variety of intensification programmes to spread throughout the country while concentrating mainly on Java. The upward trend in rice output had begun to show clearly by 1968, as can be seen from tables 84 and 91, while other staple foods were left unaffected.

The notable contribution to data for distributional analysis for Indonesia is in the form of household and per capita expenditure data obtained from national social and economic surveys ("Particulars on consumption") which happen to fall within this period of economic decline and later rehabilitation. The surveys were undertaken in 1963-64 (I), 1964-65 (II), 1967 (III) and 1969-70 (IV).[1] These data on expenditure can be substituted for data on income for the purposes of this chapter.

Unfortunately, SUSENAS 1967 was not available but this was probably the least interesting year for an appreciation of changes in distribution since production was still prevented from returning to normal by a severe credit squeeze and prices were being stabilised by large quantities of commodity aid. Instead, the last survey, for 1969-70, is included although it falls just inside the period of the First Five Year Plan.

---

[1] SUSENAS I refers to December 1963 to January 1964, SUSENAS II to October 1964 to February 1965, and SUSENAS IV to October 1969 to April 1970.

Table 86.   Annual rates of inflation, Jakarta (62 commodities)
(Percentages)

Year	Rate of inflation	Year	Rate of inflation
1963	143	1963/4	122 SUSENAS I
1964	128	1964/5	339 SUSENAS II
1965	845	1965/6	819
1966	374	1966/7	166
1967	155 SUSENAS III	1967/8	131
1968	46	1968/9	23
1969	17	1969/70	15 SUSENAS IV
1970	6.5		
1971	0.9		
1972	22		
1973	47		
1974	20		

Sources: Calculated from data from *(a)* Central Bureau of Statistics, Jakarta, (1963-66); *(b) Bulletin of Indonesian Economic Studies*, No. 7, p. 3; No. 8, p. 100; No. 6, p. 92; V(1), p. 3; VI (2), p. 18; VI (3), p. 4; VII (3), p. 22; VIII (3), p. 18; VIII (1), p. 2; X (2), p. 8; XI (2), p. 19; (1966-74).

The total period covered by the four surveys is too brief and too full of short-term economic changes to form an adequate basis for trend evaluation in expenditure distribution. But because the surveys offer the only recent hard data on distribution of purchasing power and because they cover a much debated period of economic change, they are analysed here in some detail. Since poverty in rural Java is the focus of attention in this chapter the data on Java-Madura alone will be examined.

Over the whole of this period inflation was severe, yet it was by no means running at a constant rate. The rates of inflation during the years when the various SUSENAS surveys (see below) were undertaken varied from 15 per cent in 1969-70 to 339 per cent in 1964-65. The figures for all years since 1963 are presented in table 86 since the effects of inflation in one year are bound to be felt in later years.

With such high and varying rates of inflation any evaluation of trends in income or expenditure data has to be circumspect. If short period (snapshot) estimates are made for the sake of pinpointing the exact change in prices, and therefore of real income, the results (especially in rural areas) have to take into account seasonal influences on income. If the period over which observations are drawn is even as long as three months, in order to diminish the seasonal influence, the impact of a rise in prices of 30 to 100 per cent over the survey period can lead to enormous statistical difficulties. Data on the volume of consumption of essentials by class of respondent helps to overcome these latter difficulties.

Since the only substantial data available on the distribution of income or expenditure pertain to this period and to 1969-70 they are taken together and discussed here.

Table 87. Percentile distribution of per capita expenditure in ascending order of expenditure magnitude: rural Java-Madura

Year	P_{10}	P_{20}	P_{30}	P_{50}	P_{80}	P_{90}
1963-64	45.8	61.8	75.7	100	167.3	213.1
1964-65	38.8	60.0	72.5	100	165.0	222.5
1969-70	44.7	59.2	75.8	100	153.2	195.3

Note: These data are ratios. For example, the figure for P_{90} is the ratio of the income of the top eleventh percentile (individual's income) to the median income. Thus $P_i = 100 \times \dfrac{Yi}{Y50}$

Sources: The percentile expenditures were measured from a cumulative frequency curve using the original survey data of frequencies and class intervals.

The Gini coefficients for per capita consumption expenditure in rural Java-Madura for 1963-64, 1964-65, and 1969-70 were 0.362, 0.371 and 0.330, respectively.[1] The worsening distribution in 1964-65 can be largely attributed to the regressive influence of inflation on distribution. However, when the Lorenz concentration curves were fitted to the data the curves for 1963-64 and 1964-65 crossed once, near the middle with lower expenditures showing greater inequality, and higher expenditures less inequality, in 1964-65 than in 1963-64. The curves for 1963-64 and 1969-70 crossed twice—at about the lower fortieth percentile and top ninety-fifth percentile.

Instead of merely relying on the interpretation of single coefficients, percentile expenditure distributions were also examined. The results for the three SUSENAS are given in table 87. The effect of inflation is clearly seen. The first and third years recorded show a more egalitarian distribution of per capita expenditure. However, whereas 1969-70 shows less inequality at the top end of the distribution, there is greater relative poverty at the low expenditure end than in 1963-64. The change is not great, except at the top end. Since 1969-70 marked a period of substantial price stabilisation but was too soon to reflect structural changes, apart from those induced by the widespread rice intensification programmes, the only conclusion which can be drawn is that the stabilisation programme redressed much of inflation's regressive effects on income distribution. However, the reduction in inflation did not return relative prices to previous levels. Data on percentages of total expenditure going on food (and especially rice) derived from the SUSENAS leave no doubt that amongst the worse-off there had been a shift in expenditure from non-food items to food items between 1963-64 and 1969-70.

The percentile distributions of per capita weekly consumption of rice (table 88) demonstrate vividly the impact of the rapid acceleration of inflation in 1964-65, although it must also be said that rice imports were reduced

---

[1] The Gini coefficient used here are the simple averages of upper and lower bounds of the coefficients developed by Farhad Mehran: *Dealing with grouped income distribution data* (Geneva, ILO, 1975; World Employment Programme research working paper; restricted), p. 29, in order to cope with data consisting only of income intervals and the percentage of recipients in each interval.

Table 88.   Percentile distribution of per capita weekly consumption of rice and fish in physical quantities

Year	Per capita weekly consumption of rice (kg)								
	P_{10}	P_{20}	P_{30}	P_{40}	P_{50}	P_{60}	P_{70}	P_{80}	P_{90}
1963-64	(.81)	.98	1.16	1.36	1.54	1.78	2.12	2.42	(2.82)
1964-65	(.28)	.56	.84	1.08	1.32	1.60	1.86	2.22	(2.62)
1969-70	(.55)	.80	1.00	1.22	1.47	1.71	1.96	2.27	(2.54)
	Per capita weekly consumption of wet and dry fish (kg)								
	P_{10}	P_{20}	P_{30}	P_{40}	P_{50}	P_{60}	P_{70}	P_{80}	P_{90}
1963-64	(.048)	.058	.068	.077	.092	.116	.142	.174	(.204)
1964-65	(.013)	.030	.046	.062	.080	.100	.120	.148	(.216)
1969-70	(.037)	.052	.062	.074	.088	.107	.130	.170	(.214)

Notes: (1) The survey data were given in the form of average consumption of the food item for each per capita expenditure class. The frequencies used pertained to each expenditure class. Cumulative frequency curves were drawn on these *class averages*. Whatever the disadvantages of this method they should not affect the relative positioning of the three curves and therefore the relative readings from them, except perhaps for the first and last decile readings, which are placed in parentheses.

(2) For 1969-70 the frequencies from which percentages were calculated were of numbers of persons in each per capita expenditure class. For 1963-64 and 1964-65 the frequencies from which percentages were calculated were of numbers of *households* in each per capita expenditure class. If household size remains constant over all expenditure classes, there would be no difference. In fact, poorer households tend to be very slightly smaller than better-off households, but it is not believed that this difference affected the results.

(3) In the 1963-64 survey the quantity of rice consumed was expressed in litres (volume). One litre is usually about 0.950 kilogram, but a litre can be even heavier than 1 kilogram if the grains are short.

to negligible amounts during 1965. The decline of rice consumption of the first and second decile groups was dramatic, although due to interpolation difficulties with five class intervals for 1963-64, that year's consumption figures might be too high. But actual per capita rice consumption in 1969-70 had not achieved the 1963-64 levels for any decile group; and as a proportion of 1963-64 consumption the quantities of the lowest expenditure classes declined most of all.

A major cause of this deterioration was undoubtedly changes in the system of government rice distribution (at varying but low effective prices). In 1963-64 the poorest could rely on this cheaper rice for almost 10 per cent of their rice consumption, but in 1969-70 for only 2 per cent.[1] The same data also indicate that while government rice distribution in 1963-64 was relatively (as proportions of total rice consumed), though not absolutely, egalitarian, by 1969-70 there was no pretence at even a relatively egalitarian distribution: absolute amounts of government-distributed rice rose very much faster, with total expenditure on rice, in 1969-70. Whereas in 1963-64 the per capita quantity of government-distributed rice was 8.3 times greater in the highest than in the lowest expenditure class, in 1969-70 it was 34.8 times greater.

The significance of relative price changes affecting different income budgets differently are not, of course, revealed in the Gini coefficient or the percentile estimates of expenditure. The impact of rice price changes on the poor, however, has been noted by others. H.W. Arndt, commenting on the

[1] SUSENAS, 1963-64 and 1969-70.

rise in the real price of rice between 1966 and 1973, points out that for many, higher food prices mean hardship.[1]

Unfortunately, the categories of cassava, dried cassava and cassava flour were not presented in a comparable manner in the survey data for the three years. But since rice is the much preferred source of carbohydrates the data here are considered sufficient to support the conclusion that 1964-65 was an extraordinary year and a useless base year, and that there is no evidence that the diet of the poor in 1969-70 was superior to that of the early 1960s. It is to be regretted that there are no survey data for 1959 to 1961 when the standard of living was even higher than in 1963-64.

Fish is the main source of animal protein. Data for percentile distributions of wet and dry fish were amalgamated to give the distributions of per capita weekly consumption of total fish. All the quantities are pitifully small, but the story is similar to that of rice, except that the better off rural residents gained marginally in 1969-70 as compared to 1963-64.

It was noted earlier that even 1963-64 was part of the declining period of Sukarno's administration. How would the better earlier years have compared with 1969-70? Unfortunately, comparable expenditure data for the period 1958 to 1961 are not available.

However, P. R. Deuster[2] compares real income changes of different categories of rural residents between 1959 and 1968. He shows how inflation affected categories of rural residents differently, and for this he developed separate cost-of-living indices based on the question "for a man on such an income how much must his (money) income have risen to be on the same standard of living?"[3] Applying these indices he came to the following estimates for quartile real incomes (see table 89).

Each set of quartiles was obtained for each category of rural resident separately. Thus each row in table 89 refers to a separate "population". From the listing of the socio-occupational categories it can be assumed that average income rises as one moves down the table. Thus it can be concluded that for the first four (farming) groups, the lower-income categories were more deeply affected by inflation, as their ratios to 1959 real income were lower. Moreover, by moving horizontally across the table from the right to the left, it is seen that within each socio-occupational category, the originally worse off (the first quartile) suffered greater proportional falls in real income than their better off "peers" (the third quartile). Thus the effects of inflation can be read in two ways: by moving vertically and horizontally across the table.

---

[1] Arndt, op. cit., pp. 81-82.

[2] P. R. Deuster: *Rural consequences of Indonesian inflation: a case study of the Yogyakarta Region* (Ph.D thesis, University of Wisconsin, 1971). The data used were from (i) a 1959 household survey in Yogyakarta region by a team of US economists working at Gadjah Mada University covering 245 rural and 35 urban Mada households, and (ii) a 1968 household survey conducted by Gadjah Mada University.

[3] For elaboration of his methodology see Deuster, op. cit., pp. 79-96.

Table 89.   Comparison of real first quartile, median and third quartile incomes for different occupations: Yogyakarta region, 1959 and 1968 (real income in 1968)
(Index: 1959=100)

Occupation	First quartile	Median	Third quartile
Farm labourer	64	106	108
Small farmer	64	86	98
Medium farmer	118	137	147
Large farmer	139	148	147
Transfer receiver	87	87	141
White-collar worker	92	97	110

Source: Deuster, op. cit., p. 96.

The varying influence of inflation by size of farmer is marked. Small farmers at each of the three points in their own distribution were worse off, while medium and large farmers were better off in the later period. The farm labouring category underwent a process of stratification with median and (upper) third quartile labourers doing a little better in 1968, but the poorer farm labourers being much worse off than in 1959. Later, it is shown how recent changes in rice cultivation have brought about a further stratification within the landless labouring class. But from Deuster's data it would appear that this had been occurring prior to the technological and commercial innovations of the Green Revolution. This supports a now widespread contention but summarised well by Hickson,[1] that increasing concentration of land and changes in tenurial arrangements had been occurring long before the Green Revolution.

Indeed, Deuster went on to use Lorenz concentration curves for assets.[2] He found that with total assets there was no change between 1959 and 1968, but that there was a highly significant worsening in the distributions of good rice land *(sawah)*. From this it can be concluded that inflation had lasting detrimental effects for small farmers. Again, it must be pointed out that the Green Revolution was barely under way in Java by 1968.

THE END OF "SHARED POVERTY" IN RURAL JAVA: 1969-74

For the analysis of this period data of a non-comparable nature with that of the previous section have had to be used. However, these recent years saw fundamental shifts in the relations between different rural social classes and a study of the causes of these shifts provides better indications of their power and permanence than quantitative data.

---

[1] Hickson, op. cit., pp. 330-332.

[2] Deuster, op. cit., p. 103.

The period covers exactly what is now called the First Five Year Plan.[1] One of its chief aims was to rehabilitate and, in some cases, to expand traditional exports. Over the whole Plan period approximately $3,400 million of grants and aid was given Indonesia by an inter-governmental consortium. Another aim was to encourage foreign capital and expertise to develop minerals and timber and to advance industrialisation. By August 1974 foreign investment *approvals* amounted to about $4,000 million. But the prime target was rice self-sufficiency by 1975.

The nutritional and land distribution data presented at the beginning of this chapter depicted a situation of widespread and severe deprivation. Yet observers have constantly remarked upon the superior conditions of life in Java compared with India. One explanation could lie in the theory of "shared poverty"[2] that has long been debated by Indonesian scholars. The theory postulates that when Javanese agricultural land could no longer be extended, a process of agricultural involution set in, whereby village society incorporated an intricate network of patron-client relationships (asymmetrical) between families which provided everyone with a niche in the village economy and prevented outright starvation or indigence. The theory has come under severe criticism by scholars, generally along the lines that patronage camouflaged increasing exploitation and the practice of bonded labour, and the system could perhaps be more accurately described as "poverty shared amongst the poor". Nevertheless it summarises a situation in which the disinherited were not totally redundant to the system.

The worst mass poverty is uncontestably in rural Java, particularly the central and eastern provinces. But it is also here that rice-growing, the only labour-intensive rural activity to expand output significantly after 1965, dominates livelihoods. Much of the hope for holding the line on poverty in absolute terms rests on the ability of the modernised rice industry to absorb more of Java's unemployed and underemployed and to generate mass income.

The SUSENAS household expenditure surveys, already examined, provided data only over the price stabilisation period which preceded the remarkable changes in job opportunities in Java's rice industry. In this section social processes catalysed by the new technology are examined with a view to indicating what must have been happening to the distribution of benefits and to the absolute level of job opportunities facing the large class of landless in recent years.

The implications of the new rice technology in Java are not easily evaluated since there are consecutive generations of effects as emerging attitudes to commerce and profit sharpen conflicts of interests and as capital is accumulated on a considerable scale for the first time in the villages.

---

[1] Although not actually the country's *first* five-year plan, it was described so because it was intended as the first of a new series of Plans.

[2] This was enunciated by Clifford Geertz in *Agricultural involution*, op. cit.

The technology associated with the high yielding varieties and large quantities of fertilisers is, in theory, scale neutral. And yet again and again in the literature on Java's rice sector one reads that the new technology failed to make farms of less than 0.5 hectares viable without family members also undertaking off-farm labour. Sajogyo, for example, writes that:

... in 2 out of 3 villages, that is in Pluneng, and Nganjat, for most of farmers on 0.5 hectares of riceland, even with double-cropping, it is off-farm income that enabled them to pass the "poverty line".[1]

A farm of "just under 0.5 hectares" is noted "to have enough production to be kept in operation only with supplementary income to feed the household's own labour".

Part of the reason why small farmers are unable to use the new technology to pull themselves above the poverty line is that indebtedness places restrictions on the mobility of family labour and obliges farmers to offer their labour below the going wage. A farmer indebted to another can be at the latter's call day and night. He can be up all night preventing landless labourers from harvesting the crop unsolicited and he can be offering his family's labour to a creditor when it is most needed on his own farm. Labour in these circumstances is invariably underpriced.

In this situation "the smallest farmers, mostly under 0.25 hectares, buy agricultural capital not only with the value of their labour at depressed wages, 25-35 per cent lower... but also with their labour mobility". They repay their debts by working on the farms of those who lend money and rice. Debt-labour is associated with the continued indebtedness of a large group of small deficit-farmers to a minority of those who are capital-rich.[2] Thus indebtedness prevents the smallest farms from applying the new technology and thereby increasing their income. Moreover, the increased profits from rice farming have encouraged those who are in a position to do so to exploit the position of indebtedness of the poor.

Other reasons for small and medium farmers being unable to benefit equitably from the new technology include their inability to raise working capital as cheaply as large farmers, and their consequent specific inability to purchase highly seasonal labour for the period of land preparation, a period now shorter and utilised more intensely because with the new seeds five crops can be grown within two years.

However, the way in which the new aggressive techno-commercial revolution in rice production has affected the practice of "shared poverty" is best illustrated by the spread of *tebasan*. The traditional means of harvesting was to allow a large number of villagers, men and women, to gather on a particular day and to start cropping a field without supervision. No matter

---

[1] Sajogyo: *Modernisation without development*, op. cit.

[2] Sajogyo, op. cit., quoting from R. Franke: *The Green Revolution in a Javanese village*, op. cit., provides an illustration of this from the village of Lestari in which 43 per cent of households were small deficit farmers and 7 per cent of other households were the creditor farmers.

Table 90.   Harvesting costs and returns under three harvesting conditions in village No. 3 (Kendal): dry season 1972

	Ani-ani plus customary shares of 1:6	*Ani-ani* plus *tebasan* shares of 1:11	Sickle plus payment in money
Number of harvesters per hectare	184	150	80
Average gross yield of new rice (tons of paddy per hectare)	4.72	4.72	4.72
Cost of harvesting:			
% to harvesters	14.3	8.3	1
cost in rice (tons of paddy per hectare)	0.67	0.38	1
Cost in money (rupiahs per hectare)	10 050	5 850	7 560
Return per harvester (rupiahs)	55	39	95

1 When the sickle is used no payment in kind is made.

Source: Agro-Economic Survey, Research Notes, No. 44.

how many workers there were, the farmer would hand over a proportion of the harvested crop to them. This was traditionally one-ninth but it could be one-seventh. *Tebasan*, on the other hand, which entails the selling of the crop by the farmer to a trader *(penebas)* while it is still standing in the field, has led to harvesters being hired on a cash basis, and to far fewer people being involved than under the traditional method. This reduction in the labour intensity of harvesting has also been encouraged by the introduction of the sickle to replace the flat *ani-ani* which cut each stalk separately.

The Agro Economic Survey conducted an investigation in 1972 in four villages in Central Java to determine the extent of *tebasan*. A total of 120 farmers were interviewed. An example of the changes in numbers employed in harvesting is given in table 90. Applying both the commercial and technological innovations, the number of harvesters per hectare dropped sharply from 184 to 80 per hectare, although the returns to those privileged to engage in harvesting work almost doubled.

The second labour-displacing technological innovation concerns women's traditional hand-pounding. Hundreds of thousands of the jobs are said to have been lost to the new small village rice mills which have been promoted as part of the village unit administration of rice production. The decline in hand-pounding and the concomitant rise in mechanical hulling and milling has been recent but very swift. Timmer[1] has written that in 1971 about 80 per cent of Java's rice crop was still being hand-pounded, but that in 1973 less than 50 per cent was hand-pounded. He concludes that today there is little need for hand-pounding or non-mechanised rice milling in Java. Whereas, with a crop the size of the 1971 crop, 399,000 full-time workers would have been required if only hand-pounding were utilised, if large-scale bulk facilities alone were in operation jobs would be available for a mere 33,000 workers. With small village rice mills, the previous employment would be almost halved.

[1] C. Peter Timmer: "Choice of Technique in Rice Milling in Java", in *Bulletin of Indonesian Economic Studies*, July 1973, p. 57.

An estimate has been made that about half of women's hand-pounding jobs (or 125 million days) have been lost through mechanisation.[1] This is assumed to mean a loss of $55 million in income to the women, poorly compensated by $5 million earned by male operators of the rice mill machinery. Much more is reputed to have been gained by consumers as a whole through lower cost rice (all other factors held constant), but even if rice is cheaper as a result, it represents at the very least a relative shift of purchasing power away from a class of very poor women. If they cannot find other sources of income the cheaper price of rice may not be cheaper to them, and their families, in real terms.

Whether labourers could improve their absolute standard of living depends on whether there was a compensating rise in the demand for labour. Vink[2] estimated the prewar level of labour use in rice cultivation in East Java to average 151 man-days per hectare, *plus* 98 man-days for harvesting. Data from the Philippines for 1970 suggest a figure of around 80 man-days plus some tractor utilisation for rice cultivation[3] but Sajogyo[4] quotes a figure of 51 man-days (pre-harvest) in the Laguna area of the Philippines in 1969 for farms between 1.8 and 3.4 hectares in size. It is known from the Agro-Economic Survey that on good irrigated land there were reports that pre-harvest labour requirements had risen from 150 man-days to over 200 man-days per acre on farms of less than 1 hectare.[5] Increases could be expected to be smaller on less well irrigated land. For the sake of argument let us assume that labour for pre-harvest tasks enjoyed a 33 per cent increase in demand and that on good land this was the equivalent of an increase of 50 man-days per hectare.

In contrast to this, new harvesting and post-harvest practices have made serious inroads into employment, the harvesting innovations alone leading to a fall of 104 man-days per hectare where it has been applied. On irrigated land the cropping index (number of crops per year) has risen a little. But it should be borne in mind that while the new pre-harvest practices will reach saturation point when the new seeds are extended as far as the quality of land permits, the new harvesting and post-harvest practices can be applied to all types of rice grown.

---

[1] See W. Collier et al.: "Choice of Technique in Rice Milling on Java – A Comment", in *Bulletin of Indonesian Economic Studies*, op. cit., Mar. 1974.

[2] G. J. Vink: *The basis of Indonesian farms* (H. Veenman and Sons, Wageningen, 1941), Ch. IV and Appendices I and II (quoted in W. L. Collier); and Sajogyo: *Employment opportunities created by the high yielding varieties in several areas of Java* (Agro-Economic Survey of Indonesia, 1972), Research Notes, No. 8.

[3] "Agricultural Economics", reprinted from International Rice Research Institute: *Annual Report 1970* (Los Baños, Philippines).

[4] Sajogyo: *Rural development programmes in Indonesia: village solidarity and other goals* (Bogor Agricultural University), p. 9.

[5] One particular Agro-Economic Survey report quoted by Montgomery, op. cit., p. 230, gives 293 pre-harvest labour days per hectare for IR varieties and 232.5 for local varieties – a difference of 60 labour days. But including harvesting there has been a decline from 483 to 460 labour days per hectare *per crop*.

The net impact is clear: labour's share of the product has declined. The numbers of labourers earning anything from rice cultivation and processing has been reduced, giving way to a "labour aristocracy". Thus employment possibilities in rural Java will differ sharply between irrigated and non-irrigated areas. As Mongomery has pointed out:

Employment must also be seen in terms of duration during the year. It is not a contradiction to have employment (labour days worked) rise at the same time as unemployment (per cent of the labour force finding no work) rises. This is possible if there is a rapid redistribution of who does the work. If a seasonal peak demand for labourers is flattened out by a different planting cycle, the different planting cycle can result in more days worked, but fewer persons doing the work.[1]

Thus the commercial and technological innovations in rural Java have provoked new forms of social differentiation resulting in schisms in relations between *(a)* farmers, on the one hand, and landless labourers and very small owner-cultivators, on the other, and *(b)* between those landless labourers who are offered the limited work at any one time and those who are unable to share in job opportunities.

PROSPECTS FOR THE RURAL POOR

The landless labourer's future in rural Java appears precarious from this analysis. Employment of landless women, in particular, appears to have suffered savage cuts and this may well be reflected in a new sex ratio amongst the rural-to-urban migrants.

The old idea that the intricate patron-client relationships of agricultural involution can provide everybody with a niche in shared poverty was always questioned but appears to be now no longer tenable. The result has been, as Hickson puts it, that "the Green Revolution represents only part of an ongoing process of change which had begun to 'de-Geertzify' rural Java by the 1960s and is finishing off the job in the 1970s".

That food production has risen substantially during the process is seen from table 91. Annual per capita rice production was 107.8 kg by 1973 compared with the prewar (1936-39) average of 85 kg.[2] But because of the recent decline in per capita production of other staples the annual per capita production of rice equivalents was only 162 kg, compared with 204 kg in the prewar period and 175 kg in the 1956-59 period. Furthermore, if increasing rice production is to replace imports then it is likely that an increasing proportion of total rice production will find its way on to urban markets. Declining effective demand in rural areas, via increasing mass poverty, will facilitate this.

---

[1] Montgomery, op. cit.

[2] See table 80.

Table 91. Production of foodstuffs in rice equivalents
(Thousands of tons)

Item	1968	1969	1970	1971	1972	1973	Conversion index
Rice	10844	11360	12168	12711	12377	13440	1.000
Maize	2738	2700	2531	2686	2411	2559	.989
Cassava	3441	3308	3175	3239	3060	2798	.303
Sweet potatoes	636	608	585	595	523	575	.269
Soybeans	391	362	464	480	480	402	.335
Groundnuts	435	405	426	431	414	449	1.517
Total	18485	18743	19349	20201	19265	20223	
Population (millions)	110.4	113.3	115.9	118.8	121.7	124.7	
Rice production per capita	98.2	100.4	105.0	107.0	101.7	107.8	
Foodstuff production per capita	167.4	165.7	166.9	170.0	158.3	162.1	

Source: FAO Planning Team, Department of Agriculture, Jakarta, 1974, quoted in H. W. Arndt: "Survey of Recent Developments", in *Bulletin of Indonesian Economic Studies*, op. cit., July 1974, p. 32.

Much has been said of the post-1965 Indonesian economic miracle. Does this mean, then, that Java's rural poor can find hope in other sectors of the economy if they are prepared to move?

The expansion of gross domestic product was dominated by the growth of certain relatively new sectors. The value of timber exports rose from $2 million in 1965 to $583 million in 1973.[1] Oil exports rose from $272 million in 1965 to $719 million in 1972, later to quadruple. Tin exports increased from $37 million to $86 million over the same period. Bauxite production expanded from 688,000 metric tons in 1965 to 1.2 million tons in 1973, and nickel production from 101,000 to 867,000 metric tons.[2]

Another feature of the period after 1969 was the expansion in manufacturing activity. But the rise in manufacturing production even *over the level in 1960* did not signify a clear increase in employment in industry since the new investment was very capital intensive. The example of one major industry will suffice.

The net effect of the transformation of the textile industry which formerly employed almost one-third of all workers in manufacturing has been described thus:[3]

During the period between 1966 and 1971, when production rose from 250 to 600 million metres, the industry as a whole lost more than half its workforce. The handloom and batik sectors lost all but 100,000 of the 510,000 workers who had been previously employed there. ... It was reported that "... more than 70 per cent of the total workers employed in both sectors were unemployed".

---

[1] Central Bureau of Statistics: *Financial Statistics*, VI(1) and VII(11) (Jakarta).

[2] First National City Bank: *Monthly Economic Letter* (Jakarta, June 1974).

[3] ILO: *The role of the textile industry in the expansion of employment in developing countries*, Textiles Committee, Ninth Session, Geneva, 1973, p. 65.

The estimated net increase in employment in spinning, power-weaving, knitting and finishing of 68,200 between 1966 and 1971 is poor compensation, especially when it is realised that new investment is located mainly in Jakarta.[1]

Of the investment approvals for Java virtually none was in the agricultural sector while the overwhelming share of industrial investment was in capital-intensive enterprises concentrated in West Java, and, in turn, mainly Jakarta. Central and East Java had been virtually bypassed by the huge foreign investments by mid-1973 but the new industries of Jakarta were pre-empting many opportunities for their future industrialisation. After 1973 both foreign and domestic investors were persuaded to invest a little in Java's poorer provinces but in no way can this investment be considered as a significant contribution to the reduction of unemployment.

In order to ascertain whether any creation of jobs has occurred in rural areas of large settled populations, particularly on Java, as a result of other policies, it is necessary to use agricultural production statistics.

Data on the volume of traditional primary exports since 1965 were presented in table 85, illustrating the extremely uneven performance after 1968.

Many factors operated, including changes in relative world commodity prices and the age distribution of standing perennials.[2] But one notable feature was the unequal share of gains between smallholders and estates. Rubber, tobacco, palm oil and tea are the only main export crops which have clearly moved ahead of their 1961 or 1965 levels,[3] apart from timber which is essentially a new enclave industry. Of these, estate rubber output has risen while smallholder output has fallen; palm oil is virtually entirely an estate activity; estate tea output has risen while smallholder tea production has been halved; and tobacco production, chiefly a smallholding industry, brings in only about one-tenth the earnings of rubber, less than half of coffee and about as much as tea. On the other hand copra (and copra cakes), which is almost all smallholder, has declined sharply.

The rehabilitation of estate production would have provided employment and income for rural residents, and of course much more data is needed to conclude whether the shift from smallholder to estate production had a net negative impact on mass employment and income. One comment must be made, however. Smallholders frequently practice mixed farming and decide on their own allocation of labour time. Full-time estate workers would not enjoy such flexibility between income-producing ventures. One of the reasons

---

[1] S. V. Sethuraman: *Jakarta: urban development and employment* (Geneva, ILO, 1976), p. 13, provides data which show that between 1961 and 1971 employment in manufacturing, even in Jakarta, fell from 147,000 to 110,000.

[2] In particular the average age of smallholders' rubber trees was rather high, many of them dating back to prewar days.

[3] The volume of rubber exports in 1973 was about the same as in the mid-1950s. The volume of copra exports in 1973 was half the level for 1956-57. The volume of palm oil exports in 1973 was a little higher than its level in 1957. Tobacco, which had the greatest post-1965 success, returned to a little more than its 1956 level and a little less than its 1955 level.

Table 92. Gross domestic product at 1960 market prices: value (thousand millions of rupiahs) and share (percentage) by sector, 1960-73

Sector	1960		1965		1970		1973	
	Value	Share	Value	Share	Value	Share	Value	Share
Agriculture, forestry and fishing	*210*	*53.8*	*225*	*52.3*	*271*	*47.5*	*303*	*42.9*
Farm food crops	134	34.4	142	33.0	176	30.8	197	27.9
Farm non-food crops	28	7.2	33	7.6	36	6.3	38	5.4
Estate crops	13	3.3	13	3.0	14	2.5	15	2.1
Livestock	19	4.9	21	4.9	22	3.9	26	3.7
Forestry	9	2.3	5	1.2	10	1.8	14	2.0
Fishing	7	1.8	11	2.6	13	2.3	13	1.8
Mining	14	3.6	16	3.7	32	5.6	50	7.1
Manufacturing	33	8.4	36	8.4	51	8.9	63	8.9
Construction	8	2.1	7	1.6	15	2.6	27	3.8
Trade	56	14.4	67	15.6	100	17.5	138	19.5
Other	69	17.7	79	18.4	102	17.9	126	17.8
Total	390	100.0	430	100.0	571	100.0	707	100.0
Population (millions)	95.2		109.6		117.7		125.5	
Per capita GDP (rupiahs)	4097		3923		4851		5633	

Sources: Calculated on the basis of data gathered from *Bulletin of Indonesian Economic Studies*, July 1970, pp. 144-145; A. Booth and B. Glassburner: "Survey of Recent Developments", in *Bulletin of Indonesian Economic Studies*, op. cit., Mar. 1975, p. 29; and *Indikator Ekonomi*, May 1975, p. 143. In a few cases percentages do not exactly add up due to rounding.

why smallholders showed such tenacity in the face of inflation was because they mixed export crop production with food production and the effects of inflation never operated against all their ventures at the same time. The same was true during a situation of world commodity price fluctuations. The recent trend in export cropping towards monocultural agriculture under large-scale management leaves the rural masses with less control over the security of their income.

This sectoral review ends with a summary (see table 92) of the changes in the composition of gross domestic production that occurred after 1960.

Between 1960 and 1973 (also between 1965 and 1973) the share of agriculture, forestry and fishing fell by one-fifth. The greatest proportionate decline within this group was in traditional primary exports, but had there not been such a strong promotion of rice, the same story would have been true of farm food crops. The big increases in shares of construction and trade reflect urban activities attracted by foreign money.

It should also be noted that it was the labour-intensive sectors which expanded least (except, once again, in the case of rice). The implications of these shifts for sectoral employment are startling. According to the 1961 population census, agriculture, forestry and fishing accounted for 72 per cent of employment while mining and quarrying, manufacturing, and construction took only 7.8 per cent; yet between 1960 and 1973 agriculture, forestry and fishing increased its product by only a little more than mining and quarrying, manufacturing, and construction: 93,000 million rupiahs compared with 85,000 million rupiahs (at 1960 prices). Over the entire decade, 1961 to 1971, agricultural employment rose a mere 5 per cent in the whole of Indonesia, but even less, 3.7 per cent, in Java.[1]

Official recognition of the failure of the First Five Year Plan (1969-74) to make a start on providing rural employment has been shown in many statements and in assurances that the Second Five Year Plan will try to rectify this. The excuse for the late start was that aid and foreign investment had to be encouraged to stabilise the country's finances and therefore that considerations of welfare and social justice had to be postponed. The Second Plan has been described as one in which "agricultural development receives primary emphasis in an employment policy designed to raise the income of the majority...".[2]

The agricultural sector, as the largest, can still create more employment than any other sector even if it should grow, as planned, at an annual average of only 4.6 per cent during the Second Plan compared with industry's 13.0 per cent.[3] But if forestry is to continue at a fast rate it is unlikely that the traditional labour-intensive sections of agriculture will expand at 4.6 per cent annually. These latter sections require considerable resource investment in seeds, extension services and marketing. The fall in the share of total public investment in agriculture and irrigation from 30.1 to 20.6 per cent between the First Plan and the Second Plan does not augur well for this investment, although the rise from zero to 19.1 per cent in "regional development" investment in the Plan's budget will presumably be partly for agriculture.

Nor do the aggregate growth targets of the Second Plan help in indicating from where substantial agricultural employment will come. It has been assumed in the Plan that for every 1 per cent rise in GDP, employment in agriculture will rise 0.2 per cent. With GDP rising at 7.5 per cent a year agricultural employment should rise 1.5 per cent of the present (approximate) 25 million. Over a five-year period this amounts to 1.8 million more jobs, or 360,000 a year. With annual increases in the total labour force of between 1.5 and 2.0 million, and if agriculture is really expected to find the bulk of additional jobs, then unemployment, underemployment and poverty are bound to rise.

Above all, no account has been taken in the Plan of changes in land concentration and in rural labour market stratification which are operating against employment creation. The targets cited above are not known to have accommodated these regressive factors. Unless future plans take cognisance

---

[1] Montgomery, op. cit., p. 227.

[2] Subroto: "Employment Policy and Transmigration in the Second Five Year Plan", in *Prisma*, May 1975.

[3] Repelita II, quoted in *Bulletin of Indonesian Economic Studies*, 10(1).

of the need for social development it is difficult to see where net positive employment creation in Java will occur.

CONCLUSIONS

Food consumption indicators of poverty support aggregate per capita income data in confirming that Indonesia is one of the lowest income countries in the world. The conclusion can also be drawn that the island of Java harbours some of the world's most destitute people. With land holdings already very small, increments to the rural labour force must be seen as virtually equal additions to the landless.

Unfortunately, there are no available figures for income or expenditure distribution in the 1950s, but there is no reason to believe that increasing inequality occurred over this decade in a dramatic manner. Declining food intake was overwhelmingly the result of the failure to raise the productivity of the limited land resources commensurate with population increases.

But from two separate sources (SUSENAS and Deuster's thesis) comes evidence that inflation worsened the unequal distribution of income. This inequality declined somewhat as inflation abated towards the end of the 1960s, but the official data, such as they are, suggest that standards of living of the poor had not regained their 1963-64 level by 1969-70, and were therefore clearly lower than standards in the late 1950s.

What is far more disturbing, since it signifies permanence of the greater inequality and absolute poverty, is the suggestion that there has been a worsened distribution of land. Deuster claims, on the bases of his field data, that this has happened for good rice land, *sawah*, between 1959 and 1968. The nature and direction of processes of land concentration and labour market stratification which have been greatly accelerated by the Green Revolution in Java all point towards further inequality in the distributions of income and land. At the same time the practice of "shared poverty", propounded by Geertz, is collapsing under the impact of the private returns to aggressive techno-commercial innovations.

There will be many occasions in future when economists will point out. that seasonality of labour demand is being modified, that those who do get jobs have more work the year round and that rice production is rising. All these are interesting phenomena but they do not compare in significance with the biting reality that within the last decade or so, millions of Javanese have moved from mere poverty towards the perilous state of indigence, in which there is little or no access to work and food.

GROWTH AND INEQUALITY
IN THE RURAL PHILIPPINES

11

Azizur Rahman Khan

It is estimated that 43 million people lived in the Philippines in 1975, of whom about 68 per cent, or 29 million, were in the rural areas. Agriculture is the major source of employment in the rural economy. In 1972 about 55 per cent of the nation's entire labour force was employed in agriculture and closely related activities. Within the rural economy about three-quarters of the members of the labour force were employed in agricultural activities.

The rate of growth of the rural economy has been substantial in recent decades. Table 93 summarises some of the relevant data for the period beginning in 1957. This is the period on which the present study will concentrate because the available sources of data cover it reasonably comprehensively. The four Family Income and Expenditure Surveys (FIES) carried out by the Bureau of Census and Statistics (BCS) form much of the statistical basis of the present chapter. They provide information for the years 1956/57 (for the 12 months ending in February 1957), 1961, 1965 and 1970/71 (for the 12 months ending in April 1971).

All indicators presented in the table show that the rural economy achieved rapid over-all growth during the fifteen years since 1957. Physical output in agriculture increased at an annual compound rate of 3.8 per cent between 1957 and 1971. Even allowing for the slower rate of growth in the early 1970s the annual compound rate of growth between 1957 and 1974 was 3.4 per cent, a significantly higher rate of growth than that of the agricultural population.

Column (2) of the table is even more unambiguous in that it records a rapid increase in real income per head of the rural population. (Note that the other three columns of the table show aggregates and not per capita quantities.) This series, based on the four FIES, cannot be extended beyond 1971.

Per capita rural income in real terms increased at a compound annual rate of 2.3 per cent between 1957 and 1971.[1] This, by contemporary Asian standards, was a very impressive performance.

---

[1] Column (1) of the table shows a compound annual rate of growth of physical output of agriculture at 3.8 per cent over the same period. The rural population increased at an annual rate of something between 2.5 and 3 per cent. Thus per capita physical output would appear to have

(footnote concluded overleaf)

Table 93. Growth of agriculture in the Philippines

Year	Index of total agricultural production (base 1965) (1)	Real income per head of the rural population (at 1965 prices; (pesos)) (2)	Output of food crops (million tons) (3)	Output of cash crops (million tons) (4)
1957	79.9	254[1]	6.5	2.9
1961	87.4	269	7.4	3.0
1965	100.0	309	8.5	3.8
1971	134.9	350[2]	10.8	4.8
1972	133.1	—	—	—
1973	136.6	—	—	—
1974	142.2	—	—	—

[1] March 1956-February 1957. [2] May 1970-April 1971.

Source: Production data: Central Bank of the Philippines: *Statistical Bulletin*, Dec. 1974; Real Income: FIES values deflated by the cost-of-living index of the Philippines other than Manila.

THE WORSENING DISTRIBUTION OF INCOME

The rapid over-all growth of agricultural output and rural income has, however, been accompanied by a sharp increase in the degree of inequality in the distribution of rural income. This phenomenon has been widely noted and commented upon. Table 94 summarises some of the available information on this subject. These calculations were made by the ILO comprehensive employment mission[1] on the basis of the four Family Income and Expenditure Surveys carried out by the BCS over the decade and a half.

The table indicates that there was a rather dramatic and steady decline in the share of the poorest 20 per cent of households in total rural income. The worsening distribution of income, however, was not confined to this group but adversely affected a much higher proportion of households. The share of income of the bottom 40 per cent clearly declined while the next 40 per cent was barely able to maintain their share. Only the top quintile of households succeeded in increasing their share of rural income. The combined effect of these changes is summarised in the steady increase in the indices of inequality in income distribution, the index of quintile inequality and the Gini coefficient.

Even the apparently unambiguous situation described above has been interpreted by some analysts so as to show that conditions have not been as bad as would appear from the figures in table 94.

---

grown at an annual rate of about 1 per cent. Note that this is not necessarily inconsistent with an annual rate of growth of per capita income of 2.3 per cent as shown by column (2). The difference is largely explained by the favourable movement in the terms of trade for the agricultural sector. Also, non-agricultural rural output might have grown at a faster rate than agricultural output.

[1] ILO: *Sharing in development: a programme of employment, equity and growth for the Philippines* (Geneva, 1974).

Table 94.   Rural household income distribution in the Philippines

Percentage of income accruing to	1956/57	1961	1965	1970/71
Lowest 20 per cent	7.0	5.9	5.0	4.4
Second 20 per cent	11.1	11.8	9.5	8.9
Third 20 per cent	14.7	13.5	15.3	13.9
Fourth 20 per cent	21.1	21.9	23.0	21.8
Top 20 per cent	46.1	46.9	47.2	51.0
Top 10 per cent	30.1	31.1	30.0	34.4
Index of quintile inequality	0.34	0.36	0.38	0.41
Gini coefficient	0.38	0.40	0.42	0.46

Source: ILO: *Sharing in development* . . ., op. cit., p. 10 (based on the FIES data).

One argument is that the distribution of income at the top of the income scale improved. The evidence cited is the declining share of the top 5 per cent in total income as revealed by the most recent FIES.[1] Against this one should note a number of factors. First, the income share of the top 10 per cent increased through time. Thus any decline in the share of the rich must have been limited to the households at the very top. Second, the reliability of the data for groups at the extremes of the distribution (such as the top 5 per cent) diminishes progressively as the size of the group declines. The reason for this is that the extreme values are more frequently not captured in the statistical net. Third, even if the distribution of income improved at the very top, it cannot offset the effect of an equivalent worsening at the bottom. No society would judge a given improvement in the living standard of the second top 5 per cent at the cost of the top 5 per cent to be comparable to an equivalent improvement in the living standard of the bottom 5 per cent at the cost, say, of the top 20 per cent. Even a complete equalisation of incomes for the households within the top decile would not compensate for the declining share of the lowest quintile shown in table 94.

Another argument given is that the distribution of expenditure (representing consumption) is more important in a welfare sense than the distribution of income. Thus Berry argues that the change in the distribution of consumption has been less unfavourable than the change in the distribution of income.[2] The share in consumption of the bottom quintile in the rural Philippines declined from 7.52 per cent in 1961 to 6.79 per cent in 1965 and

---

[1] This evidence is cited for the Philippines as a whole in A. Berry: *Income and consumption distribution trends in the Philippines, 1950-70*, IBRD studies in employment and rural development, No. 29 (Washington, DC, 1975). It is not clear whether the falling share of the richest 5 per cent applies separately to rural incomes because information for the years before 1970/71 for the top 5 per cent is not available for the rural Philippines.

[2] See Berry, op. cit.

6.92 per cent in 1970/71.[1] The decline in their share of income was much more severe, as has been seen. More important, as is shown below, the average real income of the bottom quintile of rural households declined in absolute terms, whereas the average real expenditure of this group, on the above evidence, would appear to have risen substantially.

Those who maintain that the distribution of expenditure is a better indicator of welfare than the distribution of income argue that an observed income flow over any given period of time includes many transient elements and is an unreliable indicator of real income. What one should try to measure is the present value of expected lifetime income or some measure of "permanent income". Expenditure, it is argued, usually is a much better indicator of this than observed income.

In the specific context the implications of the above would be:

(a) that forces have been at work to make the change in the distribution of expected lifetime or permanent income diverge from the change in the distribution of observed income;

(b) that the difference between the change in the distribution of expenditure and the change in income distribution shows roughly the difference between changes in expected lifetime income and observed income.

What are the forces that might have created a less unfavourable change in the distribution of lifetime income as compared to that in current observed income? For this to occur the lifetime income for the lowest income groups would have to be increasing much faster than current income. Such a possibility could be explained by such factors as:

(a) a sharp rise in the percentage of households in the low income groups headed by very young or very old people;

(b) a sharply rising income expectation of the younger members of the labour force (i.e. an increase over time in the variation of income due to the age of the earner); and

(c) a greater availability of credit to the households with very young earners to enable them to finance consumption in excess of current earnings.

It is unlikely that changes of this type have been sufficiently large in magnitude in the Philippines to explain the difference between the changes in the distributions of expenditure and income. Low income families indeed have a higher proportion of households headed by very young and very old people, but it seems unlikely that their proportion has been increasing over time at anything like a rate that would bring about a significant divergence between the distributions of lifetime and observed incomes. In a situation of

---

[1] The distribution of rural consumption in 1956/57 is not available. For all Philippines, urban and rural together, Berry finds an increase in the share of the bottom quintile from 5.04 per cent in 1956/57 to 5.92 per cent in 1970/71. It is uncertain whether the trend in the share of the lowest quintile of the rural households was in the same direction. That the two can diverge widely is intuitively clear and amply documented by the data for 1961 and 1970/71.

falling real wages (to be discussed later in this chapter) it seems improbable that expected income difference due to age would be increasing. There is no evidence of a massive increase over time in the volume of consumer credit for the low income families.

The change in the distribution of observed income may be an inaccurate indicator of welfare change also because of unusual and unfavourable natural or economic circumstances affecting current incomes. In such situation people probably would borrow or reduce their previous savings in order to finance current consumption in excess of current income and, in so far as the decline in income is temporary, the distribution of consumption would measure changes in welfare more accurately. But for such factors to lead to a less unfavourable change in the distribution of consumption than in income it would be necessary for the incomes of the poorer households to be affected more and more severely by such events over time. Not only is there no evidence of progressively more severe natural disasters in the survey years, there is no reason to believe that such events would temporarily reduce the incomes of the poorer households more seriously.

Is there an alternative explanation of the less unfavourable change in the distribution of consumption expenditure than in income? It seems highly plausible that the difference is due to the increasing inability of poorer households to keep up with their consumption commitments. Thus the poorer a household, the greater would be the gap between its income and expenditure needs. The only way this could be financed in the long run is by selling land and other assets or by becoming heavily indebted to landlords, perhaps to such an extent as to become some kind of bonded labourer. In either case the process leads to growing poverty of the deficit households, either through increased proletarianisation or through the lowering of wages in consequence of the exercise of monopsony power by the landlord.

Clearly, a satisfactory explanation of the asymmetrical changes in the distributions of income and expenditure must be based on information about the method of financing the deficit by those households which dissaved. Unfortunately, no information is available on this important subject. However, there is little evidence to support the view that the change in the distribution of expenditure over time is due to a corresponding change in the distribution of lifetime income. The alternative hypothesis that the poor households financed the excess of their expenditure over income by a combination of borrowing and selling their assets is considered more probable. It is not contended that this explains the entire difference between the changes in the distributions of income and consumption in the Philippines, however, but rather that much of the difference is due to adoption of improper statistical procedures in the FIES.

Table 95 summarises some of the relevant information for 1961, 1965 and 1970/71. Several features deserve special attention. In any given period, the lower the level of household income, the higher is the rate of dissaving or the lower is the rate of saving. The poorest households have been dissaving at

Table 95. Income and expenditure by household income groups in rural Philippines

Income group (current pesos)	1961		1965		1970/71	
	Average income (current pesos)	Ratio of expenditure to income	Average income (current pesos)	Ratio of expenditure to income	Average income (current pesos)	Ratio of expenditure to income
Under 500	357	2.01	319	3.51	341	4.71
500- 999	736	1.40	751	2.00	755	2.63
1000-1499	1224	1.17	1235	1.51	1248	1.93
1500-1999	1717	1.00	1718	1.24	1738	1.62
2000-2499	2216	0.89	2241	1.13	2236	1.44
2500-2999	2718	0.86	2714	1.00	2741	1.31
3000-3999	3407	0.77	3415	1.00	3442	1.14
4000-4999	4467	0.74	4410	0.85	4446	1.07
8000-9999	8719	0.67	9258	0.65	8903	0.91
10000 and over	14035	0.56	13827	0.65	—	—
15000-19999	—	—	—	—	16740	0.76
20000 and over	—	—	—	—	28239	0.44

Source: Bureau of Census and Statistics (BCS): *Family Income and Expenditures Survey* (FIES), *The BCS Survey of Household Bulletins* (formerly the *Philippines Statistical Survey of Households*), 1961, 1965 and 1970/71. Note that all figures are at current prices. Comparison between the same real income groups in different years is possible only after a deflation by some cost-of-living index. The cost-of-living index used takes the following values respectively for the three years shown in the table: 79.6, 100.0 and 141.2.

high rates. Moreover, the problem appears to have been getting worse over time. Thus the income group for which expenditure just equalled income in 1961 was 1,500-2,000 pesos. Taking inflation into account, the average real income of this group in 1965 would be about 2,150 pesos and in 1970/71 about 3,050 pesos. Yet the income groups that contained households with these incomes in 1965 and 1970/71 dissaved at very high rates. In general, for a given real income group the rate of dissaving is higher (or the rate of saving is lower) in the more recent of the three time periods under consideration. Why this happened, especially in the case of the not so poor, is impossible to explain.

Table 96 shows that the ratio of household expenditure to income rose very fast over the 15 years. By 1965 all households, on average, were dissaving at a rate of 13 per cent and this rose to 20 per cent in 1970/71. The dissaving by rural households seems to have been even greater. The rate of growth of real expenditure on consumption of goods and services implied by these data is much higher than the rate of growth of income. These results, suggested by the FIES data on relative changes in household expenditure and income, are inconsistent with independent alternative sources of information about the behaviour of the economy. For example, households are known to have beeen saving at quite a high rate and the personal saving rate has tended to increase through time.[1]

[1] For example, see the national accounts in National Economic and Development Authority: *Statistical Yearbook 1974* and the estimates of saving rates in J. H. Power and G. P. Sicat: *The Philippines: industrialisation and trade policies* (New York, Oxford University Press, 1971).

Table 96. Household expenditure as percentage of household income

Year	All Philippines	Rural Philippines
1956/57	87.3	87.5
1961	99.4	110.7
1965	113.2	122.1
1970/71	119.9	123.3

Source: Bureau of Census and Statistics: *Family Income and Expenditures Survey*, op. cit., 1956/57, 1961, 1965 and 1970/71.

It is clear that a closer look at the FIES data is necessary to establish the sources of bias. It is unfortunate that so little has been done to try to resolve these inconsistencies about a major area of quantitative information. The Bureau of Census and Statistics has given the implausible explanation that "price inflation during the decade also largely accounted for the widening gap in [household] income and expenditure levels".[1]

If one is sceptical about the data, one has the choice of suspecting the income data or the expenditure data. In determining which to reject two types of evidence must be looked for. The first set of evidence should establish whether income is understated relative to expenditure or whether expenditure is overstated relative to income. The second set of evidence should go beyond the quantification of the average overstatement in expenditure or understatement in income and show that these are distributed asymmetrically among various income groups and over time. It would not suffice to show that average income is understated in the FIES in order to reject the income data. It must be shown that such an understatement became more serious over time and that over time the incomes of the poorer households became understated to a relatively greater extent. Only then would one be justified in choosing the observed expenditure distribution as the better measure of a change in welfare. Similarly, it would not be enough to show that expenditure is overstated in the FIES. In order to justify the use of the observed income distribution as the more accurate measure of the change in welfare, it must be shown that such an overstatement was greater for the lower income households and became worse over time.[2]

In most underdeveloped countries income data are thought to be less accurate than expenditure data. Hence the income data will be examined first. It is quite possible that income is understated in the FIES relative to its true level. This by itself is not a cause for concern unless the understatement increased over time and was concentrated (and increasingly so over time) in the estimates for the poorest households.

---

[1] Bureau of Census and Statistics: *Family Income and Expenditures Survey*, op. cit., 1970-71 (Series No. 34), p. xvii.

[2] It is quite possible for the FIES to understate income (overstate expenditure) and yet give a good measure of the change in income (expenditure) distribution over time, provided there is intertemporal consistency in coverage. It is, therefore, not necessary to worry too much about the extent of coverage itself.

A comparison with the national accounts shows that the income estimates of the FIES are indeed lower, but there is no evidence that this became
worse over time, except in the last of the survey years. Nor is there any
evidence to suggest that, over time, the incomes of the poorer groups became
relatively understated. A common source of such an understatement is the
exclusion (in whole or in part) of non-cash income, since non-cash income
has a higher weight in the total income of the poorer rural families than in
the richer. A comparison of the FIES data of 1961 and 1970/71 indicates that
the coverage of non-cash income probably improved for the poorer families.[1]
Indeed the income data are more likely to understate the higher incomes
than the lower ones, and, if anything, the problem is likely to become worse
as the average income of the rich rises (with a consequent increase in the
incentive to evade higher taxes, for example).

Since an increasing underestimation of income over time does not appear to be the case, the possibility that expenditure is increasingly overstated
over time should be examined. This hypothesis is suggested by the fact that
the real rate of growth in per capita consumption implied by the FIES data is
much above that implied by other sources.

One reason for the discrepancy may be the special procedure followed by
the FIES in which information on expenditure is requested on a different
basis for food and non-food items. All information on the value of expenditure on food, drink and tobacco refers to the period of one week preceding
the enumeration. The weekly values are presumably converted into annual
figures on the assumption that the value for the enumerated week is the
weekly average for the whole year.[2] In contrast, the information on the value
of expenditure on non-food items is collected for the preceding 12-month
period. In a situation of rising prices this procedure inevitably results in:

---

[1] For the lower income groups the percentage shares of non-cash income in the total are as
follows:

Income group (current pesos)	1961	1970/71
Below 500	55.0	65.8
500- 999	45.9	54.4
1000-1499	38.7	45.8
1500-1999	30.2	40.8
2000-2499	26.3	37.7
(All groups)	(33.8)	(30.7)

Even for constant real income groups the shares have not fallen, whereas they have risen sharply
for equivalent money income groups.

[2] See Bureau of Census and Statistics: *Family Income and Expenditures Survey*, op. cit.,
1970/71, (Series No. 34), pp. ix-x, for an account of the methodology. It is clear that the weekly
expenditure thus enumerated "was multiplied by 52 weeks ... for an entry in the questionnaire
on expenditure for a one-year period". An examination of the questionnaire shows that no
information on quantities was collected and the explanatory notes do not indicate any correction
for changing prices during the year. In any case, deflation would be extremely cumbersome and
would require more information than is available with the BCS.

(a) an overestimation of expenditure on food, such an overestimation being greater the higher is the rate of inflation for food during the survey year;

(b) an overestimation of aggregate expenditure relative to income, again the extent of overestimation being greater for the years in which inflation was higher; and

(c) an overestimation of the consumption expenditure of the lower income groups relative to the higher income groups because food has a heavier weight in the budget of the former.[1]

These factors can explain much of the dissaving reported in tables 95 and 96, and the lower increase in inequality measured from consumption data as compared to income data, as well as much of the inconsistency between FIES expenditure data and other independent accounts.[2]

Moreover, some of the other methodological procedures adopted by the survey have also resulted in a relative overstatement of the expenditure of the lower income groups. In enumerating expenditure on durable goods the following practices were adopted:[3]

(a) actual payment during the year was included in cases where the payment was in cash, but something bought on an instalment plan would be accounted for only to the extent that actual payment was made during the survey year;

(b) if the article was self-produced the entire value was reported;

(c) cars, jeeps and boats bought by households were not considered to be items of consumption expenditure, whereas purchases of bicycles, furniture and appliances were treated as current consumption.

Given that the poor produce many of their durables for themselves while the rich have access to cars, jeeps, boats and hire-purchase arrangements, the methods used in the survey tend systematically to overstate expenditure by poorer groups relative to that of richer groups. Finally, it is clear from a careful perusal of the FIES that there are few offsetting factors which result in an overstatement of the expenditure (or income) of the richer groups relative to the poorer ones.

---

[1] Thus, according to the 1970/71 FIES, the lowest income group (those below 500 pesos) allocate 69 per cent of their total expenditure to food. The highest income group (those above 20,000 pesos) spend only 34 per cent. The average share of food in total expenditure was 54 per cent for that year.

[2] In the absence of detailed information about weekly movements of food prices, weekly sales of food, the exact dates of enumeration, etc., it was impossible to carry out precise calculations to show what correction for this phenomenon would be necessary. However, a crude exercise for 1970/71 was undertaken on the assumptions that (a) the respondents based their calculations of the weekly value of consumption on the prices underlying the May 1971 food price index outside Manila, and (b) that the average annual price of food was the same as the unweighted average of the food price index in the preceding 12 months. On this basis the ratio of expenditure to income for the Philippines as a whole is reduced from 1.20 to 1.11. It is possible that more detailed information, especially on the seasonality of food consumption, would explain an even higher proportion of the excess of expenditure over income.

[3] See Bureau of Census and Statistics: *Family Income and Expenditures Survey*, op. cit., p. xii.

Table 97. Real incomes in the rural Philippines
(1965 pesos per family)

Household	1956/57	1961	1965	1970/71
Bottom 20 per cent of rural households	494	446	439	439
Second 20 per cent of rural households	784	892	834	888
Third 20 per cent of rural households	1039	1020	1342	1387
All rural households	1413	1511	1755	1996

Note: Money incomes for each quintile have been estimated by applying the ratios in table 94 to the total income data from the FIES, which also supplies the data on the number of families. The cost-of-living index for the Philippines outside Manila has been used to deflate income. For 1956/57 and 1970/71 the indices have been derived by taking weighted averages of the adjacent calendar years, weights being proportionate to the amount of each calendar year included in the survey year. The indices for the four survey periods are respectively 70.0, 79.6, 100.0 and 141.2. The average size of a household in the four years was respectively 5.57, 5.62, 5.68 and 5.70. The source of the cost-of-living index is Central Bank of the Philippines: *Statistical Bulletin*, Dec. 1972 and 1974, and that of the information about household size is Augustin Kintanar Jr., et al.: *Studies in Philippines economic demographic relationships* (Institute of Economic Development and Research, University of the Philippines, 1974). As is argued in the next section, the cost-of-living index almost certainly understates the true increase in prices. It is, therefore, nearly certain that real incomes in the years subsequent to the base are overstated.

The implication of the above is that changes in welfare can be better estimated by basing the analysis on changes in the distribution of income rather than of consumption. This does not imply that the income data are wholly accurate, but they are almost certainly superior to the expenditure data for this purpose.[1]

THE ABSOLUTE INCOME OF THE LOWEST QUINTILE

Combining the income distribution data with information on rural incomes and the number of households from the FIES, and using an appropriate cost-of-living index, it is possible to ascertain the trend in real income of the various quintiles of rural households. The results of such an exercise are presented in table 97. The most important finding in the table concerns the real income of the bottom quintile, notably the decline that has occurred in their absolute real income. Moreover, this impoverishment of the poor occurred in a period of fairly rapid increase in the average income of the rural population as a whole.

Over the entire period only the lowest quintile of households experienced a drop in real family income. The second lowest quintile experienced some increase in real income during the late 1950s but none during the 1960s. All the other household groups on average experienced a substantial improvement in living standards. This conclusion about the trend of household in-

---

[1] It may be useful to state here that rejection of the data on consumption is due to these seriously biased methods of measurement. This should not be interpreted as an expression of preference in principle for income data over consumption. Indeed, elsewhere in this book consumption data have been used extensively (see, for example, Ch. 8). The general position taken is that if both kinds of information are available and appear to be roughly of the same degree of reliability then one should try to determine the reasons behind the difference in their distributions (or of changes in their distributions) before deciding which is a better indicator of the distribution of welfare.

come also applies to the per capita income of households, since there is no evidence of a significant change in the average size of household in each quintile group.

REAL WAGES IN AGRICULTURE

The unsatisfactory nature of the FIES data makes it important to look for additional evidence of the decline in the living standard of the rural poor in the Philippines. This is also important in order to enable one to form some idea about what caused the living standard of the poor to fall.

According to the FIES of 1970/71 about a third of rural households were dependent on wages and salaries as the main source of income. About 14 per cent were dependent on wage and salary earnings in agriculture (as opposed to non-farm activities) as the chief source of income. A much larger proportion, 29 per cent, were dependent on wages and salaries in agriculture to some degree. In that survey year the annual income of an agricultural labourer, on the assumption of 280 days of employment, was 938 pesos. Only 22 per cent of the rural households had incomes below 1,000 pesos. Thus an average agricultural labourer, working no more than 280 days and with insignificant income from other sources, would certainly be in the lowest quintile of rural households.[1] An examination of the trend in real wages in agriculture should provide valuable insights into the reliability of the conclusions already drawn and the mechanism of change in income distribution.

While data on industrial and urban wages abound in the Philippines, there is very little statistical information on rural wages. The Bureau of Agricultural Economics (BAE) of the Department of Agriculture and Natural Resources collects wage data for various agricultural operations in each region. The unweighted average of all these rates is the only over-all measure of agricultural wages available for the Philippines. This has been reproduced in table 98 as Series A. This series is for the period up to 1972 the latest available. The *BCS Survey of Households Bulletin*, Labour Force May Series, 1971-74, however, provides information on average daily cash earnings of salary and wage workers in rural areas. This has been spliced together with the BAE series. In comparison, additional earnings data from alternative sources (e.g. from the National Census and Statistics Office and from the ILO *Yearbook of Labour Statistics, 1975*) show that the post-1972 trend in the BCS series is less unfavourable. This is due, perhaps, to the inclusion of salaries in the BCS series, which increased more in monetary terms than wages.

---

[1] This does not mean that all or even most of the agricultural labourers would be in the bottom quintile of income earners. Favourable circumstances with respect to the number of earners per family, the degree of employment per earner, the amount of non-wage income and regional and occupational differences in wage rates could put a labourer's family above the bottom quintile in terms of income. Not enough information is available on such characteristics to permit even an approximate estimation of the proportion of agricultural labourers that would belong to the bottom quintile. There is little doubt, however, that the proportion is fairly high.

Table 98.   Wage rates in Philippines agriculture

Year	Daily money wage (pesos)			Daily real wages (pesos at 1965 purchasing power)		
	Average of all operations	Average of ploughmen, harvesters and planters only	Ploughmen only			
	(Series A)	(Series B)	(Series C)	Series A	Series B	Series C
1957	2.74	2.74	3.41	3.84	3.84	4.78
1958	2.79	2.79	3.40	3.80	3.80	4.63
1959	2.77	2.77	3.34	3.85	3.85	4.64
1960	2.79	2.79	3.33	3.69	3.69	4.40
1961	2.78	2.78	3.31	3.49	3.49	4.16
1962	2.79	2.79	3.32	3.41	3.41	4.06
1963	3.05	3.05	3.58	3.43	3.43	4.03
1964	2.93	2.93	3.45	3.03	3.03	3.56
1965	2.93	2.93	3.34	2.93	2.93	3.34
1966	3.12	3.35	3.90	2.98	3.20	3.73
1967	3.41	3.67	4.50	3.09	3.33	4.08
1968	3.42	3.75	4.50	3.04	3.34	4.00
1969	3.13	3.40	4.34	2.75	2.99	3.81
1970	3.20	3.60	4.49	2.44	2.75	3.43
1971	3.64	3.98	5.13	2.25	2.46	3.17
1972	3.78	4.25	5.30	2.17	2.44	3.04
1973	3.65	.	.	1.86	.	.
1974	4.10	.	.	1.48	.	.

Note: The Bureau of Agricultural Economics of the Department of Agriculture and Natural Resources collects the above wage data through quarterly surveys. Until 1965 wage rates for ploughmen, planters and harvesters only were collected. From 1966 the wage rates for cultivators, weeders and sprayers have also been collected. Thus from 1966 the (unweighted) average wage rate for all operations (Series A) is different from the (unweighted) average wage rate for ploughmen, harvesters and planters (Series B). For 1973 and 1974 wage rates from the same source are not yet available. The average daily cash earnings of salary and wage workers from the *BCS Survey of Households Bulletin*, Labour Force May Series have been spliced in. The real wages have been obtained by deflating money wages by the Central Bank cost-of-living index outside Manila.

The problem with Series A is that its coverage changed after 1965. Up to that year wage rates for three types of operation—ploughing, planting and harvesting—were included. Since 1966 three more operations—cultivating, weeding and spraying—have been added. Since the wage rates for these latter categories are lower than the previous ones, Series A for the period since 1966 is biased downwards as an indicator of change in money wages.

Series B in table 98 represents an attempt to avoid the problem by excluding cultivating, weeding and spraying for the post-1965 period. It shows the unweighted average wage rates for ploughing, planting and harvesting for the entire period from 1957 to 1972. Series C shows wage rates for ploughing only. While Series B and C progressively overcome the difficulty of not weighting the wage rates by employment in different operations, all three series suffer from not being weighted by employment in different locations.

To estimate real wages the money wages must be deflated by a suitable cost-of-living index. The one used is prepared by the Central Bank of the

Philippines for the entire nation outside the Manila metropolitan area. The weights of the index are based on the expenditure survey of 1965. It may be argued that, for the post-1965 period of rapid inflation, the index overstates the required adjustment in money wages by ignoring the possibility of a shift in consumption in favour of commodities which became relatively cheaper. But it is doubtful if such a shift could have been very great in view of the fact that the price increase for food, an inelastic demand category, was greater than the average.

But there are important elements of downward bias in the index as a deflator of money wages. Its weights are derived from the consumption pattern of the households in rural and urban areas outside Manila as revealed by the 1965 survey.

According to that survey an average rural household allocated 61 per cent of expenditure to food while an average household in non-Manila urban areas allocated only 51 per cent. Secondly, the rural income group earning between 500 and 1,000 pesos in 1965 (and hence representing the consumption pattern of an average agricultural labourer whose income was within this range) allocated to food 65 per cent of consumption, a significantly higher proportion than for an average rural household. Thus the use of the consumption pattern of a group which included higher income rural households and urban households outside Manila resulted in the relative understatement of the weight of food from the standpoint of what would be appropriate for the wage deflator. Since the price of food increased much faster than prices of other consumption goods, the increase in the level of prices shown by the index must be biased downward.

It is impossible to say in which direction the index, on balance, is biased. However, it is interesting to note that an official cost-of-living index for low income households for the same geographical area is available, although only for the period since 1966. A comparison of that index with the one used here shows that for the recent years the former records a sharper rise in prices than the latter.[1]

Table 98 and figure 11 show the movement in the three series of real wages. Except for the short-term recovery in 1966 and 1967, which offset the sharp decline in the preceding two years, the trend is clearly and sharply a downward one. The decline is particularly pronounced in the late 1960s and early 1970s.

It may be noted that the failure to weight the money wage rates by operations does not by itself seem to have affected the course of Series A. It is the addition of new operations since 1966 that has resulted in an understatement of Series A for the period since that year. The year-to-year changes in the three series are very highly correlated, except for that between 1965

---

[1] For 1973 the index for the low income families is 110 per cent above that in 1966. (See National Economic and Development Authority: *Journal of Philippines Statistics*, Vol. 26, No. 1, section vi). The index used here records an 88 per cent increase over the same period.

Figure 11.   Daily real wage in agriculture in the Philippines

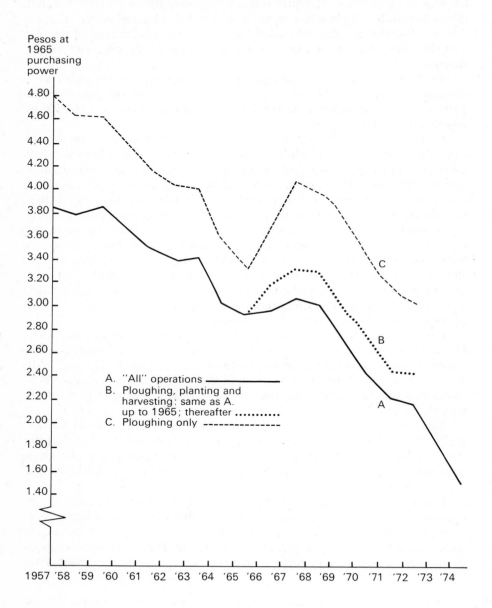

Pesos at
1965
purchasing
power

A. "All" operations
B. Ploughing, planting and
    harvesting: same as A.
    up to 1965; thereafter
C. Ploughing only

and 1966 when some new operations were added to the over-all wage rates shown in Series A. The trend in Series A is virtually identical to that in B and C for the periods up to 1965 and after 1966. Since Series B and C represent wage rates in homogeneous operations it appears that the absence of weighting by operations is not a major cause for worry; one can estimate over-all changes in wage rates by using a simple average as in Series A.

As has been mentioned, all three series are unweighted averages of the wage rates in various locations. While as a result the level of wages at any given time may be understated (because, say, high wage regions are also larger in terms of their share of employment) it is very unlikely that this would result in the rate of change in wages being understated. If the rates of change in regional wage rates diverge, then it is perhaps more likely for the regions in which wage rates are increasing at a higher rate to experience a decline in their share of the agricultural labour force. A weighted index in this case would show a lower rate of increase than an unweighted one.

SUMMARY OF FINDINGS

One must begin this summary by acknowledging the uncertain quality of the statistical information. The over-all weight of evidence, however, is too clear to leave anyone in doubt about the direction of change. While the statistical evidence cited above need not all be taken too literally, the major conclusions can be summarised with some confidence.

First, the living standards of the poorest groups of families in rural areas have declined absolutely. There may be controversy about the actual number of households and the exact extent of the deterioration, but there is little doubt that a substantial proportion of the rural households in the lowest income groups experienced a very significant decline in living standards during the last 15 to 20 years. It is probable that about a fifth of the rural households, accounting for a slightly lower proportion of the rural population, experienced such a decline. Furthermore, the deterioration in living standards was more rapid during the early 1970s, a period of high inflation.

The decline in the average income of the lowest quintile has been less than the decline in real wages. While part of this may simply be due to statistical errors, the gap is too wide and systematic to be dismissed so quickly. One possibility is that households were better able to maintain non-wage income (e.g. production of goods and services for self-consumption) than wages.

Second, the decline in the living standards of the rural poor has taken place despite rapid over-all growth of the rural economy. Output of agricultural goods per head increased rapidly until the beginning of the present decade. The value of agricultural output per employed worker, although subject to fluctuations due to such factors as short-term changes in the terms of trade, also shows a clear tendency to increase over the long term. None of these phenomena is reflected in a corresponding movement of real wages. The inevitable conclusion is that the factor share of labour has tended to decline while that of land has tended to increase.

The declining factor share of labour and the consequent downward trend in real wages are not difficult to understand even within an orthodox analytical framework. Labour supply increased rapidly as a result of demographic factors. From about the middle of the 1950s the growth of manufacturing employment slowed down and in the subsequent period barely kept pace with the growth of total employment.[1] The inflow of labour into the manufacturing sectors easily exceeded the growth in demand for labour, so that the real wages in manufacturing industries failed to rise during the 1960s and thereafter declined very significantly.[2]

Demand for labour within agriculture lagged far behind output. While some lag would be inevitable even under ideal circumstances, the dramatic decline in the demand for labour for such operations as land preparation can only be explained by the rapid tractorisation promoted directly by government policies.[3]

If the forces of the market were too powerful to prevent a downward slide in real wages, there were few attempts to offset them by compensatory actions. It is well known that minimum wage legislation has little impact on actual wages in an underdeveloped economy, especially in the unorganised rural sector. Such legislation rarely is anything more than an expression of interest of the government. In the Philippines, minimum agricultural real wages actually declined in spite of minimum wage legislation. This fixed levels as follows at current pesos per day:

6 April 1951		2.50
8 August 1963		3.50
21 April 1965		3.50
17 June 1970		4.75

Since 1963 the levels so established by law actually resulted in a minimum *real* wage that was lower than the real wage previously established.

Another possible way of counteracting the tendency for real incomes of the rural poor to fall would be by introducing land reform. The increase in the share of land rent in total income led to sharply increased inequality in the distribution of household income because of the highly unequal pattern of land ownership. In 1960, 11.5 per cent of farms were below 1 hectare in size and together accounted for only 1.6 per cent of the land. At the other extreme, 0.2 per cent of farms were above 50 hectares in size and these accounted for 12.2 per cent of the land.[4] Detailed information on the distri-

---

[1] See Power and Sicat, op. cit., pp. 53-54.

[2] See the large number of real wage measurements for various categories of workers in manufacturing industries as reported in Central Bank of the Philippines, op. cit., and National Economic and Development Authority: *Statistical Yearbook, 1974*.

[3] See Mahar Mangahas, et al.: *Labour absorption in Philippine agriculture* (OECD, 1972).

[4] Bureau of Census and Statistics: *Agricultural Census, 1960*.

bution of land ownership as compiled by the 1970 agricultural census is not available, but there is little evidence of an improvement in the decade between censuses.

It was only in October 1972 that land reform legislation was enacted[1] and it is too early to analyse its effects on the distribution of income. It is clear from the legal texts, however, that the objective of the reforms is to improve the condition of tenants by bestowing ownership rights on them. The landless labourers, the poorest of the rural classes, are not the intended beneficiaries. It is unlikely, therefore, that the land reforms will raise the living standards of those in the bottom quintile, although it may bring some improvement to those in the next quintile. The continuing sharp decline in rural real wages two years after the land reforms decree suggests that pessimism is justified.

---

[1] For an account of the land reform measures under Martial Law see Zubeda M. Ahmad (ed.): *Land reform in Asia with particular reference to Pakistan, the Philippines and Thailand*, op. cit.

PART III

THE CHINESE EXPERIENCE

THE DISTRIBUTION OF INCOME IN RURAL CHINA

12

Azizur Rahman Khan

The distribution of income and the condition of the poor in contemporary China are subjects of intense interest and controversy. Most observers emphasise the apparent similarity of the level and pattern of consumption of people from all walks of life and conclude that the equality in the distribution of income in China today is too obvious to require detailed documentary evidence. Some analysts, however, not all of whom are unsympathetic to the Chinese road to development, are dismayed about the unmistakably large differences in incomes between households, production units and regions as reported in the official sources. It is not easy to make up one's mind about questions such as the following: Compared to her own past and to contemporary poor countries how equal is the distribution of income in China today? Are there significant inequalities in contemporary Chinese society? If so, how great are such inequalities and what are their sources?

A major difficulty in providing answers to such questions arises from the lack of the usual income distribution statistics in China. The kind of household income and expenditure survey data on the basis of which Lorenz distributions could be fitted at different points of time to make intertemporal comparisons (and also international comparisons with similar measurements elsewhere) are not available for China. However, enough information is available to permit a more sophisticated analysis than could be provided merely by isolated stories and statistics.

In 1957 about 86 per cent of the Chinese people lived in rural areas,[1] and the proportion today is unlikely to be much lower.

This chapter begins by attempting to make a rough estimate of inequality in the distribution of rural income in China before the Revolution and then to trace the major steps that were taken afterwards to promote equality. Thereafter the sources of inequality within the commune system will be analysed. Finally, current policies on the distribution of income will be discussed. While the quality of the statistical analysis will be uneven and will

---

[1] H. Yuan Tien: *China's population struggle* (Columbus, Ohio State University Press, 1973).

rarely satisfy conventional standards, it is hoped that the data are sufficiently reliable to enable broad trends to emerge clearly.

POVERTY AND INEQUALITY IN PRE-REVOLUTION[1] CHINA

Table 99 contains some information about the distribution of landownership in China during the 1930s. The average amount of land owned by the 22.1 per cent of rural families in the three top groups was 10.8 acres, or 10.7 times the average quantity of land owned by the 23.1 per cent of the small farmers. The ratio of the sizes of the operational holdings—the farms—of these groups is smaller. The average farm size operated by the three top groups is 7.9 acres, while the average farm size operated by the small farmers is 1.43 acres. Thus the ratio of operational holdings is 5.5:1. The ratio of income from agricultural activities of the two groups would lie somewhere between the above two ratios because the "pure" landlords in the top group did not operate farms but received rent from, among others, the small farmers. The latter, in turn, obtained about 30 per cent of their farm land from the landlords under crop-sharing and other arrangements.

While it is impossible to obtain a precise estimate of the distribution of income among rural families some rough approximations have been attempted. As a first step incomes from farming and landownership have been estimated by combining the information in table 99 with that on cost of production, output per acre and rental arrangements.[2]

Combining all these facts it was found that the small farmers had an average family income of 759 kg of "grain equivalent" while the families in the three top groups (representing large farmers and landlords) each had, on the average, an income of 4,498 kg of grain equivalent. On the further assumption that the bottom 20 per cent of the farming families had the same average income as the small farmers (who represented 23.1 per cent of the farming and landowning families) and that the average income of the top 20 per cent of the families was the same as that of the average of the top three groups (who represented 22.1 per cent of the families), the result arrived at was that the shares of total agricultural income accruing to the bottom and top quintile groups were respectively 6.9 per cent and 41 per cent. As a first approximation, it can be concluded therefore that the average

[1] References to "the Revolution" in this chapter should be understood to relate to the establishment of the People's Republic in 1949.

[2] Information on these subjects has been collected from the works of J. L. Buck: *Land utilisation in China* (Nanking University, 1937); *Chinese farm economy* (University of Chicago Press, 1930), and those reported in Peter Schran: *The development of Chinese agriculture, 1950-1959* (University of Illinois Press, 1969). The main pieces of information are the following: *(a)* output per cropped acre for the small and medium farms was 1,096 kg of "grain equivalent"; for the large farms it was 986 kg, and the average for all farms was 1,045 kg; *(b)* cropping intensities for small and large farms were respectively 64 and 61 per cent; *(c)* rent as a proportion of gross output was 40.5 per cent; *(d)* current inputs were 10.8 per cent of the value of output; *(e)* "labour cost" was 38.2 per cent of the value of output; *(f)* hired labour amounted to 19.5 per cent of "labour cost" on the average and to 4.3 per cent and 31.6 per cent respectively for the small and large farms.

Table 99.   Distribution of landownership and farm size in China, 1929-33

Category	Percentage of farming and landholding households	Average size of farms in acres	Average size of owned land in acres	Percentage share in total land ownership
Small farmers	23.1	1.43	1.01	5.8
Medium farmers	35.6	2.84	2.00	17.7
Medium-large farmers	19.2	4.92	3.48	16.6
Large farmers	10.6	7.17	5.16	13.6
Very large farmers	7.7	12.66	9.19	17.6
Landlords	3.8	—	30.00	28.7

Note: The source of data is J. L. Buck: *Land utilisation in China*, op. cit. The categories are not defined on the basis of rigid class intervals but on wider considerations of absolute and relative conditions in various regions. There was a great deal of regional variation. In general, the share of the landlords was higher in the south than in the north. Additional information on concentration of landownership and its regional variations can be found in Institute of Pacific Relations: *Agrarian China* (University of Chicago Press, 1938).

income (and income share) of the top quintile of the farming and landholding households was about six times that of the bottom quintile.

To improve upon this first approximation the effects on the distribution of income of interest payments on debts were taken into account. Victor Lippit estimates that interest payments on all outstanding debt in rural China amounted to 2.8 per cent of the national income or 4.3 per cent of agricultural income.[1] About 56 per cent of the rural families were in debt. In the absence of information about the distribution of the interest recipients and debtors the conservative assumption was made that each of the bottom 56 per cent of the families was equally indebted and that income from interest accrued to the top 33 per cent of the families in such a way that each of them received an equal amount of interest income. On these assumptions the income share of the bottom quintile of farming households fell to 5.4 per cent and that of the top quintile increased to 43.6 per cent.[2] The ratio of incomes per household and income shares of these two quintile groups would be just over eight.

If better data had been available this crude measure could have been further improved upon by taking into account the following considerations:

(a) The assumption that the average income of the bottom 20 per cent of the farmers was the same as that of the bottom 23.1 per cent led to an

[1] Victor D. Lippit: "Land Reform and Economic Development in China", in *Chinese Economic Studies* (White Plains, New York), Vol. VII, No. 4.

[2] Charles R. Roll Jr.: *The distribution of rural incomes in China: a comparison of the 1930s and the 1950s* (Harvard Ph.D dissertation, 1974) estimates the farm income shares of the top and bottom quintiles to be 42.7 and 5.8 per cent respectively for the 1930s. His estimates of the shares of total income of these two groups are respectively 42 and 6 per cent. His estimates are based on a previously unexamined sample survey of over 1.7 million households carried out by the National Land Committee in 1934. He also makes use of the data in Buck: *Chinese farm economy*, op. cit., for comparison.

overestimate of the income share of the bottom quintile. Similarly, the assumption that the average income of the top 20 per cent of the farmers and landlords was the same as that of the top three groups in table 99, accounting for 22.1 per cent of the families, led to an underestimate of the income share of the top quintile.

(b) The above distribution was obtained for the farmers and landlords only and excluded the landless workers who were probably at the very bottom of the income distribution scale. According to available evidence such workers constituted a significant, though not an overwhelming, proportion of the rural population. Their inclusion would almost certainly have further reduced the income share of the bottom quintile of families relative to that of the top quintile.

(c) No information was available on the distribution of income of those who were engaged in non-agricultural activities. Nor was anything known about the distribution of non-agricultural incomes of farmers and landlords. It seems plausible to assume that the richer farmers had greater access to income from non-agricultural sources, but it is impossible to guess *a priori* about the distribution of income of those engaged in non-agricultural activities.

(d) There were mandatory charges which the tenants had to pay the landlords in order to have the privilege of working the land. Lippit provides a catalogue of such charges.[1] From his analysis it is clear that such practices resulted in an income transfer from the tenants, representing more heavily the lower income groups, to the landlords, included in the highest income groups.

(e) The estimates reported above are for the top and bottom quintiles of families, not persons. If family size were positively correlated with income, then the above measurements would overstate the difference in per capita incomes of the two quintile groups. In this context it is important to distinguish between the family and the household. The former can be defined to include parents, wife, children and other close relations of the head of the family and the latter to include also servants, permanent labourers and other dependants. To arrive at per capita income measurements one should take into account the size of the family and not of the household. The justification for this procedure is clear. First, the permanent labourers and servants engaged in productive activities have already been taken into account by the substraction of the wages of hired labour from the value of production to estimate income. Secondly, the consumption level of the members of the family is much higher than that of the servants, etc. Indeed the total expenditure on servants, etc., should properly be treated as expenditure on services consumed by the members of the family. The practice that is frequently adopted in studies on the distribution of income in the developing countries is to estimate

---

[1] Lippit, op. cit.

per capita income by dividing the total income of the family by the size of the household. Since the richer families have more servants and "other dependants" the result is an understatement of inequality.

From the same set of surveys on which the information in table 99 is based it can be ascertained that the average size of the household (6.2 persons) is higher than the average size of the family (5.3 persons).[1] Household size is bigger for the larger farmers than for the smaller ones. But it does not appear that this relationship applies to the same extent to family size.[2] Indeed the average family size is lower for the landlords (5.14 persons) than for all farmers (5.3 persons).

While the above discussion demonstrated the impossibility of estimating with any precision the quintile shares of rural income in pre-Revolution China, it seems reasonable to conclude that the indirect estimates of distribution derived earlier are unlikely to be an overestimate of inequality. Five additional factors have been noted for which ideally corrections should have been made in these estimates. For four of them such corrections would tend to raise estimated inequality while that for the last factor might reduce it. On the balance the indirect estimates would appear to give too low a measure of inequality. It therefore seems plausible to argue that the income share of the bottom quintile of the population was at most between 5 and 6 per cent of rural income, possibly less. The income share of the top quintile was probably close to 45 per cent or even more.

On this basis one can see that the degree of rural income inequality in China in that period was not very different from what it is in an average country in south and south-east Asia today. These countries differ a great deal with respect to rural inequality, but, on the average, the share of the bottom quintile is between 5 and 6 per cent and that of the top quintile about 50 per cent.[3]

It is even more difficult to quantify the extent of poverty in absolute terms in the absence of detailed information about the size distribution of the levels of income and consumption from all sources. Some insights may be obtained by trying to make a guess about the living condition of the small

---

[1] See Buck: *Land utilisation in China*, op. cit., table 2.2, p. 19.

[2] In the source quoted above the family size is shown only for the landlords and for all farmers. It is not shown for the various size groups of farmers. Post-Revolution data show that the average size of household varies positively with size of family, but by then the distinction between family and household must have disappeared. Once again, the family size of the former landlords is lower than the average. (See Statistical Work Editorial Committee, Data Office: "Summary material on the incomes and expenditures of peasant households in 1954", in *T'ung-chi Kung-tso* (Statistical Work No. 10, 1957), pp. 31-33.

[3] J. Stern: *Growth and redistribution*, preliminary report prepared for the ILO (Geneva, ILO, 1975; mimeographed) estimates the income shares of the bottom and top quintiles for rural and urban areas together to be 5.3 and 51 per cent respectively on the basis of the data reported in S. Jain: *Size distribution of income: compilation of data*, IBRD Staff Working Paper No. 190 (1974). The degree of rural inequality is probably a little less than that of urban inequality, but the weight of the rural distribution in these averages is overwhelmingly large. It therefore seems likely that the rural shares would be very similar. The details for some contemporary Asian countries are discussed in different chapters of the present work.

farmers in table 99. On the basis of calculations made, and after allowing for the interest payment on their debts, the retained income from farm production for an average family in this category is estimated to be 610 kg of grain equivalent. Even on the optimistic assumption that such a family consumed all its retained production of grain and financed all its non-grain consumption by earnings from other sources, this amount would provide a level of consumption well below any acceptable minimum.[1] Thus nearly a quarter of the landowning farmers had a dismally low average living condition, much below any acceptable nutritional standard. It seems highly likely that everyone in this group and many in the higher group of farmers in table 99 suffered from various degrees of undernutrition. It is in this context that the significance of R.H. Tawney's designation of the Chinese peasants as "a propertied proletariat" has to be understood.[2] When one considers that the living condition of the landless was worse than that of the small farmers the staggering magnitude of rural poverty and destitution in China at that time becomes obvious.

REDISTRIBUTION THROUGH LAND REFORM

After the Revolution the Chinese took the first major step towards reducing rural inequality by carrying out a highly egalitarian land reform. The radically altered pattern of landownership after the reforms is summarised in table 100, which is based on the findings of a sample survey of over 16,000 peasant families in 25 provinces conducted in 1955 by the State Statistical Bureau.[3] Unfortunately, the categories used in the table do not conform to those reported in table 99. It apears that the poor peasants in table 100 consist of all the small farmers and most of the medium farmers in table 99 plus the previously landless who were not included in table 99. The landlords in the two tables should be comparable, their lower proportion in 1955 being due to such factors as the larger denominator (which now includes the landless), the changes between the early 1930s and the date of the land reform and sampling error. Rich peasants in table 100 probably overlap substantially with the very large farmers in table 99, while the middle peasants may roughly approximate the sum of the pre-Revolution categories of medium-large and large farmers.

---

[1] For a family of 4.5 persons (which is below the average family size of 5.3 in rural China) at that time per capita daily consumption of grain would be 13 oz. On the assumption of 100 calories per oz. (which appears to be a reasonable average for grains of various kinds) and 20 per cent of calories suplied by non-grain items, the intake of calories by an average person in this group would work out at just over 1,600 as compared to a requirement of well above 2,000. It is, however, necessary to note that consumption for the lower income groups could have been higher than retained earnings to the extent that new borrowing exceeded repayments of outstanding debt.

[2] See R. H. Tawney: *Land and labour in China* (London, George Allen and Unwin, 1932).

[3] Statistical Work Editorial Committee, op. cit.

Table 100.   Distribution of land ownership after the land reforms

Class of family	Share of families (per cent)	Share of total area owned (per cent)	Average area owned (acres)	Net area rented in (+) or out (−) as percentage of owned area
Poor peasant	57.1	46.8	2.00	+ 2.4
Middle peasant	35.8	44.8	3.05	+ 2.6
Rich peasant	3.6	6.4	4.33	− 4.4
Landlord	2.6	2.1	1.97	+ 1.4
Others	0.9	—	—	—

Note: Source of data: Statistical Work Editorial Committee, op. cit., quoted in Peter Schran, op. cit. Class titles are based on the status of the families immediately before the land reforms. These titles continued to be applied to the households long after land reforms and collectivisation rendered them inaccurate descriptions of the current economic status. For a clear definition of the various classes see Mao Tsetung: "How to Differentiate the Classes in the Rural China", in *Selected Works*, Vol. I (Peking, Foreign Language Press, 1975), from which the following quotations have been extracted.
"A *landlord* is a person who owns land, does not engage in labour himself, or does so only to a very small extent, and lives by exploiting the peasants. The collection of land rent is his main form of exploitation; in addition, he may lend money, hire labour, or engage in industry and commerce ...
"The *rich peasant* as a rule owns land ... The rich peasant generally has rather more and better instruments of production and more liquid capital than the average and engages in labour himself, but always relies on exploitation for part or even the major part of his income. His main form of exploitation is the hiring of labour (long-term labourers) ...
"Many *middle peasants* own land. Some own only part of their land and rent the rest. Others own no land of their own at all and rent all their land. All of them have a fair number of farm implements. A middle peasant derives his income wholly or mainly from his own labour. As a rule he does not exploit others and in many cases he himself is exploited by others, having to pay a small amount in land rent and in interest on loans. But generally he does not sell his labour power ...
"Among the *poor peasants* some own part of their land and have a few odd farm implements, others own no land at all but only a few odd farm implements. As a rule poor peasants have to rent the land they work on and are subjected to exploitation, having to pay land rent and interest on loans and to hire themselves out to some extent ...
"The *worker* ... as a rule owns no land or farm implements ... Workers make their living wholly or mainly by selling their labour power."
It appears that the "poor peasants" in the table include the former workers.

Before making a comparison of the distributions in the 1930s with that after the land reforms, one important factor must be noted. The average size of the ownership unit declined from 4 acres in the early 1930s to 2.44 acres in 1955. This was partly due to the distribution of land to the previously landless during the land reforms and partly to the increase in the size of the agricultural population over the period.

Land reforms brought about a massive redistribution of income and wealth in favour of the poor peasants at the cost of the landlords and, to a lesser extent, of the rich peasants. In the early 1930s the weighted average of the ownership of the small and medium farmers was 1.61 acres, i.e. only 40 per cent of the average of all ownership units. After the land reforms, the average area owned by the poor peasants, the approximately comparable group, went up to 2 acres, i.e. to 82 per cent of the size of the average of all ownership units. While the average size of a landlord's unit in the early 1930s was 18.6 times that of an average small and medium farmer, it was so reduced by land reforms that it was slightly less than the size of the average farm owned by a poor peasant. The rich peasants were subjected to less severe measures. Their average holding was reduced to 1.77 times the over-all average, as compared with 2.3 times the over-all average in the early 1930s. The middle peasants appear to have gained in a relative sense. The average size of their holding became 25 per cent higher than the over-all average after reforms. In the early 1930s their holdings were about the same

259

size as the over-all average. These are the average patterns for the whole country. There is ample evidence of a good deal of local variation.

There is not enough information to estimate the income shares of the top and bottom quintiles and compare them with the results of the preceding section.[1] But some comparison is possible which demonstrates the dramatic equalising effects of land reforms on the distribution of rural income. Adopting the same methodology as used in the previous section, the incomes for family classes in the early 1930s were as follows:

Family class	Income in grain equivalent per family (kg)	Index (income of the small and medium farmers = 100)
Small and medium farmers	1 216	100
Very large farmers	5 029	414
Landlords	8 522	701

According to the 1955 survey total receipts per family for the different classes (expressed as indices, with the receipts for the poor peasants = 100) were as follows: poor peasants, 100; middle peasants, 158; rich peasants, 262; landlords, 102.

As indicated in the beginning of this section, poor peasants are roughly comparable with the small and medium farmers in the earlier data. Indeed the income of the poor peasants in the pre-land-reform days would have been lower than that of the small and medium farmers because poor peasants include those who were formerly landless. After land reform, not only are the family incomes of poor peasants brought into equality with those of the former landlords (who previously had more than seven times as much relative income) but the differential between the poor and the rich peasants (roughly comparable with the very large farmers in the pre-land reform data) is drastically reduced.

It is not intended to analyse every major aspect of the land reforms, but it is of some importance to highlight a few specific features. First, the Chinese land reforms were not brought about through a redistribution of land by the Government to the poor peasants. Instead the poor peasants and the landless were organised at the grassroots level by the political movement that carried out the Revolution and the peasants themselves were encouraged to take the land by overthrowing their local oppressors.[2]

Secondly, land reforms were not "class-neutral". The policy was not one of defining a ceiling on ownership and enforcing it uniformly. The landlords, those who did not engage in labour but derived their entire income from rent

---

[1] Charles R. Roll Jr., op. cit., estimates the income shares of the top and bottom quintiles of the population just after land reforms (i.e. in 1952) to be 35.1 and 11.3 per cent. Thus according to his estimates the ratio of incomes of the two groups declined from over 7 during the 1930s to about 3 after the land reforms.

[2] For an account of the process see William Hinton: *Fanshen* (New York, Vintage Books, 1966).

and moneylending, were subjected to a much greater degree of relative and absolute expropriation than the rich peasants whose role as "exploiters" was limited mainly to labour hiring.[1]

Thirdly, the promotion of income equality was not the only achievement of the land reforms. According to Lippit's estimates, about 17 per cent of the national income (i.e. 26 per cent of agricultural income) that previously accrued to the landlords and rich peasants in the form of rent, profits and other payments (and used to be consumed) was redistributed by the land reform measures in favour of the poor and middle peasants. Much of it found its way to savings in the form of self-financed investment and increased payments to the state, in the form of both direct and concealed taxes. According to the same source by 1952 about 35 per cent of the nation's gross investments were being financed by savings generated as a direct consequence of the land reform measures.[2]

Finally, land reforms severely reduced the role of private ownership of land and of the other means of production as a source of inequality of income and power. But such a role was not completely abolished. Although the inequality in the ownership of land was drastically reduced, it was allowed to continue. Land renting and even sale (see below) were permitted and continued to take place, although on a very modest scale. As table 100 shows, rich peasants rented out a net amount of 4.4 per cent of their land to the poor and middle peasants and to the former landlords. Indeed land reforms, by themselves, were not a permanent guarantee against the polarisation of land holding in rural China.

TOWARDS COLLECTIVISATION

Land reforms were completed in 1952. But the organisation of the co-operatives, the next major step in restructuring the rural society, was extremely slow until 1955 (see table 101). In July 1955 Mao Tsetung delivered his report *On the question of agricultural co-operation*[3] which made it clear that many in the ranks of the party leadership believed at the time that peasant agriculture should be the main vehicle of increased agricultural production and that it was premature to organise co-operatives on a large scale. Indeed this strand of thought was so dominant in the party that a policy of "resolute contraction" was adopted in Chekiang in which "out of 53,000 co-operatives in the province some 15,000 co-operatives (comprising 400,000 peasant households) were dissolved at one fell swoop".[4] In his report

---

[1] Since reforms were carried out on a completely decentralised basis, it is quite likely that in many areas this average pattern was not adhered to. See, for example, Hinton, op. cit., p. 592, for an account of a village in which the rich peasants were expropriated so severely as to make their per capita holdings smaller than that of the middle and poor peasants.

[2] Lippit, op. cit.

[3] Mao Tsetung: "On the question of agricultural co-operation", in *Selected readings from the works of Mao Tsetung* (Peking, Foreign Languages Press, 1971), pp. 389-420.

[4] ibid., p. 396.

Mao criticised these leaders for "tottering along like a woman with bound feet" and forcefully argued the case for agricultural co-operation.

Many of Mao's arguments were based on considerations of efficiency and the technical transformation of agriculture. He argued that socialist industrialisation was incompatible with peasant agriculture which could neither generate the required surplus nor create sufficient demand for the output of industry. But he was equally forceful in arguing the case for co-operation on grounds of equity:

As is clear to everyone, the spontaneous forces of capitalism have been steadily growing in the countryside in recent years, with *new* rich peasants springing up everywhere and many well-to-do middle peasants striving to become rich peasants. On the other hand, many poor peasants are still living in poverty for lack of sufficient means of production, with some in debt and others *selling* or renting out their land. If this tendency goes unchecked, the polarisation in the countryside will inevitably be aggravated day by day. Those peasants who lose their land and those who remain in poverty will complain that we are doing nothing to save them from ruin or to help them overcome their difficulties. Nor will the well-to-do middle peasants who are heading in the capitalist direction be pleased with us, for we shall never be able to satisfy their demands unless we intend to take the capitalist road.[1]

Mao foresaw the socialist transition of Chinese agriculture in stages. Mutual aid teams, based completely on individual farming, were in existence in the areas controlled by the Communists even before 1949. On the principle of voluntary participation and mutual benefit, the members did an equal amount of work for each other, or if one could not give another as much help as he received he made up the difference in cash. These mutual aid teams were to be pooled together into the semi-socialist (sometimes called the "elementary") co-operatives. The semi-socialist nature of these co-operatives derived from the fact that

on the one hand, [they] made unified use of land and rational use of farm tools, carried on collective labour and practised distribution according to work and had a fair amount of common property, and thus had [their] socialist aspects; on the other hand, the members still retained their private ownership of land and other means of production and received dividends on their land shares and certain payments for the pooling of their farm tools and draught animals.[2]

The third step would be to call on the peasants to organise larger agricultural producers' co-operatives which are fully socialist in nature (sometimes called "advanced" co-operatives). In these socialist co-operatives land and other means of production would cease to be privately owned and the collective product would be distributed entirely on the basis of work performed.

At the time Mao delivered his report in 1955, there were 650,000 co-operatives of the semi-socialist type, each having on average 26 households.

---

[1] Mao Tsetung: "On the question of agricultural co-operation", op. cit., pp. 411-412, emphasis added.

[2] ibid., p. 419.

Table 101.   Socialist transformation of Chinese agriculture
(Percentage of peasant families)

Year	Individual farming	Mutual aid team	Elementary co-operatives	Advanced co-operatives	People's communes
1952	60.0	39.9	0.1	—	—
1953	60.5	39.3	0.2	—	—
1954	39.7	58.3	2.0	—	—
1955	35.1	50.7	14.2	—	—
1956	3.7	—	8.5	87.8	—
1957	2.0	—	2.0	96.0	—
1958	n.a.	—	n.a.	n.a.	99.1

Source: State Statistical Bureau: *Ten great years*, op. cit., and Schran, op. cit., p. 28.

They accounted for only about 14 per cent of the rural households.[1] Mao confidently forecast "that there will soon be a nation-wide high tide of social-ist transformation in the countryside".[2] He projected the completion of the organisation of rural households in the elementary or semi-socialist co-oper-atives by 1960. He wanted the transformation of these into fully socialist (advanced) co-operatives by 1967, the end of the Third Five-Year Plan.

In July 1955 Mao was strongly urging the party "to adhere firmly to the principles of voluntary participation and mutual benefit" and recommending that for the next few years "landlords and rich peasants must definitely not be admitted into the co-operatives in any of the areas where co-operation has not been basically completed" and that, except for those who are politically conscious, "the upper strata of the new and the old middle peasants... should not be admitted into the co-operatives yet".[3] He suggested that in the formative stage the co-operatives should, instead, include only the poor peas-ants and the lower strata of the new and old middle peasants, who together accounted for about 70 per cent of the rural population.

Events moved much faster than what seemed at the time to be a very ambitious projection. Table 101 summarises the process of transformation. The pace quickened dramatically in 1956. By that year virtually all the rural families were organised into co-operatives, about 88 per cent of the families

---

[1] The estimate of 650,000 and 26 households per co-operative are from Mao Tsetung: "On the question of agricultural co-operation", op. cit. The figure of 14 per cent (to be exact 14.2 per cent) is from: State Statistical Bureau: *Ten great years* (Peking, Foreign Languages Press, 1960). It is not clear if this is the mid-year or year-end figure. Assuming this refers to the same date as Mao's estimates (i.e. middle of 1955) the implied number of agricultural households is 119 million and the agricultural population is 536 million (assuming 4.5 persons per household). These estimates do not appear to be widely off the mark. Yuan Tien, op. cit., puts the estimate of rural population in 1955 at 532 million.

[2] Mao Tsetung, op. cit., pp. 412-413.

[3] ibid. This may be a convenient place to repeat that these categories refer to the historical status of the families prior to the land reforms. Land reforms and collectivisation rendered these names inaccurate as descriptions of the current status of families. But in the Chinese political vocabulary these categories are still used to indicate the historical class allegiance of the relevant persons.

Table 102. Per capita incomes of the different classes of families in rural China (Yuan)

Class of family	1956	1957
Poor peasants	61.3	60.2
Lower-middle peasants	67.6	69.9
Upper-middle peasants	77.2	79.0
Other labourers	63.4	70.6
Rich peasants	55.3	58.7
Other exploiters	59.0	66.2

Note: "Other exploiters" presumably includes former landlords. "Other labourers" includes workers in handicrafts, peddling, etc.
Source: Statistical Research Editorial Committee, op. cit.

belonging to the advanced co-operatives. According to a survey of 228 co-operatives in 1957, it was found that 99.1 per cent of the distributed income represented payment for labour and only 0.9 per cent for ownership of land.[1] It also appears that Mao's 1955 instruction to keep out the landlords and the upper middle and rich peasants had been rendered redundant by the fact that the building up of co-operatives had been basically completed everywhere.

Table 102 contains information on the per capita incomes of the different classes of rural families in 1956 and 1957 as estimated from a survey of the above-mentioned sample of 228 co-operatives. The effect of collectivisation is clearly seen. The first notable feature is the sharply reduced income of the rich peasants i.e. of those who emerged as the top income class after the earlier land reforms. The average income of this class fell below that of the poor peasants after collectivisation.

The second important feature is that although the difference in income between middle and poor peasants was reduced from the period after the land reforms,[2] the middle peasants continued to have a much higher average income than that of the rural population as a whole. This can no longer be explained by differences in ownership of land and other assets since less than 1 per cent of income was being distributed on this basis by the time the survey was undertaken. The dependency ratios of the two groups were also

---

[1] Statistical Research Editorial Committee, Data Office: "Material on a Sample Survey of the Distribution of Income in 228 Agricultural Production Co-operatives in 1957", in *T'ung-chi Yen-chiu* [Statistical Research], No. 8, 1958.

[2] Such a comparison is not easy to make. Since the numbers of the two strata of middle peasants are not shown separately it is not possible to calculate the weighted average income of the middle peasants in 1956 or 1957. The unweighted average of per capita incomes is respectively 18 and 24 per cent higher than the per capita income of the poor peasants in these years. The estimated income difference per household between the two classes after land reforms is 58 per cent. Allowing for the difference in household size (18 per cent higher for the middle peasants than for the poor peasants) the per capita income difference between the two groups after land reforms would be 34 per cent. Thus the difference would appear to have been reduced significantly after collectivisation.

very similar.[1] Thus the difference in per capita income between the two groups must be explained largely by differences in the capacity to work. It is probable that the middle peasants were more skilled farmers with long experience of independent farm management and that for each work day they obtained more work points than did the poor peasants.[2]

Why did the rich peasants not perform equally well on the basis of the same reasoning? In the past they were more dependent than middle peasants on hired labour, a practice that probably continued under the mutual aid teams. As farm workers they were probably not as skilled as the middle peasants. It is also possible that as a former "exploiting" class they were discriminated against in the allocation of work points per work day.

In spite of these income differences it is clear from table 102 that class origin ceased to be a major source of income inequality in rural China after collectivisation. By that time factors such as regional and inter-co-operative differences in land and other resource endowment, differences in the demographic conditions of families (as reflected in the dependency ratio) and in individual capacities to work came to be the dominant determinants of inequality of income between households. As a consequence of these factors very considerable income inequalities within each class of peasants persisted in rural China. An approximate quantification of this will be attempted later. During the organisation of the communes the Chinese made a further attempt to reduce these sources of inequality.

As shown in table 101 the transformation of the advanced producers' co-operatives into the people's communes took place in 1958 during the "Great Leap Forward". The initial organisation of the communes was such that the income inequalities persisting in the advanced co-operatives could be further reduced. Two specific features of the initial form of the commune organisation were of special importance in this context. First, the ownership of all land and productive assets was vested in the commune, which was also made the basic accounting unit for the distribution of income. Since a commune was formed by the merger of a number of advanced co-operatives, this procedure abolished the sources of income inequality arising out of differences in the resource endowments of the individual co-operatives comprising a commune. Secondly, in the distribution of income, the criterion of need was assigned a very considerable weight as compared to the nearly exclusive use by the co-operatives of the principle of the capacity to work. In many communes the system of distribution was changed from one based on work points to fixed wages. Frequently the basic food ration, calculated on the basis of need, was the same for everyone. In some communes a system of free distribution of food served in the canteen was adopted. Thus greater equality

---

[1] According to the 1955 survey (Statistical Work Editorial Committee, op. cit.) the number of workers per member of the household was 0.48 for poor peasants and 0.50 for middle peasants.

[2] One intriguing question is why the income difference between the middle and poor peasants widened significantly despite a further increase in the proportion of fully socialist co-operatives between 1956 and 1957.

was promoted partly by distributing a smaller proportion of personal income on the basis of work points and partly by determining the value of work points on the basis of the average productivity over a much larger area than before, an area consisting of several former co-operatives of presumably different levels of prosperity.

It was soon realised that the rapid transformation envisaged in these egalitarian measures was out of step with the level of consciousness of the peasants. The system provoked contradictions between teams and brigades occupying land of different fertility. Members of the better-off brigades and teams strongly resented the fact that they had been pulled down to the level of the poorer brigades and teams, who in turn tended to depend on the performance of the better-off ones for their own well-being. The incentive to work was seriously weakened for both types of teams and brigades.[1] The same phenomenon occurred among households with different capacities to work within the basic accounting units.

Such a tendency to reduce the incentive to work would be of concern at any time. It was specially unwelcome in the wake of the crop failures and economic difficulties during 1960 to 1962. Reversals in policy followed quickly in stages. In 1959 the accounting unit was shifted from the commune to the brigade. In 1961 the production team, the lowest tier of the commune hierarchy comparable in size to the elementary co-operatives, was made the basic accounting unit. The distribution of income on the basis of need was greatly reduced and the principle of capacity to work was restored as the virtually exclusive criterion. In calculating work points each item of work came to be attributed a certain value which later developed widely into a system resembling piece-rates.

Thus, after 1959 the trend to greater equality was somewhat reversed. Since a production team is typically smaller than a former advanced co-operative, it is possible that inequalities due to differences in land fertility and the holding of assets by the basic accounting units became more pronounced in the early 1960s as compared with the late 1950s. It was not until the Cultural Revolution that an attempt was made to change these tendencies towards increasing inegalitarianism. Before discussing these recent policies, however, an effort is made to analyse and quantify the sources of inequality in income in rural China after the consolidation of the commune system.

SOURCES OF INCOME INEQUALITY IN THE COMMUNE SYSTEM

In this section identification and quantification of the sources of income inequality in the commune system as consolidated in a less egalitarian form in the early 1960s are attempted. The system continued in this form until the Cultural Revolution. Since then a very gradual evolution towards further

---

[1] See, for example, the account in I. and D. Crook: *The first years of Yang-yi Commune* (London, Routledge and Kegan Paul, 1966).

equality has been taking place. That the statistical basis of the following analysis is weak will be obvious. The only justification for such crude procedures is the complete absence of systematic data on which a more sophisticated analysis could be based.

Inequality within the basic accounting unit

With only a few exceptions the team, the lowest of the three tiers of the commune system, still serves as the basic accounting unit. Within a basic accounting unit the value of a work point is the same for all workers. Thus the number of work points earned per day's work can be regarded as an index of wage rates. According to the available evidence, differences in such wage rates within a basic accounting unit are limited. Table 103 provides information on the prevalent rates in 18 teams of a brigade in a Fukien commune in the early 1960s. From the available accounts this appears to be representative of the distribution of wage rates within the basic accounting units throughout the commune system. For each sex there are three wage rates, the highest rate being only a third higher than the lowest. Thus the daily wage rate for the ablest and most skilled worker within a basic accounting unit is only a third higher than that of the least able and skilled of the same sex.

The difference in wage rates between men and women within a comparable category is as great as that between the highest and the lowest rates for each sex. It is difficult to make a final evaluation of this wage differential. Some analysts have argued that "this difference between the sexes is due to the stated fact that a woman's working day in production is shorter than a man's. Part of her time goes to household work. And this household work is individual in character, and receives no wage from the collective".[1] Others[2] have suggested that this is due to the persistence of the values inherited from the old society against which the leadership has been waging a struggle.

Differences in the actual distribution of per capita income received from collective work can, of course, be much greater than differences in wage rates because of differences betwen families with respect to the dependency ratio. To what extent this factor can aggravate the income distribution problem is essentially an empirical question which will be discussed later. Here it is important to note that the commune system contains some provision which ensures against the extremes of inequality arising from demographic factors.[3]

---

[1] Jan Myrdal and Gun Kessle: *China: the Revolution continued* (Harmondsworth, Pelican Books, 1973), p. 82.

[2] For example, Neville Maxwell: "Learning from Tachai", in *World Development*, July-Aug. 1975, p. 481.

[3] In Ch'ang-sha Brigade in Lien-Chiang 27 of the 153 member households were identified as food-deficient and received free food. Sixteen of these 27 households encountered hardship due to "too many children" or illness. The assistance provided was generous. Per month of food-deficiency each person received 30 catties (33 lbs.). See C. S. Chen (ed.): *Rural people's communes in Lien-Chiang* (Hoover Institution Press, 1969), pp. 30-31.

Table 103.   Work points per day in 18 teams of the Hu-Li Brigade in Lien-Chiang

Category	Number of persons
Male	
First class (8 points each)	212
Second class (7 points each)	87
Third class (6 points each)	62
Sub-total	361
Female	
First class (6 points each)	90
Second class (5 points each)	102
Third class (4 points each)	109
Sub-total	301
Grand total	662

Source: C. S. Chen (ed.): *Rural people's communes in Lien-Chiang.*, op. cit.

Intra-commune inequality

Brigades and teams within a commune can have very different resource endowments in terms of land (in quality units) per worker, other productive assets per worker, the composition of skills and even, to a certain extent, the dependency ratio. As a result, income per head of teams within a brigade and brigades within a commune can vary a great deal. Table 104 shows the per capita income before deductions for reserve, welfare and administrative funds (which are the same percentages of income for each team) in the 18 teams of Hu-li Brigade in Lien-Chiang, Fukien in the early 1960s. It clearly shows that even within such a small community of 1,759 people the average incomes of individual groups (each on average having 98 people, the range being 71 to 128) can differ substantially. The per capita income of the richest team is 53 per cent higher than that of the poorest. For the commune as a whole the range would be greater. While it is not known that this brigade is representative of an average brigade in this regard, fragmentary information for other brigades indicates that the differential elsewhere is substantial.

Another way to obtain an idea of the extent of inter-team income inequality within a commune is to look at the differential value of an average work day of 10 points (which is the same as the average daily cash wage rate). Within a commune the ratio between the highest and the lowest work teams could be as wide as 2.[1]

---

[1] René Dumont: *La Chine surpeuplée – tiers monde affamé 1965-1969* (Paris, Editions du Seuil, 1965). Gilbert Etienne: *La voie chinoise* (Paris, Presses Universitaires de France, 1974), reports the range for two communes in Kwangtung to be even higher: in Huan-Chen commune it ranges from 0.70 yuan to 1.60 yuan and in Kwang-li commune from 0.61 yuan to 1.36 yuan.

Table 104.   Per capita income in the 18 teams of Hu-Li Brigade

Name of team	Per capita income (yuan)
Ting-chang	70
Pi-kuei	72
Pi-fa	88
Yi-shao	76
Heng-tai	68
Pi-ch'eng	85
Shui-kuan-ti	95
Neng-chih	62
Tseng-pao	80
Ting-hsieh	75
Shan-chun	63
Ch'ang-mu	65
Ting-tuan	82
Chi-kuang	64
Hua-cheng	76
Cheng-tseng	93
Cheng-t'ung	75
Chen-te	67

Source: Chen, op. cit.

Inter-commune inequality

For the mid-1960s information was obtained about the amount of collective income distributed per capita in 36 communes which together accounted for nearly a million people.[1] Once again, it is not possible to say how representative a sample they are of the Chinese communes. But they are geographically dispersed over the whole of China. Their average size (26,550 persons) is close to what is known to be the national average. The average collective income per person in these communes was 120.8 yuan per year, which seems to be close to what is believed to have been the average for all the com-

---

[1] The data were obtained from three sources: (1) Shahid Javed Burki: *A study of Chinese communes 1965*, Harvard East Asian Monographs No. 29 (Harvard University Press, Cambridge (Mass.), 1969) gives information for 13 communes for the year 1964; (2) Keith Buchanan: *The transformation of the Chinese earth* (London, G. Bell and Sons, 1970), gives information for 18 communes, of which data for 17 were used, for the year 1966; and (3) information on the remaining six were obtained for 1964 from René Dumont, op. cit. Buchanan gives information (though implicitly) on the number of workers but not on the population. His estimates were converted into income per head by using the average worker/population ratio estimated for rural China. An additional problem with Buchanan's data is that they refer to a later period. But aggregative data for China show that per capita agricultural output in 1966 was somewhat lower than two years earlier. Prices remained stable. Thus the objections to the pooling of data from different years should not be very strong.

Table 105.   Distribution of 36 communes according to per capita distributed collective
            income

Income range (yuan)	Number of communes
50 to less than 75	5
75 to less than 100	8
100 to less than 125	6
125 to less than 150	7
150 to less than 175	5
175 to less than 200	2
200 and above	3

munes.[1] These are the factors that permit a claim to some confidence in the
representative character of the sample used here, although the question
remains that even if this sample has succeeded in capturing the average it
may have failed to represent the dispersion adequately.

Once again the inequality is very pronounced. In a sense the distribution
of household income from collective sources understates the inequality between communes because of the fact that the richer communes distribute a
smaller proportion of their income among households and save and reinvest
at a higher rate.[2] In the absence of compensatory actions and policies this
would be a source of further polarisation.

Towards the estimation of a summary measure

The discussion above makes it clear that there is considerable inequality
in the distribution of income between households within the basic accounting
unit, between teams and brigades within a commune and between communes
within rural China. But there is still no summary measure of the distribution
of income on the basis of which the present situation in rural China can be
compared with that in her own past or with that elsewhere in the developing
world. This is what an attempt is made to develop next, but with a warning
that the estimation is a rather tentative one.

---

[1] Burki's 13 communes have been widely referred to as above average. The average income in
36 communes referred to earlier in this section is somewhat lower. This is the basis of this
statement.

[2] On the basis of the information for the 18 communes in Buchanan, op. cit., the following
regression was fitted:

$$Y = 68.41 - 0.04X$$

where Y = percentage of commune income distributed among members and X = average annual
wage (in yuan) per member. The coefficients are all significant at the 99 per cent level of
confidence and the correlation coefficient is -0.60. Thus for a 100 yuan difference in wages
(approximately 40 yuan difference in per capita income) between communes, the rate of
accumulation varies by about 4 per cent on average.

Table 106.   Distribution of collective income among decile groups in Liu-ling village

Decile group in ascending order	Percentage share of collective income	Cumulative percentage share
Lowest	5.1	5.1
Second	6.8	11.9
Third	7.6	19.5
Fourth	8.4	27.9
Fifth	8.6	36.5
Sixth	9.4	45.9
Seventh	10.0	55.9
Eighth	10.2	66.1
Ninth	13.2	79.3
Top	20.7	100.0

Note: The income shares for subsequent decile groups rise very gently up to the eighth decile. The jump for the ninth decile is discontinuously larger, and the jump in the share of the top decile is the biggest of all. The top decile consists of small families with a highly favourable dependency ratio.

To start with it would be desirable to estimate the income shares of the decile groups of a sample of households within a commune. No such sample is available. The only set of information that remotely resembles this ideal is the complete enumeration of the income, in cash and in kind, from collective sources received by the 46 households in the Liu-ling village in Shensi in the early 1960s documented by Jan Myrdal.[1] Table 106 shows the income shares of the decile groups of the population in Liu-ling. The data have been obtained by converting all income from collective sources into cash values,[2] calculating incomes per head and ranking all households according to income after excluding households whose chief earners work outside the village and whose incomes are not included in the reported figures.

It was assumed that this distribution was a reasonable approximation of the distribution of household income from collective labour in an average commune. There is no positive evidence to justify this assumption. But there is evidence to show that for some communes in the sample the distribution of income was almost certainly more equal. It is worth illustrating this point at some length. Commune No. 7 in Honan in Buchanan's study[3] has a minimum wage income (presumably accounting for the entire income from collective sources) of 100 yuan. On the assumption that the dependency ratio of the minimum wage earner's family is the same as the average, the lowest per capita income in the commune turns out to be 40 yuan. Even assuming that the poorest family has 33 per cent more dependants than average, the per capita income of the minimum wage earning family would still be higher than 30 yuan. If, however, it is assumed that the pattern of income distribu-

[1] Jan Myrdal: *Report from a Chinese village* (New York, Pantheon Books, 1965).

[2] The weighted average price of grains paid by the Yenan Hsien was used. Price information was obtained from Myrdal, op. cit.

[3] Buchanan, op. cit.

Table 107.   An approximate distribution of collective income among quintile groups
in Chinese communes

Quintile group in ascending order	Share of income	Cumulative share of income
Lowest	9	9
Second	13	22
Third	17	39
Fourth	22	61
Top	39	100

Note: Due to the highly tentative nature of the estimates the figures have been rounded to the nearest integers to avoid the impression of spurious precision. Note that the distribution is less equal than the one in table 106. This is probably because some of the very poor communes are very large in the sample.

tion in this commune is the same as in table 106, then the lowest decile (representing 2,559 persons) would appear to have an average income of only 27 yuan. In other words, the poorest family would have a per capita income below 27 yuan, perhaps around 20 yuan. The implication would be that the distribution of income in this commune (which is one of the poorest) is probably less unequal than would be implied by the use of the distribution in table 106. Indeed this appears to have been the case in a number of poor communes for which there is independent information on the range of wages.

The next step was to divide the distributed collective income of each of the 36 communes into ten decile groups by applying the distribution of table 106 to the total distributed income. In effect, it amounted to the assumption that each commune consisted of 10 large "families" with income shares as specified in table 106. Thus were produced estimates of the per capita income and population of 360 large "families" together consisting of nearly a million people. Table 107 summarises the distribution of income among the quintile groups of these people. The share of the top quintile is 4.3 times greater than that of the bottom quintile. This is probably an exaggerated picture of the inequality in collective income distribution in rural China. As noted above, the uniform application of the distribution in Liuling to all the communes probably resulted in an overstatement in inequality.

Private plots

The inequality in the distribution of income from private plots must also be substantial. But there are strong reasons to believe that within the commune system the distribution of income from private plots is less unequal than the distribution of collective income. This is because of the general principles which guide the management of the private plots within the commune system and thus this must not be interpreted to mean that the abolition of private plots would make the distribution of income more unequal. Why?

First, within a commune the size of the private plot is very equal for different households. Even for the nation as a whole, the size of private plots appears to be relatively highly equal in quality units since the size frequently is determined on the criterion of certain types of consumption needs.

Secondly, many families earn a low collective income because they are able to devote less time to collective work because of their preoccupation with the private plot. This is especially true of those families with only a few able-bodied workers and an unfavourable dependency ratio. Labour quotas are sufficiently flexible to permit this practice on a very significant scale.[1] In this sense the existence of the private plots is a cause of the inequality in the distribution of earnings from collective labour.

Information is not sufficient to make it worthwhile to attempt an adjustment of the estimates of table 107 for income from private plots. But some illustrations based on plausible assumptions may still be useful. It will be assumed that income from private plots amounts to 15 per cent of household income from collective labour and the private plot together. It will also be assumed, quite arbitrarily, that the top quintile's average performance on the private plots in terms of income would be better than that of the bottom quintile by a third. This seems to be the maximum differential in a homogeneous production unit in the value of work (as measured by the allocation of work points per day) performed by the best and the weakest workers. The performance of the intermediate quintiles is also assumed to be linearly located between these two extremes. On the basis of these assumptions the (collective plus private) income share of the poorest quintile of the population becomes a little more than 10 per cent, while that of the richest quintile falls to 36 per cent.

Collective consumption

Compared to a typical rural society in a contemporary developing country and in China before, the rural communes provide many more items of consumption collectively. This creates an important problem of comparison because the distribution of collective consumption is far more equal than the distribution of private consumption and income. Within a commune the access to health, education and other services is probably nearly perfectly equal. Indeed the distribution of such services seems to be designed to improve the distribution of consumption within a commune in that the fees for medical and educational services are charged on the basis of ability to pay. Between communes the quality of such services provided by the communes appears to differ less than distributed income. Moreover, irrespective of

---

[1] In Liu-ling most of the households with a very low collective income are ones which put in very few days of collective labour. Clearly they were spending more time on their private plots. While this practice could be condemned in the case of those who were trying to concentrate on private effort by neglecting collective effort, the attitude would be very different towards those who had too few able-bodied persons to allow them both to look after their private plots and work as much on the collective land as others. Indeed some families in such circumstances also received welfare payments because their only workers were occupied mainly on private plots. See, for example, Myrdal: *Report from a Chinese village*, op. cit., p. 155.

membership of specific communes, all have reasonably equal access to such services provided by the regional and central Governments. All these statements are based on reports of qualitative observations but seem to be unanimously endorsed by visitors and observers.

It is impossible to quantify how large a correction for this factor is necessary, because of the lack of information. But its importance must be recognised in making intertemporal and international comparisons. If one assumes that collective consumption is equivalent to 10 per cent of total income and is equally distributed among all, the income share of the bottom quintile rises to just over 11 per cent and that of the top quintile would fall to 34.6 per cent.

Relative prices

Another factor that should be taken into account in making international comparisons is the fact that relative prices of basic necessities in China are kept lower and that of luxuries are kept much higher than in international markets or in the domestic markets of underdeveloped countries.[1] Thus food grains cost less than half and cotton textiles considerably less than the comparable Indian prices, while bicycles cost significantly more.[2] In China the setting of relative prices seems to be a conscious income redistribution measure, and hence its effects must be taken into account in making international comparisons.

A summary of findings

In the first section it was argued that in the period before the Revolution the bottom 20 per cent of the rural Chinese population received between 5 and 6 per cent of income while the top 20 per cent received close to 45 per cent. The per capita income of the latter group was about eight times higher than that of the former. In all likelihood this is an understatement of the inequality in income between the two quintile groups in those days.

In comparison to its own past and to the contemporary developing countries in Asia the degree of income inequality in rural China is remarkably low. Considering only distributed collective income and income from private plots the share of the bottom quintile is probably no less than 10 per cent while that of the top quintile is about 36.3 per cent. Thus the per capita

---

[1] Luxuries, even by the standards of the Indian subcontinent, do not appear to enter the private consumption budget in China. The luxuries mentioned above refer to those goods which may be called luxuries by the standards of private households in China.

[2] Price information is relatively abundant. These calculations are based on the information in Myrdal and Kessle: *China: the Revolution continued*, op. cit., Ch. I. Official exchange rates have been used in making the calculations.

income (excluding collective consumption) of the top quintile is only about 3.6 times higher than that of the bottom quintile.[1]

In order to be able to make comparisons with the ratios in other Asian countries one would have to make allowances for the distribution of collective consumption and for relative price differences. If such corrections were possible, the egalitarianism of the distribution of income in China would look even more striking in comparison with the contemporary developing countries.[2]

In many of the developing countries of Asia, as in China before the Revolution, the existence of massive poverty in the form of widespread undernutrition, lack of shelter and clothing has been well documented. In contemporary China the vast rural population live an austere life by the standards of the developed world. But it does not appear that poverty in the sense of inadequate food, clothing and shelter exists. Again, some examples may be useful. Of the 18 communes on which Buchanan reports, the lowest recorded wage is 100 yuan. It was recorded in a very poor commune in Honan, the poorest in the present list. For such a poor family, income from the private plot would almost certainly be higher than average, say 20 per cent of the total. Assuming the average dependency ratio,[3] income per head from collective and private sources would amount to 50 yuan. Assuming the average calorie requirement to be 2,100 per person per day, the cost of the food grain equivalent of the food requirement per person would work out at 34.8 yuan. The cost of 7½ yards of cotton cloth would be 5.70 yuan.[4] The family would own a house whose rental value is not imputed in the income shown above. Thus nearly 20 per cent of the income would be available to pay for needs other than food, clothing and shelter. This picture is one of

---

[1] A comparison of these shares with the estimates in Charles R. Roll Jr., op. cit., for 1952 may lead one to conclude that inequality increased between 1952 and the mid-1960s. But such a conclusion would be unwarranted. Errors in both estimates must be quite significant. As has been made abundantly clear, the estimate given in this chapter is at best a rough approximation and almost certainly exaggerates inequality in rural China. However, if the two estimates are approximately representative of the distribution of income at the two dates, then it must be conceded that the income redistributive effects of the various stages of collectivisation were at best modest as compared to that of the land reforms. At this stage one should refer back to Mao's advocacy of collectivisation: "On the question of agricultural co-operation". Mao's argument was that collectivisation was needed to preserve and consolidate the income distribution effects of the land reforms. It was argued that collectivisation was necessary to prevent polarisation, not that it would lead to a dramatic improvement in the distribution of income.

[2] In this connection the reader is referred to the previous chapters. Additional information on income distribution can be found in P. D. Ojha and V. V. Bhatt: "Patterns of Income Distribution in India: 1953-55 to 1963-65", in P. K. Bardhan and T. N. Srinivasan (eds.): *Poverty and income distribution in India*, op. cit.; National Council of Applied Economic Research: *All India Rural Household Survey*, 1962, Occasional Paper 13; Subramanian Swamy: "Structural Changes and the Distribution of Income by Size: The Case of India", in the *Review of Income and Wealth*, June 1967; A. Bergan; "Personal Income Distribution and Personal Savings in Pakistan", in *Pakistan Development Review*, Summer 1967.

[3] Such extremely poor families would certainly qualify for welfare payments if the dependency ratios were less favourable than average.

[4] Total grain requirement would be 435.5 catties per year. Prices have been taken from Myrdal and Kessle: *China: the Revolution continued*, op. cit.

undoubted austerity, but it is a condition made tolerable by the fact that it is widely shared and no one has a qualitatively different life style. There has been steady improvement since the Revolution, with the exception of a temporary reversal of modest proportions in the wake of the crop failures and economic difficulties during 1960-62.

However, it must be conceded that a fairly high degree of inequality still exists in rural China. Given the stated objectives of the Chinese political leadership, the existing inequality, however little in comparison to the rest of the world, must be regarded as unacceptable. Indeed, the Chinese leadership is acutely conscious of this contradiction and has been following a policy of gradual equalisation since the Cultural Revolution. As a result of these policies income distribution in China today is almost certainly more equal than appears from the rudimentary picture drawn for the mid-1960s. These policies will now be analysed in order to understand the problems China has encountered along what is truly an uncharted course.

THE QUEST FOR GREATER EQUALITY

The main source of inequality between communes, and between brigades and teams within communes, is the difference between units with respect to the ownership of the means of production, i.e. land and other productive assets. This is due to different land/labour ratios, different levels of fertility of land and different quantities and qualities of assets, equipment and skills. Although private ownership of land and other production assets has, by and large, been abolished, collective ownership in agriculture still does not represent ownership by the "whole people". In Chinese theoretical writing this distinction is clearly emphasised. Collective ownership can be at different levels. It can be at a fairly low level (by a team representing a few hundred people), or at a higher level (by a brigade or a commune representing thousands of people). The highest level of collective ownership is that by the whole people. A system in which property is extensively owned by very low level collectives is nowhere near the ideal of social ownership. Indeed the system may strongly resemble private ownership if the low level collective is so small as to consist of friends and relations.

In agriculture, ownership by the whole people applies to only a small proportion of total assets. In the eyes of the Chinese leadership the continuation of collective ownership below the level of the whole people represents the preservation of "the bourgeois right" in this realm.[1] As long as this

---

[1] A very cogent statement of the theoretical position of the Chinese leadership is to be found in Chang Chun-Chiao: *On exercising all-round dictatorship over the bourgeoisie* (Peking, Foreign Languages Press, 1975). It should be realised that the inequality within the rural society is not the only or even the main preoccupation of the Chinese policy for greater egalitarianism. The three major differences that are most frequently mentioned as targets for gradually narrowing down are between workers and peasants, town and country and manual and mental labour. At the same time, the inequalities within each of these categories are constantly attacked in the policy pronouncements.

bourgeois right is preserved, equality among various collective units and the constituent households is impossible to achieve. Translated into the language of Western economics, unequal land and resource endowment leads to an unequal amount of rental income for different units. This is the main source of inequality between units. To abolish this source of inequality, ownership of land and resources must be pooled together and the rental income distributed equitably.

In the eyes of the Chinese leadership the over-riding obstacle to equality within the basic accounting unit is inherent in the principle of distribution under socialism "to each according to his work". The Chinese theoreticians never stop recalling that Marx clearly recognised that this *equal right* here is still—in principle—*bourgeois right*".[1] Marx was very explicit on this question:

But one man is superior to another physically or mentally and so supplies more labour in the same time, or can labour for a longer time. ... Further, one worker is married, another not; one has more children than another, and so on and so forth. Thus with an equal performance of labour, and hence an equal share in the social consumption fund, one will in fact receive more than another, one will be richer than another, and so on. To avoid all these defects, right instead of being equal would have to be unequal.[2]

From the standpoint of the Chinese leadership the existing inequality is due to the preservation of these two kinds of bourgeois rights. Unless those rights are gradually curtailed, further reduction in inequality is impossible. The experience of the "Great Leap Forward" demonstrated that the curtailment of these rights cannot be suddenly imposed on the people without serious disruption in production. The process of "the restriction of these rights" since the cultural revolution has been slow and gradual. The emphasis has been on the cultural transformation of the people to induce them to give up these rights voluntarily.

In terms of the curtailment of the "bourgeois right" in the realm of ownership, the objective is to transfer the ownership of land and other assets gradually from the lower levels of collectives to higher levels. Ownership is still concentrated at the level of the team, the lowest of the three levels of the commune organisation. "For instance, in the rural people's communes on the outskirts of Shanghai where the economy at the commune and production brigade levels has developed at a rather fast pace, commune ownership accounts for 34.2 per cent of the fixed assets owned at all three levels, and brigade ownership accounts for only 15.1 per cent, while ownership by the production teams still occupies 50.7 per cent of the whole."[3] In the nation as a whole the degree of ownership by the team is considerably greater.

In recent years a shift has been taking place in favour of the higher collectives. No information for the nation as a whole is available but "on

---

[1] Karl Marx: *Critique of the Gotha Programme* (Peking, Foreign Languages Press, 1972), p. 16.

[2] ibid., pp. 16-17.

[3] Chang Chun-Chiao, op. cit., p. 12. The reference period seems to be 1974.

Shanghai's outskirts, for example, income at the commune level in proportion to total income rose from 28.1 per cent in 1973 to 30.5 per cent in 1974, that of the brigades rose from 15.2 per cent to 17.2 per cent, while the proportion going to the teams dropped from 56.7 per cent to 52.3 per cent."[1] Detailed information about the mechanism of this change is not available, but the following seem to be the main ways in which it has been taking place. First, in some areas teams have ceased to be the basic accounting units. This function has moved one tier up to the brigades. Secondly, the rates of accumulation out of incomes generated at the brigade and commune levels have generally been higher than the rate of accumulation out of income generated at the team level.

Another change in ownership that has been taking place in some communes is the gradual abolition of private plots or joint cultivation of private plots. From available reports it appears that steps in this direction are being taken with extreme caution. It was argued above that the distribution of income from private plots was probably more equal than the distribution of income from collective work. But it was also maintained that the system of working of the private plots was a cause of inequality in the distribution of collective income. On balance, income distribution may improve slightly as a consequence of abolishing private plots, on the assumption that the work point differential would be a little lower than differentials in productivity on private land once labour is diverted from private to collective work. This is unlikely to lead to dramatic changes, however. The main reason the abolition of private plots is being cautiously encouraged is that a gradual transition to ownership by higher collectives and ultimately by the whole people is inconsistent with private ownership at the level of the household.

The above measures would tend to reduce the sources of inequality between units within a commune but would have no effect on differences between communes. It is too early to chart the course of transition of ownership from the level of the communes to that of the whole people. It is, however, not true that in China there is no active policy to reduce inter-commune inequalities. The emphasis still is overwhelmingly on self-reliance. It has been noted above that the richer communes save a higher proportion of their incomes than the poorer ones. It seems likely, however, that the difference in real accumulation is less than is implied by the difference in "financial" savings rates between communes. In the income estimates used above the imputed value of some kinds of direct capital construction (e.g. terracing land, improving dykes, etc.) does not appear to be included. The Chinese strategy of self-reliance emphasises the importance of such activities as a method of improving the condition of the poor units. It is likely that the poorer units try to make up for the low rate of financial savings through such activities.

---

[1] Chang Chun-Chiao, op. cit., p. 7.

Apart from the promotion of self-reliance, there are specific types of assistance for the poorer units from the State. Burki gives an account of such assistance during the mid-1960s.[1] In every county some backward areas have been identified. During reorganisation the geographically contiguous backward units were formed into single communes and earmarked for special treatment. Financial assistance to the poorer units is being provided in the form of credit from the Agricultural Bank of China. Finally, the recruitment policy of the industrial sector has been aimed partly at relieving the extremely unfavourable land/man ratio in the poorer areas.

There is no evidence that the method of compulsory transfer of resources between units through progressive taxation is used as a redistributive measure.[2] Voluntary transfer appears to take place on a significant scale, however, between both communes and lower units. Several reports in recent years have described such measures.[3] Advanced units lend experts and model workers to poorer units. While previously all exchanges between units were calculated in money, in recent years such exchanges have frequently been unpaid, especially when transfer takes place from a richer unit to a poorer one.

Within a basic accounting unit the principle of payment according to work has been undergoing gradual modification. There has been a gradual incorporation of the principle of payment according to need. First, the method of calculation of work points has changed. Piece-rates have been abolished. Work points are no longer calculated daily. Instead assessments are made in advance for a considerable period of time, i.e. up to several months. This brings the system closer to that of a fixed wage rate system. A "correct attitude to work" and a "devotion to the cause of serving the people" are now used as the most important criteria for assessing a worker's merit.[4] Although physical strength is still a major determinant of the work points earned, the "trend is towards ... the removal of differences in income

---

[1] Burki, op. cit., Ch. III.

[2] One may wonder why this simple measure of equalisation has not been used by the egalitarian Chinese. Indeed, taxes on communes were set on the basis of a quota output fixed a long time ago. No progressivity was built into these rates at the time and because of the higher rate of growth of the currently richer communes the rates are probably regressive by now. No Chinese "defence" of this has been noted. But it seems that in a fundamental sense this kind of fiscal strategy would be in conflict with the ideological basis of the policy of restricting and finally abolishing the "bourgeois right" in property ownership by lower level collectives. Progressive taxation is based on the concession of such rights and is aimed at reducing some of their extremely unfavourable effects.

[3] See, for example, W. F. Wertheim: "Polarity and Equality in the Chinese People's Communes", in *Revue des pays de l'est* (Editions de l'Université de Bruxelles), 1974-1, and L. Ch. Shenk-Sandbergen: "How the Chinese People Remove Polarity within their Countryside," in *Eastern Horizon*, Vol. 12, No. 3, 1973.

[4] This promotes equality in so far as the importance of physical strength and skill as the criteria for distribution is reduced. But one may also view these as efficiency measures, the provisions being interpreted as an attempt to take into account the positive external effects.

that reflect not disparities of effort and commitment to the community, but merely disparities in physical strength." [1]

Another innovation, started by Tachai, the famous brigade in Shansi, and now widely practised, is the distribution of part of the grain according to need (i.e. equal amounts per "adult-equivalent") independent of work points earned. From available accounts it appears that the present practice is to allocate at least 40 per cent of grain rations on the basis of need.[2] In many units the proportion is higher. In some, e.g. Tachai, it is 100 per cent. Since the grain ration averages about 30 per cent of collective income,[3] this means that a minimum of 12 per cent of collective income is distributed according to need.[4] In many communes the proportion is much higher.

Essentially, the current Chinese strategy for greater equality consists of a return to what was tried in haste during the "Great Leap Forward" and was largely reversed in the wake of economic difficulties.[5] From a theoretical standpoint the basis of such policies is the gradual curtailment of two types of "bourgeois right", respectively in the realm of ownership of the means of production and in the principle of distribution according to work.

After the Revolution sharp improvements in the distribution of rural income were achieved in two major steps, land reform and collectivisation. In these two steps the role of the unequal holding of the means of production (other than personal attributes such as skill and strength) between individual households as a source of inequality was ended. But very significant sources of inequality persisted. The basis of the remaining inequality lies in rights and principles which have rarely been challenged by human society at any time in history. In this sense China is on an uncharted path. Further progress in promoting equality in China will be a slow and difficult process. The gains can no longer be large and discontinuous. They can come only slowly as individual households and lower level collectives are gradually persuaded to give up their rights voluntarily. To enable this to happen, the community must cease to behave in accordance with the standard assumption of orthodox economics that individuals, households and groups work for higher material consumption. Whether the behaviour of any large group of human beings is at all capable of such a transformation has yet to be demonstrated. The great caution and gradualism exercised by the Chinese leadership makes it clear that it is keenly aware that "right can never be higher than the economic structure of society and its cultural development conditioned thereby".[6]

---

[1] Maxwell, op. cit., p. 481.

[2] ibid., p. 478.

[3] Chen (ed.), op. cit., p. 37.

[4] This refers to the proportion of personal income only. It does not include the large volume of collective consumption of health, education and various services.

[5] It would be interesting to find out whether the reversal of these policies was only due to these difficulties (aggravated by the problem of incentives) or whether this was partly a retreat before the offensive launched by the partisans of the Liu Shao-chi line.

[6] Marx, op. cit., p. 17.

INDEX